FOOD AUTONOMY
IN CHICAGO

FOOD AUTONOMY IN CHICAGO

PANCHO MCFARLAND

THE UNIVERSITY OF GEORGIA PRESS
ATHENS

Most University of Georgia Press titles are
available from popular e-book vendors.

Printed digitally

EU Authorized Representative
Easy Access System Europe—Mustamäe tee 50, 10621 Tallinn,
Estonia, gpsr.requests@easproject.com

Library of Congress Cataloging-in-Publication Data
Names: McFarland, Pancho, author.
Title: Food autonomy in Chicago / Pancho McFarland.
Description: Athens : The University of Georgia Press, 2025. | Includes
bibliographical references and index.
Identifiers: LCCN 2024043618 (print) | LCCN 2024043619 (ebook) |
ISBN 9780820369945 (hardback) | ISBN 9780820369952 (paperback) |
ISBN 9780820369969 (epub) | ISBN 9780820369976 (pdf)
Subjects: LCSH: Food sovereignty—Illinois—Chicago. | African
Americans—Food—llinois—Chicago. | African Americans—
Agriculture—llinois—Chicago. | Food supply—Social aspects—
llinois—Chicago. | Urban agriculture—Social aspects—Illinois—
Chicago. | Social justice—Illinois—Chicago.
Classification: LCC HD9008.C4 M35 2025 (print) |
LCC HD9008.C4 (ebook) | DDC 338.1/977311—dc23/eng/20241231
LC record available at https://lccn.loc.gov/2024043618
LC ebook record available at https://lccn.loc.gov/2024043619

We live here on this earth.
We are all fruits of the earth.
The earth sustains us
We grow here, on the earth and lower
And when we die, we wither in the earth.
We are all fruits of the earth.
We eat of the earth.
Then, the earth eats us.

MEXICA SONG FROM SAN MIGUEL,
SIERRA DEL PUEBLO, MEXICO
"Tlaltecuhtli: The Jaws of Life and Death by Anne Key,"
Goddess Ink Blog, March 28, 2016,
https://goddessinkblog.com/2016/03/28
/tlaltecuhtli-the-jaws-of-life-and-death-by-anne-key/

CONTENTS

ACKNOWLEDGMENTS

As you will read, many gardeners, activists, revolutionaries, artists, healers, photographers, and other community members have contributed to this work and our food movement in Chicago over the past twenty years. While you will see many of their names herein, I am unable to include all or even remember everyone who has contributed to my growth and understanding of the needs of our people. I dedicate this work to my primary accomplice, Jacqueline Abena Smith, who encouraged me, taught me, cared for me and, more than anyone, is responsible for my continued work. Rest in power. I dedicate this also to my three children. The youth give us hope. Thanks to Baba Fred Carter and Mama Dr. Jifunza Wright, who along with their son, Akin, have created a space for learning, healing, and joy at the Black Oaks Center for Sustainable Renewable Living. They are my mentors. The extended Cortez family, especially my mother and sister, nurtured me and along with hundreds of Chicanxs taught me compassion and tough lessons about how colonialism, racism, and capitalism impact our daily lives. Chicago is the "scene of the crime," and the grit, toughness and compassion of its people show me what it means to resist and be resilient. Thanks due to many of my colleagues at Chicago State University who have provided comradeship and a great environment to do this work. Our students keep me grounded and honest. Independent, and especially Black-owned and Black-managed, coffeeshops and community spaces have provided the good fuel and good vibes to learn and do the difficult work of writing. Dozens of organizations, groups, and individuals in Chicago have taught me valuable lessons about surviving and thriving as Black and Indigenous people. Much appreciation to all who have loved me and poured into me their Indigenous and African diasporan knowledge and lifeways. Each of the aforementioned have made my life exponentially better, and the best of what is in these pages is due to their strength. Of course, all the mistakes are mine. Free the land!! Mitakuye oyasin!

FOOD AUTONOMY
IN CHICAGO

PART I

FOUNDATIONS

CHAPTER 1

Okichike Ka Centeotzintli

BIENVENDIOS A MESOAMERICA EN SHIKAAKWA

At 420 N. Fifth Street in Raton, New Mexico, Jim Cortez grew cempazuchitl (marigolds), xitomatl (tomatoes), chilli (hot chiles), and ayotli (calabacita/squashes). Later, my first teacher of placed-based knowledge bought a larger lot in which he and my grandmother planted fruit trees, cacti, and an annual garden. Grandpa Jim also taught me the lessons of piñon. To enjoy the roasted, salty delight that is the piñon seed you first had to spend hours foraging for them. We would climb Goat Hill in the Sangre de Cristo mountains only yards from our home. Then, we would gather the pinecones we found on the ground or in the low-hanging branches of the evergreens. We filled large bags full of piñon and hauled them home. Later, we would coax the seeds out of the cones and wash, salt, and roast them. My grandmother, Maria Eugenia "Mary" Cortez, taught me other Indigenous foraging practices. She introduced me to wild relatives such as quelites (from the Nahua "quiltl") or lamb's quarters. I learned later that in Mexico "quelites" refers to wild greens generally, but in our part of the Mexican diaspora "quelites" or "wild spinach" was *chenopodium album*. Like pinon seed, this wild edible green, packed full of nutrition, was a common dish for our family.

In northern New Mexico we ate an Amerindigenous diet of corn, beans, squash, tomatoes, and chiles, especially local varieties from Hatch, New Mexico, and Pueblo, Colorado (Mexican Indigenous peoples, including our relations, have spread throughout much of the United States). For special occasions my grandmothers' sisters (my aunties Martha, Ana, and Sally), my mother and other adult women would make empanadas. I remember only two kinds of empanadas: "sweet" and "with meat." The meat empanadas included things such as cow tongue mixed with a variety of spices and other ingredients. As with our ancestors, special occasions called for tamalli (tamal in Spanish) usually purchased from a local tamalera but sometimes made at home. Our diet tied us to the thousands-year-old food arts and sciences of our Amerindigenous ancestors.

My grandparents were my first teachers of Indigenous foodways. Since in many ways we were deindigenized and assimilated, I didn't know that I commonly ate ancient foods from Abya Yala/Turtle Island/Anahuac/the Americas. Our assimilation included a loss of many of our foodways. That we ate flour tortillas instead of corn illustrated the degree to which our colonization had been successful.[1] While the adoption of wheat flour tortillas suggested assimilation for many of us, adoption, adaptation, and flexibility have always been part of Indigenous resiliency and ability to live well under difficult circumstances. The use of wheat for tortillas by our Indigenous ancestors illustrates how they used the ingredients at their disposal to continue and expand their culture and foodways and that an assimilationist lens is too simple for understanding our relationships with our food.[2] Nonetheless, by the time I was born, European wheat culture had been successful in replacing centeotzintli (our sacred maíz) for many of us Mesoamerican diasporans/Mexican Americans/Chicanxs. Our trips to fast-food joints, "Chinese" restaurants, and steakhouses demonstrated how Anglo-America and late capitalism have successfully penetrated our culture and colonized our foodways.

My connection to land, place, and Tierra Madre included a rural small-town Illinois birth where nature engulfed us and a move to the Southwest in my eighth year. Across the street from my home at the foot of Goat Hill, we ran in and jumped over centuries-old irrigation ditches. The ditches no longer served as a technology of sustenance for the Nuevo Mexicanx and other Indigenous people who have lived in the area for centuries. While they no longer served an agricultural function, they were an important marker of a rural-small town New Mexican culture. The ditches irrigated the fields of chile and frijol that still form the foundation of a northern New Mexican diet. I daily walked into the kitchens of my grandfather, grandmother, aunts, uncles, and mother to experience numerous types of chiles and chile preparation techniques. Each year during the local harvest season, we bought fifty or more pounds of chiles to roast and freeze. I learned to make a northern New Mexico enchilada casserole with red chile powder and a salsa with dried red chile flakes, both of which continue to please dinner and party guests. Ranching and hunting played important roles in our food culture. My tías and tíos would cook venison or steak with green chiles, garlic, and onions. The all-too-common, in my opinion, dinners of tripa (animal intestines) and menudo were always spiced with chile. Whether I liked it (which I most often did) or not (as in the case of menudo), the ancient chilli (in Nahua) formed much of my diet and informed my identity. I have vivid memories of my grandmother chiding us to see who could prove their "Mexicanness," defined as toughness, by eating a raw jalapeño. As a light-skinned "coyote" (biracial) boy, I always took the bait and learned to love the burn in the process. It formed my cooking and eating style. Today, everything gets some form of chilli.

Frijoles, primarily pinto beans, accompanied most things during my youth. Our kitchens were often a sensory wonder as we could smell, hear, feel, and taste frijoles. The seemingly giant pot or equally giant pressure cooker sputtered with

FIG. 1. Images of McFarland-Cortez family.
Photographer unknown.

boiling beans that included chilli, onion, garlic, and salt, sometimes with a large scoop of manteca (lard). Burritos of beans, chilli, cheese (cheddar or American, usually bought from a store but sometimes received through government subsidy programs), and onions wrapped in warm tortilla de harina (wheat flour) were probably the most common food item in our household until my teen years. Beans were taken for granted. This familiarity often brought discomfort and embarrassment as it symbolized being Mexican—that is, being brown, foreign, and racially othered. We were "beaners," after all. However, today my reindigenization requires a love of northern New Mexican food and nature as well as an exploration of pan-Indigenous foodways. Las tres madres (the three mothers or three sisters for some), beans, centeotzintli and ayotli, fill my annual garden beds, my kitchen, and my pantry. My infrequent restaurant outings to spend time with my children find me eating burritos, enchiladas, or huevos rancheros, always with chilli, beans, and centeotzintli at El Gallo near my current home in the Morgan Park neighborhood in Chicago. To the degree that I can, mine is an antiauthoritarian, anticolonial, alterNative (AAA) food practice using the Indigenous foodways of my friends, family, and community as well as the political thought and strategies of Indigenous freedom fighters.

My personal journey out of New Mexico through the pursuit of a PhD sharpened my understanding of the ills of capitalism, colonialism, White supremacy, and heteropatriarchy. Attempting to indigenize our understanding, I use the term "Wetiko" (also, "Windigo," the Algonquian monster of greed, selfishness, and destruction[3]) to describe our society. The Zapatistas and their revolutionary insistence on being themselves as place-based peoples was my first education in the food injustice of Wetiko. They unashamedly claimed their dignity and indigeneity. They fought and died to be themselves and help create a world in which all worlds fit (un mundo donde caben todos los mundos). These inheritors of centuries-old maíz culture struggle to maintain ecologically sound, culturally appropriate food and lifeways. From them I learned lessons in the importance of local struggle "against neoliberalism and for humanity."

My associations with anarchists and other antiauthoritarians deepened and further politicized my understanding of self-determination and community, first taught by my grandparents, and reinforced by the Zapatistas. Anarchists in Texas introduced me to community-supported agriculture and provided me with the first real examples of community living and collective decision-making. They brought my attention to the centrality of food to the global capitalist system and how to create an anarchist food system.

My explorations and experiences led me back to Colorado in the late 1990s and early 2000s. There I focused on environmental justice, confrontations with the industrial-agricultural food system and practical alternatives to the capitalist, colonialist status quo. I found the sustainable design system, permaculture, and began taking workshops on biodiesel, herb spiral creation, alternative transportation, and other related topics. Amid my work in Colorado Springs and Fort Collins I purchased Rosemary Morrow's *An Earth User's Guide to Permaculture*. Her lucid writing and confident voice attracted me further and had me convinced that a free future required permaculture. Since then, I have earned two Permaculture Design Certificates and taught dozens of classes on permaculture and Indigenous growing systems online and in my gardens. I continue to be convinced that permaculture is an essential tool in our revolutionary, decolonial toolbox. Much controversy surrounds this design science first organized and articulated by White Australians Bill Mollison and David Holmgren, based on an Indigenous scientific and moral foundation and including the best European scholars such as Buckminster Fuller, Peter Kropotkin, and James Lovelock. Nonetheless, I find it a valuable design system to bring colonized, assimilated folks and non-Indigenous, non-Black people to a revolutionary loving relationship to the land and one another.

Shikaakwa/Zhigagoong (Chicago) taught me the words "food justice." Living and working in working-class Black and Mexicanx/Chicanx communities deprived of access to healthy, dignified, culturally appropriate food introduced me to the unjust realities suffered by Black, Indigenous and other people of color (BIPOC) in Wetiko's urban environs. The abundance of liquor stores and corner store junk-food outlets and fried fast-food options, as well as the lack of fresh produce and meats at "grocery stores," vividly illustrate the symbolic violence of Wetiko's food system every time I step outside my door. The resistance of Black and Brown community gardeners, social justice activists, and revolutionaries makes evident the possibilities for a different social order. They argue for food justice, autonomy, and sustainability with Indigenous, place-based values and organization as the basis of a new world.

This book is a dialogue about food autonomy and the food movement between distinct yet similar place-based traditions. The political traditions and practices of revolutionary communists and anarchists contribute to the food movement and my participation in it. But they have a lot to learn from the political thought and practice of the African Diaspora/New Afrikans/Black Americans and Nican Tlaca (American Indigenous or Amerindigenous): How might Black and Indigenous/ Mexican horticulture and their biocentric values be used to frame our thinking about food autonomy and the practices of food advocates and revolutionaries? What role can revolutionary communists and anarchists and their theories play in developing a food-autonomy framework? What can revolutionaries learn from African diasporic people and Nican Tlaca? How do we work to remember our ancestral foodways and reindigenize? What are the consequences if we don't? What role can permaculture play?

The chapters and dialogues in this book analyze the food movement in Black communities in Chicago through my participation in them for more than fifteen years. They form a new millennial maíz narrative and an adaptation of African diasporan rice narratives.[4] The texts, maps, and codices of the Toltec, Maya, and Nahua-speaking peoples, the murals, banners, and flags of the Chican@ movement of the 1960s and 1970s, and the hip hop of the urban Mesoamerican diaspora all recount an anticolonial history of the thousands-year old maíz-based and rice-based cultures.[5] My experiences detailed and analyzed in this book illustrate the continued migration, resilience, and adaptation of maíz-based culture through examination of how Indigenous foodways are interpreted and practiced in the Black agrarian tradition (BAT) in an urban context and how a reindigenizing Chicano interacts with, interprets, and adapts Amerindigenous and Black American traditions. This is a story of reindigenization/re-Africanization.

Thus, it is auto-ethnography or autohistoria-teoria. I agree with "some Black feminist anthropologists [that] there is no hard and fast distinction between 'us' as researchers and 'them' as the community in which we serve."[6] Like Xicana feminist scholars, I understand that scholarly work and theorizing in BIPOC communities by BIPOC researchers requires a decolonizing methodology that begins with our very own bodies as "lived in" communities. Patricia Hill Collins uses the concept of "passionate rationality" to explain Black feminist methodology. She describes it as a "caring, theoretical vision with informed, practical struggle."[7]

I also reject the faux objectivity and value-neutral stance of traditional European and Euro-American scholarship that would distance researchers and our emotions from the "subjects" we study. As Black food scholars show, those driving our understanding of Black food culture are often not of the Black community and thus often focus on lack and further a narrative of "Black" as a problem category.[8] Dara Cooper uses the example of the ubiquity of the term "food desert" to describe the terrible conditions that many Black communities are in to show how an "outsider" with no ties to Black communities can circumscribe the narrative around Black foodways.[9] The "food desert" perspective predictably frames Black communities through the lens of lack, thus cutting off inquiry into vibrant Black food cultures and the ways that Black people and communities thrive despite the neglect and violence of anti-Blackness. On the other hand, Black geographer Ashante Reese offers the concept of Black geographies of self-reliance demonstrating agency and how "Black folks navigate inequities with a creativity that reflects a reliance on self and community."[10]

Gloria Anzaldua and many others who have followed in her scholarly footsteps use the term "autohisteorias" or "autohistoria-teoria" to describe a decolonial methodology. She explains,

> One of the essays I'm writing focuses on what I call autohisteorias—the concept that Chicanas and women of color write not only about abstract ideas but also bring in their personal history as well as the history of their community. I call it "auto" for self-writing, and "historia" for history—as in collective, personal, cultural, and racial history . . . I use my life to illustrate the theories.[11]

My analysis in this project concerns me and the movement to which I belong. It is necessarily subjective and begins from my standpoint as a reindigenizing anarchist of Mexican descent living, working, and fighting in Black Chicago. I examine the movement from my perspective and my experience as an activist-scholar employed by a state institution of higher education. I have experienced the dilemma of being an anarchist in the academy for nearly thirty years.[12] The entire structure of the academy builds on hierarchies and logics that anarchists and Indigenous people reject. While universities and research institutions are steeped in liberal-reformist (ultimately, reactionary) intellectual engagement, anarchists, Indigenous scholars, radical Black scholars, and others manage to make revolutionary scholarly interventions. Many of these are incorporated into my methods for investigating the food movement in Black Chicago.

My approach resonates with Graeber, who concludes:

> Obviously, what I am proposing would only work if it was, ultimately, a form of auto-ethnography—in the sense of examining movements to which one has, in fact, made some kind of commitment, in which one feels oneself a part. It would also have to be combined with a certain degree of utopian extrapolation: a matter of teasing out the tacit logic or principles underlying certain forms of radical practice, and then, not only offering the analysis back to those communities, but using them to formulate new visions. These visions would have to be offered as potential gifts, not definitive analyses or impositions.[13]

Following Black and Chicana feminist scholars as well as Graeber, I offer this book as a gift to my numerous communities, especially my food community in Chicago, but also to my fellow anarchists and other revolutionaries fighting for a better world— earth warriors who see the connections between local crises and global political economic practice—and Chicanxs and other Indigenous peoples working for peace, power, and freedom in occupied territory. This project is not simply a book but a larger effort to create a more ecological, free, and democratic world through fierce local struggle and global solidarity. As I gather information and write about our movement, I work through ideas and approaches with my accomplices and mentors and apply them in our gardens and organizing work.[14] This approach has proved an effective means to address community needs in a dialectical fashion.

I work as a member of a vibrant, dynamic, and potentially revolutionary movement. I am not an ally in the Black food movement but rather a member of a community attempting to live by the best of our ancestors' principles in this age of advanced computer and military technology, ecological devastation, and capitalism's decline. My journey in this movement began in 2005 when I become a member of Healthy South Chicago and joined my community garden in 2008. I worked hard to learn as much as I could at my community's garden. Two seasons later I began taking responsibility as a leader and began to extend my associations in the food movement in Black Chicago. My desire to learn about horticulture, urban growing, and food arts led me to meetings, workshops, workdays at other community gardens, markets, and other such spaces. From there I taught a class on food justice at Chicago State University, a predominantly Black institution where I began teaching as an assistant professor of sociology in 2005 and began introducing the CSU community to our gardens only blocks from the campus.

I learned of the Healthy Food Hub (HFH) in 2010. This hub of Black food, sustainability, and pride provided me with much of my education in the Black food movement. They and the movement that surrounds the HFH engage in a form of direct-action politics that make food "a point of entry for discussing how African Americans might gain control over their lives."[15] Like many others throughout the country, the HFH and the Black Oaks Center for Sustainable Renewable Living (BOC) provide spaces for healing, safety, resistance to the corporate food and health systems, and renewal of the BAT tied to Black liberatory politics. Black Oaks helped nurture the development of the Green Lots Project (GLP), the focus of most of my service in the food movement. The founder of GLP, Dominique Bowman (now Vining), created it through conversations and workshops at BOC. HFH and BOC's' eco-campus in Pembroke, Illinois, have influenced hundreds, perhaps thousands of Black Chicagoans and others, in our efforts to be more sustainable, freer, and healthier. My association with Black Oaks and the HFH has been my primary point of entry into the dynamic, life-enhancing food movement/community. Cofounders of BOC, Baba Fred Carter, Mama Dr. Jifunza Wright, and Akin Carter, deserve much of the credit for the positive things I have been able to learn and do in our movement.

The politics of a non-Black identified person in a consciously Black political and cultural space are fascinating and complex. All parties, including me, who enter into the spaces of the Black food autonomy and sustainability movement bring their experiences with, knowledge of, and baggage from our entanglement with

Wetiko. Since the spaces of the food movement are mostly segregated and since conscious Blackness is central to the spaces in which I work and live, race becomes a crucial lens through which to understand justice, health, culture, history, and social movements. This lens, like all lenses, has its limits, and some of these are witnessed in the failures of the movement. In particular, knee-jerk reactionary variants of bourgeois Black nationalist and Black capitalist thought infiltrate the spaces of our food community. Lacking a class analysis limits our ability to ask important questions about key issues of food production, distribution, and consumption. In addition, a race lens without an appropriate understanding of colonialism and the global nature of our interconnectedness often limits our ability to understand the problems we face, who our enemies are, and who our allies and accomplices might be. The race-exclusive lens used by some means that BIPOC engage in interracial or interethnic conflict, place blame on other colonized/racialized people, and develop shallow analyses of our connections and the common threats of the system arrayed against us. Moreover, the simple race lens often fails to understand Blackness internationally and our intimate, though hidden, connections to people all over the planet. It often keeps Black urbanites from seeing the obvious connections between them and Mexican migrant farmworkers, for example. Xenophobic comments about Mexicans, Whites, or "A-Rabs" go unchallenged, and with very few referents for reordering our mistaken racial notions, stereotypes build and get reproduced. I argue that this orientation keeps us from fighting our struggle well. On the other hand, there are promising interethnic collaborations around food and liberation. Groups like Urban Steward Action Network (USAN) and Inner-City Muslim Action Network (IMAN) began to consciously fight through the divide-and-conquer mentality and enact an extremely diverse multiethnic, multigender soil politics. Similarly, in 2022, Baba Fred Carter, Dr. Jifunza Wright, and I taught a Resilient Community Design course that was equal parts Black American and Indigenous/Mexican American with a few White accomplices.

My intention is that through the stories, analyses, and conversations in this book we can better understand race as it affects us personally, in the food movement, and in the broader struggles for autonomy. As a revolutionary intellectual intervention, I intend for this work to go beyond a deeper understanding of race to the active dismantling of this crippling concept and the divisive ideas that prop up Wetiko such as "authenticity" and "ally." Thus, this is a pedagogical project that desires to grapple with what it means to be human, to have culture, and to be free.

The rest of this introduction describes further my approach to understanding this movement and the important aspects of it that I address. Each of the central topics of the study and how they intersect with our movement requires engagement with different scholarly traditions. I have ordered the book so that each of the main topics—pedagogy, race, gender, spirituality, and movement politics—has its own stand-alone section that places what I have found in dialogue with the relevant literature.

Learning and Teaching Ancestral Foodways

A central goal of the food justice, autonomy, and sustainability movements involves reclaiming, reworking, remembering, and reteaching the place-based wisdom of our ancestors. Many of us, deindigenized or de-Africanized urban dwellers, relearn our traditions in the food movement. Sometimes we learn important things from books by BIPOC food autonomy activists/scholars. More often the reteaching occurs with our hands in the soil, outside engaged in earth stewardship and community building.

This book attempts to illustrate something of the pedagogical principles of the Black food movement in Chicago and how I have incorporated these principles into my food autonomy pedagogy. Part II, "Anticolonial CommUnity Pedagogy," describes the passing on of traditions through the formal and informal spaces of the food movement. In addition, student-gardener-teachers assimilate the principles of the food movement through dialogue and study of global traditions and implement them through organic, sustainable, and just practices in the garden. My methodology and pedagogy use standard and radical academic practices, including participant observation, ethnography/oral history, archival research, Freirian pedagogy of the oppressed, service-learning approaches and deschooling. However, the primary pedagogy/methodology in our movement relies on dialogue: communications between older and younger; Black, White, and Chicanx; men, women, and queer; city folk and rural dweller; etc. Importantly, my primary collaborators in the development of this project have been elder Black men and women. Thus, my primary perspective in the project has been elder epistemology/methodology. It is similar to Rodriguez when he writes:

> My research methodology includes my research protocols, collaborative relationships, and elder epistemology; that is, listening to elders and acknowledging, rather than seeking to validate, their knowledge. Elder epistemology includes respect for stories and oral traditions and respect for the elders who pass on their knowledge.[16]

What I know about food autonomy and land stewardship in Chicago results from what I have learned from elders. I have, as their example directs, put it to use and taught it in the gardens of the Roseland neighborhood and others. Using elder knowledge in the gardens creates the conditions for further learning. The land, our empty lots in the city, also teaches. Using a land pedagogy and elder epistemology/methodology, we see what grows and what doesn't. We learn about our community and the people in it. We learn how the earth responds. We learn about the hazards of a neglected and abused sector of the city. We teach these lessons and implement them in the gardens and community organizations, and the pedagogical cycle continues.

Our ancestors knew that careful attention to the land teaches all one needs to know to survive, prosper, and live right according to the "Original Instructions," those guidelines passed down for millennia by Indigenous people as a result of deep relationships with land.[17] Many of us in the food autonomy movement on the South Side of Chicago approach our work with this same humility. Keen attention to the land and the beings residing on it opens infinite opportunities for learning about how to relate to one another and all our relations. From the starting point of the land, we can better understand "urban social problems." Violence, poverty, ill health, depression, and drug abuse and trafficking become better understood from a land-based perspective. The land teaches us about the cycles of life and struggle. With this understanding I wrote several short essays for *The Environmental and Food Justice* blog between 2009 and 2013 to theorize and analyze my experiences and rework them into my movement praxis. These early observations, lessons, and essays formed the basis for my apprenticeship with the land and my praxis in the garden.

Learning from the land, other members of the food autonomy movement and I adopt a "land pedagogy." Leanne Simpson provides us with Indigenous concepts that can aid in our pedagogy within the food movement as well as provide food warriors with new ways of seeing and improving our work. For Simpson recovery of Nishnaabeg intelligence is required to overcome the ills of colonialism and eventually to completely decolonize. She argues that the goal of decolonization cannot be realized without community- and land-based intellectuals focused on the resurgence of Indigenous knowledge.[18] This belief and practice can be found throughout the food autonomy movement in Chicago. To solve our urban social problems and to sustain community empowerment and self-determination, we need to develop pedagogical methods that teach young people to prioritize community needs. The wide diversity of perspectives in the food movement can be seen in the myriad approaches to teaching children in our communities.

Nishnaabeg knowledge and pedagogy have several characteristics that can be found in differing degrees throughout the growing spaces in Black Chicago. First, pedagogy in Nishnaabeg requires doing. Simpson writes that "if you want to learn something, you need to take your body on to the land and do it. Get a practice." Second, learning is a process that includes the whole being. To learn, to accept the gifts of knowledge, one has "to be fully present in all aspects of your physical and spiritual body." Third, Nishnaabeg intelligence is spiritual. Accessing it requires "being engaged in a way of living that generates a close, personal relationship with our ancestors and relations in the spirit world through ceremony, dreams, visions and stories." Fourth, individuals are responsible for their own learning. Fifth, meaning does not come from a set of abstract, decontextualized ideas but from "a compassionate web of interdependent relationships." Sixth, learning is lifelong. Seventh, teachers have the responsibility to "wear your teaching," or model the behavior that they are teaching. Eighth, learning is not coercive. Finally, the land and nature (or "aki," which "includes all aspects of creation") are our primary teachers. Her explanation of land pedagogy describes well what many of us are attempting:

> The Anishinaabe have long taken direction about how we should live through our interactions and observations.[19] Within the environment people regulate their behavior and resolve their disputes by drawing guidance from what they see in the behavior of the sun, moon, stars, winds, waves, trees, birds, animals and other natural phenomenon. The Anishinaabe word for this concept is qikinawaabiwin. We can also use the word akinoomaage, which is formed from two roots: aki and noomaage. "Aki" means earth and "noomaage" means to point towards and take direction from.[20]

Conversations in Black food autonomy spaces in Chicago illustrate how these pedagogical principles are being used and developed. This does not mean that our pedagogies are always decolonial, resistant, or freedom-seeking; sometimes we cause harm. However, the best of what we do follows the principles of land-based pedagogies. In fact, BOC relies on the Black agrarian tradition (BAT) and pedagogical practices and permaculture principles that are a synthesis of Indigenous practices from around the globe. The BOC offers courses in indigenized permaculture that make its Indigenous knowledge (IK) explicit and push back on a movement that is seen by many as appropriating our knowledge base.[21] In addition, many of my accomplices use the land and its lessons to teach young people about life.

Finally, my teaching and learning strategies are heavily informed by permaculture. By June 2021 I had taught over three hundred hours of permaculture courses to students all over the planet. Moreover, as I will discuss, permaculture informs all my teaching and learning. Pushing through and struggling with the Whiteness of the permaculture community, I have learned to love the brilliance of Bill Mollison's work. Fortunately for me and my students, I learned permaculture from Black teachers (Fred Carter, Dr. Jifunza Wright, and Matthew Stephens) steeped in love for Black people and all our relations. They challenge Whiteness, cultural appropriation, and any attacks on our communities.

Mothers of Our Movement

Rice surreptitiously arrived in French Guiana in the hair of African women enslaved and brought to South America. Later, women escaped enslavement and brought rice to maroon communities, resisting their enslavement by running away and establishing free towns and villages. Rice arrived to the Saramaka maroon communities of Suriname through the formerly enslaved Paanza's ingenuity and daring.

> Paanza ... one day decides to flee as she is harvesting rice on a plantation. But before she runs, Paanza scoops up some grains of ripened rice and stuffs this seed rice in her hair. She escapes, and brings the grains to the maroons living in the forest. This, Saramaka descendants recount, is how they came to grow rice.[22]

Elders also tell of how in Para, Brazil, an enslaved African mother fearing separation from her children took the all-important rice seed and hid it in her children's hair. In their stories, mothers are responsible for the maintenance of the rice-based cultures and resilience of African peoples in the Americas.

In the "Ancient History of the Birth of Maíz," the grandmother passes on "huehuetlahtolli or the ancient word" to her grandson. The grandmother explains:

> You should understand the things you need to know about the earth and how to work it. This way you can live and you will not suffer in life. You will know how to plant, you will know how to till the soil and where you will plant the maíz ... You will water the chile seeds where they are already planted and also the seeds of the tomato. And you will learn the secrets of how to make the chile hotter ... This is ancient practice. That is the word of the elders. All that we eat is our life sustenance, it is what keeps us alive and thus we work. We care for it and appreciate it. We offer prayers before Mother Earth and we offer prayers before our Father Sun.[23]

"The age of maíz (w)as a time when women became more central to food production." It became an age of balance in which men and women both played important roles. The account above from Nahua elder, Tata Cuaxtle Felix Evodio, describes the central role women played in teaching the traditions of Mesoamerican maíz culture. Rodriguez adds that "the post-harvest process is viewed as women's technology. Once the corn has been chosen for consumption, it is women who prepare it in a variety of ways; it is primarily women who grind the corn on a metate or molcajete with a mano, in a process that is perhaps close to five thousand years old."[24]

Like their Amerindigenous sister from Tata Cuaxtle's account, Paanza and other women passed on the food arts and sciences of their land-based Indigenous African people. Maroon societies were able to resist slavery and survive until current times in French Guiana and elsewhere in South America because of rice, which "is a woman's crop."[25] That is, women were responsible for rice dispersal and the development of maroon rice culture and technology. In more recent times, Black and Indigenous women have continued passing on African heritage knowledge (AHK)/IK, as evidenced in the stories of how Black women interact with chicken "as a tool of self-expression, self-actualization, resistance, even accommodation and power," economic empowerment, family and community uplift and activism,[26] and in supplying food and AHK in Detroit[27] and elsewhere in the United States.[28]

The important task of processing staple grains among Mesoamericans, other Amerindigenous people, and African communities in the Americas fell to women. In these pre-Columbian societies women held a great deal of power, especially as concerns food. Brit Reed helps us understand the central role of women in pre-Columbian food systems, arguing that "in some tribal nations, such as the Choctaw, where agriculture was a major source of food production, women were responsible for tending the fields and growing the food. As such, they held power over the distribution of food within their communities and to outsiders"[29] Through traditional foodways, women have played a central role in the survival and thriving of African people in the Americas as well as in Amerindigenous communities.[30]

As colonialism, slavery, and capitalism devastated African and Indigenous people in the Americas, the central role of women in food production came under attack. Yet many millions of these women along with African and Indigenous men persevered largely due to the maintenance of their rice- and maíz-based cultures and the ingenuity they demonstrated through adapting their ancestral foodways to new physical and political-economic environments. Surviving Wetiko for Indigenous people required that women and men cooperated. Each had their roles in these communities and continue to do so in many. In addition, two-spirit people performed crucial roles. But as colonialism ravaged Africans and the Amerindigenous, patriarchy separated women from men, attacked two-spiritedness, and denigrated Indigenous land stewardship, which colonizers associated with savages and women.[31] The Indigenous sex-gender system and family structure formed the foundation of our "rebellious" lifeways. Thus, colonizers attacked our families and religions, which provided us with the Original Instructions needed to live well and in peace upon our land.[32] The colonizer's sex-gender system has been successful in undermining Indigenous people. Far too often in many of our communities, including those where I live and work, our response to disrupted families and lost culture is a retreat to heteronormativity and heteropatriarchal ways with the nuclear family and Wetiko gender roles and identities. On the other hand, in our movement women have asserted themselves and taken leadership roles. Of course, this hasn't been without a great deal of struggle. As a new generation of BIPOC land stewards asserts itself, they have us confront our contradictions around queerness/two-spiritedness. I strive to overcome my personal and our collective imprisonment in Wetiko's ideology, which directly attacks Indigenous sex-gender systems that typically employ a nonbinary view of gender, sex, and sexuality. Two-spirit accomplices and their experiences and worldviews add to my and our understanding.

Women seem to do most of the work and leadership in the food movement in Black Chicago and in the maintenance of AHK. Key personal teachers and leaders in the movement include elder mothers Dr. Jifunza Wright, Carolyn Thomas, Naomi Davis, Paula Roderick, Jessie Avraham, and Paula Anglin as well as younger women such as Dominique Bowman, Jacqueline Abena Smith, Safia Rashid, Mecca Brooks, and Dr. Mila Marshall. They represent much of the leadership of the movement. Other Black women in Chicago and elsewhere, including Erica Allen, Naya Jones, Dr. Bonnie Claudia Harrison, A. Breeze Harper, LaDonna Redmond, Kenya Sample, Latrice Williams, and Dara Cooper, have also been teachers. In addition, my experiences in the food movement are replete with dialogues with Black women gardeners and community organizers. In my more than fifteen years of involvement in Chicago's food movement, women have always represented most of the attendees at organized meetings of community groups, gardens, coalitions, and policy working groups and participants and teachers at workshops, conferences, and demonstrations.

In a fashion after Harriet Tubman (Araminta Ross), Fannie Lou Hamer,[33] and scores of African/Indigenous women in the Americas and beyond who did/do much of the food production and care work to maintain our cultures and traditions, our Lifeboats Permaculture Guild consists of primarily older Black women fighting to keep traditions alive. In my experience and that of many others in this movement, they are the primary teachers of AHK. Their work keeps alive the resistant and resilient foodways of Africans in the Americas. They exhibit the "innate agrarian artistry" that has been pivotal to the survival and resilience of African peoples for centuries.[34] The "mothers" of the movement that I have had the good fortune to learn from illustrate agrarian artistry with their practice of the healing, growing, and nurturing arts. They follow in the footsteps of Mama "sheroes" of Black resistance and regeneration.[35]

The observation that Black women do most of the work of the food movement in Chicago and in maintaining AHK does not intend to diminish the crucial and complementary roles that men play. Black men, mostly older but some middle-aged and young adults, redefine the feminized image of caretaker, earth steward, gardener, and teacher. Their skills, power, generosity, openness, and sincerity challenge the all-too-common stereotype of Black and Amerindigenous men as violent, uncaring, unintelligent, criminal, hypersexualized, and immoral. While some Black and other men in the city reflect the hypermasculine norm of our heteropatriarchal society in their interpersonal relations and while many others engage in hypermasculinity through their positions within powerful institutions, the Black men in our movement illustrate a more complex masculinity. Elders like Fred Carter, Dwight Dotts and Gregory Bratton, middle-aged men including Mike Tekhen Strode, and younger men develop an alternative model of masculinity through their teaching, caring, and stewardship. Akin Carter, Dwight Dotts, Julian Sample, Daryl Gibson, Kevin Triplett, Floyd Banks, Austin Wayne, Matthew Stephens, and others in Chicago have also taught us about various ways of growing food, community, and revolution in Chicago. Black and Amerindigenous male food scholars and activists like Will Allen, Kevin Thomas, Michael Howard, Ron Finley, Devon G. Peña, Bryant Terry, Tezozomoc, Blain Snipstal, Michael Twitty, Enrique Salmon, and Malik Yakini provide leadership for the growing numbers of food warriors across the country.

This work aspires to deepen relationships and build bridges between communities. While my experience of urban food struggles is informed by Black men and women, my understanding of freedom and right livelihood begins from a Xicanx upbringing and intellectual-activist training. Like my Black-identified teachers in Chicago and elsewhere, Xicanxs inform my work, experience, and understanding of food autonomy in Chicago. These Xicanxs include my grandparents; mother, Virginia Marie McFarland (née Cortez); and extended family, including Lucile Cole, Anna Martinez, Virginia Cortez (great-aunt and *madrina*), Luis Cortez, Roger Cortez, and Jesus "Jesse" Cortez. Scholar-activists like Manolo Callahan, Gustavo Esteva, Dinah Ramirez, Subcomandante Marcos, Ruben J. Martinez, the farmers of the San Luis Valley, and the example of the South Central Farmers added to my understanding of food and freedom, and their work is reflected in the best of my practices.

The mezcla of my affiliations discussed throughout this book include my associations with anarchists, Marxists, and other revolutionaries. All this experience and living as learning is brought to bear on my work in a Black food autonomy movement in Chicago. Mezcla or mixing is a key principle in Indigenous agroecology, nature, and human communities. A politicization of diversity, mezcla, or mestizaje yields revolutionary polyculturalism, and it is revealed and practiced in our gardens and broader movement. I offer Indigenous/Black anarchism to create our desired society and overcome the limiting factors of race, nation, and heteropatriarchy. In the final chapters of this study, I propose an antiauthoritarian, anti-colonial, alterNative (AAA) masculinity to revolutionize and indigenize our sex-gender practice and theorize and synthesize anarchism and radical Indigenous and African traditions into an urban anticolonial theory/praxis.

Teosinte, Collards, Frijol, Ngumbo

The history of food and culture in the African diaspora is replete with adoptions, adaptations of, and exchanges with Amerindigenous foodways and other cultural traits.[36] Black American food thrives on a foundation of ancient African technology while adopting and adapting technology of the myriad cultures they have encountered. This process continues in the gardens and farms of the Black food movement in Chicago. Gregory Bratton teaches to always grow the "three sisters." In addition, the Amerindigenous developed the tomatl, camotl (sweet potato), and many of the chiles that now grow in all vegetable gardens on the South Side. At the same time, "traditional" Black foodways influence the food arts and sciences of many people of Mexican descent in Chicago. Greens and ngumbo (okra) grow alongside Amerindigenous-origin crops.

Diversity plays numerous roles in food autonomy. As land stewards we know that polyculturalism is a law of nature. No ecosystem can be sustained if it does not include diverse species in mutually beneficial interdependent relationships.[37] Industrial agriculture with its monocultural production techniques breaks this primary law, and the soil, water, and air suffer. Moreover, this law does not simply apply to "nature" outside humanity. Work with our relatives in gardens and farms teaches the lesson about the primacy of diversity. Many have begun to apply this law to human society. Well-ordered societies require diversity of opinions, ages, sexualities, ethnicities, and interests. Again, the best of our work implements the natural law of biodiversity, mixing African, Amerindigenous, and European foodways and horticultural technologies while communing with diverse groups of people.

Space, Place, Territory

Perhaps the key concern of people in the food movement in Chicago is the control of urban space. No matter where one or one's group is on the political spectrum, if you are involved in growing food in Chicago (or anywhere else), you are concerned with who controls the land, how it is controlled, and what is done with it. This major concern of the food autonomy movement puts it in league with recent antistatist movements in Latin America. Many in our movement in Chicago recognize that focusing on demanding rights or equality or justice from the state has largely been a failure. In the realm of food, the state and corporations form a junta that enforces profit-making over citizen and consumer health and welfare.[38] Thus, many in the movement have moved away from a civil rights discourse and speak about sovereignty, self-determination, "commUnity" wealth, and empowerment. In our January 2015 conversation, Austin Wayne articulated this position when he critiqued the concept "food justice" as one of dependency. Black food activists like Wayne (though he would reject this description of himself) refuse "the politics of demand":

> a politics that, no matter how it wears the guise of defiance, ever positions us as humble petitioners waiting to be acknowledged, recognized, included by the state as a neutral arbiter, a monological consciousness that, upon request, dispenses rights and privileges in the form of a gift.[39]

Radical Indigenous scholar/activists similarly reject colonial, capitalist norms regarding land and the notion of "justice." The politics of recognition is a settler-state strategy to maintain dominance over Native people. The state uses a combination of exclusion and assimilation as means to dominate Indigenous peoples. Reserves, reservations, and ghettos are examples of exclusion, as are limiting access to educational or other resources. Assimilation includes the notorious boarding schools responsible for the kidnapping and murder of Indigenous children and violently forcing Christianity and European thought and habits on to them. Recognition is an assimilationist politics that aims to reinforce state power through bestowing upon Indigenous people citizenship rights and inclusion in the Canadian, U.S., or Australian body politic. Assimilation illustrates the vast power difference between settler states and Indigenous nations. It is not decolonial in that it does not return land or resources to Native people and does not seek to retrieve, develop and further Native culture and identity.[40]

Landmark cases, *Pigford I* (1997) and *Pigford II* (2001), are examples of how the politics of recognition "stymies the production of alternative social projects beyond the fiscal logics of the U.S. government." Politics of recognition further legitimates colonial, White supremacist institutions leaving the Black food "movement vulnerable to co-optation." Relying on governmental redress of grievances through such mechanisms as *Pigford* mires Black and other colonized communities in a civil rights discourse that ultimately reinforces dependency.[41]

Large numbers of Black food activists in Chicago do not humbly ask the political elite for "rights and privileges" to live the lives they desire. They refuse the "politics of demand," recognition, or "begging" as Wayne calls it. They have learned that relying on Wetiko's anti-Black, anti-Indigenous political structures and practices cannot lead to Black and Indigenous surviving and thriving.[42] Instead, they strive for commUnity empowerment (as Dr. Jifunza Wright would frame it), by building collective adaptive capacities that will help them survive and thrive in uncertain and difficult times. To be self-determined, communities must have control of the means of production—primarily, the land.

Raul Zibechi's analysis of autonomous, nonparty affiliated, antistate movements points to how the most marginalized and disempowered have begun to "take the everyday life of their people into their own hands . . . They have become producers, which represents one of the movements' greatest achievements in recent decades, in terms of autonomy and self-esteem."[43] They have been able to do this through a redefinition of land and the reterritorialization of spaces neglected and deprived by the agents of capitalism and the state. They open "territories of resistance" where noncapitalist, nonhierarchical social relations can develop. Some anarchists describe this strategy as the creation of counterpublics.[44] In Latin America the subaltern rural and urban populations have been manipulated by capital and the state into increasingly dystopic spaces on the margins. Massive population shifts have been a common strategy of capitalists since the seventeenth-century enclosure acts. The hundreds of thousands of dispossessed peasants throughout Latin America have created rebellions such as Movimento dos Trabalhadores Rurais Sem Terra (the Landless Workers Movement) in Brazil and the Zapatistas in Mexico. In cities the masses of unemployed in Latin America create hyperlocal movements that fulfill their members' needs in ways that the state and market are unable to. In Chicago and throughout the United States, gentrification destabilizes the neighborhoods of the inner city. The rapid destruction of Chicago's housing projects and subsequent relocation of tens of thousands has led to several responses including the development of new community organizations.

Many in our food movement have begun to see the possibilities created through this urban "renewal." As neighborhoods are abandoned and left with little employment, few food resources, and numerous vacant homes and lots, groups like GLP begin to see space differently. Instead of lack, we see human potential. Like decaying life that provides food for other life, urban decay could mean new life for those left behind. Instead of lots of vice and violence, we create green lots filled with gardens and other means of sustenance for our communities. We reject imposed identities and instead redefine ourselves, our spaces, and our communities. We create autonomous, democratic, and nonhierarchical community gardens as counterpublic spheres to practice a new urban right livelihood. The final chapter of the book includes an analysis of community gardening and the food autonomy movement as potentially revolutionary direct action and as a redefinition of self, community, and space.

An important strategy of new movements that seek autonomy, nonstate forms of social organization, and noncoercive human relations involves exile from capitalism, the state, and its culture. In Abya Yala/Turtle Island Black, Indigenous and other people of color have been using this strategy of exilic self-activity since the early days of colonialism and slavery:

> Spaces of exilic self-activity represent not only an escape from the state, but exit from the totality of hierarchical relations that form the capitalist world economy, of which the state is only a part. What distinguishes exilic self-activity from other instances of exit is that it assumes an alternative construction as well as a characteristic spatial organization.[45]

To develop effective resistance to capitalism and the state, people need spaces of relative freedom from agents and institutions of domination.[46] These spaces are not peripheral to larger revolutionary behavior but are a prerequisite for it. It is in the free spaces, counterpublics, or autonomous zones where we can have the interactions that can develop our exilic logic, where we can decolonize and re-indigenize our minds. Much of the food autonomy movement in Black Chicago resembles the exilic self-activity of maroon societies and other Black liberation behavior as well as the new movements in Latin America and elsewhere in the developing world—what some have referred to as "fugitivity."

While developing counterpublics and exilic behaviors are crucial to improving the lives of the subaltern working classes and marginalized, and are required of revolutionary politics, the fact that a space may be liberated for a time does not mean that it will automatically meet the criteria of an AAA community. The culture of domination enforced by Wetiko is omnipresent. Moreover, exilic self-activity takes place within a global capitalist system. Engaging in this strategy means a constant negotiation with the state, the market, and the insidious cultures that develop from them. Dropping out like the yippie strategy of the 1960s in the United States risks devolving into individualism or tribalism which are key practices of Wetiko society. To best understand the food movement in Chicago, the threats to autonomy within the food movement must also be understood. Racism, selfishness, heteropatriarchy, classism, and consumerism prove to be formidable foes of food autonomy work. In addition, liberal capitalist ideology in the movement leads to struggles for reforms or "crumbs off the master's table"; we are left to beg the state or corporations for food instead of autonomy.

Writing about the Movement

This book began with an invitation by Devon G. Peña to contribute to *The Environmental and Food Justice* blog. We decided that analysis of the food justice movement in Chicago would broaden our discussions about food justice and help create new relationships. I accepted the challenge and decided to title my occasional blog series, "Food Justice in the City." I wrote my first blog post, "Key Concepts" (expanded as chapter 3), as an introduction to important ideas to ground the food environment in Chicago in the broader discussions of food justice, community gardening, and urban agriculture. Later essays focused on specific experiences that I was having in the movement. Parts of these essays have been expanded and updated in this book.

Given the centrality of teaching and learning to the movement, I have spent more than fifteen years learning, understanding, analyzing, developing, and implementing pedagogical strategies appropriate to the goals of the movement. Many blog posts focused on pedagogy and my development as a teacher and student of food autonomy and community empowerment. In dialogue with elders of the food movement, I learned of their pedagogy and placed it in critical, positive tension with other liberatory pedagogies. I discuss the results of this development throughout this writing.

My frustration with explaining the revolutionary politics of the Black food autonomy movement to "communists" fully invested in a Marxist-Leninist worldview prompted me to write the chapter, "Indigenous/Black Anarchism: Liberation Thinking in the Food Movement" (chapter 10). I felt that the lack of understanding of others' movement traditions confirmed the original intent of my project to broaden dialogue and develop new alliances. Each of the groups and traditions that I work with rarely consider the others. For me the goals of anarchists, Indigenous people, and members of the Black food autonomy movement had natural affinities and similarities that made dialogues and the development of networks between these groups obvious. As it turns out, capitalist ethics, racism, stereotypes, racial supremacy, and other ideologies and practices of domination keep distinct groups from seeing these affinities as clearly. I believe that an Indigenous/Black anarchist praxis can overcome the myriad challenges to Black, Indigenous, and working-class solidarity.

The food autonomy movement in Black Chicago emphasizes community, collectivity, and nonhierarchical relations. Throughout the writings I discuss these qualities. However, the essays, while informed by dialogue and careful attention to my colleagues, accomplices, and elders in the movement, reflect my own individual understanding. They are from my individual perspective and reflect a variety of hierarchies. In the end, there is not likely to be a satisfactory solution to this problem. However, this realization changed the book in important ways. Instead of only having the essays sprinkled with knowledge and wisdom from conversations I was having with movement accomplices, I decided to foreground a diverse array of voices from the movement. I asked my comrades and accomplices to tape dialogues with me in which many of the ideas I had heard and begun to write about could be discussed and debated. Important parts of the dialogues appear throughout the various sections of this book to add depth to my analysis.

"Beggin to Be Free"

AUSTIN I. WAYNE ON JUSTICE AND PROTEST POLITICS AS DEPENDENCY

AW: *I'm gonna tell you right now, before we get started. I'm not on that food justice shit.*

Austin wanted to make it clear before we started to record our dialogue that he disagrees with the food justice frame. I responded, "Great! This is exactly what I want from these dialogues." He started to explain his critique of "food justice." I stopped him to turn on the digital recorder. We began the taped dialogue with his critique of justice as dependency. Throughout the more than two hours of conversation, we returned to

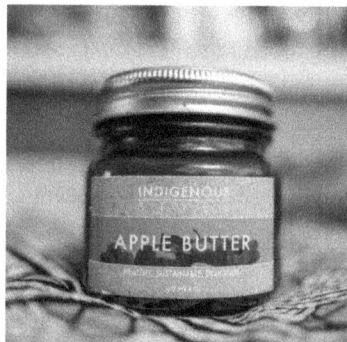

FIG. 2. Apple butter from Austin Wayne's Indigenous Style Foods. Photo by Tafari Melisizwe.

his fundamental problem with how we understand the work that we do in the "food movement." In addition, this conversation with Mr. Wayne is a good place to begin our examination of our movement since in it he discusses key issues such as sovereignty, self-determination, our disconnectedness to nature, movement tactics, health, and more.

PM: Some of the stuff you have been saying is what I have been learning about food from the justice frame. But it also includes a lot of things that you would include in the way you are approaching sustainability. When I said, "Autonomy," you said that makes sense to you, right?

AW: What's the definition of justice? Let's look it up.

PM: I think people would say fairness, being treated fairly.

AW: Yeah and equally. But equal to who? Equal to who?

PM: It's not about comparing yourself to somebody else but about living how you wanna live.

AW: That's saying it right there that you don't belong to yourself. Being treated fair. Who do you belong to? Are you your own person? Am I my own man? That's the kind of conversation I'm on.

PM: When I think of justice I think of those terms: sustainability, self-determination, autonomy. I do. But I see what you are saying. It's still a dependency frame.

Later in the conversation I respond to some of the definitions of "justice" that he looked up.

PM: Fairness was the first thing that came up. So we are doing this book. I'm editing this book of pieces on Indigenous, Mexican, Mesoamerican food ways and more in the United States. How those folks have always been mixing and stuff like that. But what does it look like today? We were going to call it . . . One of the frames we were going to use is "decolonial." They were gonna call it Decolonial Food for Thought. They decided to change it, but that's kind of a frame too. Part of getting your mind right. Part of taking back your . . . who you are, self-determination. Not only creating things but creating who you are. Being able to define yourself instead of letting someone else define you.

AW: Exactly.

PM: That's part of the decolonial process . . .

AW: And that's what's got to happen in order to become sovereign. "Justice. Fairness. State of affairs in which conduct or action is both fair and right given the circumstances. In law it more specifically refers to the paramount obligation to ensure that all persons are treated fairly."

PM: So is part of the problem with that is the way they define justice is that you are asking for compensation from somebody. Would that be part of your problem with that word?

AW: Yeah. Somebody's obligated to ensure that all persons are treated fairly. So, you [are] asking.

PM: So justice as a concept, as an idea, always has to go back to someone being in charge, someone on top. Every one of those things you read comes back to that. The justice frame is limiting in that way.

AW: Exactly. That's the way I feel. It's limiting.

PM: It doesn't allow us to really think more about terms like "freedom." I do use "justice," but . . . "freedom," "autonomy," "self-determination," those are terms that feel more comfortable to me in terms of how to think about what I am doing and how to talk to people about what I am doing.

Mr. Wayne sees protest politics, protests, demonstrations, and the like as futile. More than just ineffective, these actions take away from the goals of self-sufficiency and sustainability. Perhaps, more importantly, protest politics, or what he describes as "asking" or "begging," changes a land-based value system into a deeply entrenched dependency. Being on the land, working with nature, creates an understanding about how life works, its cycles and its lessons that most people living in the overdeveloped world do not have the opportunity to learn. The desire for material objects detached from their origins and relations of production (à la the Marxist idea of commodity fetishism) robs us of a land-based ethic and appreciation of life processes. Land-based ethics and experience exist in harmony with the self-sufficiency and sustainability emphasis of many of my accomplices in our food movement.

Mr. Wayne continues his critique of what he sees as the dependency frame of "food justice" and its consequences:

AW: When you learn that from all the social justice people, I mean protesting and slave reparations and revolts and stuff, slave insurrections and stuff and revolts and stuff, it never worked. We still in the condition that we are today. Even worse. We probably even worse because now we stripped from the land. Back then we was . . . the land was more . . . society was more plantation based, land-based. Even though it still is, but more back then. Now we off the land . . . People don't even wanna think about getting in the dirt. You got these girls without a pot to piss in looking at these rich women on TV and wanting to look rich too. It's the value system too at the same time.

PM: So you think that kind of value comes from being stripped from the land and the loss of that relationship, that understanding.

AW: I would say it play a part in destroying the value system. Being on the land you got more appreciation of how things work. You gotta make yourself warm at night. You gotta grow your own food to eat. If you want cherries and blueberries, you gotta make sure that blueberry patch is straight so y'all can have blueberry pie.

We discussed some of the fundamental principles and strategies in the food autonomy movement: accountability and responsibility. We know that to be healthy—mentally, physically, spiritually, and otherwise—we must do it ourselves with our community. We must be responsible and accountable to one another and ourselves.

Austin's critique of an underlying dependency in the food justice perspective leads us to discuss contemporary social justice movements. At the time of our conversation, hundreds of thousands of people in the United States were in the streets protesting, slowing commerce, shutting down highways, and confronting the police in response to the continuous callous lack of regard for Black life as illustrated vividly by police murders of unarmed Black men. The murder of Black teen Michael Brown by Ferguson, Missouri, police officer Darren Wilson was the catalyst for the 2014 protest movement. People all over the world were incensed by other police murders of Black men and boys including the videotaped police choking murder of Eric Garner in New York City (allegedly for selling loose cigarettes) and the shooting of teenager Laquan McDonald sixteen times in the back by Chicago Police officer Darren Wilson and subsequent state coverup by Mayor Rahm Emmanuel (former chief of staff to President Barack Obama). Because Austin has familial and community ties with Ferguson and spent his youth in the area, this was a perfect opportunity to explore the differences between current protest politics and work in the food movement. Protestors and food movement worker proclaim to want improved conditions for the poor and people of color and would seem to have many affinities. Our conversation revealed how different these social movements are.

PM: You see the unbroken line between slavery and dependency in the United States and what is happening today. It's the same stuff. Right?

AW: Yeah.

PM: And what it is is not what we call slavery or plantation. It's dependency. We're still controlled and [made] dependent upon. That's the relationship to someone who is more in power.

AW: They talk about, you know, slavery. The picture that we get ain't always the picture that it was, especially in North America. I'm not gonna say it wasn't bad and all that, but, you know, they talk about they didn't have bad relationships with their masters. Masters left them they land after they died.

PM: Which doesn't diminish slavery; it just helps us understand where we're at today.

AW: That's what I'm sayin.

PM: Slavery was horrible but so is what is happening today.

AW: We're still enslaved. It never ended. Now it's just more broad. Everybody is a slave. Everybody is a number. It's a business. This is a business.

PM: It just changed its form a little bit; some legal changes, some other things happened.

AW: The United States is a business. It's a corporation. It's clear how everything works. It's a business. So, like, I don't see us getting nowhere wasting our energy yelling. Unless I'm yelling down the field telling you that here I come. I got some watermelons down here too.

PM: So the whole protest politics and that you don't see as very valuable?

AW: Yeah. No, because you're begging to be free. What you beggin for? What you beggin for? Huh?

Wayne continued his critique of protest politics by arguing that it is ineffective and hypocritical. Protest politics amounts to asking (not demanding) from a more powerful entity that you be treated fairly. In addition, Austin argues that the people who want to disrupt and protest the police will run to the police when they are needed. He sees protesters as hypocritical, too, because they rely on the capitalist economic system to supply their sustenance. They are dependent upon the same system that they argue they want to replace. Moreover, police violence against young Black men has roots that most do not examine. The extreme power differential between the state in the form of the police and Black people and other disempowered people makes it foolish to act other than in deferential ways when confronted with their power. However, the strategy is to build "alternative institutions" while surviving under the current conditions of master's house. Austin uses the metaphor of living in your parents' house to explain this strategy for seeking self-determination and sustainability.

AW: They [are] gonna call the same people [police, authorities] who they were talking crazy about asking for justice from. It's nuts. It's nuts. That's why I keep going back to, it's no difference from being in your mama and daddy's house. You do what the hell you are told and whatever you can do until you can get up outta there. Right now we [are] some kids. Minorities. That's what they call us. It's minor. That's what they mean. There are way more of us than it is of them. It means minor, feeble-minded . . . It's all by design. People are protesting about all kinds of shit around the world, around the country. I'm so tired of hearing about damn protests! For real.

PM: I was going to go down to Ferguson and be a part of that. I thought it was important to be around where there was a fight against the state.

AW: What the hell am I gonna do locked up in jail but miss the [Healthy] Food Hub and miss money and get further away from my goals? That's all that's gonna happen to me going down to Ferguson. My other mother lives in Ferguson. I'm from around there. I didn't go down there not once. What the hell am I gonna do locked up?

PM: But the counterargument is you could be locked up anyway, so you want to fight to change it. This is the argument I'm saying. So that's why you would do that so you can try to fight for change with a bunch of other people.

AW: How could these people do that? Stop what they doing and go. How can you afford to do it? You got days to put away and miss money to go yell? That means you don't have no goals for yourself. That means you are looking to somebody else for security.

PM: I got you, but the point is still we are living in this thing whatever you want to call it. We're not free or whatever . . . The fact of the matter is that you can be attacked and killed. OK? It doesn't matter if you go to Ferguson [to protest] or not. So why don't you fight?

AW: It's not about to change. That's the simple fact of it that Michael Brown wasn't the first nigga that got killed in St. Louis. You feel me? It's like maybe a few dozen niggas got killed since Michael Brown got killed by each other. People got robbed . . . First of all, it's not changing nothing. It's not happening to everybody. Police are not about to roll up to me and blow my mother-fuckin head off. All police are not on that. They not on that. I don't care how much they coming through the neighborhood and hate you and all that. Your vibrations can change their vibrations quickly. I done did it. I'm telling you. If I see the motherfuckin police, I'm not gonna act like I got more power than he do. Because he can take me to jail right now and fuck up my whole day. Feel me? I ain't about to act like I got more power than him. I ain't about to talk shit. That's why I don't mess around with these young dudes cuz they hot. I know when that police rolled passed him telling him to get the fuck out the street, they went off on his ass cuz they probably didn't have no pistol or no weed on them. They clean. They talk to the police when they clean. That's how young dudes do. They talk to the police when they clean. That's stupid. Ya hear me? That's dumb. That right there is dumb. Those people get killed by the police. Talking shit to the police like they got more power than they do. They don't. You don't.

PM: Let me ask you so that I'm clear on what you are saying. You're saying that the protests are taking away energy from things you need to do, your goals and stuff, and, at the same time, it's wrongheaded in that way, strategically it doesn't change anything either.

AW: Put it this way. If I was protesting, I would be wasting my time. I wouldn't be changing anything. I would be just biting the hand that feeds me and yelling for nothing. That's what I would feel like if I were to go protest. I ain't gonna say nuthin about nobody else. Let them go do what they do. At the end of the day, they probably don't know what to do. That's what people who don't know what to do gonna do. Get mad and yell.

PM: I have disagreed with people in my circles, too. I have other circles besides the food community. Other people, political, revolutionaries, and all that. I have this argument with them. I'm trying to figure out how this fits in with the book, too. What we are doing. Whatever you wanna call it, sustainability, food justice, urban ag, all these kinds of things. What we are doing is really, you talk about revolution and all this, you are trying to fight the state and all this but [you don't]. What we're doing is we are actually, really taking our power in some ways. Anarchists call it direct action. We're doing it for ourselves. They want to have an armed revolution against the state or they wanna protest or they wanna pass out literature and stuff like that. I'm saying . . . if the problem is our health and our welfare and our mindset, that's what we need to, we're doing that. What your revolution [the protests] is doing, again, it's almost like a dependency thing. Asking for better conditions . . . What allows you to do that is that you have a nice job or whatever. You're not really being self-sufficient. You're being something else.

AW: People comfortable in this world they live in watching scandal, artificial stuff. People comfortable. That's one thing about people. They get comfortable quick. Ya know?

PM: So that's a problem of comfortability. We are at a high level of comfort in our illusions or delusions.

AW: Comfortable with it but not comfortable at the same time. Comfortable with it but got something to complain about.

CHAPTER 2

People, Places, and Spaces
OUR COMMUNITY

In the introduction, I mentioned many of the people who I have interacted with in the food movement in Black Chicago and described my methods
of analysis as auto-ethnography. In this chapter, I introduce important members
of the movement and set the scene for our work in the food movement and my
work as a scholar examining it. Most of my interlocutors have been my teachers
and co-workers in the movement. Others have been people who have influenced
me from a slight distance. Each has their own unique perspective and story. This
diversity and the multiplicity of relationships that it engenders is extraordinary
and one of the reasons this movement provides hope.

Additionally, I develop a history and analysis of the work of the Black Oaks
Center for Sustainable Renewable Living, the Healthy Food Hub, and Green Lots
Project through documents and eighteen years of field work in Chicago's abandoned lots turned garden oases and similar spaces where food autonomy takes
place in Black Chicago.

GLP: Community Gardening and Food Autonomy in Roseland

My entrance into the food movement began in 2005 when I met Dinah Ramirez, a
long-time activist and resident of South Chicago, my new neighborhood. I moved
to South Chicago based on a suggestion by the dean of the College of Arts and
Sciences at Chicago State University, Rachel Lindsey (later she would serve as
interim president, 2016–2017, and chairperson of the board of directors of BOC).
When interviewing for an assistant professorship in sociology at CSU, I asked if
she knew of a working-class neighborhood relatively close to CSU and preferably
diverse with a Mexicanx and Black majority. I landed in the historic community
that was one of the first destinations of large numbers of Mexicans in the early
twentieth century. The steel mills provided a degree of comfort and safety (though
racialized violence and struggle for limited resources was not uncommon), so that
a solid working-class neighborhood of Mexicans, Blacks, and immigrant Europeans developed. Once the steel mills closed due to deindustrialization in the 1980s,
South Chicago saw an extreme economic downturn that coupled with the economic devastation of Black communities and the dispersal of thousands of Black

families from Chicago's housing projects destabilized South Chicago by the time I moved there in 2005. I arrived to find a mix of gangs, illicit activity of all sorts, violence, and extreme poverty as well as families working hard, community gardeners making a difference, and activists fighting for justice.

In the fall of 2005, I asked Danny Block, PhD, professor of geography and director of the Neighborhood Assistance Center at CSU, if he could suggest people to speak to about getting involved in community work. He recommended Dinah, who was serving as the executive director of Healthy South Chicago. I soon joined HSC and became president of its board of directors. I learned that their four areas of engagement included access to health care and healthy habits. One of our most successful projects was assisting a neighborhood organization with maintaining their garden two blocks from my apartment in the particularly troubled section of the neighborhood called The Bush. Dinah hired Gregory Bratton to manage the garden. I met Gregory in the HSC offices and got to know him.

In 2008, I called Gregory telling him that I was ready to fully engage in community gardening and asking if he knew of a garden in my new neighborhood of Roseland. I moved to Roseland for family reasons, and it has turned out to be one of the most important relocations of my life. In Roseland I learned so much about Chicago, inequality, and the problems facing Chicago's working-class Black community and about the rich and dynamic movement of which I have become involved. Roseland is a community on the far South Side of Chicago. Early in its history, it served the Pullman railyard with many of its residents working in the industry. From the time of its creation in the mid-nineteenth century till the 1960s it was also overwhelmingly White. More recently its reputation has garnered it the nickname, "The Wild 100s." Roseland and its fifty thousand residents, 97 percent of whom are now Black, have a history that repeats itself in Black neighborhoods throughout the country. As the neighborhood changed from White to Black, Whites fearing displacement mobilized. In 1943, they protested new housing intended to attract Black residents. Finally, in a last-ditch effort to keep Blacks out, Whites erupted in the Fernwood Riots in 1947. White residents beat Black newcomers to keep Black migration east of the railroad tracks.[1] The unsuccessful riots took place on the streets outside my former home, where my children attended elementary school at Fernwood Elementary and on the very spot where our Sacred Greens Community Garden (407 W. 104th Street) was located. Of course, the riots were unsuccessful, and Roseland became a middle- and working-class Black community.

In the 1970s and 1980s, Black middle-class flight to the suburbs left the once stable Roseland with few professionals and Black business owners. The dismantling of the vast federal housing projects and their community networks established by long-term residents led a new population of the marginalized to migrate to neglected areas of the city such as Roseland. The result was a further breakdown of the community. The gutting of Roseland included a lack of food options. Today, Roseland is considered a "food desert" or, perhaps, food junkyard, as there is not a single full-line regional grocery chain in the geographically large community. A few small and discount grocery stores complement the dozens of fast-food and corner-store junk-food outlets that dominate the foodscape of Roseland. The community, like all communities suffering under food apartheid, has more than just the problem of a lack of food. The average median income was $10,000 less than that of Chicago as a whole and the poverty rate of 27 percent compared with the city rate of 21 percent. Yet the average rent in Roseland is higher than in the city average. One in five households is headed by a single woman, and women outnumber men by more than five thousand. Roseland can be tough on its residents, including a crime rate twice that of the rest of the city, older housing stock, and few natural spaces to help us cope with the concrete, crime, and crack.[2] Despite these difficulties, many in Roseland such as Diane Latiker of Kids Off The Block and Daryl Gibson of Southside Economic and Environmental Development Systems, Inc. have created spaces of healing and resistance. Some of these spaces include gardens. Over the years I have learned to see Roseland in all its fullness and resist the urge to see Roseland in stereotypical anti-Black racist fashion as a community solely characterized by lack and pathology.[3]

Upon my arrival in Roseland in 2007–2008, Mr. Bratton pointed me to the Roseland Community Friendship Garden (later renamed the Roseland Community Forest Garden, RCFG) where I met Dominique R. Bowman and the other members of GLP. Dominique envisioned turning the lot on the northwest corner of 104th Street and Wabash into something of an outdoor community center with a garden as a central meeting place for neighbors to build community and better health and to employ neighborhood teens. She worked with Fred Carter and Dr. Jifunza Wright of BOC to develop an organizational structure, set of principles, and strategy for achieving her vision.

With their influence, Ms. Bowman developed several founding documents including the following GLP "Mission Statement": "GLP is committed to inspire and educate communities across the country to grow food in environmentally sustainable ways and create community food systems where fresh, affordable, and locally produced food is available to all." The document also discusses GLP values, including access to land for all, sustainable small-scale agriculture, education for community improvement, community self-governance, and collaboration and valuing local knowledge.

Keeping the mission and values in mind, a small group of us worked the two city lots. With no water source on site, our neighbor graciously let us use his outdoor spigot to turn the lot into a lush productive space for community involvement. When the task of organizing GLP members fell to me two years later, I hit the pavement and worked to raise awareness about this community resource. My position at the university located only blocks from the garden in a section of the neighborhood called Rosemoor provided me with many opportunities to speak with students, faculty, and staff. Dozens of members of the Chicago State University campus provided labor, donations, and friendship that helped the garden grow. In addition, I began to seek out alliances with people and groups doing similar work. As a result, I was asked to speak at several different venues about the work we were doing. More people joined GLP. Most came out infrequently, and some worked with us for an entire season learning how to bring seeds, some soil, and water together in a neglected part of the city to provide healthy eating options for the community; a small number continue to work with us.

The hunger for healthy food, community, and beauty led many to seek out GLP to assist on garden projects. In 2010, CSU student intern Ebony Johnson, organized an elders' gardening club at a senior citizens' home one block from the RCFG. Each week Ebony and I worked with a dozen or so elders raising seedlings, planting them in their raised beds, and caring for them. Unfortunately, a change in personnel at the home led to a dissolution of the project, a problem that small community groups like ours encounter regularly. We tried again in 2011 when another former CSU student asked us if we would install and help maintain a garden at an elder's community in the historic Black neighborhood of Bronzeville. Five of us, including my two oldest sons, Gregory Bratton, and CSU student intern Tre Thomas, built a garden in Bronzeville. The elder's gardening group consisted of a dozen enthusiastic members. Many of the elders held critical African heritage knowledge (AHK) they learned from the southern Black agrarian tradition. They had sufficient knowledge to make a garden grow but lacked the resources and labor power. GLP and the elders bartered. We supplied most of the labor, and they passed on critical AHK that would assist us in our growth as urban land stewards and growers.

In addition to our initial garden and the elders' garden in Bronzeville, we offered our labor and expertise to community gardens throughout the South Side. Importantly, we began a partnership with Southside Economic and Environmental Development Systems (SEEDS), Inc., a small group of committed neighbors in Roseland. SEEDS developed from the needs of parents in the neighborhood and one staunch antipoverty, pro-education activist. Daryl Gibson (a parent) and Paula Roderick (a North Side activist and lawyer) worked with Dunne Elementary School to secure a site for the creation of a "mini-farm" where they could grow

FIG. 3. Ebony Johnson and Maurice Walls. Photo by Tafari Melisizwe.

healthy food, teach children academic subjects and life lessons, and provide job opportunities for them. This small group had almost no growing experience, yet they saw the need for and potential of a community garden to contribute to alleviating some of the numerous social ills in Roseland.

Over the years, human and nonhuman beings have ruined large parts of the garden. Sometimes maliciously and at other times out of a desire to help, individuals mowed over, trampled, or incorrectly harvested some of our plots. We determined that for the garden to produce at its best and to have a space to teach we should erect a fence. We wanted to have a teaching space and, at the same time, have an open space for members of the community. We did not want to alienate members of the community by locking up the garden. This would go against our vision of including as many people as possible in our work. Yet we felt frustrated, angry, and disappointed when we came to a workday and found parts of the garden destroyed.

On the advice of Emmanuel Pratt of Sweetwater Aquaponics and the Aquaponics Center at CSU, we enclosed a small portion of the garden. Mr. Pratt told a story about confronting the same issue during a previous project in which he was involved. In this project the group decided to enclose most of their garden with a fence but were sure to plant plenty of space outside the fence with vegetables that anyone could access. With a small teaching grant from Chicago State University, my "Food Justice" class built an Outdoor CommUnity Classroom at the Roseland Community Peace Garden. CSU intern Tennille Birden organized the effort in which we erected a chain link fence around a third of the garden space, built tables and a bench, and created a small discussion space using logs.

With work on the RCPG/RCFG going smoothly (more or less) we decided to begin a new project. In 2012, we partnered with Chicagoland Prison Outreach, a nonprofit Christian ministry dedicated to assisting formerly incarcerated men develop skills in welding and computers. The land on which CPO trains its clients is located one block from where I lived. Dan Swets and Corey Buchanan invited GLP to take over a large garden that had been created by a group of men from the Cook County jail's "bootcamp" and teenagers from Dayton Christian School in Ohio. As part of longtime Cook County sheriff Tom Dart's reform plan to change the horrific conditions at the jail, he created a bootcamp that engaged men in a variety of skills-building events. Unfortunately, the gardening effort ended as soon as they were done with the initial building and planting of it. The garden was built and planted but then left with no one to maintain it. GLP stepped in at the end of the season to plant greens and harvest the abundance of food that was growing haphazardly there. In between the 2012 and 2013 seasons, Dan, Corey, Jacqueline Smith, and I met to work out an arrangement for GLP to take over the garden. In recognition of the spiritual nature of both CPO and GLP, we named the garden "Sacred Greens" and began work in March 2013. The solid GLP crew consisted of new members Karlita Jefferson, Linda M., Dwight Dotts, Rashon, Salvador, Malik, Jacqueline, and me. In our gardens we got help from CSU students, CPO students, and others throughout the South Side.

In the same season we began work on a garden for Ashburn Community School. Roderick Cox of Metropolitan Family Services, Principal Diaz, a parent advisory group, and GLP worked out an agreement to build a large community garden for the school children, their families, and others in the neighborhood. Our plans fell through due to concerns from the Catholic archdiocese that owns the land on which the school sits. However, the Ashburn Lutheran School and Church just down the block welcomed us to create a much smaller garden on their property. GLP and Mr. Cox got busy and built a small garden consisting of seven 6-by-4-feet raised garden beds. There Jacqueline and I taught a small afterschool group about square-foot gardening, nutrition, and IK/AHK. With so many bureaucracies working on this effort, the project sputtered along for two years. Chicago Public Schools, like many throughout the country, place financial importance in areas other than nutritional education and home economics. Chaos at Chicago Public Schools caused the project to be unworkable in the third season. The all-too-common story of good intentions of community activists being thwarted by city politics led to the project's demise in 2016.

At the urging of Kevin Triplett, a communist friend (in the Marxist-Leninist tradition), we began a new garden in 2016. As a communist, Kevin believed in the elimination of the wage system and money and in the kinds of collective work that we were doing in community gardens. In the fall of 2015, Kevin and I, following advice from Jacqueline, developed plans to turn an abandoned garden in the lot next door to his home in the Auburn Gresham neighborhood into a thriving, collectively worked garden. Kevin wanted to use the opportunity to show members of his community how communism could work and how a society organized under communism could produce better and create a better quality of life than that afforded by the capitalist economic and social system. Although not a grower himself, he wanted to work on a garden with his neighbors with GLP lending support and advice in a space originally owned and operated by St. Sabina Catholic Church, the home church of well-known activist priest Father Michael Pfleger. Church members built the garden and whimsical wooden raised beds but later abandoned it. For years, Kevin and his son labored to keep the lot from being an eyesore. Kevin wanted to use the GLP garden as a model whereby members worked the land, produced abundantly, and gave away excess produce. At the same time, he could teach communist ideas and reach his community with a communist message in a more effective manner than he was used to seeing with the efforts of communist organizations with whom he had been affiliated. He had grown weary of "coffee shop communism" where members of organizations sat around discussing the minutiae of communism together but doing little to reach people as well as the aggressive protest politics of some who showed up at every protest event speaking loudly about communist politics in a manner that was more alienating than endearing. So in March 2016 we purchased twenty yards of manure to supplement the soil and woodchip mulch already at the garden and brought CSU students including men from the African American Male Resource Center, neighbors, and concerned others in our circles to spread and mix it and repair the small, decorative growing boxes made by the previous gardeners from St. Sabina. We "guerrilla" gardened at this site and called it a liberated space or temporary autonomous zone. We dubbed it El Jardin Izquierdista/Community Garden of the Left. We turned the eyesore into a thriving garden without anyone's permission. Like Austin Wayne, we refuse to beg someone for the right to live well and create community.

In September 2018, at the end of the growing season, with El Jardin Izquierdista thriving and new members Carolyn and Donnell participating enthusiastically, the garden turned into a lesson in private property under capitalism. St. Sabina Church and community had been wanting to get rid of the property at 8557 S. Loomis for several years. Kevin had tried to negotiate with them to purchase the lot before our gardening on the site, but communication proved difficult. One day

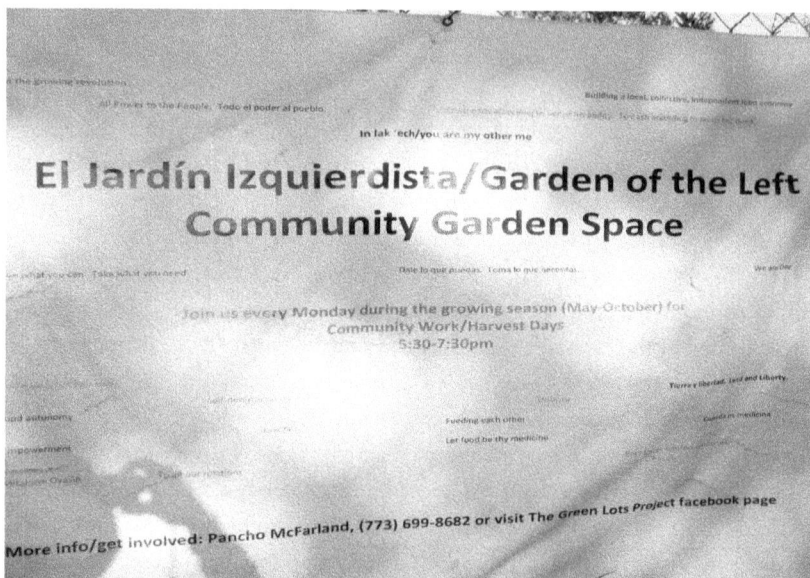

El Jardín Izquierdista/Garden of the Left
Community Garden Space

Join us every Monday during the growing season (May-October) for
Community Work/Harvest Days
5:30-7:30pm

More info/get involved: Pancho McFarland, (773) 699-8682 or visit The Green Lots Project facebook page

FIG. 4. Sign at Jardin Izquierdista. Photo by author.

Kevin saw strangers appraising the garden space. When he inquired, he found that a minister from a nearby church had purchased the lot. He hoped to put a community garden on the site! The irony, of course, is that we were already clearly doing this, and we had announced our activities clearly with a large sign that included our contact information. So the pastor purchased a thriving community garden and displaced its community gardeners without consulting them, so that he could put a community garden on it. Even in this instance the land teaches. We learned about property relations and how sustainable, just land practices mean little without land title. Our arguably healthy, community-oriented practices on the land have zero value in the eyes of property owners, even those owners who ostensibly believe in and practice community improvement and stewardship. For about four years the lot remained empty and once again began to become an eyesore. Recently, the lot was purchased, and a few flowering bushes and other plants now grow there. In 2022, the new garden included a few beds for vegetable growing.

Besides the unpredictable human element in urban settings, urban community gardeners have several problems. First, the land on which we grow is often contaminated with all types and number of toxins. In general, we do our best to cap and build on top of the existing contaminated soil. We place a barrier down and then bring in new uncontaminated soil and build raised beds on top. Second, water is often an issue. Many of us have found great abandoned spaces on which to build a garden but find that it has no water source. We encountered this problem at the RCPG. Initially, GLP received permission from the City of Chicago to use a hydrant one-half block west of the garden. This involved lugging large amounts of heavy hose down the block each time we needed to water. Of course, this manner of watering caused numerous problems including the time required to set the hoses up and that we had only one key to the hydrant. If the person with the key was unavailable, then the garden did not get watered. Soon our neighbor just to the north of us came to the rescue and allowed us to use the water from his external spigot. We used this source for several years, but when the homeowner became mired in legal problems and a dispute with the Water Department our source of water dried up. We again sought City permission to use the hydrant. In the 2013 growing season, we used a combination of the fire hydrant and the neighbors across the street to water our garden. Neither source was a good solution for our problem. The next season the city changed their policy on allowing the use of hydrants for community gardens. It became almost impossible to get permission. We relied on our neighbors from across the street to help our garden grow for the 2014 and 2015 seasons.

A third problem with community gardening in the city involves participation. Participation fluctuates greatly from week to week and season to season. When I was able to bring a class of students to manage the garden for ten weeks during the summer, we had a steady set of hands for a good portion of the growing season. When that labor source ended in 2013, it was up to GLP members and occasional volunteers to care for the garden. But the all-volunteer labor force could not be counted on, especially during the cold days of late winter/early spring when we do the important preparatory work and during the hot dog days of summer when we are tired from a few months of gardening work and just want to sit in our air-conditioned homes. For us, this problem has yet to be solved, though our solid core group is enough to grow abundantly.

As a result of the problems of water and participation, we decided in 2012 to fill the RCPG with perennial plants including herbs, berry bushes, and trees. Mama Dorothy began implementing the plan by planting herbs throughout the garden and in a lovely herb bed; novice volunteers helping to "put the garden to bed" (shut it down for the winter) destroyed many of Mama Dorothy's herbs at the end of the 2012 season. However, her mint and comfrey were saved and continue to produce abundantly for us and numerous others throughout the South Side. In the same season we planted raspberry bushes. Since a large section of the garden on the west side of the lot went unused most seasons due to lack of labor power, we decided to place a berry bramble there hoping that it would grow and fill in the space in the coming years and provide delicious, nutritious berries for the neighborhood kids and GLP members. The berry bramble performed multiple functions (a key principle of permaculture[4]) not limited to being a source of food, including serving as a windbreak for annual crops, a habitat for small animals, birds, and insects, a source of food for pollinators, and a living fence and outline for pathways.

With the success of the mint, comfrey, and raspberry bushes, we were emboldened to add more perennial elements. We began studying perennial plants and permaculture design. Two of us spent time at the BOC learning from Baba Fred and Mama Jifunza, including an incredibly informative two-day session with Dr. Ross Gay. With this new knowledge in hand, we began to redesign the RCPG into a forest garden. We planted more raspberry bushes and added perennial herbs. In 2015 we teamed up with Openlands and Gabriela Naveda, who offered native fruit and nut trees to community gardens. By the end of the season, we had planted sixteen native trees and thirteen native berry bushes. We designed a seven-layer forest garden using Indigenous knowledge and the permaculture idea of guilds. We used nature as a guide (biomimicry) and planted complementary plants that would work together to provide all the nutrients needed.[5] Our guilds consist of a primary element (usually a tree but sometimes a berry bramble), a ground-cover and herbaceous element (often the mint that Mama Dorothy planted those years ago), a bioaccumulator (comfrey and rhubarb), a root layer (onions, garlic, and lilies), plants to attract pollinators, and other elements.

As of this writing, the experiment is successful. We decided to rededicate and rename the RCPG. It is now the Roseland Community Forest Garden. Due to the water and other problems, we chose not to plant annuals between the 2014 and 2018 growing seasons. Instead, we maintain the forest garden by pulling weeds, mowing grass, maintaining pathways, and picking up trash while harvesting the abundance of food growing without our help. The food and medicinal plants we planted during the 2014 and 2015 seasons and wild edibles such as dandelion, plantain, clover, and lamb's quarters provide members and neighbors with remedies for all kinds of ailments and nutritious food. Importantly, the neighborhood children enjoy the berries which bring them closer to nature and pique their interests in healthy food and the environment. More than four hundred people came through GLP gardens in the 2015 season. Most worked briefly at the Roseland Community Forest Garden and were given a tour of it. The tours, which last between one-half hour and two hours, include discussions of horticulture, permaculture, home economics, IK, urban social problems, traditional medicine, macroeconomics, and other topics. The problems of water and participation were turned to our advantage (Mollisonian principle: "The problem is the solution"), and the creation of the forest garden provided numerous opportunities to further our mission and

FIG. 5. Adults constructing a water catchment system. Photo by author.

spread knowledge about urban growing and self-determination. At the end of the 2018 season with the design and building assistance of Baba Eugene Mason, a graduate of the Lifeboats Permaculture Guild, we built a 255-gallon rainwater catchment system.

Importantly, GLP attempts to break down barriers between various communities. Chicago is historically the most racially and ethnically segregated city in the country. In addition, the city is segregated by class and many ethnic and racial communities are segregated by generation. GLP crosses ethnoracial boundaries encouraging Latinxs and Whites to work and share in Black communities. Additionally, we make great efforts to bring different generational groups together. Our workdays include a mix of children, young adults, and elders. Each group contributes to the overall effort in different ways and interacts with others learning from and loving one another. The work of student volunteers, primarily from Chicago State University, challenges class boundaries and breaks down divisions between the academy and the community.

The GLP mission includes helping to develop a local food economy whereby people can have much more control over the production and consumption of our food. Besides maintaining community gardens, GLP leads workshops, gives tours, works with other groups, and helps coordinate a number of growers to take steps toward developing a local food economy through growing, aggregating, and distributing produce and other food products within a fifty-mile-long area stretching from Kankakee County to the South Side of Chicago. We also sold small amounts of produce at extremely low prices to local markets, especially the HFH providing healthy options for community members in Roseland and other South Side neighborhoods that have few opportunities to eat healthily.

GLP members give lectures and workshops to numerous audiences. Schools, after-school programs, and churches are the primary audiences for these activities. Besides educational activities, GLP shares plants, seeds and produce with countless others. For three years GLP had a tomato-plant giveaway at the beginning of the season. Tomato plants first purchased from HFH grew abundantly at the RCPG as the plants dropped their seeds and reproduced the next season. We always had hundreds of tomato plants growing in our garden beds and only cared to grow a couple of dozen each year. We hated to throw such a great resource away but could not use so many plants. The tomato-plant giveaway developed to use the plants and to introduce more people to our garden and our organization. Over the three years that we held the giveaway, several hundred plants were given to dozens of people. Each of these plants provided a great source of nutrition and enjoyment as well as more tomato plants in subsequent growing seasons. In 2017, as part of my final project for my Permaculture Design Certification at BOC, we installed a "CommUnity Nursery" that has provided several gardens with berry bushes, onions, comfrey plants, and medicinal herbs. In this way we multiplied our efforts to extend traditional foraging knowledge and "earth care, people care and fair share" (the three revised permaculture principles of ethics). In addition, we joined coalitions such as the Roseland Pullman Urban Agriculture Network, the Chicago Community Gardeners' Association, and the Greater Roseland-West Pullman Urban Agriculture Network. Our associations with others serve as a form of mutual assistance in which we traded and borrowed tools, knowledge, seeds, seedlings and produce.

Black Oaks Center for Sustainable Renewable Living

The Black Oaks Center in Pembroke, Illinois, fifty miles or so from Chicago, is the locus for an important part of the Black food movement in Chicago and my and GLP's primary collaborator. On their website they explain that Akin Carter, Fred Carter, and Dr. Jifunza Wright "formally established [BOC] in 2008 [but] its true beginnings date back to 2003 when the family became aware of resource depletion and climate change. The family made a deep commitment to bring information not only to our communities who were totally unaware but most importantly begin to create a path to solutions to our impending energy descent."

Baba Fred Carter explained further that his knowledge of the impending energy crisis and the lack of preparedness of "the Black community" for it spurred him to work hard on BOC:

> They [people in the alternative energy and permaculture communities] said the community that was gonna suffer the most was the community that I came from because we don't know anything about it. In fact, Richard Heinberg [author of *The Party's Over: Oil, War and the Fate of Industrial Societies*], I was angry at him. I thought he was a racist when he made the statement, "Fred, if we understand that people in your community are played as fools. And we know you all don't have any more room to put anything else on your plate." What do you mean you don't have room to think about whether or not your baby is gonna be here in ten to twenty years? Anybody's got room for that! You know? Thinking about that knowing these things are occurring. They are happening for real. No matter what you like or dislike about them. And it's gonna impact your children in a way that you have no background to even think about. Black folks got room on the plate for that. You know? And then at first I thought it was a racist statement, but it was true. Young guys are so full of other problems. So [now] we understand cuz we did the research. Now he tells me he did all the research on the problems in our community. He's from California. And I was angry. He shared this with me when we was in Peoria, Illinois, at a conference on peak oil. I was the only brother. I was sitting at a table at a restaurant with all these White guys and they're talking about what they're gonna do in their community around this concern around energy and around environment.
>
> That blew me away when he said that. I thought he was a racist. But later on, I really got the impression that he wasn't racist. He was just stating the truth. And so we decided after that event in Peoria and then Yellow Springs, that we needed to come back to our community and educate us, so we're prepared for what's gonna happen so. We're just not total victims, which is what we normally become. The last one to know and the first one to go. You know? And that's what they were saying. "I'm not gonna make it. I don't know anything about it. We don't have no preparations in our society. Not educating our children about it; not doing anything about it." We have no clue. You know? So we started Black Oaks.

BOC honors the key species of the dwarf black oak savanna ecosystem and the Black farmers/stewards who migrated from the South to escape the violence and oppression there and turn their skills and AHK into a prosperous life, including, as Dr. J likes to discuss, that the area was the largest hemp-growing region in the country during the World War II-era (hemp being a plant that Doc and Black Oaks are returning today as a sacred plant and economic engine for the region).

Unfortunately, Pembroke's prosperity lasted only a few decades as multiple factors, especially racism in the markets and at governmental agencies, have led to a dearth of Black farmers in Illinois and throughout the country. The Pigford case (*Pigford v. Glickman*) found a "well-documented pattern of discriminatory lending practices employed by the USDA against Black farmers."[6] Those Black farmers who remain "receive fifty percent less government support in terms of loans, conservation programs, subsidies for crop production and disaster insurance than the average farmer of any race."[7] Black Oaks and the Carter-Wright family work tirelessly to bring back BAT and the self-determination and empowerment that goes along with it. An important part of their mission is to train Black farmers. They explain this goal in an email from the HFH on June 1, 2015:

> Black Farmers & Ranchers [*sic*] are less than zero point one percent of all farmers in the United States. It is up to us to pick up where the Elders left off to take black farming to the next level; to be local food system developers, to be producers that play a key role in feeding our communities, our region, our nation. We are at a unique advantage: we have land. We have more folk that want to pay to eat our food than we can supply. Let's fill the gap and harvest the wealth from seeds our Ancestors toiled long ago.

The above email message was sent to members of the HFH, which is an African-inspired market started in 2008 by BOC at Trinity United Church to fulfill some of their goals. The market has struggled over the years and has been located at and relocated to the Betty Shabazz International Charter School, the Good Foods Garden, and the Quarry Events Center, and other locales on the southeast side of the city. In 2018 and 2019 BOC contracted with Cook County Health Services to provide a revamped HFH at Cook County medical sites. In 2020, during the COVID-19 pandemic, Black Oaks began strategizing about a mobile market. In 2021 the HFH became a delivery service. While the HFH is effective in bringing affordable and sometimes free food to the community, it has lost its place as a community-building practice.

In our taped conversation Baba Fred explained how HFH evolved:

> We actually started at my wife's medical practice. It was a food buying club. It was called the Organic Food Buyers' Club or some name we had. And it wasn't a HFH because that came later after Trinity. So she used food as medicine. So we all fell in love with Whole Foods. But her patients kept telling her, "Well, I can't afford that, Dr. Wright?" So we started the food buying club with the patients. We'd buy collectively, split it up at the office twice a month.

At every market day for years, an important ritual would begin when Baba Mike Tekhen Strode took the microphone and announced a "mission break." During the mission break Baba Mike quieted the crowd with a loud call of the Akan "ago" ("attention") and crowd response, "ame." Then, he proceeded to remind us of the rest of the ritual. First, he would recite the HFH mission statement, and then we would "hold" the mission together as a community by repeating it slowly:

> Our mission is to create a just, holistic local food system to transform urban to rural communities through education, entrepreneurship, and access to healthy, affordable food.

Holding the mission together, we were a congregation committing ourselves to the goals and values of the HFH and BOC. The commitment of Baba Fred, Mama Jifunza and Akin, and the community around BOC includes a spiritual calling. In 2016 the BOC website described this commitment:

> In honor of our Ancient Ancestors who mastered the skills of sustainability, we have come to understand that land is to be shared. We are doing all we can to care for the land we have been given and to foster harmony and balance, to protect life and defend against all that threatens it. We invite those who share our vision to come and create safe healing spaces here on the land with us.[8]

The mission of the HFH and Black Oaks includes working toward developing a local economy bringing in local businesses to supply needed products to a resource-starved and resource-denied community. The market includes educational workshops, movies, discussions, demonstrations, planning sessions, and gourmet-quality food cooked freshly from locally sourced produce and eggs. Kemetic yoga, tai chi, and other healing arts are practiced occasionally. Music and dancing breaks out often with Baba Mike leading the music and small groups dedicating love to the community and family by singing.

Black Oaks is a complex, ambitious project, as their Values, Visions, and Mission statements attest. According to BOC documents, BOC values include collectivity, cooperation, and "honoring the sacredness of life." The BOC "Vision Statement" includes the following: "Our vision is to create safe, healing spaces founded on the principles of environmental stewardship and social equality." They want to teach as many community members, especially Black and other BIPOC, to be "lifeboats thriving during an energy descent." Thus, their "mission is to foster resilience." To accomplish their goals of developing skills for community resiliency, they prioritize educating and "empowering children," creating rural-urban connections, and providing opportunities to work collectively. Their work is organized around four areas: renewable energy, sustainable building, sustainable agriculture, and resilience.[9]

Black Oaks has continued to evolve over the years, and the members have engaged many coalitions, networks, and institutions to realize their dream of creating a local food economy, including working with local and state political entities. In 2017 BOC began the Lifeboats Series with a Local Food System Development with Permaculture Design Certification. Late in 2016 Doc and Baba Fred invited me to collaborate with them on designing the course and serve as one of a three-person team of teachers. The course began in February 2017 and ended in October 2017. The unique course taught permaculture design through a hands-on and multilayered cooperative pedagogical model discussed in part II of this book. As of this writing, I continue to serve on the board of directors of BOC. Their latest programs include hemp growing and processing along with specialty grains as economic drivers for their other projects and for Pembroke Township as a whole, and in 2021 they began a struggle against big-energy interests in Pembroke and their state of Illinois and local government officials who wished to engage in a land grab through a natural-gas pipeline project.

I taped a dialogue with Baba Fred on March 2, 2016, at the Starbucks on Seventy-First and Stony Island, a block from Mosque Maryam, an important Nation of Islam mosque, and where he and Dr. Wright were engaging in food business later that day. I asked him to describe how he got into the food and sustainability movement. After 9/11, the transportation industry "tanked" in his words. Within two years he had to sell his company when transportation companies could not pay their bills. He began to take his interest in solar energy seriously. He explains:

> I didn't know what to do with myself. It was time for me to re-create myself. So in the crash of 9/11 I had to re-create myself, my whole career. I looked at where could I go. My wife, her practice was going real good at the time. So she said, "You are out of work, figure out what you want to do." The thing that came to mind was I always wanted to know about solar. So I thought of these ideas. I thought about geodesic domes and aquaponics and stuff like that.
>
> I took the energy class up in Wisconsin first. Very racist environment. I was the only Black person there. The only person that was speaking was the instructor. He was a great old hippy. I can't tell you his name now. But he did something that just blew me away. I had never thought about environmental stuff. Never thought about anything that had to do with anything. I ended up spending close to $800 on books because I bought everything that he said to buy. They had a bookstore up there. They had a renewable energy class annually. It was the largest in the Midwest. So I took the class in solar hot water. And he said, "You gotta read this one book, Fred. This is gonna change your life. It's called, *The Party's Over* by Richard Heinberg." And right now he is one of the top in the world in sustainability and energy. Peak oil. I read the book.

After his early exposure to the energy crisis and peak oil, he began taking classes on sustainable energy, energy all over the country. Empowered with a great deal of knowledge, he and his family incorporated the BOC for Sustainable Renewable Living "in order to bring this information back to [their] community."

Baba Fred's partner and wife, Dr. Jifunza Wright, is an important healer in our community. She has an MD and is a holistic medical practitioner. I met Dr. Wright at the HFH in 2008 when it was held at the Betty Shabazz International Charter School. "Doc" (as I call her) or "Mama J" or "Mama Jifunza" (as others call her) plays numerous roles in the community. First, Doc's leadership at HFH is a central component to the success of the community. She generally manages HFH during market days and works with others to enhance the market. Without her, the market would be a very different thing. She heals as part of her formal work as a doctor and informally through advice on diet and other lifestyle issues at the HFH or BOC. During the six-week-long Spring Community Cleanse, Dr. Wright brings together dialogues and workshops to help us cleanse. An email to members of the HFH on August 5, 2016, described Dr. Wright in the following way:

> Jifunza Wright Carter, M.D., M.P.H. is a family physician boarded in Holistic Integrative Medicine. She has gone from an organic farmer and food system builder to now take her rightful place at the Quarry [Events Center] to work in team to provide health care, local healthy food, plant medicines and other antidotes as the CommUnity Wealth Wheel comes together.

Dr. Wright is the busiest person I know. She plays several roles at BOC and within our community. So I had difficulty pinning her down to tape a dialogue with her. I was finally able to record some of her words on May 5, 2022, and recount some her words that she uttered during the Resilient Community Design course that she, Baba Fred, and I taught together in the spring of 2022. Doc explained that she had always been attracted to plants. She said, "I have been growing food and medicine since I was a little girl." For Doc, maintaining her connection to her African and Indigenous roots are important. While she is a Black woman and works primarily within the Black community, she recognizes the crucial role of her Amerindigenous family. Doc explained that when she was young, she remembered her "aunts who would be speaking the language. They would be cooking, or it would be late and they would be speaking the language." Her calling to be a holistic doctor who uses plant medicine and nutrition as her primary healing modalities came early from both Indigenous backgrounds.

Numerous members of the food autonomy movement have been mentored, encouraged, and supported by Doc and Baba Fred. Dozens of people have gone through their farmer training programs, worked on projects associated with BOC or the HFH, or taken the Lifeboats Permaculture Design Certification (PDC). As of 2023, their latest educational programming includes the Pembroke Farm Restoration program, several workshops each season, and permaculture courses.

My Accomplices

Over the years I have had dozens of conversations with important people in the Black food movement. I decided that I should record some of those that have influenced me and subsequently, the work of GLP. Chief among my influences in this movement is Mr. Gregory Bratton. Mr. Bratton has worked with numerous organizations to build dozens of gardens; he provides materials for community gardens and consults on urban agriculture projects. At the time of our recorded dialogue, he was the executive director of I Grow Chicago/Intergenerational Growing Project. He explained, "Our true mission is to have a 100 functioning city gardens by

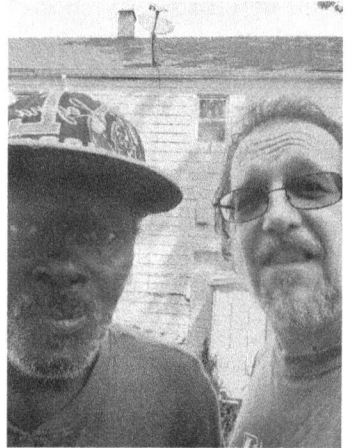

FIG. 6. Gregory Bratton and Pancho McFarland. Photo by author.

2020. The reason for that is that the equivalent of 100 functioning gardens in the city would be the equivalent of feeding 385,000 people per month."

He explained his longevity in the food movement and dedication to urban agriculture and the problem of food access for working-class Chicagoans when I asked him about his motivation:

> At one time I thought it was just one of my pleasures or a hobby. As time went on, I feel it became my calling . . . I find great pleasure in knowing that I'm feeding people and saving lives as well as teaching people. You know? Because we possess the knowledge of growing anywhere . . . So we teach people sustainability and how to grow anywhere on any surface at any time. Even through the winter.

In the above statement, Mr. Bratton touches on community, sustainability, and pedagogy, important emphases of the food movement that run throughout our discussion, his teachings, and this study. I learned a great deal directly from Mr. Bratton at the Roseland Community Peace Garden, our elders' garden in Bronzeville, numerous gardens in South Chicago and Englewood, and in workshops.

Dominique R. Bowman (now Vining), founder and first executive director of

GLP, reintroduced me to Baba Fred, who I had met the year previously working with Mr. Bratton. From my association with Baba Fred and Dr. Jifunza Wright, I became deeply involved in the movement. I met many of the interlocutors in this book at the HFH and many of my other teachers are somehow associated with the HFH and Black Oaks, Baba Fred, or Mama J.

At the HFH, I met Mecca Brooks (2010), Austin Wayne (2010) and Safia Rashid (2012), accomplices and friends who agreed to tape dialogues for this book. Mecca described her introduction to the food autonomy community around Black Oaks in our taped dialogue:

> For four years I've been working at the intersections of food, gardening and I'd go beyond food justice and say overall people of color justice. Sustainability justice would be a better, more accurate word for it. Really looking at how those three things come together in public space and public space as a notion of shared space … This summer I worked with Safia Rashid, who I know from the HFH with Your Bountiful Harvest … I'm in this group called Sustainable Leadership Network. The purpose of the group is to bring voices of color together around the sustainability movement.

When we taped our dialogue, Ms. Brooks from the New Jersey and Philadelphia areas lived and practiced "sustainability justice" in the historic Black community of Bronzeville in Chicago. She is part of a growing cultural renaissance in the area that includes professional arts and educational institutions as well as several grassroots initiatives.

I taped a dialogue with Austin Wayne at his residence on December 17, 2014. I met the twenty-something native of St. Louis four years prior at the HFH where he had just begun to work. During our dialogue he explained that in 2009 as a teen he had begun to change his life. He moved to Chicago and became acquainted with HFH. Since then, he has been a part of the Black[10] food community serving as the market manager for HFH for a number of years and owner-operator of Indigenous Style Foods. In 2017 he began working an empty lot in a neglected part of the South Shore community. In this garden young Black men and women who have been written off by society work to improve their lives. As Austin wrote in 2017, this garden is "bringing kale to the hood." Since we met in 2010, we have had dozens of conversations at markets and other places where food work occurs.

His critique of "urban" and the urban lifestyle illustrate his desire to be landed, sovereign, and moving and working at the pace of the land:

AW: It's an urban way or language, though. The justice thing. It's urban. The whole urban thing is by design. It was a money thing.

PM: Right. So the idea is that the development of the European city was that you bring populations from the country together in one place so that they could make stuff to make people rich.

AW: Then, you gotta depend on them [owners] to live. They [workers] work to live. They pay the money right back . . . keep all going around. To keep the system going. What "urban" is is to keep the system going. If it wasn't for urban, I don't think that we'd have this system.

He uses IK and AHK in his efforts to marginalize the system and achieve his goals of independence for his family. His company, Indigenous Style Foods, demonstrates his commitment to land and community. He sells his medicinal food products at HFH and other places. Austin explained that to solve some of the problems plaguing our communities we need medicinal food. He believes that changing the gut microbiome will change how people think, which is the first step toward changing society. His marketing and selling of kimchi and his gardens are steps in his effort toward this change. In addition, his hummus, apple butter, and apple sauce were staples in the pantries and medicine cabinets of many who frequented the HFH.

I met Safia Rashid and her husband, Kamau Rashid, PhD, around 2012 through HFH. A mutual friend introduced Kamau and me at a market day at the Betty Shabazz International School, an important Afrocentric educational institution founded by Black literary legend and former faculty colleague at CSU, Haki Madhubuti, and wife, Carol D. Lee, along with Robert J. Dale, Anthony Daniels-Halisi, and Soyini Walton in 1998. I first learned of Safia soon after when she led a discussion of "community" in the local food movement. Safia and Kamau have three impressive children who are involved in entrepreneurship and maintaining and developing their understanding of African diasporic traditions. I have since interacted with Safia and Kamau on numerous occasions including a shared car ride to Detroit with Safia, Mecca, and Jacqueline Smith to attend the Black Urban Grower's Conference in the fall of 2014. We recorded a conversation in the spring of 2015. During our conversation she discussed how she became part of the food movement through her desire to contribute to the "Pan-African nationalist movement" and her desire to become healthy. She said,

So being a vegan, a vegetarian, then a vegan. Well, a meat-eater first. Meat-eating, [then] went to college [and] became vegetarian. Then, shortly after having my son being vegan. So it kinda came up because of the movement and saying, "What else can I do? What else can I contribute? There are these five levels of institution building . . . through the sankofa movement we learned that. You know they talk about food, health care, shelter, etc., etc. One thing I thought about was the food.

Like, you know, growing up things kinda centered around food cuz we didn't have a lot of money.

In addition to her Pan-Africanist roots, Safia began growing to improve the lives of herself and her family. She explains her concern about the effects of Wetiko's food on their health and using that as a catalyst for participation in the food movement and developing her own urban farming business, Your Bountiful Harvest, where she educates primarily Black people in autonomous, ecological growing in the city:

> For me, I already started this journey of trying to eat healthy. Learning about GMOs. Learning about all these different things just came to a head. How do we grow for ourselves and for our people? Coincidentally, just after I had my daughter, maybe six months in or so, you know, she started having these allergies, suffering from these allergies. But at the time we didn't know that they were allergies. But we learned about the allergies. Because conventional medicine wasn't working, we went to a natural doctor. She right away was able to point out that this was eczema on your face and that it is probably linked to food allergies because you are nursing. And it may be some environmental things as well, but I had already been using natural almost everything in the house. So she's like, "It's probably linked to your food." So that got us really going. So we started in our little apartment with pots. From there I grew with the pots when we moved back here, back to Chicago in 2009. We got the backyard and started back there.

Notably, Safia played an important role in the Lifeboats PDC in 2017. She offered several lessons including an important crop-planning class. For years Safia arranged a seed-swap event at the HFH. In 2017 she and Kamau visited the RCFG where we traded perennial berry and herb plants for some of their annual seedlings. Her leadership and commitment to the food movement and community empowerment is unwavering and inspiring.

HFH intersects with dozens of others in the movement including the Roseland-Pullman Urban Agriculture Network initiated by the efforts of Dr. Danny Block at CSU. While I met Jacqueline Smith at a coffee shop near my former home in the Beverly neighborhood, I got to know her better, in part, through our mutual affiliation with HFH. At an Roseland-Pullman Urban Agriculture Network event at the Aquaponics Center on the CSU campus in which Fred Carter was the featured speaker we discussed her joining the GLP. After some discussions, Jacqueline agreed to serve as project coordinator for GLP and began designing gardens and providing our organization with her extensive expertise regarding BAT and Indigenous land stewardship. In October 2014 she described herself in a biographical blurb advertising her appearance on the Café Yeye Show hosted by Marian Hayes on the CSU radio station, WCSU radio:

> I am the great granddaughter of a Mississippi sharecropper; agriculture is the industry of my focus, but gardening and farming are my ministries. As a Chicago South Side native, I witness and live in a food desert; therefore, I have been self-motivated to empower not only myself but other South Side residents to grow and secure their own food to be food secure. I seek to nourish my small business GrowAsis Urban Garden Consulting in order to carry out its mission and fuel my passion by advising and educating others on how to grow food sustainably in efforts to combat the food insecurity epidemic.

As a thirty-something, Ms. Smith represented a new generation continuing the traditions of Black diasporan women's struggles for freedom and for the maintenance of AHK. Her food experiences, interests and participation in the food movement resulted, in part, from being Chicago born and raised during the period of late capitalism, rapid increase in inequality, and climate chaos. She engaged questions of food security and earth stewardship from multiple vantage points. Ms. Smith had a great deal of urban gardening and teaching experience. At the time of our recorded dialogue, she had been involved in growing food in Chicago off and on for nineteen years. Her work with several community-based and nonprofit organizations generally revolved around growing but she also worked in other areas of service especially with young people. She wrote about food justice including a study of the impact of faith-based organizations on food insecurity in Chicago and an article about the Black Urban Growers Conference in Detroit in 2014. She wrote about urban growing and related topics for online publications and blogged and vlogged for her own website. She also gave lectures and presentations about food at conferences, workshops and classrooms and permaculture courses for The Permaculture Institute of Chicago including a Permaculture Design Certification that we taught together in 2021. In 2019, she began working with a wide variety of groups and coalitions including Urban Steward Action Network, Urban Growers Collective and Three Little Birds community garden. On March 5, 2021, Jacqueline died of complications from diabetes and gastroparesis. As a master of small-scale design, she used "indigenous food cultivation" to design a small homestead on the South Side of Chicago complete with thirteen chickens and medicines and foods that addressed her health challenges as a diabetic. Her lectures, workshops, classes, and tireless community-building efforts modeled the best of our community and gave us an example of how to implement permaculture and Indigenous knowledge. As a result, she is a revered ancestor of our community whose legacy is continued through various programs and memorial gardens.

Our dialogues and gardening work began in 2013. In 2014, besides launching her garden consulting business, GrowAsis Garden Consulting, Inc. and teaching sustainability in a summer youth program, she became a central figure in GLP. She, more than anyone in Chicago, impacted my thinking and work in food autonomy and became my most important collaborator before her untimely death at thirty-nine years old. As GrowAsis grew, Ms. Smith deepened her ties with and responsibilities to the Black food community in Chicago. Between 2014 and 2016 her pickled vegetables and herbs from her gardens and locally grown sources became a mainstay at HFH. Like Safia Rashid, Ms. Smith served our community well through her participation in the 2017 permaculture course. Her appearances at workshops, on panels and as a guest speaker at food events increased significantly in the last two years of her life. We taped a dialogue together on November 4, 2014.

Ms. Smith is responsible for making stewardship a regular part of my vocabulary and recurrent theme in my work. She later began to use the phrase "co-steward with nature" in recognition of the active and co-creative relationship that she and many of us strive for. Our dialogues often centered on notions of home, land and stewardship. In our taped conversation Ms. Smith pointed to her great grandmother as the origin of and model for her own values. Jacqueline often spoke about key themes in the Black food autonomy movement: identity, spirituality, and tradition, and its maintenance in the efforts of Black growers in Chicago.

Through Jacqueline I have met many wonderful people in Black food and related movements. Her connection to BOC and the HFH began at the important Black activist hub, Trinity United Church of Christ, where as a result of her work with its Green Ministry she helped Baba Fred and Mama Jifunza establish the first markets of the HFH. She introduced me to Paula Anglin, master gardener, Green Ministry member, gardening entrepreneur, professional actress and head gardener at Trinity's George Washington Carver Garden where we met in the spring of 2014 and where on August 25, 2015, we met to tape a conversation. Ms. Anglin had a serendipitous beginning to her gardening vocation explaining:

> I started gardening like in the '80s. My grandmother had, here in Chicago, had a garden. She had a corner building. And when she had her garden I wasn't interested in it. But I had an injury to my knee. I had to stop the job I was working on. And somehow I found my way to her yard. And it was a mess. But I just started weeding it and, you know, getting it organized.

Later, she became involved with Trinity's Green Ministry, practiced gardening there, read books on gardening and took some classes. According to Ms. Paula, the Trinity United garden on Ninety-Fifth Street across the street from the church began around 2000. She explained the garden's origins:

> Pastor Moss named the garden. We were sitting in church one day . . . and he said, "George Washington Carver." He said, "Wait, I think I just named the garden." That was his plan. I don't know. I heard him say it.

Trinity was the home church of President Barack Obama and his family and is the church of many influential Black South Siders including politicians, educators, and business owners. For many years Reverend Jeremiah Wright presided over the congregation. Wright, a leading Black liberation theologian, is renowned for his fiery speeches critiquing governmental policy and its effects on Black communities. The church has had a social justice mission for decades and is a leading voice for Black uplift in Chicago. In recent years, especially under the guidance of Reverend Otis Moss III, the church has emphasized environmental justice, sustainability and food justice. This focus continues the work of the national United Churches of Christ whose study and activism in the 1980s were watershed moments in the early years of environmental justice work.

Trinity is among many churches that participate in the food movement. God's Gang, created by Carolyn Thomas and family, developed out of "St. Mary's Church at 51st and Dearborn." Ms. Thomas created God's Gang in the 1980s at the height of gang violence in the projects surrounding St. Mary's. She explains how the organization developed:

> We had a lot of discord with the community, with the kids. Kids couldn't go out while church was going on or they would get beat up . . . But my son thought that the reason they couldn't get along with the kids, [why] they couldn't get on the court . . . They couldn't get time on the courts because they thought, in his words, we were better than them. We sort of promised that we would change that kind of feeling because every kid thinks their dad is better than your dad. Their dog is better than your dog. How could they think that, and we are all Black? And he said, "They see us coming in here and we're always dressed up and we get out of these cars and we come and do what we are gonna do. And we worship and we have a picnic out front or out back and then we leave. We never go to where they are."

God's Gang and St. Mary's began to bridge the divide between the church kids and kids who lived in the Chicago Housing Authority projects next door to it. This eventually evolved into a food pantry and then to a community gardening and social justice organization. I met Ms. Thomas at a meeting of a group of food activists who eventually became the Roseland Pullman Urban Agriculture Network. Ms. Thomas and I taped a conversation on a very cold day in November 2015 beginning outside at the Passion of Pullman Garden and finishing at the Ranch Steak House in Roseland; two spots that illustrate the struggle between unjust Wetiko food (Ranch Steak House) and community efforts at food autonomy (Passion of Pullman Garden).

The Roseland and Pullman neighborhoods are key to this story since most of my work has taken place in Roseland which also houses CSU founding home of the Roseland-Pullman Urban Agriculture Network and the Neighborhood Assistance Center. Danny Block, director of Neighborhood Assistance Center, has assisted the food movement in Black Chicago and has made CSU an important venue for food movement work. I met another member of the movement at CSU. Mila K. Marshall was a biology student at CSU when we met in 2008. After graduating from CSU, she attended graduate school at the University of Illinois at Chicago. We became reacquainted in 2010 when she invited me to speak at the Urban Resolutions Bridging African Americans to Natural Environments conference at CSU that she was organizing with Michael Howard of Eden's Place, another significant site of Black food struggles in Chicago.

Dr. Marshall and I met at the Iguana Café, a coffee shop north of the University of Illinois at Chicago, to tape a conversation on December 1, 2015. She described herself in this way:

> I am a struggling graduate student. I won't say struggling doctoral candidate at the University of Illinois at Chicago in the Ecology and Evolutionary Biology Department. So the work that I do focuses on the intersection between urban agriculture and environmental justice here in the city. I'm unlike many urban ecologists because I have a big interest in understanding how diversity and segregation within cities changes the environment for people to grow food or to grow high-quality food. It could be based on location next to industrial corridor. It could be because you are located right next to a busy expressway or even a bus depot or truck depot.

In addition, she works tirelessly for environmental and social justice. She hosts conferences and brings working groups together to impact government policy related to the environment and BIPOC.

I also met Paula Roderick through CSU. I heard about the Dunne School Mini-Farm from the Neighborhood Assistance Center in 2011. I showed up at a community workday and began meeting the members of Southside Education and Economic Development Systems, Inc. (SEEDS) shortly thereafter. Paula, a lawyer by trade and human rights activist by conviction, lives in the Edgewater neighborhood on the North Side of Chicago far from the food inequality and stifling oppression of Roseland where she engaged in food activism.

Her insights as an outsider to the Black South Side have long been valuable to me. During our interview she spoke about her understanding of racist oppression and poverty as manifested in our food system:

> I talk about my drive down from Edgewater where I live from the far North Side of Chicago down to Roseland because it is kind of a metaphor of what we're talking about. I come from my neighborhood where I have access within walking distance or a very easy bus ride, to two Jewel's, now a Whole Foods, it used to be a Dominic's and the Edgewater Market. I'm thinking I'm close to four different farmers' markets on different days. Then, I drive down twenty miles, not quite a twenty-mile drive, down Lake Shore Drive, some of the richest neighborhoods in Chicago and I see thousands of dollars of resources that are spent on maintaining the green spaces around Lincoln Park down Lakeshore Drive. Thousands and thousands of dollars are spent to keep those flowers looking well-watered and beautiful to get down to I-94 and you start coming south of the Loop and you see less and less and less. Less well-kept green spaces.
>
> I mean, then we get down to Roseland and the grocery store is Save-a-Lot. There isn't a choice. I can't even explain except that I know what it does for me . . . That doesn't make me smile . . . I look at the fruit and I go like, "I go back up to my neighborhood and I've got like thousands of choices." I thought "food deserts" doesn't really explain what's going on here. There's a lack of jobs . . . a neighborhood where there is 70 percent unemployment. Then, I can go up north, you know. So it's not just about the food and the quality of the food and the choices of the food. Someone today was saying she had to go to her physical therapist and it's two bus rides. It's a long bus ride to get to a physical therapist. Well, I've got chiropractors and physical therapists and hospitals all close to where I live.

Paula and I have had many conversations and worked together on a few projects. A memorable project included creating an on-site market stand at the Dunne School Mini-Farm in 2013. That year GLP sold dozens of pounds of purple-podded pole beans for a very low price to Roseland neighbors. For years later, people from the neighborhood asked me when the purple beans would be back. In addition to her local work, Paula sees the larger picture concerning the global food system and attempts to connect the concerns of the Black South Side with those of Palestinians who suffer similarly.

Dwight Dotts is the second longest continuing member of the GLP. I met Dwight in 2013. He came by the RCPG/RCFG, which is less than a block from his home. A gardener in the community of South Chicago who was affiliated with Gregory Bratton told Dwight about our garden. Since our initial meeting, Dwight has brought his wife and grandchildren with him to the garden and has provided quality informal education to dozens who have come to our gardens. In our 2018 taped dialogue, Dwight explained his approach to the work we do:

> The Caucasian race, they have the concept of ownership of everything. And you and I are kinda like, "I don't own the land. I'm only a tenant at this time . . . and this place . . . taking care of the land and it's hopefully to leave it in better shape than what I got it or at the same place when I got here. It is no worse for me to have lived on the planet so you can have enough to be comfortable when I'm gone." It's not the thing where I have to take every darn thing or I need to pull the oil out of the land. I don't need to pull the gold outta the land. No. There's enough. We should be able to feed everybody in the world. I think America if they put their heart to it, they could feed everybody in the world . . . I think there is enough land and the way that things are resourced, North America, the United States or Canada or both of us working together say "You know what? We're going to feed the whole damn world tomorrow. And you know what? We don't care about your affiliation, your government. We don't care about your religion, your gender. We don't care about your sexuality. I don't care. Are you hungry? Yes? You can eat." We could end the wars, the foolishness, all this foolish stuff that is going on. A man don't want to fight with you if you feed him.

In late 2021 after the COVID-19 scare, I began dialogues with accomplices again. Much had happened in the years since I first taped dialogues and felt that additional dialogues were necessary to reflect these changes and conclude the project. I had a dialogue with Dr. Bonnie Claudia Harrison (Alalade Feyisara) on November 5 using the newly discovered (at least for me) technology of the Zoom video conference call. So Dr. Bonnie (as some of her students refer to her) and I decided to record a dialogue from the comfort of our respective homes. Our recorded dialogue lasted ninety minutes and covered all the topics that the preceding dialogues and my experiences had shown were central to the movement. I anticipated that this would be the case and felt that this dialogue would make for a good summary of all that I had been thinking about for years regarding our movement.

I have known Dr. Harrison longer than anyone in our movement community. We met at the University of Texas at Austin in the late 1990s when we attended graduate school there, she in anthropology and me in sociology. We reunited in Chicago around 2010 when we found each other attending HFH. I then learned that she was married and had a child. I regularly saw her and her family at the HFH and we began to discuss working together. In 2017 she and her husband joined the Lifeboats PDC. Since then, we have worked together on many projects. Even while she told me that she doesn't see herself as a food activist, she and her family are deeply entrenched in the food community that surrounds the BOC, especially through the family property named CoGro Biodynamic Farms. As a professor at Kennedy-King Community College in Chicago, she has for two decades informed, trained, and organized the overwhelmingly Black student body in social justice. She says that more than a food activist she is a social justice trainer. In addition to political education and organizing tactics, as an Ifá priest she leads her students and comrades in understanding the connections between the spiritual, emotional, and the "political." Her keen insight into the human condition and her experience in movements causes her to question taken-for-granted knowledge. She challenges religious dogma and recognizes "race" as the ideological wool pulled over our eyes that keeps us from coming together. She explained in our taped conversation that to create a new world we "need to transcend the categories that our masters gave us."

When we began our dialogue, I asked her to tell me who she is. She responded:

> My best and most favorite place is standing in the prairie. I got to do that on my grandfather and grandmother's farm growing up in the summer and on breaks. I did that with my family. My people have forty acres here in the South Suburbs which didn't used to be the suburbs, here in Chicago Heights . . . I know the difference between standing in the prairie and standing in the city in Hyde Park, Forty-Eight, and Lake Park . . . If I had to choose, it would definitely be in the country. So I'm a country girl raised in the city.
>
> My grandfather practiced the Yoruba tradition on the land along with Indigenous practice. He self-identified as Native American, my grandfather . . . I wanted to go to Africa cuz my other side of my family is Afrocentric. I was raised Afrocentric in the city. My great grandparents were Garveyites. My grandmother was an activist in women's rights in the sense that Black women were not afforded the luxuries of beauty and grace and womanliness.

Again, using the power of video conferencing I recorded a dialogue with Bee Rodriguez, on November 18, 2021. I met Bee in 2019 when they took my Social Class and Stratification course at CSU. By the end of the semester, we had started working together on garden projects. They had established an organization dedicated to improving the community through tending a garden and working with young people of Mexican descent. Their organization, Reclaiming Our Roots, scouted their Gage Park community for an empty abandoned lot upon which to establish a garden. They found a space and began to guerilla garden on it. For two years their garden was a thriving outdoor cultural space that hosted events, healing circles, temezcales (sweat lodges), and rituals. They terminated this project after feeling threatened by a local gang member in 2022. Bee worked with Gage Park

Latinx Council, a women and queer-led community organization. In our recorded conversation, I asked about who they is in this movement:

BR: That question is always evolving. I went to get coffee before this, and I think right now I'm in a space that I'm understand that I'm always changing. That my physical, mental, spiritual body . . . I'm an ever-evolving being. At the time right now, I am an urban farmer, urban gardener, urban agriculturalist, however you want to call it, urban campesino and put the @ at the end. Cultural educator, creative writer, and an elder to many young people . . . I'm a friend to those young people that are coming to the green spaces that I organize in Chicago. I am somebody that is learning and reconnecting to my ancestry. A lot of the stuff that has made me who I am today, this urban campesino, if you may, is ancestral and it extends beyond my generation . . . it has been happening for years and years and years which is Indigenous land management. I am somebody who is trying to preserve that knowledge, that IK, within my own family. Right now, here in the United States, at least, out of all my family I am the only individual who is still practicing and trying to tend to the land. Not only ways of tending to the land but also reclaiming our spirituality that is related to tending to the land.

PM: That is who you are right now. That was the first thing I heard you say that I resonate with. I just finished this morning . . . Octavia Butler's book *Parable of the Sower*, which talks about change. She has her little verses about change, right. God is change. Change exists. I think it is one of the subtle ways in which Indigenous minds work and that colonial minds don't. There's a rigidity to that mindset that wants to control everything and doesn't want to accept change. I think as far as I understand there was an acceptance to change and that change and adaptation . . . that is what nature is. Nothing lasts forever.

BR: The way that I've seen the colonial rigidity is how we related with the land. We go down south in southern Illinois, and you see all these monocultures, mono-cultures that are not only monocultures but that are hurting the land because of a lack of diversity and the lack of, like, fluidity that exists within those green spaces. In comparison with, like, our milpa, our garden. In our garden this year we grew corn, but at the same time with the corn emerged a lot of other stuff that we didn't know were going to emerge. We had a lot of native plants. We had a lot of mint that popped up that we placed there to be in relation with the corn. Rather than colonial agriculture, which wants to kill everything and be rigid and just grow corn and kill the environment, you know? I learn a lot about my identity through those practices and I want to be more like the milpa, you know. I want to be more like the milpa. More diverse. More complicated, I want to say, more complex.

Bee's desire "to be more like the milpa" in its diversity, resilience and tradition epitomizes our food movement. Their efforts as a twenty-something urban campesino reflect the new generation of Black and Indigenous food activists for whom diversity is a given and flexibility, adaptation, and change are their modus operandi.

CSU also indirectly contributed to my relationship with Kevin Triplett. I met Kevin through my camarada at CSU, Dr. Floyd Banks. Floyd, Paul Gomberg, John Boelter, and a few other colleagues had a significant presence on campus as members of the Progressive Labor Party, a Marxist-Leninist/Stalinist revolutionary organization notorious for its confrontational actions and absolute commitment to ending racism. As a result of their commitments, we often ran into one another at political events and actions. I got to know Paul, John, and Floyd and started to attend Progressive Labor functions. I met Kevin Triplett at a salon held at Floyd Banks's house. Floyd, Kevin, and I had Sunday breakfast together for a couple of years where we solidified a friendship and learned of one another's politics. Kevin had been a long-time active member of the Progressive Labor during which time he made a career teaching grade school children in Chicago Public Schools. Kevin's deeply held convictions for creating a better world around communist principles and his experience as an active member of his Chicago community led him to working on a project with me.

I asked Kevin in April 2019 about how and why he decided to jump into the food autonomy movement in Chicago. He responded:

> The dialectic is there are things that are contingent and there are things that are necessary. The contingency was that there just happened to be this plot of land where I lived, and the other contingency was that I knew you as a member of this movement. The opportunity presented itself to say, "Hey, given what I know about you, given what I know about the neighborhood, given what I know about food, why not try to do this?" That was the genesis. An opportunity presented itself and personal relationships and politics were there to take advantage of it.

Kevin and I managed El Jardin Izquierdista for three years with the help of Jacqueline Smith and several community members and students. Kevin, GLP, and I learned a great deal about Wetiko from the rise and demise of this garden.

Finally, I interviewed a filmmaker and my former student at CSU, Maurice Walls. As I explain in the "Epilogue," Maurice has long been an admirer of our work and has an activist spirit. He contacted me in 2021 about making a short public service announcement around gun violence. The result was a short video shot at Sacred Greens Community Garden called "G.R.I.P. (Guns Rest In Peace)." We spoke over the phone in October 2021.

These are some of the important people I have shared struggle with over more than seventeen years. My work and the successes of the movement result from the tireless labor that my accomplices have performed over the past two decades. These folx have been my inspiration and teachers. The best of my work reflects them. What follows is an analysis of the struggles we have been engaged in together with all our relations.

Baba Fred and the Energy Conversation
RESILIENCY AND BLACK SURVIVAL

FRED CARTER: OK, I read this book. It's called *The Party's Over* by Richard Heinberg, and right now he is one of the top in the world in sustainability and energy, peak oil. I read this book. Screwed me up. I was really screwed up. I never thought about energy having to do with anything. But the oil embargo. They had gas lines and rationing. You're too young.

One of the exercises in the book said go down to the downtown section and imagine 10 percent less energy. I went on to the lakefront and thought about the aquarium, planetarium, and looked at the skyline downtown. I tried to imagine what it would be like if we had 10, 20 percent less power. Just imagine all the energy to move this downtown activity. People going to work, lights on, cars traveling and then I looked at it. I've been in business most of my life. How would you re-create a business without considering energy? I said, "I'm going to re-create myself." That to me is a cornerstone of being resilient, re-creating yourself. So I'm re-creating myself, but I didn't know what I was re-creating. I took the first energy class, got all this information about energy and the environment and all of that. Just bought the land.

PM: I wanted to ask you about these philosophical kinds of issues that I see in your value statement of Black Oaks, your mission statement. Things like collective and sustainability, resiliency. I just want to ask you what those things mean to you and why they are important.

FC: I mean sustainability has been so contaminated now.

PM: That's why I've got to ask the question because everyone means something different. You know, even the capitalists are talking about sustainability, sustainable development, and those kinds of things.

FC: The war machine's got a sustainability department.

Our interpretation of what sustainability is is to live a lifestyle that's perennial. And what I mean by being perennial is a lifestyle that can last for thousands of years without disturbing human or nonhuman. Perennial principle versus an annual principle that we live in now. It's not a perennial garden. Permaculture is not in the conversation. But sustainability is a principle driven by more perennial practice. So your actions are designed long term versus quick hit and don't worry about the consequences, what the outcome might be long-term. Although it's being used all over the place, "I want a sustainable military system." Wal-Mart has their green sustainability. All these companies have changed the original meaning. To me the original interpretation of sustainability from the ecological factor was about these perennials, biological systems that have been here for millions of years. Right? So we mimic their behaviors so we can maintain a lifestyle that's always something left for the future. So that's how I view sustainability. I get the military and the corporations want to be sustainable. Every living entity wants to be sustainable even if it's not healthy. Cancer wants to be sustainable. So that's where resiliency comes in. You know, our communities, what we've learned, used to be resilient. When something happened to us, we always seemed to survive. Not just survive we thrived. We improved. I mean there was a betterment. Constant improvement.

PM: Resiliency when I hear you talk about it is being able to survive and thrive no matter what happens. If there's no energy, if there's no oil, if there's no, you know, water systems, we're able to respond to that.

FC: Be able to psychologically manage yourself and the system manage itself and still play the game of life. And we lost that as a community because we don't control any of those key elements like the food, the water. We don't do that. We don't control any of that. We don't control our community. So we need to come out with an alternative safety net.

PM: Terms like "self-determination" and "community determination," "control over community resources." Is that the key to resiliency?

FC: The key to resiliency is control over what makes life work. And I don't mean control, like, I can control the movement in and out of it but control in the sense that if that's not there, if it's not available the way it used to be, your community is able to survive and come out with a state of well-being. To me that's the biological model. So your body loses balance, homeostasis, and then it comes back to a state of balance and health. So you went to hell and, you know, you came back from out of hell and you are still thriving and healthy. To me that's resiliency. So how do you do that in a community? I mean that's the question. I don't even know why I'm doing this when I think about it cuz it's crazy. I mean to talk about trying to have a conversation with people about something they can't even imagine. It's unimaginable to not have good water. I mean, that's unimaginable. Who can imagine that unless you are in Africa somewhere or someplace where it seems like it's a common thing. But on Seventy-Ninth Street or in Flint? People don't have clean water out there, man. My food is not what it used to be. I don't have any control over those things. When you go back in time that was something I grew up in the revolution. The plate was the most political thing that could be. The brother that really started that I think was in Kenya. I think they killed him. The most political act that anybody could do. He told everybody "Turn around and look at your plate. Whoever controls your plate controls your life." And, uh, I said, "Wow! If we could control our plate." We used to control our plate. My family was farmers. It's been a degraded thing. You know, dirt. You're in dirt. We've got a problem. How do you have that conversation in our community who don't see any relationship? Our commitment at Black Oaks is how do we create the language to where people can see this to survive.

PM: About what we might call Black culture or whatever we want to call it or Afrocentric culture or something like that and how that comes into play in the work that you do around self-determination, resiliency, and all those kinds of questions.

FC: Well, because the first I don't know if you ever seen the sister who wrote The Power of . . . , we need to see that again. Her name was Dr. . . . what's her name? From Kenya. She won the Nobel Peace Prize.

PM: Wangari Maathai.

FC: When you look at our cultural history, all our cultural history, even the European, was based on resiliency, being able to sustain yourself with your environment. So somewhere along the way we've lost that. So it's like Black people could just go back to our cultural principles. If you want to call it Indigenous or whatever you wanna call it. It was a principled way that we related to the environment that we don't do now. Also, there was a principled way that we related to one another based on that principled environmental relationship that we don't have anymore. In fact, all our stories, spiritual, mythological, all of them, came from our relationship with the environment. When you look back . . . I didn't really get it at first. People would say, "Boy, you look dead as a chicken." "Sly as a fox. Sly as a weasel." I didn't know what that meant until I saw a weasel flying in to kill fifty-five of my own birds. OK? I mean it was always wisdom that was galvanized from our relationship with the environment.

We built great stories around it. From the wind, the water. All these, what they call the Orishas, ancestors worshipped. My wife has more of an Afrocentric nationalist background than I do. I had a different experience here. I was a revolutionary in the 1960s and 1970s. That's how I grew up. It wasn't like what later on become Afrocentric. To me it was like intellectual, people were being very intellectual, but they didn't really practice. What I call a porcher. Yeah, a porch revolutionary. They sit on the porch talking about, philosophizing, while other people were being shot at and going to jail. So the Afrocentric part comes from the fact that I just happen to be born in Black skin. So I was born in this Black skin, and I have a history, a cultural history. When I look at it, I mean, it's what I saw. Then, the other part come around about being conscious, about being Black and all that. Cuz at the end of the day every race has a sustainable past. Even Europeans have that.

PART II

ANTICOLONIAL
commUNITY
PEDAGOGY

CHAPTER 3

Key Concepts for Our Food Fights

As I describe in the next chapter, the place-based commUnity pedagogy that I use in my food autonomy work involves formal classroom-based instruction at CSU and the Permaculture Institute of Chicago and hands-on work in the Outdoor CommUnity Classroom and other food autonomy spaces. In classroom settings at CSU, I introduce key concepts required for the study of food autonomy to a primarily nontraditionally aged, working-class Black student population. In this chapter I describe these concepts and begin to define a framework for a food autonomy perspective that places our food work within revolutionary autonomous activity. In addition, this chapter serves to place the work that my camaradas and I do within some of the central conversations occurring in food autonomy work, both in the academy and in activist circles. These larger discussions and analyses of the food system and the movement to change or replace it influence the work of gardeners and food activists in Chicago who regularly receive and discuss information about food and sustainability issues from across the planet. These global linkages are part of the context in which we do our work and live our lives.

This text and the work that it analyzes can only be a revolutionary intervention if it helps us to act autonomously around food and our other needs as individuals, communities, and as a species. To begin to act in self-determined and autonomous ways, we require some fundamental knowledge of key issues, ideas, and practices. Primary among the knowledge that we need to act with freedom is an understanding of the current food system, which springs from the four-headed monster of colonialism, capitalism, White supremacy, and heteropatriarchy. The greed of Wetiko knows no bounds as the Algonquin and others taught us. The invasion by Europe unleashed a tidal wave of misery for Indigenous Americans and Africans. What we call Wetiko and others call "the winning of the West," "development" or "American exceptionalism" illustrates the greed, materialism, and drive for power of the imperial state and the psychopathology of those who will to dominate.

However, equally important to liberated-food thought and action is knowledge of alternatives to Wetiko and its system. I start an examination of these alternatives in this chapter and show throughout this work how we in the food movement in Chicago develop these alternatives. To begin, I briefly examine what we call our work and why.

The Food Movement in Black Chicago: Justice, Autonomy, Sovereignty

As discussed earlier, the food movement of which I am apart contains several different people with different motivations and politics. While my emphasis is on autonomous behaviors and aspirations, the diversity of the movement makes it fascinating and a joy to be a part of. My participation and how I define my work owes a debt to all this diversity. Food "security," "justice," "autonomy," and "sovereignty" are among the important frames used by members of the movement in Chicago who I have worked with. Each of these terms comes from distinct historical and political traditions that place slightly different emphases on our work and as such allow us to develop a more complete understanding of the food movement in Black Chicago.

Food security as a frame for some movement participants suggests that the key issue is getting food to people who do not have enough.[1] Food security can be defined as having enough food to meet the daily nutritional needs of you and your family. The 2020–2023 iteration of HFH as a mobile market and the efforts of several gardens exemplify this frame. While it addresses access to healthy food, this frame does not include production factors, environmental factors, ownership, land issues, or other issues important to our movement.

Many with whom I work and encounter in the food movement in Chicago use the food justice framework (a derivative of environmental justice) as it fits well with the currently popular frame of "social justice." However, "justice" comes from a liberal-democratic tradition emphasizing fairness in resolving disputes. Thus, "food justice" would suggest an equitable distribution of food within the dominant capitalist arrangement. Without discussion of cultural relevance, autonomy in production, distribution and consumption of food, private property, environmental impacts or workers' and peasants' rights, such a framework is unsatisfactory for many of us. Baba Fred questions "justice" from a similar perspective:

> "Just" to us means that people are not trying to stop us from doing that. Not "Please give me some food. Feed me. Help me. Don't violate." I don't mean just in that sense, but a just political system, which means that you won't stop us from doing it. We are trying to take care of ourselves. History has shown that they've stopped that. Look at the history of co-ops. Co-ops formed in this country by sharecroppers, Black sharecroppers, in order to keep them from buying from the owners. The sharecroppers' store . . . My grandpa and them, my father. That's what they did. They formed a cooperative. That they collectively bought things together and leveraged it collectively versus an individual farmer and it took off because they were able to buy collectively. And the guy couldn't rip them off anymore. Then it spread to the White farmers and when the White farmers started doing

that then the government came in and destroyed it. They said, "We just can't have these people being self-reliant. We can't have y'all free of the system." Cuz this system, sharecropping, is a capitalist system. You can never get out of debt.

He explained further that what many others mean by justice is "the sense of equitable integration and sharing." His work at BOC begins from a more liberatory interpretation of food justice. The use of a justice frame for the work of BOC results from the cultural cachet that "social justice" has today. The mission of HFH reprinted earlier includes "justice." He explained that "the mission statement was created by people, younger people. They're active. Dara [Cooper], Mike [Strode], Mama Safia [Rashid]. These were young people. It was not our interpretation. They gave it the social justice kinda theme." Fred prefers terms like "resiliency," "self-reliance," and "sustainability" to describe his work as a farmer and key figure in the food autonomy movement in Black Chicago. However, Fred, even while he questions the liberal-democratic interpretation of food justice, doesn't fight the trend. He simply places a more radical spin on "food justice." His radical spin can be seen from his mention of the origins of Black farmer cooperatives. Food justice as collective community self-determination mirrors what some of us call food autonomy.

Austin Wayne's critique described earlier suggests a food sovereignty framework. He argues that "justice" is part of a dependency framework in which the individual depends on someone with power over them. Instead of justice, which he describes as begging, he works toward and asserts his individual "sovereignty" over his body, mind, and family to produce what he needs in the way he wants. Sovereignty can be defined as "the right of a community to define its own diet and therefore shape its own food system."[2]

Nonetheless, many Indigenous activists and revolutionaries in Canada and the United States rely on the idea of sovereignty to achieve freedom, well-being, and a reclamation of indigeneity. Use of "sovereignty" in a manner consistent with self-determination and autonomy is crucial to many food struggles. Some Native people argue that food sovereignty includes autonomous Native governance and Native government support for traditional agriculture and other foodways. Examining food sovereignty, Mihesuah quotes the 2007 Declaration of Nyeleni:

> The right of peoples to healthy and culturally appropriate food produced through ecologically sound and sustainable methods, and their right to define their own food and agricultural systems." The declaration also asserts that food sovereignty "ensures that the rights to use and manage lands, territories, waters, seeds, livestock, and biodiversity are in the hands of those of us who produce food." To be

a "food sovereign" tribe ideally would mean, then, that the tribe has the right to control its food production, food quality, and food distribution. It would support tribal farmers and ranchers by supplying machinery and technology needed to plant and harvest. The tribe would not be answerable to state regulatory control, and would follow its own edicts, regulations, and ways of governance.[3]

Like many of my accomplices in Chicago who advocate for food sovereignty, Mihesuah recognizes that central to any notion of food sovereignty is power and the recognition that food sovereignty is not separate from community or tribal self-determination. Others in our movement assert that "food sovereignty is important as a liberation practice because the ability to decide what and how we eat is at the very center of our relationship with ourselves, with each other, and with our planet."[4]

Some quarrel with sovereignty since it can only be achieved within the confines of a nation-state organization of the planet. It derives from a European nation-state jurisprudence and implies state power. Autonomists of various sorts reject the state, and some de- and anticolonial rebels see the use of sovereignty as a concept foreign to Indigenous lifeways. Peña details five "contradictions" in the common usage of "sovereignty," including the acceptance of the European human rights paradigm, an anthropocentrism (human-centered perspective) that values human life over the planet and all our relations, and commitment to the capitalist idea of "sustainable development."[5] More fundamentally, Klee Benally explains that colonizers have replaced Indigenous ways of social organization with sovereignty: "A politic rendered legible by violent imposition of settler authority and temporality in service of civilization."[6]

We can begin a discussion of food autonomy with this useful definition: "a people's or a community's ability to independently and fairly control both the quantity and the quality/appropriateness of their food as well as their collectively owned knowledge about food."[7] Revolutionary traditions of autonomist Marxism, autonomia, and anarchism have emphasized autonomy as a goal for societal organization based on maximum individual freedom with community responsibility. Indigenous political and ethical systems, with their emphasis on relationality and connectedness and without a notion of capitalist private property, provide a model of autonomy or autonomía. From this perspective, we "are guided by awareness that our movements do not seek permission from the state or corporate acquiescence in order for us to act in solidarity."[8] Food autonomy places emphasis on community control of food production and distribution and broader political self-determination. While engaging with the state and the capitalist markets out of necessity, many in our movement use other methods of exchange and distribution of resources including barter, the labor exchange practice of time-banking, skills-sharing, crop-mobbing (working in groups at one an-other's growing sites), cooperatives, and gifting. These practices of autonomous, self-organized economic behavior challenge Wetiko's food system at the levels of production, distribution, work, and "ownership." These practices are detailed throughout this study and in some ways are at the core of what we do in the food movement on the South Side of Chicago.

In the end, different individuals, groups, and organizations call what they are doing a wide variety of things. Those who I have worked with vary in how they see our work, and, again, this is what makes this movement so intriguing, important and, even, revolutionary. Throughout this text I will mostly use food autonomy to describe my work and most of the work we do in the Black and BIPOC food movement in Chicago. But, first, an understanding of the current dominant food system helps us develop solutions to the problems of food insecurity, food access, food injustice, and the lack of autonomy and sovereignty for Indigenous people, Black people, and other people of color.

Wetiko's Food

Capitalist social and economic practices dominate the global food system. For this reason, those of us in the food autonomy movement require a deep understand-ing of capitalism, colonialism, White supremacy, and heteropatriarchy (in a word, Wetiko) and how it works in the food system.[9] Wetiko's food system results from the bourgeois need to accumulate profits through the exploitation of labor and consumer, and the manipulation and destruction of the environment. Wetiko's food makes huge profits from the creation of monopolies, the intensive use of fos-sil fuels and petrochemicals, and massive damage to farmers, farmworkers, and their communities. Colonialism and its variants, neo- and internal colonialism, are required for the development of capitalist superprofits and wealth consolidation. In the past, we have called this process primitive accumulation. However, given the ongoing facts of colonialism, we might abandon the idea that the enclosures of land and primitive accumulation is a stage of capitalism and instead understand it to be a necessity for capitalism at any stage. Wetiko has used the power of the state through violence and theft of people's land and labor. Wetiko's global land grab continues to reap profits and power for a few using violence and new legal apparatuses such as the World Trade Organization, free trade agreements, and in-tellectual property rights on genetic material.[10]

In North America, British, Spanish, and French colonial violence shrank the Indigenous land base by 90 percent. Along with the loss of land and Indigenous people, we suffered the loss of Indigenous knowledge (IK). Indigenous land man-agement and governance were replaced by inappropriate crops, values, and techniques and private property. This paved the way for the development of U.S. agri-business. Agriculture remained the primary economic driver of U.S. capitalism through the early twentieth century. The Green Revolution of the middle part of the twentieth century led food production away from sustainable farming methods and toward intensified use of polluting off-farm inputs, including machinery and petroleum-based products. The Fordist production techniques have led to a new form of agriculture whereby massive fields are planted with a monoculture. This unnatural exploitation of the land requires that industrial farmers use toxic fossil fuel-based products to gain high yields and high profits. The hormones, pesticides, and herbicides required for Wetko's food ruin our food and water and creates superpests and superweeds that further challenge food production. These same agribusiness practices harm micro-organisms in the soil, beneficial insects, and pollinators such as bees, birds, and butterflies. In addition, the total reliance on petroleum to run highly mechanized agribusiness and for the development of chemical fertilizers and other key inputs has negative consequences for our earth and other beings.[11] That the U.S. government and corporations developed these industrial agriculture inputs originally for war is the perfect metaphor for the violence of Wetiko's food.[12]

The latest adulteration of our food supply results from genetic modification. GMOs (genetically modified organisms) or, perhaps more accurately, transgenic organisms (TOs), are organisms that have had the genes of another organism directly inserted into them and then bred to create what amounts to a new species. GMO/TO technology is the latest and scariest of capital's tactics of control over food.[13] Reports from scientists across the globe point to numerous reasons why TOs should be banned. A 2003 report argues that GMOs pose several problems. They include the following: lower crop yields than initially claimed; escalating problems including major crop failures; non-GMO crop contamination; no proof of safety; ill-health effects in lab animals; infertility in some male plants due to terminator technology; increased toxic herbicide use; rise in superviruses; GMO use linked to cancer and antibiotic resistance in humans.[14]

Transgenics are a major threat to the global food supply and the environment. TO crops have assaulted the livelihoods of Indigenous and the health of the urban poor. Kierin Gould writes, "Trans-genics (bio-tech foods, terminator seeds, etc.) effect sacred and staple plants and ways of thinking about them, as well as adding to input costs, yet they have not proven to be more productive or nutritious in the long run or to serve any particular consumer needs."[15] Importantly, the proliferation of transgenic corn from the United States and its deadly monopolistic control by a few megaseed companies has serious consequences for the health and welfare of the poorest and most vulnerable. Many with limited access to healthy food will consume "food-like substances" containing TOs, since corn products especially in the form of high-fructose corn syrup are a significant part of the processed, fast-food, sugary-drink, high-carbohydrate standard American diet (SAD). In response, Calvo and Esquibel urge a return to a pre-Columbian Mesoamerican diet since European colonization has led to the adoption of unhealthy eating and a loss of food knowledge represented by SAD. They quote la Red en Defensa del Maíz, a coalition of Indigenous and peasant groups fighting against TOs and for food autonomy in Mexico who state:

> The planting of transgenic maize is a frontal attack against the native and peasant peoples and a violation of their rights. For the peoples that constitute Mexico, maize is not merchandise, but the origin of a civilization and the foundation of peasant lives and economies. We will not let our seeds be lost or contaminated by transgenes owned by transnational companies. We will not comply with unfair laws that criminalize seeds and peasant life ways. We will continue protecting maíze and the life of our peoples.[16]

TOs are heralded by the world's wealthiest as the solution to the world-hunger problem. Multinational companies and "philanthropic" organizations claim that TOs will save the world and go to great lengths to get small farmers in the colonized world hooked on them. They undermine food autonomy and food sovereignty by forcing the new technology on to vulnerable farmers. The effects on Indigenous communities and peasants are numerous. Dependence is among the most alarming consequences. An example comes from southern African agricultural systems in which "we see and fear a great deal of social dislocation, of collapse of our farming systems—and it's already happened. In industrialized-agriculture countries like South Africa, farmers have become completely deskilled and divorced from production decisions, which are made in laboratories or in far-away board rooms."[17]

Not all are convinced that TOs are a threat worth concerning ourselves. Many in our food movement pay scant attention to the issue. In our dialogue Mila Marshall expressed the idea that the fight against GMOs is far removed from urban realities of food security.

> Don't get me started on that because people get so angry when I talk about GMO. That's privileged talk in my opinion. When you live in a desert, you need to grow whatever you can. That's what I'm saying. Food is an entree into so many other discussions. "You can't do this. Genetically modified food is wrong." No, what's wrong is your $700 pair of jeans that some little five-year-old was making in China . . . You don't want to talk about that. You want to talk about GMOs.

Dr. Marshall asserts that there are more important issues relating to food production and unequal access than GMOs. Having heard too many privileged activist-types discuss GMOs, she is convinced that they misunderstand food and environmental issues in Black America.

With the extensive documentation of the problems with Wetiko's food, why do we not know of the extent of the problems? Importantly, systems of domination require that the subjugated populations believe in the legitimacy of the system. Rulers and dominant classes accomplish this using ideology. I use the term "ideology" in the sense that Marx and Marxists have. Marx and Engels famously write about the need for a ruling class to have its ideas dominate: "The ideas of the ruling class are in every epoch the ruling ideas . . . The class which has the means of material production at its disposal, has control at the same time over the means of mental production."[18] To maintain an exploitive system of production from which they profit immensely, the ruling classes need a system of ideas or an ideology that justifies, normalizes, and naturalizes the system. The role of ideology in capitalism, then, is to convince workers that the inequalities and vast differences in the distribution of societal goods and bads are not injustices caused by Wetiko but, rather, the result of the failures of individuals and groups. About the contemporary problem of unequal distribution of food, capitalist ideologues would argue that they do not result from a horrifically oppressive and violent system but to the failures of individuals to make the proper decisions and take the proper actions that would ensure that they eat well. Moreover, colonialism requires a racist ideology. In the United States and much of the overdeveloped colonial world, White supremacy fulfills this role. The divide-and-conquer strategy of the colonial and capitalist bosses pits different "racial" groups against one another with Whiteness being an esteemed identity and valued resource. The dispossession of Natives, Mexicanxs and Blacks from land in the United States illustrates this strategy.

Ideological apparatuses such as the media and public education assist Wetiko foodways.[19] As a result of media hyperconsolidation whereby six companies control 90 percent of the media outlets in the United States, a couple of hundred media executives control the information concerning food and other key aspects of our lives that four hundred million in the United States consume.[20] They have taught us not to question the dominance of Wetiko, and they have limited access to information that would help us take control over the food system. Additionally, BIPOC deal with White supremacy and its various manifestations in the food system, including dangerous farmwork, poisoned land, and abandoned lots, poor food options in our neighborhoods and attacks on our foodways. At every level, Wetiko ideology justifies food poverty and ill health. The powerful agribusiness lobby, and their public relations arms make sure that in the United States we are not even allowed to know whether our food contains TOs. Agribusiness and other toxic industries have successfully maintained their control and enormous profits by ensuring that school curricula exclude concepts, ideas, or perspectives that would help children make good decisions about food, health, and the environment. Most of us are incapable of growing our own food because we were taught that food labor was inferior labor and that others would produce our food for us. BIPOC learn that the IK of our ancestors constituted backward slave labor, savagism and "old wives' tales." Americanization programs, notoriously including boarding schools for Indigenous people in occupied territory, tore IK from our ancestors leaving us helpless without the "benevolence" of our colonial masters. During this period, we lost knowledge of maíz and how to learn from plants and other of our more-than-human relatives.[21] Instead of the plant-based medicines of our ancestors, we learn to entrust our health and nutrition to governmental regulatory agencies, agribusiness, health-maintenance organizations, and pharmaceutical companies. Wetiko ideology obscures the truth concerning how the system ruins lives and limits our capacity to do something about it even if we knew the truth. This knowledge gap is a primary driver of food inequality, food junkyards, and food poverty.

Food Apartheid

Since the term "food desert" was coined in the mid-1990s, it has gained in popularity to describe unequal food conditions. By 2010, people outside food policy, advocacy, and scholarship began to hear the term. The U.S. Department of Agriculture provides the following definition: "Urban neighborhoods and rural towns without ready access to fresh, healthy, and affordable food. Instead of supermarkets and grocery stores, these communities may have no food access or are served only by fast food restaurants and convenience stores that offer few healthy, affordable food options."[22] Additionally, residents in communities with little access to food find that if healthy food can be found at neighborhood corner stores, it is much more costly than at supermarkets in other neighborhoods. Healthy foods at these stores are also more costly than highly processed and nutritionally lacking foods. Thus, working people are often forced to purchase unhealthy food.[23]

The popularity of the term concerns many. It potentially furthers misunderstanding in several ways. It contributes to an inaccurate understanding of desert ecology and cultural diversity found there. Importantly, the phrase does not immediately invoke the power relations that cause food inequality. The term fails to reflect residents' understanding of their communities and the abundance of skills, ideas, and resources found in communities that suffer disproportionately from industrial agriculture. For these reasons, many food autonomy advocates prefer

terms like "food inequality," "food junkyards," and "food apartheid." Food apartheid emphasizes the colonial and racist conditions at the heart of food discrimina-
tion. Leah Penniman explains her preference for the term "because it makes clear
that we have a human-created system of segregation that relegates certain groups
to food opulence and prevents others from accessing life-giving nourishment."[24]
The term also invokes the spirit of the youth of Soweto who fought back against
the White supremacist South African regime. Eventually, the youth destroyed
apartheid. Like those youth, we hope to rid ourselves of food apartheid. To do so,
we must learn "negative" lessons, including that Wetiko is resilient.

Whatever we decide to call it, we can easily see the oppressive nature of Wetiko
food. A drive through working-class, particularly Black urban communities, and
then on to middle-class White neighborhoods only a few short blocks away vividly illustrates the problem. A four-mile-long drive down 103rd Street in Chicago
from Cottage Grove in the Pullman neighborhood to Western Avenue in the Beverly Hills neighborhood provides an example. Driving east to west from Cottage
Grove to State Street, we first encounter Christ Community Church and then four
neighborhood bars including my old favorite, Judy's, three liquor stores, four corner stores, nine fast-food joints, two cut-rate grocery stores, and one bank. Continuing west from State to Vincennes, which marks the boundary between affluent
Beverly and impoverished Roseland, we see a Walgreen's with some limited food
options, a Jehovah's Witness building, two dollar stores, two liquor stores, two bar-
bershops, one corner store, a place to buy cheap phones, three small churches, a
day care, and a Harold's Chicken, the famed "fried chicken shack." The drive from
Vincennes to Western through Beverly offers a wider variety of food and other
options including a Starbucks, a CVS, one church, a Hawaiian ice shop, antique
and boutique stores, one hairdresser, one Walgreen's, and a Jamaican restaurant. A
two-mile drive from Ninety-Fifth Street and Western Avenue to 111th and Western
offers a couple dozen food options.

Students in my Food Justice course complete an assignment that maps available food and other resources and challenges in Roseland and an affluent neighborhood, Hyde Park. These two communities provide valuable comparison since
both contain universities. Hyde Park houses the famed University of Chicago,
which has stirred controversy for years due to its "land grabbing" and gentrifying
of nearby Black communities. Roseland, of course, houses Chicago State University, a predominantly Black institution. This tragically underresourced university
offers our predominantly working-class, nontraditionally aged, Black students an
opportunity for a high-quality education denied to them at places like the University of Chicago. The educational segregation at these institutions mirrors the
food apartheid that we experience and study. From our cars (or, better yet, bikes).

while comparing the available options for purchasing food. we bear witness to food apartheid. Wetiko food distribution creates a situation whereby the wealthy and middle class have access to an overabundance of healthy food options and annually throw away tons of food while the poor and working classes live in areas where access to healthy food is limited or non-existent.

To make matters worse, food junkyards are also transportation-poor as few cheap public transportation options are available and many lack access to personal vehicles. For example, in the food junkyard community of South Chicago, nearly 30 percent of residents do not have personal vehicles. They must take the bus or walk to distant full-service grocery stores. In Chicago, a bus trip to a grocery store easily costs five dollars. Food junkyards lack not only food but also most other resources. "Food desert" limits our understanding of the causes of food insecurity to a lack of grocers, instead of encouraging us to locate the causes of it in the maze of private and governmental practices that is Wetiko in action.

Obstacles to accessing healthy food mean that hungry children are often given a couple of dollars to run to the corner store or liquor store to grab some chips, candy, and a soft drink for dinner. Of course, this poor eating leads to illnesses including chronic and life-threatening diseases. In fact, studies have shown a correlation between food access and diabetes and obesity.[25] Pattrice Jones describes these problems that we encounter in Black communities in Chicago as dietary racism and dietary colonialism resulting from a profit-obsessed Wetiko economy. The drive for capitalist profit led businessmen to conquer Amerindigenous and African lands "forcibly replac[ing] subsistence crops with cash crops, an approach that continues with trade globalization policies that make it cheaper for poor people to eat at fast-food restaurants owned by multinational corporations than to buy healthy food from local farmers and vendors." Today, the earlier theft of Native land by colonizers and their settlers has resulted in food poverty and its diseases. The effects for Black urban dwellers are that the manufactured "desire for the steaks and shakes and deep-fried mystery meats that clog the arteries of so many African-Americans might best be seen as a form of literally internalized colonialism."[26]

Political and Ethical Considerations

Achieving food autonomy requires combating the inequalities of Wetiko food. Since this food system relies on racism and heteropatriarchy to supply its profits, food autonomy requires ending racism, sexism, and colonialism. It requires truly democratic and local politics— a radical democracy.[27] Starvation, hunger, malnutrition, and disease caused by Wetiko food can only be eradicated if people control politics and economics. The control of food is a weapon wielded by the powerful against the poor. Specifically, we know from our study of Marxist political economy that the capitalist economic system and the continued domination of the ruling class result from the private ownership of the means of production or the means of life. Thus, the land, food, machinery, and knowledge to use them confronts us as a powerful weapon. With capitalism intact, the wealthy and their political functionaries make closed-door, backroom decisions that manipulate the lives of billions through their policies and investments. Without control over the food we eat, we are forever beholden and dependent upon the ruling classes.[28]

A central problem of the organization of our world is that the systems we have created are beyond the human scale.[29] They are global in scope and thus incoherent to the vast majority and out of our control. Since they are out of our control, they are antidemocratic. A potential antidote to this antidemocracy is a radical localism that brings our systems down to a human scale in which each of us can participate, debate, organize, and engage in mutually beneficial agency. It includes radical democracy. Such a democracy is a true form of democracy in that the people rule. Every adult in a community participates in governance. The autonomous communities of the Zapatistas are organized on such a model. This form of governance takes time, but, perhaps, this is a virtue as capitalism requires speed and efficiency. Slowing down may help undermine it.

Radical localism includes radical democracy and "locavorism" (an ethic of eating locally). To have food autonomy, people must have a say in food production, distribution, and consumption as well as how land is used. Locavorism, at its best, is an orientation toward food that privileges local food systems that are kind to the earth and all our relations, respectful of Indigenous food practices, and supportive of noncapitalist methods of food production and distribution. Locavorism encourages us to eat food produced with minimal use of nonrenewable resources. Eating locally also helps solve the ecological problems created by the Wetiko food system that imports foods from thousands of miles away. Food miles is a "measure [of] the distance food travels from where it is produced to where it is consumed." Shipping food contributes to climate chaos and requires additional toxic-chemical inputs to account for the long-distance travel. This distance also does not allow consumers to participate in the production process or to observe and resist the exploitation of farm workers who otherwise remain faceless and invisible. Advantages of local food systems include:

> Localized, biodiverse ecological agriculture can reduce greenhouse gas emissions by a significant amount while improving our natural capital of biodiversity, soil and water; strengthening nature's economy; improving the security of farmers' livelihoods; improving the quality and nutrition of our food; and deepening freedom and democracy.[30]

As with all strategies, radical localism and locavorism have their detractors. Importantly, critiques of the locavore movement point to the potential dangers of insular localism and the local trap. Vasile Stanescu criticizes the locavore movement's major proponents, Joel Salatin, Michael Pollan, and Barbara Kingsolver, warning against nativism, xenophobia, racism, nationalism, and sexism. He sums up his concerns stating that his goal is "to expand the struggle to include a consideration for the full panoply of social justice issues that a truly just and therefore truly 'green' diet must entail."[31] Additionally, the local is not inherently good and that an evaluation of the justness of any food system or strategy must take into consideration the strategy in context and seek structural changes that will allow people, especially marginalized and disadvantaged, to practice local production and consumption.[32]

Without dismissing the potential problems of the local trap, the food movement in Chicago that I participate in focuses heavily on developing a local, community-controlled food economy. The BOC, through many of its projects including the HFH and their permaculture design courses, emphasizes Black control of the food put into Black bodies in Chicago. Its concerns about industrial agriculture and racism have led it to conclude that local is the best way to go to attain Black self-determination and freedom. This ethos animates much of our work.

To counter the ideological domination of the proponents and wealthy beneficiaries of Wetiko's food system, we require a new ethic, one that is inclusive and focuses our understanding and analysis of our interdependence. Thus, a central component of our food autonomy is an Indigenous biocentric (life-centered) ethic exemplified in the Lakota "mitakuye oyasin" (all my relations), the Lacandon Mayan notion of "in lak' ech" (you are my other me) and the Bantu "ubuntu" (I am because we all are). An autonomous food system requires regaining a community and love ethic, a philia which recognizes that all living beings are my relations. Thus, many strive to be good stewards of the land and our brothers' and sisters' keepers. A food ethic based on IK means we act locally and participate directly in the production of our food. We act as relatives with responsibilities to care for all our relations and not simply as consumers of commodities or exploiters. We support local farmers, community-supported agriculture and community markets at the same time that we produce in backyard and community gardens. We tread lightly on the earth and encourage biodiversity. We do this while recognizing and combating injustice wherever it occurs. We work with all our relations from all over the planet.

An additional consideration of what constitutes an ethics of food autonomy comes from the ethical vegan community. Several important high-profile arguments for becoming vegetarian, vegan, or drastically decreasing consumption of animal products have brought to the mainstream ideas that ethical eaters have been discussing for decades. Michael Pollan's series of books have perhaps done the most to bring this debate to light. However, for our purposes of examining food issues in Black Chicago, the collection *Sistah Vegan* provides important lessons concerning the relationship between food, race, gender, sexuality, violence, and class. The Black women authors point out that many vegans have adopted the lifestyle due to their concerns about the violence done to animals and our speciesist orientation. Speciesism is the "belief that nonhuman animals exist to serve the needs of the human species, that animals are in various senses inferior to human beings, and therefore that one can favor human over nonhuman interests according to species status alone."[33] Vegan sistahs examine the relationships between the violence of speciesism, ecocide and racism, nationalism, sexism and homophobia. Similarly, ahimsa-based veganism suggests "conscious harmlessness, nonviolence and respect for life."[34]

Black female vegans are a diverse crowd and have different stories about coming to vegan consciousness. However, they all argue that eating meat and many other products of Wetiko food costs humanity, the earth, and all our relations. Some claim we are addicted to a "meaty-dairy" diet chock full of pesticides, hormones, and antibiotics.[35] This addiction began with European imperialism and the Atlantic slave trade. The attack on Africans in the Americas and the linking of White working-class Europeans to horrendous factory work resulted from sugar addiction.[36] As we travel through the early history of the United States, we see continual attacks on the Black body through food. This has led us to the current situation in which working- and middle-class Black Americans exist on an illness-inducing diet. Some Black vegans believe that Black liberation is impeded by fast-food addiction and the "soul food diet." Dick Gregory argued, "I personally would say that the quickest way to wipe out a group of people is to put them on a Soul Food diet."[37] Following this logic suggests that a prerequisite for liberation is to eliminate disease-causing diets such as "soul" food, fast food, and SAD.

One of the most ironic and disheartening things about Wetiko's food is that those who do the work of feeding us are impoverished, marginalized, criminalized, and, in many cases, starving. Farmworkers and their families live with food insecurity while fresh vegetables surround them in the fields. A 2007 study found that "45 percent of the workers in the most productive agricultural county in the U.S. [Fresno] are food insecure" while another study of Salinas, California, found 66 percent of farmworkers interviewed were food insecure.[38] Farmworkers earn on average $13,800 per year. They endure the lowest wages of any job sector in our nation, which leads them to eat SAD. This has high costs in the long run as diet-related illnesses plague them. Farmworkers' low pay leads to substandard housing in overcrowded conditions and lack of transportation. Farmworkers are exposed to other health hazards. Cancer and birth defects top the list of threats to farm-worker lives as toxic pesticides are dumped on them in the fields.[39] Some endure enslavement and physical violence.[40] Madrigal shows how an "expectation that human workers in agriculture can be treated as a disposable and bonded labor market continues to be deployed to this day."[41] While the political and economic systems are stacked against workers in the food system, activist-scholars and others point out how workers, especially Indigenous Mexican migrant workers, are organizing themselves in myriad ways to survive and thrive, to create community and place, and to revive food and lifeways.[42]

Resilient Polycultural Local Food Systems

How do we achieve food autonomy in an urban setting? Baba Fred and others in our food community look toward IK for answers. He emphasizes resilience and community engagement. I often hear him state a version of the following: "You can't be a resilient individual. If I'm food secure but my neighbor isn't, then what's gonna happen?" Indigenous peoples of the today's southwestern United States and northern Mexico have maintained many of our traditional foodways through "resilient persistence." "Cooperation and adaptation" are the keys to the continued existence of our peoples, cultures, lands, and, ultimately, the planet.[43] Moreover, native resiliency emphasizes a spirituality rooted in relatedness and biocentric ethics.

We are part of movement creating local, democratic, ecologically sound food systems. Through a combination of community-supported agriculture, farmers' markets, community markets, food sharing and giving, backyard gardeners' networks, food forests, and innovative community gardens, thousands are participating in alternatives to Wetiko's food system. While the food movement continues to grow, the challenge is to include more people and more communities in these confrontations with Wetiko's food system and social organization. We need to examine these alternatives and understand their strengths and weaknesses, their liberatory and authoritarian aspects, their successes, and failures. Examinations of previous and ongoing projects to establish and strengthen urban communities and local food systems can help us realize food autonomy.

Resilient autonomous food systems recognize and encourage diversity and polyculturalism, an understanding and respect for the multiple and complex connections that we share with multiple peoples and beings.[44] Polyculturalism suggests that we learn from and exchange foodways with multiple peoples with whom we interact. Autonomous food systems are not authoritarian regimes requiring adherence to a dogmatic orthodoxy. They work from a rhizomatic pattern of interconnected, self-organized, and self-governed units.[45] Anarchists and permaculture designers would call them decentralized.[46] Self-directed units may include communes, co-ops, or autonomous communities. Such food systems increase diversity and interconnectedness. This visibility of our dependence on one another reinforces our ethic of mitakuye oyasin, in lak' ech, and ubuntu, or in permaculture's version, earth care, people care and fair share. Thus, we come to the crux of the problem: ideology. Wetiko ethics and practices have disconnected us from the land and one another so that we no longer have a communal land ethic. In fact, city dwellers are far removed from an Indigenous ethic that would begin to repair the damage caused by Wetiko. Recognizing this, those of us in the food movement in Chicago focus a great deal of our time on learning and teaching an Indigenous community ethic and practice.

Paula Roderick Sows SEEDS

PUBLIC SCHOOL & commUnity-BASED PEDAGOGY

FIG. 7. Paula Roderick.
Photo by Tafari Melisizwe.

PAULA RODERICK: I didn't get started with this doing food work. I got started about five years ago with trying to design a mentoring program to be able to work with youth in Roseland and it started out as I was asked by one of the members of what is now SEEDS to sign my name on to the board and come in and try to do this organization working around a youth mentoring program at Fenger High School. There was a greenhouse at Fenger High School. Fenger High School had been put on the list of the worst performing high schools in Chicago. Darryl who now is the board president came to me and said, "Will you come on board? What we want to do is work with the type of students at Fenger High School in this After School Program and we're just gonna go in and work in the greenhouse." And it started with the intent of community activists wanting to come in and participate in any way that I could with working with young people in an at-risk school.

Now the reason why food seemed to work so well is that I had gone to an alternative high school that was pretty progressive even for its time. It was a private school in Vermont, and it had a working farm and the principle was that it started with this idea that students ought to have some work that they were engaged in, some learning that they were engaged in, and some physical exercise that they were engaged. So the school that I went to had a working farm. And everyone was expected to do some kind of work project on the farm at some point while you were in school, and I was familiar with the idea of using the garden as a teaching tool, as a way of building independence in young people. It certainly did it for the group that I was with in high school.

So the idea that we could do that again in Chicago . . . I just thought it just seemed like a natural.

PM: It was about five years ago that you got together with this group that then becomes SEEDS. Tell me about SEEDS.

PR: SEEDS stands for Southside Education and Economic Development Systems, Inc. So SEEDS is an acronym. It also stands for that idea that from a very small seed you can grow a very big enterprise. So SEEDS the mission has a sort of big vision of connecting outdoor classrooms to actual classrooms in poor minority communities, which is what we started at Dunne Tech Elementary. To use the garden not just for the students that are directly connected to the elementary school but [also] for students within the community to come in and learn from the garden at varying levels. And to use the produce to benefit the community. So the philosophy was [that] in communities like Roseland a school garden had to be more than just a pretty flower garden. It should actually be a garden that produced goods for the community to benefit the community. So this overall vision was that even though we were on elementary school property, this rather large garden that we started at Dunne—it's about a quarter acre—would be used throughout the year for education, all different levels, not just elementary school. We've worked with high school students. We've had college students come in and work with us. We've had a postgraduate come in and work with us. So at all levels of education as well as the community members coming in to learn and then hopefully benefit from the food that we are growing.

PM: This is sort of where we crossed paths because a lot of what you are saying is part of the philosophy that I'm bringing to our project, GLP. A lot of that community pedagogy is what I'm calling it: a philosophy and practice of teaching in the garden not only for our members but for a larger community. That's where we came in. When we met maybe three years ago. Four years ago?

PR: Four years ago, yeah.

PM: I saw what you guys were doing and I wanted to be a part of it. It was in Roseland. It was right down the street from where I was living, maybe six blocks from my house and another few blocks from the garden. So it made a lot of sense to get together with you guys and see what you were doing and try to create something, you know, partnerships and networks and coalitions.

PR: We started with a really broad vision of what community education should look like and so we worked closely with Danny Block and the Neighborhood Assistance Center at Chicago State. We've worked with

Growing Power. We've worked with and been a very strong member of the Roseland-Pullman Agricultural Network, which is an organization of gardens in Roseland and Pullman. Trying to build a support group for community gardens. I'm sort of hesitating because it was such a broad idea of how it should work and I know that we've kinda have fallen short of the goal, but that education, I called it pre-K to postgrad pipeline, that SEEDS ought to work with universities to encourage college students to come back, to learn from the garden, to learn some sociology perspective of what community organizing should look like at a cellular level. So we've worked with DePaul. The Center for New Learning. We've worked with Loyola. Loyola students have come in and helped us do a design for what the garden should look like. We have just reached out to other community organizations such as the Food Network, The Greater Roseland [West Pullman] Food Network, because initially when we started with our produce we quickly learned that after you plant the garden things grow, which is a good thing. And after things grow, you have to find a way to distribute.

The youth? We backed into this. We really did. We backed into with the thing at Fenger had come just after the incident with the young gentleman who was killed just outside Fenger High School.

PM: Darrion Albert

PR: Darrion Albert. And so we being a loose consortium of community activists. So there were several members who had been parents of children in Roseland schools. Darryl's children had already graduated. They were older. Helen's a grandmother. Her children were also older, but they were from Englewood. So we had parents that had interacted with Chicago Public Schools for years, and I came in from this sort of lofty idea from a private school perspective [and] would say, "Yeah, of course, hands on learning makes sense." It makes sense on a cellular level of reaching and connecting students to what they're learning. That doesn't take place in the formal classroom. So we just sort of came in with, yes, there was a need. We knew that the high school students at Fenger weren't bad students. They weren't bad youth. They were in a very difficult situation in a school that hadn't been properly funded and they were underresourced, but they weren't bad youth. What was lacking was the kind of community that surrounded the high school to support it that other communities have. So we said, "We can't fix all of what's wrong with Fenger. What we can do is one sort of after school program." We can do that. We can find a way to get adults in the community that were willing to come with us to mentor, you know, high school students. We started out and we had a group of about fifteen high school students from Fenger. We had a small group of almost, our numbers have gone between five to fifteen and sometimes it's a little bit bigger sometimes less of adults.

PM: So, really, it wasn't about teaching food necessarily, right? It was just about mentoring.

PR: It was about teaching food. The food part came in. It goes back to where we are. It goes back to Roseland cuz this is where we started. Roseland was identified as a food desert. I come from an area of Chicago that is not a food desert. So I came in with sort of really high expectations of what would be available in the community. I didn't know what being a food desert meant on a day-to-day, daily basis to the people who live here with the schools, with the community members that we work with. It was eye-opening for me.

And I think that the people we were working with. We didn't know how to really grow food. We just knew that we could do it.

PM: You guys weren't necessarily teachers, and you weren't really farmers either?

PR: We weren't really. We had, I call him, Bill, who was a gentleman who lived in the North suburbs and knew a lot. I'm not sure what his educational background was. He wasn't a farmer, either, but he knew a lot about farming. So he was our kinda, like, technical adviser. Since then we have added a lot of people who do know alot about farming. But, again, it seemed as if from my point of view, and I'm not speaking for SEEDS. The members come with different experiences. It seemed to me that we had . . . I looked and said, "Wow! We've got the University of Illinois, which had an agricultural component, teaching component. Chicago State. We were with DePaul University in Chicago. Loyola. I went to Northwestern. What I don't know, I'm gonna find out. Chicago is rich or should've been rich or has the capacity to be very rich in experts in all sorts of areas. So the idea that I came in . . . I don't know a lot about growing vegetables. But I know how to pick up the phone and call somebody. I thought what seemed reasonable would be that there would be organizations, in particular, educational institutions, [which] would be excited about the idea about helping the community.

What we have done is we did the Saturday Barbecue or cookout. Whatever way we could get vegetables out. So we had people would come in and sort of in an organic way we had these older women that love to come into the garden, and they're our best gardeners. For instance, I had never seen poke salad growing. I didn't really know what poke salad was. We had one of our older women came in, and she was walking through the garden the way she did with her bags. She could harvest things in ways that I hadn't . . . We still, the younger ones, don't know how to do. And she walked by and said, "That's poke salad." She knew it in an instant. We didn't know what it was. And, sure, didn't know how to cook it. And we didn't know what it could do for you. We all, the ones that were there, learned about poke salad. We also learned about different ways of cooking, um, we had an African green that was growing in our garden and I think it was called . . . Cynthia Mackay talked about a way to put rhubarb in a muffin. Which we never heard of. So in terms of the volunteers as a community, the people that are coming into our garden, we've learned, I've learned a lot about healthy eating!

My friends always ask me. "Why do you go down there?" By the way, I had three community gardens. If I just wanted to do community gardening, I could walk out my door and I've got one half a block away from me and one three blocks away from me and then there's one a little bit farther away. So I can do gardening if that's what I wanted to do. But I come down here because I think this is where it's needed. This is where it can make an impact. Yes, it seems like a small thing for one high school girl to find out that she had skills that she could use and make her feel good about herself. That's worth it, I think. We, ah, I guess I get on my soapbox about why we do this. There's two parts to that. Yes, there's a lack in Roseland. There's things that are just not here. Basic things like the choice between if I want to go to the physical therapist, I have a choice. Close by and whatever. So then those kinds of things. But there's, also, there's a goodness here in Roseland so that it's sort of, you know, if you have a penny and it's all covered in dirt it doesn't look very valuable but if you shine it up it looks valuable? And so one of the other things that happens is that the assets that are here in Roseland there's so much that covers over it you don't see it. You can't see it. We talked about Ms. Mackay and the older women that come into the garden. There's an incredible wealth of knowledge about agriculture in Roseland that I won't find in my community. I don't know that I would find somebody that would just walk through the garden and go, "Oh, that's edible. You think it's a weed but that's edible. And this is poke salad and this is how you cook it." Skills. And people here don't know that they have those skills because they don't know how to share that information. There's not enough space to share.

PM: The garden certainly can provide that community space.

PR: So there we were I mean I told you about Ms. Mackay, who's older in her seventies. Just at the end when we were getting ready to leave putting our tools away, an older man comes into the garden and starts talking to Helen and Cynthia, and he goes, "I've got a garden." Now his garden is about two blocks over. He's got a garden. So he was talking, he and Helen and Cynthia were talking about the things that were growing and how we could grow better. And he said, "Maybe I could come in and show you some things." And what I noticed was Helen and I sort of looked and went . . . this is not a diplomatic way of saying this. He's in his eighties . . . He takes care of a really substantial sized garden on his own. So his physical and mental acuity is out of hand. The same way with Cynthia. She outfarms us, the younger people, me and Helen, and she's healthy and vigorous and intellectually curious and all sorts of things that go along with having that expertise. Having an interest in the diet that we eat. Our older people have this knowledge, having that sense that, you know, we pay thousands of dollars to go to the gym. They go and plant a garden and spend the whole day bending and stretching and picking weeds and up and down and do much of the same thing. You know? And so you are laughing, but I'm going like, "They're in better shape." Are we gonna be in that shape at that age? Not if we eat fast food and make poor food choices. So part of it is they've learned how to make better food choices because they grow their own. And by growing your own even when you go shopping, you make better choices. You just do. And they take care of themselves in a way that is different. Now how do you take that knowledge and pass it down through the ages?

CHAPTER 4

Learning from the Land
commUnity pedagogy in place

Within our movement, we value passing on knowledge related to growing and stewardship, and our Indigenous ways of being. While land stewards use
a variety of tactics and strategies to pass on information about horticulture and
freedom, we have in common a place-based "living as learning" approach as our
primary pedagogical strategy. The commUnity pedagogy (CP) approach that I
use begins with this place-based foundation and incorporates several pedagogical
strategies. My teaching and learning results from interactions with "organic" land-
based intellectuals throughout the food movement including the many elders in
Chicago who have generously engaged me and my accomplices. I apply a place-
based CP informed by Indigenous and anarchist practices. In addition to my primary teachers, the land and elders, I have been influenced by radical pedagogues.
CP draws insight from Paolo Freire, Leanne Simpson, and bell hooks and relies
on Antonio Gramsci's insights regarding organic intellectuals. I use a mix of liberatory pedagogies to teach social science and humanities subject matter and apply
the knowledge gained therein to act toward solving the problems plaguing our
communities. It requires engaging the subject matter through interaction with and
embeddedness within communities outside the university. In my case, I use land
stewardship and community gardening as means of interacting with and expand-
ing our community. With this pedagogical approach I hope to help build stronger
communities and self-actualization among university and community gardener-
students, especially the young Black and Brown on Chicago's far South Side who
suffer the brunt of the so-called War on Drugs and mass incarceration, attacks on
their ethnoracial identities, and Wetiko's food. In this chapter, I detail pedagogical
strategies that I and others use to fulfill the myriad goals of our movement.

Placed-Based Pedagogies

At root the commUnity pedagogy we use is a land-based, Indigenous pedagogy.
It requires active engagement with the land and the place that is Chicago's food-
and resource-deprived communities. CP aspires to using the best practices of
our Indigenous African and Turtle Island ancestors to teach food autonomy and
self-determination. Often books are used to teach principles associated with inter-

national food autonomy efforts. However, the primary teacher is the land. Both Simpson's "land as pedagogy" and Prakash and Esteva's "escaping education" and "living as learning" provide insight into place-based CP practices.[1] This type of Indigenous alterNative education challenges colonial structures because we decolonize our minds and bodies as our indigeneity resurges and reforms.

Wetiko education amounts to an attack on Indigenous people and our place-based cultures. The education provided by settler governments "is the road to ignorance of the local culture."[2] Settler-colonial school systems homogenize education while beating our indigeneity out of us. The brutal system of residential schools and Americanization programs for "foreigners" was a primary site of genocide and ethnocide while the current school system asks our children to see Indigenous people as characters in an ancient history. The pluriverse of Indigenous knowledge systems are abandoned for the assimilative, competitive, sorting colonial-education system. Wetiko education divorces learning from living as Indigenous people are separated from our land where we learned the intelligence of our communities. "Grassroots cultures" or "place-based people" learn by living and not by being educated. For example, Andean Indigenous people respond to the damage done by colonial education by using our IK beginning with respect for life. Andean elder-teacher Grillo discusses conversation in their traditions.

> Here, conversation cannot be reduced to dialogue, to the word, as in the modern western world but rather here conversation engages us vitally; one converses with the whole body. To converse is to show oneself reciprocally, it is to share, it is to commune, it is to dance to the rhythm which at every moment corresponds to the annual cycle of life. Conversation assumes all the complication characteristic of the living world. Nothing escapes conversation. Here there is no privacy. Conversation is inseparable from nurturance. For humans, to make chacre, that is to grow plants, animals, soils, waters, climates, is to converse with nature.[3]

Andean knowledge is a pedagogy of land. Similarly, Simpson explains that Nishnaabeg (Anishinaabe) intelligence is not learned through abstract, decontextualized processes as found in European pedagogy and science. Grounded normativity, the basis for Nishnaabeg intelligence, results from an openness to learning with community and the development of "a compassionate web of interdependent relationships."[4] Indigenous people learn how to live by doing; interacting with and observing nature.[5] They learn how to behave by taking guidance from natural phenomena. The Anishinaabe word for this pedagogical practice is "akinoomaage, which is formed from two roots: aki, noomaage. 'Aki' means earth and 'noomaage' means to point towards and take direction from." Earth and, by extension, all natural phenomena must be focused on and acknowledged as teachers. In addition, the development of "Nishnaabeg-Gikondaasowi or Nishnaabeg knowledge" "takes place in the context of family, community and relations."[6]

Anishinaabe storytelling teaches and passes on land-based knowledge. Simpson tells the story of Binoojiinh, who in her retelling is a gender-nonconforming child who learns from their more-than-human relatives. Binoojiinh (child in Anishinaabe) learns the importance of preserving food and preparing for the winter from Ajidamoo, the squirrel. In the story they lay down underneath a tree and observe Ajidamoo's behavior. Through imitating the acts of their more-than-human relative, they learn to get "sweet water" from the tree. Binoojiinh takes the sweet water to their grandmother. They cook with it and learn how to make sugar from it. They take the whole community to see Binoojiinh's discovery. Ever since that time the Anishinaabe "collect that sweet water / and boil it up / and boil it down / into that sweet, sweet sugar /all thanks to Binoojiinh and their lovely discovery, / and to Ajidamoo and her precious teaching / and to Ninaatigoog and their boundless sharing."[7]

In the story the Anishinaabe community learns from loving attention to aki. But it also illustrates other key aspects of Indigenous pedagogies including intergenerational communication, love, "whole-body intelligence," interdependence with all our relations, kinetic learning, and individual responsibility for learning. The story shows how the "context is the curriculum." Place and land play a central role in teaching and learning. In the European context we learn in the hierarchical "banking method" so well described by Paolo Frieire and within the confines of a square sterile box where nature dare not intrude. In Indigenous pedagogy the context is aki, the land.[8] The Anishinaabe believe that "Intelligence flows through relationships between living entities" and requires love. John Borrows said, "As long as we love them [the animals] they will provide for us, and teach us about love and how to live well in the world." Meaning results from "a compassionate web of interdependent relationships that are different and valuable because of difference."[9]

Indigenous pedagogies conflict with Wetiko education. Indigenous education requires land—the very same land that Wetiko covets for its wealth. Thus, Indigenous pedagogy is a revolutionary decolonial pedagogy. Decolonization requires

a generation of land-based, community-based intellectuals and cultural producers who are accountable to our nations and whose life work is concerned with the regeneration of these systems rather than meeting the overwhelming needs of the western academic industrial complex or attempting to "Indigenize" the academy.[10]

To create land-based, community-based intellectuals, we let land lead the lessons. However, implementing land-based pedagogy in the context of the postindustrial city at the beginning of the new millennium requires an adaptation of Indigenous pedagogy and attention to other liberatory educational perspectives. Hip hop pedagogy, the "organic intellectual" of Gramsci, Freire's "pedagogy of the oppressed" approach, and the political education of Black radicals are used in a variety of ways in the food movement on the South Side of Chicago.

CommUnity Pedagogy in Chicago's Food Movement

Food is central to the social, cultural, political, and economic spheres of every society. As a result, using food as our primary unit of analysis provides insight into a wide variety of subjects and social problems. In addition, the food autonomy perspective actively critiques the dominant food system through direct action. This strategy facilitates active student learning as well as the development of community. Properly teaching food autonomy ultimately requires a place-based commUnity pedagogy whose dynamism and effectiveness rest on the crossing of invisible, but nonetheless real, boundaries between the university and community, elders and youth, and teacher and student.

To begin, CP attempts to develop a group of organic intellectuals whose "function [is] in directing the ideas and aspirations of the class to which they organically belong."[11] Organic intellectuals draw their support and intellectual foundation from their class. They share many traits with Simpson's "community-based intellectuals." Gramsci explains:

> Every social group, coming into existence on the original terrain of an essential function in the world of economic production, creates together with itself, organically, one or more strata of intellectuals which give it homogeneity and an awareness of its own function not only in the economic but also in the social and political fields.[12]

Organic, community-based intellectuals develop out of every social group including the Brown and Black urban working class. These intellectuals "give awareness" through culturally relevant pedagogical methods. They help provide coherence to the groups' beliefs and identity. The Black and Mexican urban working class in Chicago and elsewhere serve specific economic functions in a postindustrial economy. This unique class has created a group of intellectuals that help it develop a consciousness of itself as a class. Artists, musicians, comedians, bartenders, barbers, professors, activists, community gardeners, organizers, and elders, among others, are the organic intellectuals of the inner city.[13]

CP requires that intellectuals be active members of their communities. It is not enough for them to think about, theorize, or research urban social problems. Organic intellectuals must experience and strive to eliminate them.

The mode of being of the new intellectual can no longer consist in eloquence, which is an exterior and momentary mover of feelings and passions, but in active participation in practical life, as constructor, organizer, "permanent persuader" and not just a simple orator.[14]

The permaculture education provided by BOC and the Permaculture Institute of Chicago is dedicated to getting "the key potential resource" (information) to Black and Brown/Indigenous people in Chicago and beyond. The members of these educational institutions actively seek Black and Brown students and provide more free education than tuition-based education. Each of the faculty members of these institutions is of Black, Indigenous, or Black-Indigenous heritage and speaks directly to our communities of origin.

Paolo Freire's insights have also influenced the place-based CP I use. His concept of conscientizacao is useful for understanding the goals of CP. Conscientizacao focuses on examining the social, cultural, political, and economic contradictions of a society and action to end its oppressive elements. Conscientizacao is achieved through dialogue and communication with the various sectors of the working classes and Indigenous peoples and through a process of reflection/theory development and practice. The dynamic process involves commitment to community and willingness to act on behalf of oneself as a community member. "While no one liberates himself by his own efforts alone, neither is he liberated by others." Conscientizacao is "a search for self-affirmation."[15]

"Any radical pedagogy must insist that everyone's presence is acknowledged . . . Often before this process can begin there has to be some deconstruction of the traditional notion that only the professor is responsible for classroom dynamics."[16] Using this principle, educators can help students in a process of self-actualization instead of dependence on an authority for imparting knowledge. The common practice of the "check-in" exemplifies this orientation toward learning. Since co-teaching a PDC with Fred Carter and Dr. Jifunza Wright in which Baba Fred took the "check-in" very seriously, I have also used this tactic in my classes. The technique aims to simply understand the mental-emotional-physical-spiritual state of each of the participants in the class. Doing so signals to participants that they and their thoughts, feelings, and so on are important and valuable to the collective. We strive to empower all who come into our circles of learning. Second, it provides content for class discussion. In addition, community land stewardship provides opportunities for self-actualization through solving numerous practical problems that arise in community gardens and through diverse and constant interactions with fellow stewards. The notion of a classroom community is expanded to surrounding human and more-than-human communities and so, too, are the opportunities for learning and identity development.

The denial of community and exalting of individualism in Wetiko society and education makes this process of creating an empowered space in which to learn through place-based CP difficult. In the university setting this problem seems insurmountable as universities rely on hierarchy, individual achievement, and competition, and in community spaces Wetiko often creeps in to make learning and organizing difficult. Through land-based CP strategies we attempt to mitigate the effects of Wetiko's educational system. In the educational spaces of the food autonomy movement, we challenge Wetiko's education as we adapt CP strategies.

Finally, the focus on community in CP adds diversity of opinion and experience contributing to much richer and deeper learning. Community requires engagement with urban social problems and racism through direct interaction. Community implies action. CP is hands on. Poverty and hunger aren't merely statistics and abstractions but real-life problems to be solved. The flourishing of the community garden produces visible results that positively affect our communities. Two important results attract our attention. First, community is developed, expanded, and deepened through bringing diverse people together for the goal of making positive change. Second, hundreds of pounds of food are produced using the food arts and sciences of BIPOC.

Using Place-Based CommUnity Pedagogy

For many years my Principles and Practices of Food Justice class at CSU partnered with the members of GLP, the RCPG and others. Students spent half their class time during the ten-week long summer semester in a traditional classroom at CSU and the other half at the Outdoor CommUnity Classroom (OCC) at the RCPG. University and community students acted as caretakers of the garden and exchanged information and experience.

Time spent in the traditional classroom focuses on an examination of the dominant food system, key concepts and theories of the food justice perspective, and alternative food systems. Our class readings and discussions emphasize issues pertinent to our immediate surroundings, the far South Side neighborhoods of Chicago. Many of the students come from food deprived communities or communities otherwise affected by poverty and racism such as Roseland where our university and the OCC are located.

In the OCC students become student caretakers of a community resource that intervenes directly in the social problems we examine in the traditional classroom. Through caretaking they use and reinforce knowledge gained from class texts. Major issues examined in readings, films, and discussions, including developing alternatives to the dominant food system, loss of ancestral knowledge, health inequalities, and poverty, are confronted through the production of food and medicine. Scholarly knowledge combines with IK to address these social problems materially.

Importantly, Blackness, Mexicanidad, indigeneity, and the working class are re-examined through the lens of food autonomy and IK. We spend the season working with and learning of the vast knowledge of Africans and Amerindigenous. Instead of seeing people of Africa and Abya Yala as backward, we present them as highly advanced in the food arts and sciences and in sustainable living. The botanical and moral legacy of Africa and Abya Yala are presented as essential to the development of food and moral systems across the planet and for saving the planet from Wetiko-generated ecological disaster.[17] While the tragedy of slavery, land theft, genocide and colonialism are discussed to advance our understanding of the causes of urban social problems, the core of CP and food autonomy involves the examination of how people have survived these conditions and how their food arts and sciences continue to be essential aspects of that survival.

Beans and Greens: Rethinking Black and Mexican History

The dominant narrative concerning Black and Mexican/Indigenous history and contemporary Black and Mexican/Indigenous life depicts us as tragic.[18] Wetiko's violence, while important to the understanding of our history, are far from the only significant factors in our lives. What interests many of us is how Africans and the Indigenous survived and thrived against such odds. Examining history from this perspective fills gaps in our overall knowledge and allows us to see BIPOC as more than victims and tragic figures. Rethinking Black and Mexican/Indigenous history in terms of triumph with a focus on ancestral wisdom, IK, and survival strategies can be empowering for BIPOC students and our communities.

Thousands of years of land steward technology allowed for the survival of enslaved Africans brought to Abya Yala. For example, the story of the yam is one of survival and resistance. "One of the first food crops domesticated, the yam was subsequently developed as an important tuber of the humid tropical forests of Nigeria and Cameroon." Archaeological evidence suggests that African food cultivation began at the latest between 5000 and 4000 BCE. In free African communities throughout the Americas, enslaved Africans who escaped captivity (maroons) grew yams as one of their central crops due to its high carbohydrate content and hardiness. Afro-Caribbeans prized the yam since hurricanes do not affect root crops as they do aboveground yielding crops.

> The tubers introduced to the New World from Africa—yams, plantains, and
> taro—were ideally suited to slave subsistence plots because they demand little attention, are high yielding, and are readily prepared as food. Root crops hold a dis-

tinct advantage over cereals in hurricane-prone areas, as the underground edible part usually survives when struck by storms that routinely occur in the Caribbean. The tubers moreover can be continuously harvested, as needed.[19]

Students in the OCC and other spaces learn important lessons about food and the land and, more importantly, the predominantly Black gardeners learn empowering lessons about themselves and their history. At the OCC we learn about greens. We raise several different kinds with collards and mustards being the most popular. Along with growing practices, students learn about the cultural and historical importance of greens as we share memories and knowledge from our families and communities and discuss the historical evidence regarding their domestication in Africa and transplantation in the Americas.

While working in the various greens patches in the garden and sitting on chairs made from storm-felled trees from around the neighborhood, we examine how mustard and collard greens came to the Americas from Africa where for centuries women had been using them in countless ways in soups, salads, and side dishes. In kitchen gardens enslaved Africans retained the practice. They, like many contemporary Black Americans, preserved the food arts and sciences of Africa. We learn that "greens contribute crucial stores of vitamins, minerals, and micronutrients to the diet" and have many medicinal uses.[20] Student gardeners see the ubiquitous and humble greens prepared by grandmothers, aunties, and mothers in new ways after learning this. Greens become decolonized. Ms. Thomas and God's Gang emphasize their African/American roots through growing greens, cotton, okra, and African heritage foods. She explains that she and God's Gang not only teach Black children about African and African diasporan history and culture but also use food to teach them about other traditions:

> We always try to grow cotton. We try to do things that when kids come is new, different and historical. We always grow gourds. Every kind of gourd we can. Sourghum. And that provides that lesson. We also do Chinese cucumbers. We do artichokes. I love the way artichokes look. It's real primitive looking and something different for them to eat and taste. Not only our ethnicity but others . . . [At Elliot Donnelly Youth Services] we built a garden and, in fact, it had five different gardens. We had a Hispanic garden which was kinda like a mandala [design].[21] It had those kinda crops. We had an Indian garden with squash, corn and beans. Then, we had a southern garden with collards. We had okra in our African garden and melons and peanuts and things that were appropriate.

The students not only learn about the historical genius of African, Indigenous, and diasporic foodways but also how to employ this genius in their own lives. In

Indigenous food systems throughout the world complementary planting is used as a technique to improve plant growth, resist disease and pests, and develop soil. "Las tres madres" teach students a practical lesson they can employ in their plots as well as further illustrate the genius of Indigenous people. Along with teaching complementarity, soil conservation, and polyculturalism, las tres madres teach survival, subsistence, and spirit. Members of GLP plant the important Indigenous Mexican triad of teosinte, yetl, and ayotli. We discuss how the ideas of complementarity have been adopted by the larger organic and sustainable farming movement. These practices have become in vogue and a standard that all of us in these movements learn. What many do not know is that these practices are ancient in the Americas. Corn has over five thousand years of history here. As we tend the milpa the story of corn domestication by ancient Mexicans further illustrates the power of IK.[22] Our discussions and readings develop a maíz narrative that includes the on-going five-hundred-year-long colonial attack on corn and hijxs de maíz as well as our resistance.

We focus on the lessons of las tres madres or three sisters, as many of our English-speaking Indigenous relatives call it. Through touching the seeds and lovingly tending them, we learn the deep lessons of reciprocity that they teach. We see how they provide a model for human relationships and the values of respect and interdependence central to Indigenous social organization. We see how the uniqueness of each is nurtured when they grow together. The mothers teach us that life requires diversity to thrive as their yields increase in direct proportion to their cooperation. We also learn about our unique gifts and responsibilities as humans. We learn that our tres madres garden is

> a Four Sisters garden, for the planter is also an essential partner. It is she who turns up the soil, she who scares away the crows, and she who pushes seeds into the soil. We are the planters . . . We are the midwives to their gifts. We cannot live without them, but it's also true that they cannot live without us. Corn, beans, and squash are fully domesticated; they rely on us to create the conditions under which they can grow. We too are part of the reciprocity. They can't meet their responsibilities unless we meet ours.[23]

In the indoor classroom students learn an interdisciplinary perspective on Mexican land traditions. We learn of the "Mayan Managed Mosaic," a system of land use practices and IK in accord with the notion of in lak' ech. The Maya "created a mode of production that allowed the forest to alternate between domesticated and wild (self-willing) states. Forest users maintained a shifting balance between subsistence production and biodiversity. Maya farmers developed impressive knowledge of horticulture and agroforestry."[24] Mayans developed agriculture techniques such as biomimicry (imitating nature), polyculturalism (planting multiple species together), ground covers (low-growing plants), raised beds, and complementary planting.

Through the focus on the IK and habits of Africans and Indigenous people, we hope to counter the prevailing White supremacist mythology that imagines our people as backward, uncivilized, and victimized. Rethinking Black and Mexican/Indigenous history through food autonomy and IK lenses allows for learning that 1) social science and Ethnic Studies theories, perspectives, and concepts related to food autonomy, poverty, urban problems, White supremacy, colonialism, geography and the like; 2) techniques for growing food in sustainable, culturally responsive ways beneficial to ourselves and families; and 3) information about our traditions that helps our goals of strengthening identity and self-esteem and developing land-based, community-based intellectuals.

Redefining Work: From Slave to Autonomous Steward

The completely abject "slave," that overemphasized trope of Black history, can be usefully interrogated when placing the work of enslaved Africans in the Americas and their knowledge in proper context. Seeing the enslaved as skilled and knowledgeable and food cultivation as dignified resituates the powerful BAT handed down over centuries in Africa and on to the Americas where it was adapted further to thrive in the soil of the new environments. The continuous emphasizing of food as the central aspect in our lives helps us also to re-examine our relationship to those responsible for feeding us; namely, farm workers, food processors, chefs and other restaurant workers, and grocery store employees. Many of these workers come from the much maligned Mexican "migrant" population.

With this perspective in mind, gardens can teach numerous lessons as we engage in the most useful and dignified work of growing food. We learn to see our past in terms of triumph and learn to see others and our relationship to them in deeper, more meaningful ways. Gardens teach us these most important of lessons from our Bantu and Mayan ancestors: ubuntu and in lak' ech. We are intimately connected through food, and this becomes easily understandable as we think about food systems and the food arts and sciences of our ancestors. Importantly, manual labor in the community garden amid food poverty teaches us to examine Wetiko's food system, alternatives to it, practical political and home economy, and the nature of human labor. For most of us in the working classes work is a means to an end, often loathed and rarely celebrated. Work is where exploitation and abuse take place. Often, the goal of working-class people is to get as far away from the arduous manual labor of the fields and factories as we can. A lesson from a workday at the Roseland Community Peace Garden illustrates this problem and solution:

"I feel like a slave," Amina exhaled loudly.[25]

I responded, "It's hot, right?"

The high humidity and 90-degree temperature at 10 a.m. made work difficult. Amina and a few other students affirmed that the weeding and seeding of a large, raised bed made them feel "how slaves must have felt on the plantation" as Amina described it.

After a brief discussion, the crowd began to develop a consensus that the hot humid air and hard work were unbearable even as they smiled and joked. I took this opportunity to suggest that this work and slavery were, in fact, the exact opposites. "This work is the exact opposite of slavery. The collectively worked community garden can provide true freedom. Know what I mean?" When no one responded affirmatively, I continued. "What made slavery horrible was not the agricultural work but the relations of production. In fact, the work that slaves and migrant farm workers do today is some of the most dignified, noble, and important work that can be done. We are fed from their labor." Students recalled how earlier in the week we read a similar line of reasoning regarding socially useful, dignified work with the land.[26] Now they were getting a chance to experience the theory.

The small crowd of students grew as their attention was piqued by this line of argument regarding slavery and work. Their understanding of the slave and sharecropping eras caused them to equate manual agricultural labor with the horrors of slavery. Repositioning agricultural work as a highly dignified, yet denigrated, craft was something that most in the discussion were willing to explore, if only once a week while in class.

I continued with the impromptu lecture on dignified versus alienated labor, slavery, racism, and liberation: "The problem with slavery was twofold: First, a human owning another human is obviously wrong. Second, is the superexploitation of a person's body. Their work and bodies, which we know are dignified, become degraded as the products of their labor are claimed by the owner for self-enrichment. The owner now owns the amazing, wonderful product made with the blood, sweat, and tears of another's labor. In essence, the owner steals the product of slave labor. If the slaves owned the products of their labor, it, first, would not be slavery, nor would the labor seem undignified and horrendous." Some took the long, deep pause for reflection as a chance to get back to the (in some ways) easier labor of weeding and harvesting a bed of purple pod pole beans. Others wanted to continue the conversation in the shade.

I argued, "As we have been learning in class, we have very little control over the products we consume, especially food. What we eat and how it is produced are determined by others. Having no self-determination is the very definition of slavery. Then, without the ability to determine what and how you eat (remember food sovereignty?), your health and, by extension, your life and that of your family and community is controlled by someone else. Their concerns for profit will always determine what they provide. Your health goes unconsidered."

Connecting the dots, Amina responded, "That's like when we did our community maps. We found that there were no good stores in Roseland. But, in the place where the better-off live, they got rich White people there, they have that store with the health food and organic food."

Intern Tre Thomas added, "That's because they don't care about Black people. All they care about is making money."

"Right!" I interjected. "So how can community gardens and a local food economy solve the crises of food access, junk food and the lack of access to real food in the hood, and food sovereignty? How can the work we do in the gardens help us achieve greater freedom? Remember when we all stood around and discussed what we wanted to plant in the four new beds we had just weeded? The students nodded. "How did we decide?"

Brian said, "We talked about the food we liked and about what would grow this late since it is late in the summer." I responded, "That was a collective, community process! We decided. We are growing it. Not wage slaves on a corporate plantation. We had control over our labor and the decisions about what we would eat. Freedom." The conversation continued in this vein for a few more minutes until it was time to resume our weeding and harvesting. Those who took greens home also took a new way of seeing the much-maligned greens that generations ago helped Black people survive the atrocities of slavery, sharecropping, and lives of limited opportunity and structural violence under Jim Crow segregation.[27]

Students connect food and labor activities with the hard life in the South. This attitude is reflected in another oft-heard remark in the community garden and food justice classroom: "My grandma left the South to get away from this." Birdie added to the line of critique one day, explaining her grandmother's journey to Chicago: "She said the White man worked them like slaves, and sometimes they had their way with the women. You couldn't even walk down the streets because if a White person walked on the sidewalks you had to move into the street. She had to escape late in the night to get away from the South."

A chorus of students chimed in telling stories that elders in their family had told them about the South. What became evident during this conversation was that none of the complaints about the South during the early twentieth century had anything to do directly with agriculture and rural life itself but with the racist apartheid system that controlled Black people's right to move or even live, and that degraded or dismissed their skilled artisan and farm labor. I used this as an opportunity to share an alterNative history, geography, and political economy:

People's experience with nature and their surroundings is determined, in good part, by how their political, economic, and social systems are structured. It's important to differentiate between the factors that made rural and agricultural life for Blacks intolerable and those factors that didn't necessarily cause them anguish . . . When we watched the movie about Immokalee,[28] remember? We talked about questions of labor and food justice. The migrant farm workers, Mexican and Haitian, provide the tomatoes that we eat in our tacos from Taco Bell. Everyone benefits except for the workers. It's the structure of labor that people hate, not necessarily the labor itself. For example, the pace of work in these sweatshops in the fields is inhumanely high since the workers' wages are determined by a piece-rate system that pays them mere cents for a fifty-pound bucket of tomatoes. If workers controlled the pace, product, and other factors of their labor, then it wouldn't be so awful. If they owned their labor and the products of their labor, like we own this garden, they may not have developed the same feelings regarding agricultural labor.

The young stewards all nodded in agreement and Amina smiled, a knowing smile that came from this newfound sense of the dignity and skill in her own work in the RCPG and that of her ancestors from the South.[29]

Experience working in autonomous community-controlled gardens illustrates how labor takes on the conditions of its organization. We understand that our experiences and feelings toward work result from the relations of production under which we labor. Under capitalist relations of production, we suffer for a wage. We are not compensated for the true value of our work, and we recognize our exploitation. We become "alienated" from work, its products, and our fellow workers. Of course, it is not the work but our dependence on and exploitation by bosses that causes us to despise work. Since we collectively organize the labor in the garden with no coercion (except for those who must fulfill course requirements), we experience the work differently than we would as slaves, sharecroppers, or migrant farm workers.

In addition, feeding people is a useful contribution to our society and thus it is dignified.[30] Garden work provides many of the things that make work attractive: short duration, variety, conscious usefulness, and pleasant surroundings.[31] Within an oasis full of flowers and beauty, we work only a few hours per week on innumerable, complex tasks that feed people. Moreover, our work is made more attractive by its collective nature and the relationships that we develop doing it. That our work provides a service to all our relations adds to the dignity of the work in growing food. We strive like others in the food autonomy movement to redefine tending the land by using ancestral ways. The farmworker members of Community to Community (C2C) in Bellingham, Washington, express this transformative process:

> By respecting traditional ways of learning and growing foods, we hope to remember that growing food was not always the shameful and devalued work that we know today as farmwork. We try to remember that growing food is a dignified, necessary, and valued skill that our parents and ancestors learned and passed down. The oppressive realities of farmworkers are the result of corruption in today's food system and are not inherent in the act of growing, harvesting, and processing food.[32]

However, because our bodies are not used to the strenuous labor and due to the overwhelming historical associations of this work with enslavement and indignity, the garden experience is fraught with contradictions for many. The lesson about self-organized work, while easily assimilated by many, meets with resistance from others mired in historical and ongoing trauma or who simply do not want to do the work. In addition, food autonomy and time spent cultivating land will not get us any closer to the "good life" as defined under the capitalist consumerist ideology. Freedom under late capitalism means the freedom to purchase, not self-determination. This ubiquitous ethos often wins workers and BIPOC over to individualism and consumerism, which undermine our autonomous impulses. These among many other problems plague CP as a strategy of radical intervention.

Elder Pedagogy

Intergenerational communication occurs daily in food autonomy spaces. Elders pass on foodways and culture to children and young adults. Teens and children express their fears and joys and thus help adults better understand urban social problems and their effects on young people. Without such transmission of culture, the wisdom of African and Indigenous Mexican peoples is being lost to the seductions of the Wetiko lifestyle. Through planting, watering, weeding, and harvesting, dozens of boys and girls begin to learn self-determination, empowerment, and dignity. They learn how to provide for themselves in ecologically and culturally appropriate ways without reliance on Wetiko. They learn collective labor and broader connections to all our relatives. They learn and practice community. Through active listening to young people, adults learn a different way to understand our world and its problems. Collective work and communication provide profound liberatory educational opportunities.

GLP gardens offer students of all ages freedom to explore and learn. The controlled chaos of a dynamic and evolving forest garden ecosystem in a neglected sector of the postindustrial city provides untold, unpredictable moments for passing on IK. On a cool September day in 2010, I witnessed an example of intergenerational interaction when I overheard Mama Dorothy tell Salvador about the proper way to pick greens.

> Come over here and pick these turnip greens. No, not like that. Come here, Salvador. Like this. Get down, like this. All the way down to the ground. And snap it off. Right there, where the stem meets the tuber.

Teaching local youth appropriate methods for harvesting turnip greens and other horticultural techniques is among the most important work we do in community gardens. Mama Dorothy's exchange with Salvador, who was twelve at the time, is duplicated daily in our community gardens. Here an elder communicates AHK to a preteen. Passing on such knowledge is important if a community or other group formation is to achieve food autonomy. Importantly, this exchange about Black foodways occurred between an elder Black woman and a Black-Mexican boy on land stolen from Indigenous people and turned into a ghetto by Wetiko. This is an example of how we reclaim (or reterritorialize) the land using the landed, elder pedagogy of IK. Mama Dorothy is an organic intellectual.

If a culture is to exist, it must determine its own food system. This is the essence of sovereignty and why many Indigenous activists and authors argue that we cannot be Indigenous without our land. The people making up the cultural community must have requisite knowledge of land stewardship, hunting and foraging, food preparation and preservation, and the culinary methods and techniques of previous generations. Otherwise, BIPOC communities lose their independence and become or remain food colonized. Most in our movement charge that the loss of food autonomy is a key cause of hunger, malnutrition, and related maladies in many working-class urban areas.

The ubiquity of fast-food and prepackaged Wetiko food-like products in BIPOC communities in Chicago tears at the fabric of Black and Indigenous foodways and culture. IK and AHK are lost in urban food-deprived communities marked by the (dis)array of fried and processed, sugar-laden, fat-saturated, and preservative-tainted industrial foods; the "meaty-dairy" SAD.[33] The pace of life in the city, the effects of poverty and food policy, education through formal schooling,[34] and the media all contribute to the loss of knowledge. By tilling, planting, watering, and harvesting, Salvador and two dozen other boys and girls at the RCPG began learning how to provide for themselves in an ecologically and culturally appropriate manner without reliance on the capitalist market or governmental handouts. They were learning while practicing community autonomy.

"Tell your Mom what three things a plant needs to survive and bear fruit," Baba

FIG. 8. Jacqueline Smith and Evon McFarland. Photo by author.

Jim encouraged six-year-old DeShaun. DeShaun enthusiastically replied, "Water . . . the sun, . . . and food from the soil." DeShaun, of the night-watering crew in the RCPG, had been watering the crops with a hose and harvesting and eating broccoli for most of the summer when his mom came to the garden to bring him home. She was impressed by her son's knowledge of gardening. His almost daily walks down the block to the community garden provided him an opportunity to interact with elders in his community and learn how and why to care for the garden. Through the spreading of love, good intentions, and important community survival knowledge, youngsters like DeShaun and Salvador can appreciate and care for the life of their community. Elders in the community offer this gift of care to the youth knowing its importance to community survival.

Biking to the Garden: Pedagogy on Wheels

My sons and I spent many summers and autumns of their youth biking to the RCPG. Biking through our neighborhood, Roseland, taught us about alternative energy, health, community problems, urban policy, ecology, and community empowerment. The four of us learned so much from our sustainable transportation that I now refer to this as "pedagogy on wheels."

The short bike ride illustrated how neighborhoods are spatially arranged, including the way in which institutions such as schools, the police, and liquor stores circumscribe neighborhood life. In addition, we talk about how the underground economy influences the patterns of community life around our garden. Many aspects of life are affected by illegal and barely legal activity common in our underresourced neighborhood. On the one hand, we have the typical drug dealing, gang violence, and prostitution. On the other hand, we have the violence of the market in the form of poor-quality retail and food outlets and the presence of the state, especially through minimal social services and the ever-expanding police force. These forces can hold community members hostage. As a result, there are few spaces that we can transform into places that provide opportunities to learn and practice community empowerment.

The bike rides demonstrate governmental neglect. While the police seem to have a bottomless budget for containment and surveillance of the community, fewer public resources are invested toward efforts at community-building and the maintenance of culture. For example, the 2021 City of Chicago budget included tremendous increases for the Chicago Police Department. The U.S. federal government allocated $1.2 billion to Chicago in COVID-19 Emergency Relief funds. Mayor Lori Lightfoot, who ran primarily on identity politics as a Black lesbian, used $281.5 million of these funds for police wages and other expenditures.[35] Public resources in the form of educational programs and institutions to encourage access and knowledge concerning healthy food. The food movement steps in where governmental neglect leaves people vulnerable.

From the vantage point of our bike seats, we see things differently than from our car. We experience, literally, every bump on the road. We can see firsthand the effects of urban policy and corporate greed. After seeing evidence of the devastation wrought in poor neighborhoods, we often discuss what we saw. We have read about the concept of food deserts and issues related to ecology, poverty, and race. The core ideas of a land-based CP develop through an organic process of direct lived experience, dialogue, and participatory and collaborative research.

This deep pedagogy is a wholistic undertaking, an approach akin to Freire's generative pedagogy whereby the situation and participants determine the content and nature of the course. It is a learning by doing method central to Black and Indigenous lifeways. In this deep pedagogy on wheels and in the garden, student-teachers learn about societal issues and problems, our place within the social structure, and how to empower our communities through taking away capitalism's central weapon—our dependence on capitalism for survival. Not only do we think about our food, health, and vulnerability vis-à-vis the Wetiko, especially agribusiness, but we also take our health and food into our own hands through kinetic learning. On the bike and in the garden, we build stronger bodies, minds, and spirits. We begin to take away the bosses' control over our lives. This approach also incorporates a biocentric perspective, deep ecology, critical race analysis, and anticolonial and antiauthoritarian positions.

It is deep in that it tries to get at fundamental questions and solve keystone problems. The teaching and learning are democratic, challenging hierarchical organizational models. It is deep also since it relies on Indigenous knowledge with its deep roots in this place. Each participant is a student and teacher. Each person holds responsibility for the entire group's learning. We are learning through discussion, reading, and research about Indigenous nonhierarchical modes of community organization and knowledge exchange.

Cultivating Quiltl: Wild Plants Are Our Teachers

In 2013, I decided to let quiltl take over much of my home garden space as well as allow them to be an important part of the garden design at GLP gardens. At the forest garden we simply weed and tend pathways. I let the "wild" edibles like verdolagas (purslane) and quiltl (wild greens but, for our family, lamb's quarters[36]) sprout up among the "volunteer" cultivars that decided to grow from previous seasons' fallen and wind-blown seeds. I planted a few things at home and worked with GLP to carve out neat growing spaces at the community gardens, but I decided to let nature lead and learn from quiltl, other wild edibles, and all my relations.

A new gardener pointed to a quiltl plant and said, "This is a weed, right?" The discussion of wild edibles began organically with this question. The small group working in the OCC began talking about what constitutes a weed. How do we define it? Can you identify one when you see it? I pointed to a dandelion nearby. "Is that a weed?" Everyone immediately agreed that it was. The dandelion is probably the most well-known and easily recognizable "weed" in the country. The gardeners formed a circle, and we pulled a dandelion to examine. I held up and then passed around my copy of *A Field Guide to Medicinal Plants and Herbs of Eastern and Central North America*.[37] I explained how to use every part of the dandelion for some form of sustenance and nutrition. "The beautiful plant has leaves to eat fresh or lightly cooked like other greens, flowers to eat in salads or fried, and roots to make a coffee-like substance. I have some dandelion leaves drying in the basement. Soon it will be a key ingredient in household teas."[38]

It's all about context and knowledge. If you want it in your space, then it is fine. If you do not, then it is a weed. A dandelion is a weed to most in the suburban context of a monoculture grass lawn because we don't know how to use it and learn to despise that which we don't know. For our community food development course, Baba Fred shed important light on "weeds." In our interactions with all our relatives we are supposed to act morally, which requires patience, respect, and knowledge of our relatives. So he defined a weed as "a plant that you don't know how to use." It is human ignorance and not anything inherent in the plant that causes it to be a problem, a "weed." Divorced from the knowledge of its usefulness and value, the highly nutritious and useful dandelion becomes a weed. The monoculture landowner assaults the dandelion and other "weeds" with herbicides in pursuit of the perfect lawn; chemical warfare is declared daily by the monocultural grass-lover. I told my fellow gardeners that I solve the "dandelion problem" by simply eating them. A perfect example of the permaculture principle of "the problem is the solution." So along with dandelion, quelites, and verdolagas, GLP members have learned to use chicory, cup plant, clover, burdock, and many others for food and medicine. We have begun to learn the lessons that our wild plant relatives teach.

I remember eating quiltl as a kid, but my memories are a bit hazy. My sister, on the other hand, has clear loving memories of eating quiltl. She described to me how our grandparents made "wild spinach" with bacon and butter. Given my distance and time away from New Mexico, it makes sense that I would have lost some of my memory of this food tradition. It took me a few days to realize that the lamb's quarters growing everywhere in the community garden were the same quiltl I ate as a kid. My recognition of quiltl led to new insights regarding time, geography, memory, class, imperialism, and tradition. Quiltl began to teach me valuable lessons useful in my food autonomy work and life. This is what it means to say that the land teaches.

I recall my experience with quiltl to teach a lesson about the history of the Mexican diaspora, some of our oldest history and newer trends. Our ancestors foraged for quiltl ultimately cultivating them in their gardens and food forests. Mesoamericans continued the tradition. In fact, the name "quelites" is ancient in the Americas as it is derived from the Nahua word "quilitl." It was a key green in home gardens. Amerindigenous people valued it for its high nutritional content. It is high in vitamins A, C, and K, as well as in iron, fiber, vegetable protein, and various minerals. It is prepared easily like spinach and grows abundantly. What is not to like about quiltl?

With European imperialism, the diets and horticultural traditions of native Mexicans changed dramatically. The Spaniards brought a new "ecological revolution" that included an attack on native foodstuffs.[39] Sometime between the Spanish colonial era in Mexico and the 1970s in New Mexico when I was a child, quiltl became a weed. Yet we still ate it. Mexican Americans of New Mexico recognized quiltl and others such as piñon and verdolagas as wild edibles. However, imperialist ideologues and missionaries deemed them unsuitable for cultivation in our gardens, so most of us don't grow them.

My personal story of the loss and recovery of an Indigenous food practices illustrates further a story that is altogether too common a part of the Mexican and African diasporic experience. Today, few of my friends and family eat quiltl. Our diets have been colonized and wild edibles are certainly not part of the standard American diet. We have turned over our diets to corporations and advertisers. While many in New Mexico, for example, still eat roasted New Mexico chile (chilli in Nahuatl), piñon seed, and red chile with venison, or hunt as part of the way to obtain our food, as people move out of the geographical area or up the economic ladder, distance is placed between us and our Indigenous food traditions. Of course, dietary colonialism in the form of ubiquitous fast-food "restaurants" and the continued denigration of things Mexican and Indigenous along with land loss are the primary deterrents to maintaining our ancestral foodways. I moved up and out. So quiltl was lost to me. My loss mirrors that of "most Mexicans living in the United States [who] no longer 'know the maíz or the bean.'"[40] Fortunately, the food movement and the tenacity of Indigenous people in the face of the colonization of our diets has led to a remembrance of quiltl and other Indigenous Mexican foods. As a result, I and other members of the GLP "know quiltl" and other wild edibles. We know it intellectually as an important, highly nutritious foodstuff. I also now know it intimately, spiritually and emotionally.

My recognition of quiltl and decision to let nature guide my hand in the garden and to encourage others to do so in our community garden taught me to see colonialism and decolonialism in two important ways. First, I experienced a real-life example of our dangerous tendency to want to control and colonize nature. I, like many gardeners and farmers, too often attempt to impose my will on nature. I pull weeds with vengeance when I only want one row of crop in each bed. If it is true that a primary characteristic of nature is that it is fecund, then it seems foolhardy to attempt to eradicate "weeds."[41] Instead, I should take more seriously the idea of complementary or companion planting that our ancestors gave to the world so many thousands of years ago—the elegant principle of the polyculture milpa. I should understand the importance of wild edibles and native plants instead of shaking my head in frustration as the "weeds" outproduce my vegetable plants. Letting quiltl teach leads us to the realization that nature produces perfectly. We should, like our ancestors, practice biomimicry; a principle in which we "imitate the diversity and layers of the local native flora and fauna and their habitat."[42] This is the same understanding that permaculture designers inherited from Indigenous forest management. The ideas of complementary plant guilds, forest gardening, and food forests so popular with permaculture designers result from IK. Cooperation, complementarity, and mutual aid are important to how an ecosystem works without human intervention. Permaculture designers and traditional Indigenous food movement workers and thinkers argue that these natural principles should be applied to human systems if we are to create a new society that would be environmentally and socially just.[43] Can we even imagine what our world would look like if we incorporated just these three natural principles into our human-human interaction? How might we change, individually and as a society, if we get to "know" our wild edibles and the secrets of all our relations?

Second, remembering quiltl along with my fellow gardeners brought forth a history that illustrates the material consequences of colonialism. Loss of food traditions results from the colonial process in which all that is native becomes vile, savage, and backward, whereas all that comes from the settlers becomes idealized, overvalued, and esteemed.[44] Quiltl becomes a weed, and "civilized" people don't eat weeds. To the colonizer and victims of capitalist ideology, it is a marker of my backwardness that I now do cultivate and eat quiltl, Jerusalem artichoke, mulberries, and other "wild" foods.

Quiltl with its high nutritional content[45] was a primary factor in the survival and prosperity of millions of native Mexicans for centuries. As with the loss of corn to wheat and the concomitant rise in obesity and related problems, the loss of quiltl, a key source of affordable nutrients, offers insight into the health consequences of colonialism.[46] We lose quiltl, verdolagas, tortillas de maíz, and nopal (cactus) and have them replaced with chemically preserved, packaged, and "fast" foods. We lose health as we lose tradition. Colonialism takes the very resources necessary for our survival, our food traditions, arts, and sciences. Our traditions are hidden away or turned into a commodity. Either way, we lose the ability to determine our own food choices; we lose autonomy over our survival.

Quiltl has taught all of this. What else might we learn if we just pay attention to our self-willing plant relatives?

Lifeboats Learning: CommUnity Pedagogy as Praxis

The Lifeboats Series: Local Food System Development with Permaculture Design Certification course exemplified the pedagogy used by many in the food autonomy movement. The BOC and I developed a permaculture design certification course (PDC) that incorporated a CP understanding of the uniqueness of our community, being Black American, urban, and working class. Our PDC extended urban permaculture design to new levels by focusing on IK and the Black agrarian tradition (BAT). Baba Fred, Dr. J, and I analyzed the ever-present ethical challenges that are the biggest hurdles to transforming our society. In our course-development meetings, we spoke about how we would teach permaculture techniques while insisting on attending to the spiritual and emotional healing needed in our community. We organized the course into equal parts people care, earth care, and fair share.[47] The goal was to learn the skills and develop the community trust necessary to become lifeboats for one another in the current energy, food, water, climate, and political crises as well as to extricate ourselves from the Wetiko mindset.

As it turns out, the most needed of the three ethics was people care and work on Zone 00. In permaculture design a strategic mapping system uses different zones that will help the designer organize the land.[48] Baba Fred added Zone 00 to the accepted zone system that usually begins with Zone 0, which includes the home and family. Zone 00 is the inner self. It became apparent early in the class that a great deal of time would be spent on working through the barriers caused by Wetiko's violations to our spirits. White supremacy and individualism have turned us, our cultures, and our relationships into commodities. bell hooks's work on love informs my understanding of this crisis of the commodification of life and relationships. She examines the consequences of a society adrift without a love ethic. Regarding consumerism and its connection to community mental health, she explains:

> Isolation and loneliness are central causes of depression and despair. Yet they are the outcome of life in a culture where things matter more than people. Materialism creates a world of narcissism in which the focus of life is solely on acquisition and consumption.[49]

She examines how the pursuit of material goods to fill our emptiness leads to unethical behavior that often traumatizes ourselves and those around us. "When greedy consumption is the order of the day, dehumanization becomes acceptable. Then, treating people like objects is not only acceptable but is required behavior."[50] Greed erodes bonds and breaks down community.

My experience in community organizing and activism in Chicago showed that many of our responses to the trauma of Wetiko have been to mechanically turn to consumerism and materialism for psychic relief. Deprived of dignity and care, we are convinced that "the good life" requires a large quantity of material objects. Our emphasis on the acquisition of things means we spend a disproportionate amount of our time attempting to acquire them and use them in isolation from others. We don't have time for deep relationships. Baba Fred likes to talk about "being present." Without practiced attention to being present in our relationships, we lose the ability to communicate intimately. In the Wetiko mindset "the good life" emphasizes things over being. Even many of us who consider ourselves activists, organizers, and revolutionaries seek the acquisition of more things as our end goal. We believe that our struggle is to have all the things that the "White man" has. This perspective and value system turns us away from IK and knowledge of self in relation to our world.

Baba Fred, Doc, and I concluded that our permaculture course would be indigenized and decolonized. We would not, as others in permaculture have done, simply teach design concepts and techniques. Nor would we encourage individual material gain and unsustainable consumptive behaviors. Our goal was to create community so that together we could develop our local, community-controlled food system. Thus, we returned many of the ethics, principles, and practices of permaculture back to their original Indigenous conceptualizations. For example, alongside the conventional ethics of earth care, people care, and fair share, we studied Indigenous ethics. We replaced earth care with mitakuye oyasin; people care become in lak' ech; fair share became potlach. These common Indigenous ethics of relationships, respect, and reciprocity and became the ethical foundation of our course. We studied Indigenous thought to gain a better understanding of our proper relationship to all our relations. We relearned how to think, feel, see, and act relationally. We learned to be in place with all our relations.

At the end of February 2017, we embarked on an eight-month journey. In the first phase of the course during the cold winter months when we were not work-ing in our growing spaces, we met together at the Quarry Events Center in the South Shore neighborhood. There we learned principles, ethics, and design con-cepts. We sought to understand one another as well as collectively work through individual design issues under the guiding ethic of in lak' ech. Each student took on an "eco-practicum" whereby they could implement and learn permaculture more deeply. Through lectures and small-group work, we supported one anoth-er's learning and project implementation. We emphasized not only design but also developing a community-controlled food system, and in lak' ech/people care we took time to figure out how each of our eco-practicums could work in tandem with others to build commUnity wealth. During the first weeks of class, we established interest-based groups. Teams were formed to strategize how to work together most effectively. For example, people interested in using perma-culture to design sustainable energy projects often worked together. Those fo-cused on healing formed a group that became the Family Healing Circle. Others formed a group focused on food production projects. Students worked together across groups to ensure that the projects complemented each other. Those who had land worked with those who didn't so that their projects were mutually ben-eficial and coordinated.

As the class developed organically from the needs of the people in the class, we spent most of our mitakuye oyasin section of the class at the homes, gar-dens, and farms of class participants. We would tour the land while the student directing the day would describe the objective of their eco-practicum. We used each of these periods of the class to emphasize permaculture design concepts. If the student hadn't already done so, one of the three teachers would ask how the project used permaculture. The question invoked deep analysis on the part of the student designers and worked to reinforce permaculture concepts for the rest of the class.

During some classes we worked on eco-practicums together collectively. We developed our "crop-mob" or "barn-raising" ethos and technology. Working together with a common goal we could accomplish our individual and collective goals. We planted trees, made medicine, harvested, built earthworks and water works, and cared for gardens in the city and at BOC. Knowing the extent to which we have been trained in Wetiko lifeways, we focused on unlearning and decolonizing our interactions and thought processes. Unfortunately, collective decision-making, follow-through, and accountability often failed, showing us how far our decolonization has yet to go. Moreover, any number of material and personal troubles resulting from our social positions as Black and Mexican working-class people under Wetiko kept us from successfully learning collective ways of being and working.

Always with in lak' ech guiding us, we ate together and included our children. Our collective meals also illustrated the ethic of fair share or what we called potlach after the egalitarian, caring ethic of the Indigenous peoples of northwestern United States and southwestern Canada. We modeled the fair share ethos in other ways. Students with knowledge in particular areas shared it with others. Many of us shared the abundance of our seed, rootstock, and cuttings from the previous seasons' savings. Student-teachers and teacher-students shared materials, seeds, and harvest. Jacqueline Abena Smith, Safia Rashid, Eugene, and Dr. Andrea Mason, and others offered their expertise through lectures and workshops. Importantly, the year of cooperative work between Dr. Wright, Baba Fred, and I illustrated the first, and perhaps most important, principle in Permaculture: "cooperation, not competition, is the very basis of existing life systems and of future survival."[51] To this end we established the Lifeboats Permaculture Guild that aspires to continue the work of building a community-controlled food system and developing our individual and collective skills associated with growing food and designing our spaces. The guild engages in skill shares, permaculture education and mobilizes when members are in crisis.

In 2020, Jacqueline Abena Smith and I took the lessons from the Lifeboats PDC to heart, and along with a great deal of other permaculture education and experience we taught our first PDC together for the Permaculture Institute of Chicago, as well as other courses including her course Black, Indigenous Women, POC and the Land and our co-taught course with Matthew Stephens, Permaculture POC. Jacqueline and I carefully recruited students through our years of work in the community and online. We began our PDC in January 2021 with nine students: two African students, one White-identified disabled woman, two Black women, and four Latinxs. Four students graduated as financial problems caused many to have to discontinue the course. In addition to teaching Mollison, we focused on the usefulness of permaculture to each of our decolonial and reindigenization projects. We incorporated the work of Indigenous authors and activists such as Devon G. Peña, Leah Penniman, and Robin Wall Kimmerer. Aspects of the class—such as Jacqueline's explanation of permaculture principles through the AHK sayings of her Mississippi-born father, Tommy Smith, my PowerPoint presentation on pattern understanding among Mesoamericans, and assignments designed for students to explore native plants and Indigenous uses of them in medicine and food forest design—challenge White colonialist permaculture that further disengages White middle-class environmentally-minded people from issues of justice and decolonization and turns off many BIPOC. Moreover, during check-in and throughout the class, we spoke to the challenges of being Black and Indigenous permaculture designers in this world. We discussed the challenges we are experiencing as we attempt to design our lives in an Indigenous manner. Jacqueline and my PDC continues to bear fruit as two of our graduates have co-taught courses with me and served as teaching assistants in our Resilient Community Design course. We continue to develop anticolonial land curricula and work on various projects together.

Touring the Forest Garden with Landed Organic Intellectuals

Most of the educational work I and others perform at food movement sites is informal. Lessons arise when problems and pleasures do. The land provides the "curricula." However, my Food Justice course, organized tours of school kids, university classes and groups, and internship programs, the Seedkeepers Collective, and Jacqueline Abena Smith Scholars, provide formal teaching moments. As a result of our community connections, many tour GLP gardens and often contribute labor and in-kind donations of plant material, tools, and the like. GLP accommodates as many groups and individuals as we can. Jacqueline Smith and I normally conduct formal tours of the gardens. Tours include tasting and smelling and last between forty minutes and two hours. We examine numerous home economics and social studies topics. Importantly, the learning occurs through live and growing examples of IK/AHK and permaculture practices. In a typical tour of the RCFG, we cover the following: complementary planting, compost, soil conservation, guild building, vertical growing, medicinal herbs, foraging, wild edibles, native plants, vermicomposting, perennials/annuals, biological pest management, ground covers, crop rotation, pollination, food preparation, environmental racism, food inequality, capitalism, alternative food systems, decolonization, poverty, and public health. Some tours have specific topics or speak to the interests of the group. For example, Danny Block's graduate Urban Geography course visited in 2019. The discussion not only included the previously mentioned topics but also focused on space and alternative uses of space in the city. In 2021 a group of young people from Gage Park Latinx Council and members of the Lifeboats

Permaculture Guild visited our gardens. We focused our discussion on decolonization. The event, titled "Decolonizing Our Mind-Body-Spirits in the Urban Garden," included collective work and a "Forests, Foraging and Deep Foods Tour" of the recently damaged Roseland Community Forest Garden. The RCFG provided numerous opportunities to develop our understanding of Wetiko as we discussed the destruction of half our garden. Through teaching about wild plant relatives, how to care for them, and how to make medicine and food with them, Mother Earth provided lessons on how to be in right relationship with her. At the end of the 2021 season, a class on eco-spiritual traditions took an introduction to permaculture course from me at Sacred Greens Community Garden. With the divinity school students, I let the land lead as we discussed the spiritedness of the garden and how its being spoke to us.

Importantly, in most cases we discuss community empowerment, self-determination, and cultural resurgence. We focus on AHK/IK while doing it in the garden. Often elder community gardeners use garden tours to teach. Dwight, Sandra, and Liza were the most consistent members for four growing seasons where they shared their knowledge of the garden, medicinal herb gathering and preparation, cooking, and Black history and politics during the tours or whenever someone listened. Younger members such as DeVonya, Jason, and Bee have used their youth and savvy to teach younger camaradas about right livelihood. While I take on the responsibility of organizing the tours and preparing work and information for our guests, other GLP members take on the role of organic intellectual.

These organic intellectuals sow the seeds of AHK/IK learned through family experience and interaction with others in the food movement. Dwight offers his travel experience and decades of food study to the garden guests. His knowledge of food art, science, and history is as broad and thick as his graying moustache. Liza has dedicated her free time to learning about medicinal plants, food preservation techniques, and foraging. She often shares her spiritual practices with other gardeners while tending our herb and flower gardens. Liza intersperses her advice to forest garden tourists concerning medicinal plants and their preparation with detailed, sharp criticisms of politics, power, corporate dominance, and survival. Her smile belies the seriousness of her message about how the community garden contributes enormously to solving the problems of Wetiko. Jason brings the "young homies" whom he mentors and helps to see alternatives to the street life. Most appreciate the opportunity to experience nature and quiet in the city, to slow down and feel peace. Similarly, Bee works with neighborhood youth in the chronically plagued Mexicanx community of Gage Park to help them develop an Indigenous way out of the "barrio." When not teaching and mentoring young people in the Reclaiming Our Roots garden that they collectively manage and guerilla garden, Bee teaches at GLP gardens.

The impromptu, informal education interventions made by GLP members demonstrate the collective approach to education that I call commUnity pedagogy. The very nature of the garden as a dynamic, evolving microecosystem means that new learning can take place at any moment and in any nook in the garden. Sharing knowledge while working sets the stage for multiple members to take leadership as organic intellectuals.

Intergenerational interactions provide a key ingredient to CP. In the food autonomy movement, we recognize that communities of color are at the mercy of Wetiko food since few have the requisite knowledge and material resources to grow and prepare our own food. Years of colonization and miseducation of BIPOC have led to a loss of our ability to care for ourselves. Traditions and wisdom of our ancestors have been lost or stigmatized while commodities have taken on a value far beyond their usefulness. Many in working-class and BIPOC communities lament the deterioration of community and find that a communication and respect gap between elders and children is both symptom and cause of this breakdown. Our Indigenous communities required a system of intergenerational interaction whereby the cultural heritage of communities was passed on generation after generation.[52] Without such an Indigenous system of education, ages-old traditions of survival are lost. In place of these traditions are ethnocidal and genocidal practices that we often refer to euphemistically as "urban social problems." We recognize also that material deprivation and legal barriers keep those without money, especially BIPOC, from becoming self-determined.

Many in the food autonomy and related food movements in Chicago believe that the survival of Black and other deindigenized people requires a return to intergenerational Indigenous educational practices. Today urban social problems affect all people of color and working-class people living in the city. However, young people experience them differently than elders or middle-aged people. Understanding our communities' problems requires recognition and respect for age diversity. The community gardens provide opportunities for strengthening intergenerational bonds.

Organic Intellectuals

My practices of commUnity pedagogy rely on an applied approach in the university classroom and a land-based pedagogy in the gardens. It combines the activist-oriented lessons of Ethnic Studies, the direct-action principles of community organizers and anarchists, the most progressive service-learning approaches, and most importantly, Indigenous knowledge to offer a holistic, organic learning opportunity to university and nonuniversity students alike. Both the OCC at the RCFG and Sacred Greens Community Garden break through the multiple barriers erected by the academy and by our societal prejudices. CP ensures that the examination of social problems and sociological phenomena does not remain at the theoretical level but is literally rooted in place. Through bringing students into working-class Black and Mexican communities and into scholarly interactions with people other than students and professors, CP puts the content learned in classroom materials to an experiential test. The OCC and similar community classrooms do not allow the passive, banking method learning that plagues students.[53] Material examined within the walled classroom of the university is reinforced and sometimes challenged in outdoor classrooms. Both body and mind are exercised as a way of learning develops that privileges the kinetic alongside the cerebral.

For BIPOC students, Eurocentric classrooms prove to be a barrier both to academic success and to their individual development. Often, even the most well-intentioned professors and teachers of race and ethnicity reinforce a negative approach to understanding Indigenous/African history and identity. Black and Indigenous history are taught with little reference to AHK and IK, especially the ingenious traditions of survival and resistance illustrated so well by our food arts and sciences. Teachers weave together a historical narrative filled with the injustices and indignities of slavery and colonialism. The evaluative lens applied to these histories condemns agrarian lifestyles and food production conflating these aspects of Black and Indigenous cultures with the capitalist relations of production under which rural laborers had and have to toil. Instead of recognizing and teaching the genius of our ancestors, Black and Indigenous culture is further stigmatized. CP in urban community gardens relies heavily on the horticultural traditions of our ancestors, explaining and illustrating their wisdom at every turn.

Place-based CP requires landed organic intellectuals and aspires to develop more of them. Through a process of political and cultural conscientizacion, students re-examine and understand anew Blackness, indigeneity, Mexicanidad, and their own unique subjectivities. Confronted with the stark differences between the Eurocentric classroom and the community classroom and with the stark realities of poverty, deprivation, and food insecurity, students develop a different relationship to knowledge and their communities.

Moreover, student gardeners participate in collective labor that benefits working-class BIPOC communities under food apartheid. Thus, place-based CP offers the lesson that alternatives do exist and that the social problems that we examine can be impacted. Importantly, the lack of community that is often identified by students as an important effect of a lack of self-determination and racial oppression can be confronted head on. The community classrooms I have taught at and many others where I have been a student offer students opportunities to effect positive change in their lives and the lives of their neighbors through the direct application of knowledge. At the garden classrooms managed by GLP, we apply IK and AHK communally with reverence and respect for all our relations. It allows us to engage in living as learning and to practice community.

Lessons on Work, Private Property, and Resistance

A drizzly April day was the perfect occasion for a group of about forty to work together in the RCPG. The young, middle-aged, and elders alike, under the organization of Intergenerational Growing Projects, GLP, and CSU, braved the rain to clear out weeds, till soil, collect garbage, start the compost pile and plant seeds. It took them approximately two hours to accomplish all of this on two large city plots. Working and laughing together presented an untold number of opportunities to commune and learn.

EJ described the task of weeding a raised box and planting eggplant seeds as "easy." Mr. Cortez said, "It is, right? If a lot of people work a little together, then no one has to do a lot. We try to work smarter and together to get much more done together than we ever could separately." The older man explains to the young adult men that we must gain more control over our food. The failure of the government and the private sector to provide healthy food for many communities means that people in these communities have to provide it for themselves. Cortez says, "This area is a food desert, you know?" The younger men who have heard of food deserts in their classes nod in agreement. Many grew up in similar neighborhoods and easily identify the problems in Roseland. They have seen it all before. They have grown up with lessons of inequality. So in the RCPG we focus on learning technologies of resistance and our ancestors' IK.

Lessons about the failure of the state and market to provide for Black and Mexican communities was physically, mentally, emotionally, and visually learned in the community garden in a way that no other method could have. Being in place in the working-class Black community vividly reinforced numerous lessons that could be easily taught in traditional classroom settings but never as effectively. EJ, Cortez, and the other student-teachers saw the neglect of the state and market in the community and its obvious hardships. They also saw people coming together, sharing, and resisting.

A major obstacle to community participation in the community garden and larger food justice movement is the initial visceral response that many must experience seeing young people of color engage in agricultural labor. Importantly, the visual of young and older Black people engaged in agricultural work around the work leader, me, who is not Black undoubtedly adds to the apprehension.

One certainly couldn't blame passersby for looking at this scene and seeing a twenty-first-century version of slavery. Many in the Black food movement have pointed out that the trauma of plantation slavery is not easily overcome. One man upon seeing his son engaged in the dignified work of seeding yelled at him to "get up off of that ground. I didn't work this hard to see you in the dirt!" Penniman explains using a quote from Black farmer Chris Bolden-Newsome:

> "The field was the scene of the crime [of slavery]." Hundreds of years of enslavement have devastated our sacred connection to land and overshadowed thousands of years of our noble, autonomous farming history. Many of us have confused the terror our ancestors experienced on land with the land herself, naming her the oppressor and running toward paved streets without looking back.[54]

Without the knowledge of community, solidarity, and collective work that goes on at hundreds of gardens in Chicago, one can easily see only Black toil in the hot sun. The relations and organizational forms of production are rarely analyzed by passersby or gardener-students themselves unless a point is made by one of our teachers to examine the topic. Instead, the type of labor and the wages earned through it become the basis upon which the work is evaluated and judged. As a result, collective land stewarding in community gardens can be miscast as akin to agricultural labor under slavery, sharecropping, or migrant worker-dependent agribusiness factories in the fields.

The notion of private ownership, especially of land, is another factor obstructing participation in community gardens. Many have a hard time believing that something can be collectively owned and managed. Their only exposure to ownership is individual, private ownership. Capitalist relations of production characterized by the private ownership of the means of production are deeply ingrained in our legal, moral, and ethical systems. The veracity of this claim is illustrated often when first-time visitors, gardeners, or others inquire about the "property" and how it is managed. Many ask about ownership and decision-making in the garden. Half the land at RCFG is owned privately, while the other half is controlled by alderperson's office. GLP has been given permission to use it while the land remains in the hands of the current owner. Production, distribution, and other questions are decided by consensus of collective members. Questioners' looks of confusion and amazement and their probing questions illustrate how difficult collectivity is to understand for people possessed by Wetiko.

Given the context of slavery, anti-Black racism, the denigration of AHK, and capitalist individualism, it is difficult for many to imagine a society characterized by autonomy, democracy, and cooperation free of capitalist relations of production and individualist ethics. The idea that the workers can own the products of their own labor and that a collective could own a productive enterprise often creates misunderstandings about the community garden and the nature of self-determining and unalienated labor therein. It is a central goal of our work to overcome these barriers to community self-determination.

Three incidents further teach gardeners and community members about private property and resilience: the loss of El Jardín Izquierdista/Community Garden of the Left, the destruction of half of the RCFG, and the Chicago Transit Authority's seizing of the land on which Sacred Green stood for nine years. These gardens illustrate the importance of land access to any movement for liberation. As mentioned earlier, we lost El Jardin Izquierdista because we had no legal right to the land. We were guerilla gardening. Instead, the legal owners, St. Sabina Catholic Church, and legal buyers, a Protestant church, exchanged the land and kicked us out. The destruction of half of the RCFG puts an exclamation point on this lesson. In 2020 some as-of-yet unknown entity ran a very large machine across the northern half of the garden. They scraped a two-foot layer of soil from a 25-by-50-feet section of the garden. They uprooted and threw away a peach tree, three berry bushes including a 10-by-4-feet stand of goji berries, dozens of herbs, a living black raspberry fence, comfrey, Jerusalem artichoke, and much more. While we may never find out the story including identifying the perpetrators of the crime, we learn the lesson. Without ownership, power, and control, all our efforts are vulnerable to state or corporate desire; Wetiko can easily gobble up our efforts to heal the earth and justly feed ourselves.

Finally, as of this writing in 2023, Sacred Greens will soon be destroyed as the legal owner of the land, Chicagoland Prison Outreach, is negotiating with the Chicago Transit Authority and other local and state entities to sell the land or part of it to be used for the next elevated rail stop on 103rd Street. In June 2022, I was informed by CPO president Corey Buchanan that the City would begin a soil-bearing test in July as part of the negotiations. The soil bearing test would destroy the unique place that has seen over two thousand visitors since its founding. This refuge for humans and more-than-humans included several herb gardens, fruit trees, guilds, annual keyhole beds, "three sisters" gardens, and a Zone 5 or wild section that provided habitat and food sources for numerous relatives as evidenced by the loud and numerous birdcalls we hear any time we visit. Few places in the city can replicate this sanctuary. Unmoved by the sacredness of Sacred Greens and unmindful of the food crisis gripping Roseland and similar Black communities in Chicago, the Chicago Transit Authority and CPO worked out a deal to convert this sanctuary and healthy food source into a rail station or parking lot. We, GLP, as visitors and guests of the legal owners, have no say. Yet we steward the land in the best way we can until we finally left in 2023.

About Resilience under Wetiko

Community resilience for urban working-class BIPOC requires the maintenance of our food cultures. Wetiko's food based on profit and petroleum, the industrial-capitalist model, is authoritarian. It is based on the exploitation of producer, consumer, and provider (the earth).[55] This exploitation involves the control of food "from seed to table" using toxic chemicals, fertilizers and pesticides, altered genes, and other ultimately unsustainable and extremely damaging agribusiness practices. Since only a few corporations control the global food system, it is, by definition, undemocratic and authoritarian as capitalist colonialism has always been. Most peoples of the world suffer because of Wetiko. The dominant industrial-food system can accurately be described as a continuation of the colonial process through means of food.

As with all aspects of colonialism, many of us have begun to "decolonize our diets."[56] High on the list of priorities of those who work for democratic change and community, (food) autonomy is an elder epistemology and land pedagogy that relies, in part, on the development of organic intellectuals. Education takes numerous forms. Simply being together as a community creates opportunities for learning. Elders who have acquired a wealth of IK and new and diverse techniques to develop and maintain community resilience interact with younger or less knowledgeable members of the community. Through work elders teach stewardship and the ethical lessons of Indigenous people. The young are provided with living models of community empowerment through control of their food system. Time spent with our hands in the soil brings each of us closer to Indigenous lifeways. This is landed, elder pedagogy. This is "living as learning"[57] for the urban, Black, and Indigenous working classes of the United States in the twenty-first century.

Gregory Bratton, Elder Teacher

At a visit to the headquarters of Inter-generational Growing Projects (IGP) I heard Gregory Bratton telling this brief story. "See that hoop house. I made it from these bails of plastic wiring. Here, over there. That pile of plastic that's what I used for the structure of the roof. I found it in a lot." The small group assembled at IGP headquarters saw firsthand the Black agrarian ethic of resourcefulness and resilience. Will Allen writes about the "ethic of making do." He cites the ethic as learned from his grandmother, Rosa Bell, whose life was "deeply rooted in the virtue of making do," and George Washington Carver, whose career at Tuskegee was a model of developing tremendous practical scientific knowledge and technique with few resources.[58]

FIG. 9. Gregory Bratton. Photo by Gregory Bratton.

The hoop house that Mr. Bratton constructed from found materials is keeping hundreds of seedlings warm and giving them a head start. These seedlings were moved to community gardens throughout the South Side and later supply dozens of families with fresh vegetables for months.

The possibilities for teaching, learning, and building community through inter-generational interaction and unity through a common goal motivate Mr. Bratton and those he teaches. On visits to IGP, one has constant opportunities to learn about gardening, community activism, and related topics. The headquarters contains dozens of varieties of edible plants in varying stages of growth and growing in a number of ways: grow boxes, found plastic containers, growing flats, berms or mounds, in the ground, hanging, on trellises, and so on.

A wealth of information can be found at every step at IGP. Anyone who visits gets a visual lesson in the ever-developing traditions of Black agrarian culture. Mr. Bratton translates what he learned in his home state of Arkansas into the current realities of growing in the urban confines of Chicago. This he passes on to visitors, volunteers, and members of his various projects and gardens. If you stay long enough, Mr. Bratton will find work for you to do.

On August 11, 2015, I spent three hours with Gregory Bratton watching him teach teenage workers how to build a fence and chicken coop at the Good Foods Community Garden in the South Shore neighborhood and check on a shipment of materials for his latest project in South Chicago, a few blocks over. These are just two of dozens of gardens and growing projects that Mr. Bratton and IGP support. We ended our afternoon at the Good Foods Vegetarian Restaurant, which is feet away from the community garden near Seventy-Third Street and Jeffery in order to record a thirty-five-minute conversation.

PM: Mr. Bratton, I want everyone to know when I write this up that you were my first mentor in urban agriculture. So it is very important that I have this conversation with you. I ask everybody similar kinds of questions. Can you tell me about your work in gardening, in food, in horticulture, justice, all that kind of stuff?

GB: Well, first off, I have two masters' degrees. One in horticulture. One in agriculture. I've been growing and gardening for about ten years. I've been an urban farmer for eight. The difference between gardening and urban farming is that you are growing for yourself when you are gardening and [with] urban farming you are growing crops to feed other people. The difference between urban farming and general farming is that the majority of land in Chicago is contaminated, so you have to know how to not eliminate the contamination but to eliminate the threat of the contamination. Meaning, knowing how to grow without the threat of poisoning someone . . .

You said, "Food justice." What really needs to be said is "food knowl-edge." I'm using myself as an example, and a lot of people at our events have become vegetarians or lean toward eating healthy now because of what they didn't know. Education is a very big part. A good example is I would ask you a question such as, Do you know how many varieties of tomatoes there are? And then could you tell me the name of the tomatoes that you get on your sandwich, your tomato paste from, or your hot sauce. All right? There are thirty-eight different varieties of tomatoes. And the same tomatoes that you get your sandwiches from are not the same as the tomatoes that you get your hot sauce from or your tomato paste from. We have workshops such as "The 3 Ps: Preparing, Planning and Planting." We have "Three Sisters." We have "Potatoes in a Bag," where we teach our youth and some of our elders how to grow twenty-five pounds of potatoes in a garbage bag. It's all about the knowledge of how to grow, where to grow, when to grow, and why. We do them in gardens. In the wintertime we do them inside. We usually have a space at the YMCA in South Chicago. We have started, eight years ago, the

Backyard Gardeners' Network. Where we started a workshop called "The Backyard Gardeners' Network" with thirty people. It's about three thousand people now.

PM: How does that work? What is the Backyard Gardeners' Network?

GB: We started with the workshops: how to grow; if you didn't have enough space, how to use containers; how to weed. Different perspectives of gardening or problems. How to get rid of certain ones using [nontoxic to humans] pesticides. We have this pesticide that we use called burnt ash and charcoal ash. We explain that and it is commonly known that insects do not like the burnt taste. It doesn't destroy the insect, but they do relocate. Those are the kinda workshops that we started. And through those workshops we created the Backyard Gardeners' Network. Which through that we started what we call the Backyard Gardeners' Farmers' Market, which is called the Community Market. "Community-grown, community-owned." In late fall sometime, ten to twenty, last year it was thirty-five, of our backyard gardeners got together and half of their yard, what they grew, they brought to market. They brought the price real reasonable to the community because it was community-grown and it was extra grown in these backyards. There were peppers, tomatoes, corn, potatoes, peanuts. Whereas the price of the tomato was at two dollars and sixty cents at Jewel's or Dominick's for two to three tomatoes, you got five tomatoes from the Backyard Gardeners' Community Market. So it wasn't . . . we didn't anticipate that. It came about from that. Now we have the Rainbow Beach Farmers' Market, which are backyard gardeners.

"We're Five Generations Urban"

DR. MILA K. MARSHALL ON
FOOD CHALLENGES IN THE CITY

FIG. 10. Dr. Mila K. Marshall. Photo by
Taylor Larue.

MM: The other part of my work looks at the impact of how being in a segregated [community] also limits your network. So thinking about not just a "food desert" but at times it's a "knowledge desert" also. So for African Americans we have . . . we're the most underemployed. We're also undereducated. We often lack resources, educational resources, and our networks are very homogenous, which means that if you live in Chicago or in any of the rustbelt cities it is highly unlikely that you live, work, play, or network with anybody that is not African American. What that means is that for people that are working in gardens, that are trying to grow food, [they] don't have access to people with resources that could help that garden be more productive.

We're also four to five generations urban. So while people say, you know, "Well, we came from the land. We worked the land," that was five generations ago. We don't return down south to live with grandma. Grandma is up here living in the city with us. So we've lost the ability and the skill set to work the land. So we're also first-generation farmers. And many people in cities are first-generation farmers. So you take that, and you couple that with the impact of climate change and the diversity of growing environments due to just city . . . And you need a person that knows what they are doing. That includes pest management. That includes soil nutrient management. It includes water management. It includes the fiscal health of growing food. The ability to hire people, maintain resources for the garden including tools and equipment. So you get somebody that doesn't have the money, doesn't have the wherewithal, and doesn't have somebody in their network to make that happen you end up with a garden that has lower production, lower quality food, and sometimes doesn't even make it past a season. So when you think about who acquires the skills, the know-how and the understanding to grow in the city, it would be people of color and they're also in some of the most environmentally degraded areas that are even more complicated to grow in and require even additional resources.

You know, also, you get people who not only have the sickest land, but they also have the least amount of understanding to get it to level that it needs to be productive. So that's the other part that I work on.

PM: What do you propose or what do you do about that? Or what do you propose we do in a larger context of movement or community to alleviate the knowledge . . . I don't like "desert" . . . but knowledge whatever it is.

MM: Absence of knowledge or limited knowledge or you could even go as far as agricultural knowledge or growing knowledge.

I guess the first thing to ask is, Why is it that you are doing it? If you're growing food because it is therapeutic, your experience becomes your teacher. So every day, every season, you're out there and you're out there and you're learning intentionally and you're present. And you're taking that knowledge from last year, "Oh, the tomatoes didn't do well, or the tomatoes I bought from here . . ." Your intent drives your acquisition for knowledge. I don't know if many gardeners understand that growing food is a science. Intentionally growing food for, you know, to go to market, whether that's a farmers' market or a secondary product, requires a plan. And that plan means that you have to know what you're putting in in order for you to get something out. I believe that some of the absence of knowledge is due to people seeing things grow and they think that it just grows. You know. "All I have to do is put it out there and it will grow." That's true, but when you are talking about a managed system when you've taken your garden from "Oh, we just want to grow because it's a living thing and it's going to be beautiful" to "I want to feed twelve families for the next year." That's a totally different system. So I don't think that people understand that this earth, it's natural, and it goes through these cycles and seeds will sprout. When you have plans for that seed to turn into profit or to turn into nutrition for a human, then you better well know what you are doing. It better well be intentional. Um, I don't think they see earth and earth systems in that way. It's like it's just this disconnection of what it takes to grow food. We are so far removed from farming.

I think the problem could be an artifact of just the city. You know, of life in the city. We live in a society where we can, you know, go buy seedlings and pop 'em in. We don't have to germinate them. We can buy half mature plants and put 'em in. And we can speed up the process. Many people have never been to a farm. They don't know what it takes to grow food. They've never seen a farming system and how managed it actually is in terms of even how much water is applied and when it is applied is chosen for that crop. The crops are planned out even in advance.

PM: People don't even have yards. They live in apartments.

MM: So they need to have these alternative ways of growing food which even if you were familiar with traditional farming don't necessarily apply to the city. So you have . . . that's why I said it was an artifact of the city. You have people that were raised on farms that may be able to take some of that understanding and transfer it into a city, but they're still learning and adapting what they've learned. That's very different than learning from scratch. They have something to go off of. And they can experiment, and they can do it a lot faster. And they're more intuitive. So a person that also wasn't raised on a farm all of a sudden is growing food on their patio or stoop or whatever, um, isn't reading a book, isn't going to meetings or conferences or training sessions or seminars. They really just trying, but many of them have these social goals of transforming their block or transforming their community through these efforts but not understanding that growing food really does require a set of skills that takes time to learn and takes resources to get access to. And some of those resources are time. You know? If you work a full-time job, growing food is another full-time job.

So there are two strategies that I think work and one of them is lesser applied. You have the teaching by passing down knowledge like how to sample your soil. How to create a garden plan. Those are skill sets that can be passed from one garden person to another garden person. And essentially, they don't change. You can adapt them because of whatever is going on. Another thing is teaching people in the garden to create and generate their own knowledge. Which is to a lesser extent is talked about and supported within Black gardens, which I think is to their detriment. So I have this saying that I live by, which is "Don't just celebrate Black history. Make it." It's funny how Black people don't realize that we're in control. We don't need permission to tell our stories. We don't need permission for somebody to call us an expert. You say you are an expert because you say you're an expert. You've gone through this rigorous training, and we respect you for such. So you've been in this community, and you've been Black all your life. You get to say that "I'm an expert in my community. I'm an expert in understanding my system." So helping support people within a growing framework is to create your own knowledge. If you're interested in growing collard greens for whatever reason, cuz you want to know how much water, ask that question. Develop a plan to answer that question. You have the ability to ask and answer your own questions that are of interest to you. And often I think Blacks feel that other people are studying us and studying the things relative to us. That doesn't mean that you can't do the same thing. Like, to generate . . . whether it's a newsletter or, you know, I don't know. It can be anything. But what I've seen is that a lot of gardeners don't recognize their power in the generation of their own information.

So through my relationship with Chicago State and who was there at the time, Dr. Juanita Sharpe, I was able to make a conference, which is URBAANE, Urban Resolutions for Bridging African Americans with Urban Environments. You can tell I came up with that name because scientists love acronyms. But we also realized that there were very few opportunities for people within the community to engage one another at a higher level. Like, it's OK to go and kinda have the sharing sessions of like, "We're angry. This is what happened." That's kinda what we do. We vent a lot. But we wanted to kinda create an experience that connected people of color also to the institution because Chicago State is there for community. But a lot of people don't recognize that it's their college, that there are opportunities to engage with the institution. So we thought that was a great opportunity. So we were able to put together the theme of the conference around one of them was vacant lots and the use of them and the diversity of how people are engaging them. One of them was about climate change and disaster preparedness. Another was a symposium for the next generation of environmental student, and it was all packaged to be specific to working with and for Black communities. So that also gave me more experience as a scientist. That is what we do. We don't just write papers and do research. Learning how to put together a conference. Learning how to draw people in to shape the conversation. That's power. I have never felt so present in this as when I was able and over a hundred people showed up. That blew my mind. I really tried to reign in my . . . what I think that conversation should be. You know? I had to really do some soul-searching and scanning for what's bubbling up. Right?

Further along in the conversation our examination of education turned to nutrition. Tying a wide variety of social problems together with ecological and food knowledge, Mila stated:

That's the part that I feel doesn't get the attention that it deserves. We don't understand that nutritional deficiencies lead to psychological issues. When you are not well nourished or you are malnourished, you are not able to make decisions, control your emotions. Like how people act is impacted by the quality of food that they eat. So I'm not surprised when I see kids wilding out when you are eating flaming hots every single day for breakfast. You are eating. You have food. But it has absolutely no nutritional value.

PART III

RACE, PLACE, GENDER, SPIRIT

CHAPTER 5

Race Other

My nearly two decades of learning and working within the Black food movement in Chicago has meant that especially during the growing season I interact mostly with Black Americans who are politicized in a nationalist or Pan-Africanist perspective. As a "racial outsider" in a racially conscious community, I experience both the joys and pains of Black-Mexican-origin relations under Wetiko. I have become part of the Black food community surrounding the HFH. However, it seems that the racial system so highly ingrained in us limits the degree to which I attain first-class citizenship in my community. On occasion people have approached me and asked some version of the question, "Why are you at the HFH?," a place where I had gone weekly for approximately ten years. Many have questioned my relationship to my dark-skinned, African featured son. In the 2017 growing season, I served my ninth year as executive director of GLP. My duties included managing and caring for three gardens and co-teaching the Lifeboats Permaculture course with BOC. An elder who I had worked with in GLP gardens more than eight years prior and who knew my children well joked about whether I could be trusted. In the same season students of the permaculture course argued in our October 7 class against allying with non-Blacks as we move further in our efforts to solidify our community. This after I, a non-Black identified person, served as one of three teachers for the course that led to the guild that they were benefiting from and had been sought out as a mentor.

My community work has included many other projects with Black groups. In them I am guardedly accepted. Because of this I hear all manner of Blacks-against-everybody rhetoric. I feel an "inbetweenness" because of my simultaneous acceptance (even esteem as many use the honorific title of "Baba" as part of my name) and suspicion in Black community circles. As a border-crosser, I see and experience Wetiko in a unique fashion. I see how Wetiko's race ideology has a tight grip on us and despite our best efforts we are unable to fully see ourselves in the "racial Other." In an interview Angela Y. Davis addressed this problem thoughtfully.

> Spending time with 'one's own group' needs to be interrogated. How would
> you define one's 'own group'? For African Americans, would that include every
> person who meets the requirements of physical appearance or every person who

identifies as African American, regardless of their phenotype? Would it include Republican African Americans who are opposed to Affirmative Action?[1]

Race has taught us that Black people are substantially and unalterably different from people of Mexican descent. Today, many of us run to the "genealogy industry" ("big business [that] reinforces mythology about race and biology") to confirm who we are and who we are not.[2] Most of us gladly accept the teaching and create our own racial superiority theories. Often, "the desire to know more about our origins runs the risk of compromising our relationship to historical fact, reaffirms white supremacist and capitalist rationales, and threatens our privacy, all to gather dubious information."[3] The attacks on our bodies and identities leads many of us to challenge the ongoing slander about who we are. Unfortunately, we use master's tools (race) to attempt to dismantle the master's house (racism) and create new myths that often lead to self-misunderstanding and more often lead to exclusionary practices. Claims to racial purity, unalterable biological race differences, and racial superiority furthers Wetiko's work and fails to lead us to freedom or, even, "justice."

I agree with Chairman Fred Hampton (Chicago Black Panther Party leader killed by the Chicago Police Department on December 4, 1969), who explained that "we don't hate the white people; we hate the oppressor, whether he be white, black, brown, or yellow."[4] I hope and believe that with an understanding of how race is used to prop up White supremacy and Black, Indigenous, and White working-class oppression, we can adjust our thoughts and lives in the manner of the Original Instructions. Our permaculture course emphasized this Indigenous manner of being even though not wholly integrated by our student-growers as illustrated by the October 7, 2017, conversation. At the same time, though the course only partially succeeded, it illustrates the potential for food work to serve as bridges to overcome racial divides. To help build the bridge, we also must be well versed in the complex and contradictory history of relations between African and Amerindigenous people. The following describes some of that "invisible" history through our food.

Latinx-Black Relations in Chicago

Despite at least five hundred years of African-Indigenous interaction, the existence of African Mexicans and other Afro-Indigenous people, and the Mexican American-Black American co-creation of and participation in a good deal of popular culture over the last two centuries, Mexican and Black relations in Chicago are far from ideal.[5] The racial antipathy and confusion I experience is not unique. Heightened anti-immigrant sentiment, ongoing virulent anti-Black racism, and the struggle for limited resources have often caused misunderstanding, suspicion, dislike, and conflict. In October 2017 Hurricane María devastated Puerto Rico. The news that Chicago might be a major site of resettlement alarmed many in the Black activist community who believed that the "Puerto Rican agenda" would further displace Black people and make their lives even harder. A screed of racist Facebook comments by some Black activists and their friends included the following:

> "I'm for the improvement of the quality of life for black people not against yours."

> "Who the hell are people of color? I'm black, and I'm insulted at a description that lumps me in with any other group."

> "It's not about being against Puerto Ricans. It's about being for those already here."
> (Willie Preston, FB Live, October 25, 2017)

> "I think it's time for everyone to experience what we as blacks deal with on a daily basis and nobody cares but the one who can level the playing field and make things right, it's not natural disasters, it God, we have suffered long enough. Now it's somebody else's turn." (Yvonne Clark)

> "I'm talking about Black Chicagoans. IDGAF [I don't give a fuck] about Black Puerto Ricans. Hell no. Fuck them [Puerto Ricans] if they are not for our issues."
> (Mark Carter)

Similarly, activist Maurice J. Robinson sensationalizes racial violence and racial antipathy on his *Alternative Thought* radio show. The October 26, 2017, show, "The Harold Washington Theory Is Dying" (Que4 Radio, 1680 FM), featured a conversation between the host, Mark Carter, Grady Norwood, and Willie Preston (at the time, Democratic candidate for state representative for the troubled Englewood community and former comrade in struggles at CSU). The show argues against racial coalitions or what they call the "Harold Washington Theory" (after the former Chicago mayor and coalition builder), claiming that Latinxs are foes in the battle over scarce resources. They discuss with a caller the claims initially made by Mark Carter that "the Mexicans burned Blacks out of Compton" and Aurora, Illinois, among other places, and that Mexicans were responsible for several murdered Black teenagers at Farragut High School in Chicago. They purposefully leave out key information about historical relations between Blacks-Latinxs, never acknowledge the existence of Afro-Latinxs, and distort gang-related tragedy created stemming from Wetiko.

Willie Preston, in his Facebook live presentation, explained that the politicians in Chicago are creating another disaster in the Black community by bringing Puerto Rican refugees and suspending rules to allow for them to be here. After several racially inflammatory Facebook posts and others defending his opposition to Puerto Rican relocation in Chicago, he finally states at 19:00 minutes into the video that "I want to suspend the rules for everyone." While not stating it, Preston's contradictory statements show the difficulties we encounter in understanding Black-Latinx relations when we do not focus our analysis on how politicians cynically offer poor Puerto Ricans or undocumented Mexican immigrants a few crumbs and make them the new racial Other for many Black Americans.

In Chicago, Black folks commonly report racist comments and other behaviors from Latinxs. Many Mexicanxs have accepted the racist lie of White supremacy. The ugly back and forth between many Blacks and Mexicanxs came to a dangerous head in 2020. With the COVID-19 pandemic in full swing heightening anxieties and fears of the Other, the police murder of George Floyd capped years of police violence against Black people that included the 2014 murder of seventeen-year-old Laquan McDonald in Chicago that led to weeks of aggressive, multiracial rebellion in Chicago. Many Black people along with White, Latinx and other accomplices began to aggressively challenge Wetiko. Activist and journalist Charles Preston (no known relation to Willie) described the response by people in the downtown area as multiracial and multicultural. People of various races/ethnicities are getting fed up with state violence. A few broken windows of corporate representatives of Wetiko, some minor looting, and other property damage resulted. Sensationalist media reports of the resistant behavior of Black people led many to arm themselves in the face of what they have been primed to believe is a "riotous mob of Black criminals." Several business owners in Latinx communities hired gang-affiliated young men to "protect" their property. These young men and others driven by racial hatred and fear and perhaps their own racial trauma began a series of attacks against Black people in communities such Pilsen, Cicero, and Gage Park that lasted three days. Many framed these attacks as examples of Latinx racial hatred toward Blacks. A GLP intern called me and asked why our "Latin brothers" have turned on "us." The lack of attention to a long history of solidarity work between these communities and the current media sensationalism that fails to report on current co-resistance between Blacks and Latinxs lead many to question Black-Latinx race relations. The self-defense patrols created by Latinxs activists to safely escort Black people through violent spots and the several rallies of racial solidarity went widely unreported by the local capitalist media, though activists recorded the events well on Facebook and other social media.

When you don't realize the true nature of race as a tool of Wetiko, you blame other poor people, racialize them, and attempt to deny them resources. Ultimately, you support White supremacy.[6] This behavior has repeated itself in many ways throughout the history of Black-Mexican relations in the United States. Many of us believe that the teaching and implementation of food autonomy can assist in this effort to reassess African-Amerindigenous history to struggle together for an autonomous future.

The Rise and Fall of Emancipatory Internationalism

Before examining how we got to the current state of racial animosity that exists between some in Black and Mexican communities and within our food movement, we should be clearer about how we got here. To do so, we must disabuse ourselves of the colonial logics that created the categories "Black," "Mexican," and "Indian" and overdetermined how these groups relate to one another. Two recent works address the "master's categories" challenging us to see this history (and thus our future) differently. Both Kyle T. Mays's *An Afro-Indigenous History of the United States* (2021) and Paul Ortiz' *A Black and Latinx History of the United States* (2018) offer convincing rereadings of the history of race in this country. These two texts offer a few lessons to help us unlearn settler-colonial history and see ourselves differently.

First, Mays's work adds detail to an assertion that some of us have been making for several years: that Black people should be considered Indigenous; that inherent, though hidden, in Black diasporic culture are cultural retentions and underlying worldviews based in African Indigenous being:

> The African peoples were in fact Indigenous peoples who were violently ripped from their homelands. The ancestry of Black Americans, or the descendants of the enslaved, may not originate in North America, but they are Indigenous . . . It might seem controversial to call Africans and their descendant Indigenous peoples, but it is not. To reclaim, insofar as we can imagine the Indigenous roots of Africans in the diaspora is neither an attempt to replace Indigenous peoples of the U.S. nor to act as settlers in some real or imagined return to Africa, as previous generations have done.[7]

The culture of today's Black Americans, especially their food culture, results from thousands of years of Indigenous development as well as kidnap, slavery, and anti-Black racism. Importantly, Mays steers clear of the claims made by many whom he describes as hoteps ("hypermasculine Black male[s] who [have] an ahistorical, Afrocentric conception of [themselves]"[8]) inspired by the debunked pseudo-scholarship of Ivan Van Sertima that Africans sailed from the West coast of Africa tens of thousands of years ago, populated the Americas, and established all of the mother civilizations of today's Latin Americans and Indigenous Americans. Instead, his study shows that Africans brought to the Americas were Indigenous, that is, place-based.

Second, both works show that African-Amerindigenous relations have been a mix of tragedy, violence, and animosity *and* cooperation, mutual recognition, respect, and cultural exchange. Third, Africans and Indigenous people in the Americas have suffered similar albeit different tragedy at the hands of Wetiko. While in our popular imagination we equate slavery with the treatment of kidnapped Africans in the U.S. South, the truth about slavery in the Western Hemisphere is more complicated and tragic. Many millions of Indigenous people here were enslaved, while some such as the so-called five civilized tribes of the U.S. Southeast held African slaves. In addition, both groups were forcibly taken from their homelands and relocated to the benefit of White landowners. Chicanxs and African Americans have served as the workhorses of U.S. capitalism and have constituted the superexploited classes that often justify the exploitation of White workers. Seeing U.S. history from a class- and race-based perspective shows not only how the "wealth" of the United States has resulted from this superexploitation but also how these groups share class interests and struggle. Joanne Barker explains that "the anti-imperialist struggles of Indigenous peoples to reclaim governance and territory is not dissimilar to the struggles of Africans, Arabs, immigrants and others comparatively oppressed by imperialism's racism and capitalism."[9]

Fourth, each group resisted their treatment at the hands of the European foreigner and "have always resisted in little and subtle ways."[10] We have also participated in larger scale resistance, whether in wars of colonial emancipation, strikes or demonstrations, and other tactics. Dr. King, Fannie Lou Hamer, Malcolm X, Vine DeLoria Jr., Stokely Carmichael (now known as Kwame Ture) and others worked in solidarity and discussed the importance of combining Red Power and Black Power to undermine White supremacy. The Poor People's March of 1968 and the work leading up to it exemplify the interracial cooperation that has been more common in our history than most of us acknowledge.[11]

Fifth, Black, Indigenous, and Mexican populations in the United States until recent times have been international in outlook. This orientation challenges contemporary hypernationalist understandings of ourselves that limit our ability to act as a unified whole against Wetiko and for humanity (to paraphrase the Zapatista principle). Ortiz uses the idea of emancipatory internationalism to express how Black Americans and Latinx people understood their relationships to racial or ethnic others. The struggles of Haitians and other Caribbeans, Mexicans and other Latin Americans, Asians and Africans inspired Latinxs and African Americans whose Indigenous humanistic traditions led them to struggle alongside the oppressed of these countries. He explains, "This idea of emancipatory internationalism was born of centuries of struggle against slavery, colonialism, and oppression in the Americas." The positive interactions and beliefs about each other shared by many Mexican Americans and Black Americans were born out of struggle. Mexicans, other Latin Americans, Indigenous peoples, and Black Americans fought alongside one another in our attempts to gain freedom and dignity.[12]

Huey Newton and the Black Panther Party made struggle alongside colonized people all over the world a central part of their theorizing and work. Newton and company developed the concept of intercommunalism as method of struggle and organizational principle. Newton believed that the world had no nations but rather empires and colonies. From the people's perspective, we had communities. It is in these communities that we struggle and form alliances. He and the Black Panther Party developed a Black anarchistic outlook as the organization developed. Nations and states have never been agents for freedom for Black people; I would add that Amerindigenous people have experienced the same. Black anarchist William Anderson adds, "Nations and states have long treated this planet and its resources as always being for someone" and not others.[13]

For our purposes, a general rereading of history using the insights of Mays, Ortiz, Anderson, and Newton allows us to develop a revolutionary anticolonial identity. How we understand our history and ourselves, of course, has a powerful effect on how we behave toward one another and the planet.

The Roots of Black-Mexican Relations

A common starting point for discussing Black-Indigenous-Latinx relations is the Spanish invasion of the Americas in the early sixteenth century.[14] In the early sixteenth century, Spanish colonization of the Americas and trade in African slaves brought Africans and Mexican/Indigenous into contact as colonial subjects. Spanish colonizers brought hundreds of thousands of Africans to Abya Yala. Under these conditions, Indigenous Mexicans and Africans became the co-creators of Mexican society and culture. Significantly, they and their "racially" mixed offspring resisted exploitation and violence at the hands of the conquistadores and hacendados. In 1609, Yanga led a slave revolt that created the first free African town in the Americas later renamed in his honor. Dozens of similar towns would eventually be created in Mexico's Veracruz and Costa Chica regions. Eventually, Indigenous, African, and mestizo/mulatto resistance ended Spanish rule in Mexico. Men like revolutionary Vicente Guerrero were, in part, descendants of African slaves. In the spirit of Yanga, they fought for self-determination.[15]

During the Spanish colonial years, African and Indigenous cultures mixed and mingled to create what we now know as Mexican culture. While we are aware of Spain's contribution to Mexican culture in the form of the Spanish language, patriarchy, racial hierarchy, Catholicism, and architecture, many are unaware that the bulk of Mexican culture is Indigenous and African. Marco Polo Hernandez

Cuevas focuses our attention on the African contributions to Mexican cuisine, language, music, and dance, among other important aspects of Mexican culture. Traditions such as mariachi, fandango, the consumption of barbacoa and tripa, and the central place of the verb "chingar" in Mexican working-class language use result from Africans and their interaction with Indigenous/mestizos.[16]

Despite the divide-and-conquer strategies of Spanish, and later Mexican, elites that led to both anti-Black and anti-Indigenous racism and the exalting of "Hispanidad" and "mestizaje" (racial mixture) à la José Vasconcelos's influential concept "la raza cósmica," the history of cooperation between the Africans and the Indigenous continued in the nineteenth and twentieth centuries. Mexico abolished slavery in 1829 (nearly forty years before the United States did so). Some enslaved Africans from the U.S. South chose to go south to Mexico instead of north. Enslaved Africans in the United States were often assisted and encouraged to settle in Mexico. Black Americans often received a positive reception in Mexico leading people like the iconic heavyweight champion boxer Jack Johnson to encourage Black settlement there. Further, Mexico provided opportunities for Black baseball players and artists that were absent in the United States. At the same time, Blacks and Mexicans in the United States encountered one another on the West Coast. Here they co-created zoot-suiting, lowriding, street style, the U.S. third world resistance movement, and West Coast rap/hip hop and breakdancing.[17]

Though we have a large and largely unknown body of evidence for positive, co-creative relations, structural factors have imposed strife and tension between the two communities. This begins early in the colonial period when elites imposed a racial hierarchy that placed Africans below the Indigenous and mestizos. Through their *casta* paintings and complex social behaviors, the Spanish racial hierarchy took hold in Mexico. Later, the African presence and contributions to Mexico and its culture were rendered invisible in part by José Vasconcelos's raza cósmica thesis.[18] In addition, Blacks were depicted negatively in Mexican popular culture of the twentieth century. The U.S. racial hierarchy, xenophobia, and popular culture representations contributed to Mexican-Black conflict. Today, economic downturns have created tensions between the two groups as the worsening economy causes both to suffer and the media portrays Blacks as lazy and criminal and Mexicans as foreign and usurpers of Black jobs.[19] This is nothing new since "the white settler state helped construct the image of Black and Indigenous peoples in ways that allowed them to continue to be dehumanized and treated as separate political, economic, and social structures."[20] The role that White elites have played in constructing dehumanizing images and imparting a fear of the racialized Other in Black, Indigenous, and Mexican people cannot be underestimated. This barely visible "third party in the room," as Bee Rodriguez described it, has played a determining role in how we see and behave toward one another.

It is this determining role that has led to incidents like the 2020 attacks on Black residents in Chicago and the vitriol about Mexicans coming from Black pundits and activists on outlets such as WVON radio. Recent expressions of ADOS-supporters (American Descendants of Slaves) have further marked Mexicans and all other noncitizens as enemies of Black Americans. This new movement relies on an old divisive sentiment that Black Americans are separate and different from other so-called people of color and that their enslavement and building of this country gives them sole right to demand money and other concessions from the U.S. government. They believe that all non-Black people of color and non-U.S.-born Blacks are interlopers and are here to take what the United States owes Black Americans. For example, the ADOS website explains their position that affirmative action should be "streamlined as a government program only and specifically for ADOS."[21] Their stances align closely with Republican anti-immigrant talking points, and ADOS leadership regularly communicates with hard-right conservative figures such as Ann Coulter. Its central proponent, Yvette Carnell, can be seen draped in the U.S. flag wearing a "Make America Great Again" hat worn by far-right xenophobic followers of Donald Trump.

In Chicago, the premiere, influential Black talk radio station, WVON, regularly argues such a divide-and-conquer strategy. During the Latin American refugee crisis of 2023 in Chicago, "The Black Excellence Hour" host, P. Rae, advised Black listeners to call ICE on people they suspected to be illegal immigrants.[22] Morning show host Maze Jackson asks listeners to tell him "What's in it for the Black people?" While Jackson's vigilance regarding local, state, and national politics as concerns how they affect Black people may be warranted given the historical and ongoing anti-Black racism perpetrated by these entities, his zero-sum game and scarcity perspective leads him to emphasize conflict over cooperation with Latinxs and to assume racism on the part of Mexicanxs and other Latinxs instead of seeing the all-too-common similar interests and relationships to the power structures. His regular undermining of coalition-building efforts and lack of larger national and international context for understanding local events has the effect of supporting the divide between Black Americans and Latinxs. The afternoon show with Kimberly Egonmwan reinforces the "us vs. them" perspective of many middle-class professionals and activists in the Black community who listen to the show and call in to express similar racialized, colonized perspectives. WVON is in line with the more conservative aspects of Black movements such as the Nation of Islam (NOI) that has attempted to work with the Ku Klux Klan, Nazi organizations, and recently with the white nationalists (fascists) of former president Trump's administration as evidenced by Ice Cube's overtures to them.[23] The NOI and its conservative nationalism have had an important presence in Chicago since Mosque Maryam became NOI's its headquarters in 1972.

Minister Farrakhan, the NOI leader, has a heavily guarded compound of houses in the Kenwood/Hyde Park neighborhood in Chicago. Many people connected to the food movement of which I am a part are members of Mosque Maryam or have connections to the NOI.

The right-wing isolationist turn of many Black liberals is a far cry from the emancipatory internationalism expressed in the nineteenth and first half of the twentieth century by influential Black media outlets. Black people had a great deal of concern for international struggle and solidarity with other dispossessed people and for a general humanism. A 1915 Chicago *Defender* article exemplifies this internationalism:

> The people of Latin America ethnologically are very little different from the
> Afro-American of this country . . . They have Indian blood in their veins; so have
> we. They have African blood in their veins; so have we . . . It is only a difference
> in degree.[24]

Black people before the twenty-first century "link[ed] together the fate of African Americans with their embattled brothers and sisters in Latin America." During the U.S. war on Mexico to extend slavery and White elite landholding, many Black Americans, including the Black press and Frederick Douglass, "kept Mexico at the forefront of their hopes for future liberation."[25] Later, Rev. Dr. Martin Luther King Jr. expressed Black emancipatory internationalism as he reached out to migrants of the United Farm Workers and denounced the U.S. war on the Vietnamese people.[26] Black leaders and the Black press expressed an understanding that "slavery and imperialism were fatally intertwined."[27]

With this history of contradiction, conflict, and cooperation as backdrop, the food autonomy movement in Chicago strives to be revolutionary. Some ask how we can overcome barriers between marginalized and food-deprived communities. In recent years, many land stewards have recognized the importance of solidarity and have created Black-Latinx-Indigenous organizations of food autonomy advocates.

Local Food and Black-Brown Coalitions

Those of us engaged in developing local food systems in urban areas can build BIPOC and White revolutionary coalitions to struggle against Wetiko's destructive food system and for a just and better future. A key component of local food systems, and perhaps, its most important, is the education in food production that results from community members working together to feed themselves. In gardens, urban consumers become producers who gain firsthand knowledge of food production from seed to table. This "doing" instead of consuming is an Indigenous way of life.

Nishnaabeg society, for example, is "a society of makers, rather than a society of consumers . . . We didn't just control our means of production, we live embedded in a network of humans and nonhumans that were made up of producers."[28]

Conversations and formal and informal classes on organic, sustainable, and culturally relevant food practices teach not only about organic practices but also about how agribusiness does its business. Discussions about the importance of diversity in a garden plot and polycultural techniques such as intercropping and companion planting translate easily into acknowledgement of diversity and polyculturality in our human communities. We integrate the lessons of ubuntu, in lak' ech, and mitakuye oyasin into a plan for a successful community garden and food system. These lessons come alive as the gardens grow and food is harvested and shared.

The growing of our ancient Amerindigenous las tres madres only feet away from collard greens and okra (ngumbo) becomes a living metaphor for the possibility of relations between Black and Mexican/Latinx people. When recipes are shared, a new conviviality develops that would be impossible under Wetiko's food regime. Convide (the sharing of food among neighbors) reinforces a sense of community and mutual aid that is part of nuevomexicano culture and the cultures of many African, Mexican, and Indigenous diasporas. Convide "is an idea that has allowed our communities to survive and thrive when it comes to eating healthy food." In northern New Mexico, for example, such practices made it so that for centuries no one went hungry. Convide and similar concepts and practices of African-origin peoples are essential in the struggle against Wetiko that separates Blacks and Mexicans and that threatens our communities with poor quality food.[29] Through convide and similar Indigenous ethics, we aspire to create local food systems that bridge the gaps between different racial/ethnic groups and between producers and consumers of food.

However, such practices require vigilance to be successful. We must be aware that societal pressures continually threaten the development of Latinx-Black and consumer-producer relations. Misreadings and selective readings of history, real present-day competition, a media that fans the flames of fear and anxiety of others, urban and rural social problems, and an economy that not only denies BIPOC access to important resources but also does untold psychological and spiritual damage to us creates a situation in which the lessons of conviviality taught through the mutual production of healthy and culturally relevant foodstuffs can be overlooked. The lessons of one community garden in Chicago in which Black and Mexican-origin community members worked serves as a warning about how the ambitions of Black-Brown coalitions can be easily undermined. In South Chicago, which had been predominantly Mexican and Mexican American since the 1920s but had begun to transition to a predominantly Black neighborhood in the late 1990s, the tensions around race and class led to a palpable animosity between some in the two groups by the early 2000s. A community garden in a Mexican-origin part of the neighborhood drew both Blacks and Mexicans. While the excitement of building a beautiful award-winning garden eased tensions in the beginning, soon pride, fear, and racism caused problems. Fights over space, grant money, and which vegetables to be grown led to the garden being overtaken by the Mexican-origin members who felt a certain entitlement related to their sense that the garden was in their neighborhood and that the newer Black residents were interlopers. Racial epithets were hurled between groups with leaders trying in vain to resolve the problem. The parent group, Healthy South Chicago, mediated the conflict but racial antagonisms ruled the day and the Black garden members began to stay away.

Thus, we should be aware of the barriers to conviviality that result from Wetiko culture that teaches fear of other and extreme individualism. The problems that erupted in this garden required attention and education. Members needed to remind one another of the convivial belief systems of our ancestors. This situation required more than learning organic, sustainable horticultural practices. It required a critical analysis of our society from Indigenous and food autonomy perspectives that connect the problems of food production and environmental destruction to that of human-to-human relations. This example shows how we can create a beautiful community garden while we undermine practices of conviviality under Wetiko. The garden fed some people well but failed to produce in a just, democratic, and egalitarian manner.

My experience as a non-Black identified Chicano in the Black food movement in Chicago shows me that the practices of community gardening and the development of local food systems combined with lessons in conviviality and respect for all our relations can produce an equitable social system. Overcoming a capitalist ethos that hides social relations of food production and offers ahistorical understandings of difference and otherness requires IK and knowledge of our mutual interdependence and the complex history of our relations to one another. This is essential if we are to escape from Wetiko food and other inequalities and work toward food autonomy and un mundo donde caben todos los mundos. In the short run it is essential for each of us in the movement to arm ourselves with this way of knowing Mexican/Indigenous-African/Black relations.

Indigeneity as the Way Through

As mentioned throughout, I believe that a connection to land is key to our survival. In the case of Black-Mexican relations our common precolonial Indigenous past may hold the key to the way through the crises we face. What if we saw ourselves and one another as Indigenous people with a set of anticolonial, anticapitalist, alterNative (i.e., Indigenous) principles in common? Why not see ourselves as communities with the same Wetiko enemy and who essentially want the same things? What if we used Indigenous governance structures and ethics to encounter one another and build a new society? Why not just drop the colonially imposed labels of Black and Mexican-origin and just be Indigenous? What are the problems with adapting or adopting indigeneity as an identity for Black and Mexican-origin people?

Place-based connection rooted in our Indigenous African and American traditions holds promise for overcoming racial hostility and environmental ruin. Many, especially the younger under-forty crowd, in the movement see this possibility and have begun to form alliances that go beyond the labels and categories offered us by Wetiko. One such group is Urban Stewards Action Network. On their website USAN describes themselves like this: "Urban Stewards Action Network (USAN) is an action-based transformational network focused on Black and Brown relationship building to cultivate connections and provide peer-based mutual support within the food system in Chicago."[30]

The members of USAN recognize the similar struggles of BIPOC folks around food and other issues including high levels of food insecurity in the City. They take a food justice perspective. About their work they write,

> USAN works to address social justice through a focus on food justice. We believe food serves as a symbolic and historic tie binding people across cultures while reflecting injustices such as access to land, diet related disease, low paying jobs in the food sector, access to affordable healthy food, contaminated soil, among many other issues. Food is a focus for celebrating diverse cultures while providing direct projects and policies in which communities can collaborate.

USAN membership is restricted to BIPOC stewards and growers. They state that their priorities are "on the ground Black and Brown solidarity" and uplifting BIPOC communities.

Multiethnic organizations focused on Indigenous ways of relating to one another, and the lands we are responsible for provide models and experiments in a potentially revolutionary urban reindigenization. The work of USAN, ChiResists, Chi-Nations Youth Council, Reclaiming Our Roots, Urban Growers Collective, and GLP shows us a red, black, and green way forward and out of the climate crisis and related horrors of Wetiko.

CHAPTER 6

Diasporic Foods

RACE, PLACE, AND IDENTITY

The problem is the generations of people with no real knowledge of African American history... Devoid of this knowledge, they are ill-equipped to identify modern-day versions of berating images, or worse they could not care. PSYCHE A. WILLIAMS-FORSON on the history of food-based anti-Black imagery (*Building Houses Out of Chicken Legs: Black Women, Food and Power* [Chapel Hill: University of North Carolina Press, 2006], 223)

Over the years, discussions with Black and Latinx university students about Blackness and Latinidad inevitably center urban culture. What it means to be Black or Latinx is tied to an urban cool. Younger Blacks and Latinxs tend to describe their identities in two ways: 1) as tied to urban youth culture including music, clothing, language, and a tough "street" attitude; and 2) as victims of White racism. Never do these young adults highlight agrarian culture, attachments to land, or horticultural traditions. The extensive history of Black/African and Indigenous respect for and understanding of our interrelatedness has been made invisible by Wetiko, and this invisibility is key to understanding Blackness, Latinidad, and indigeneity as consumerism.[1] Moreover, African diasporan traditions such as the BAT developed in the U.S. South are stigmatized as representative of a racist past. Nor do they often discuss Black and Latinx resistance or agency beyond electoral politics or a "Black Pride!" or "Viva la Raza!" slogan. However, once exposed to community gardening and Black/Indigenous land traditions, these students and others often begin to see the work of growing food differently and sometimes reveal memories of an agrarian past. This chapter examines what we can learn about the identities of BIPOC through work in community gardens and in the spaces of the food autonomy movement and how many in the movement attempt to influence identity and self-esteem among Black Chicagoans.

A politicized reading of the concept of "diaspora" can be useful to our understanding of identity in urban settings and in the development of movements for community food autonomy and self-determination. I explain how the concept helps us understand issues of race, place and identity in the community gardens and local food movement in some Black communities in Chicago. Additionally, some in the communities in which I participate see indigeneity and place-based identities as central to their struggles.

A Politicized, Indigenized Diasporan Perspective

Etymologically, "diaspora" suggests "a scattering which is also a sowing."[2] This metaphor is perfect for our understanding of the relationship between those in the food autonomy movement in Black Chicago and their natural surroundings as seen through community gardening. "Diaspora" is not simply a term that suggests displacement and victimization. Diaspora is the dispersion of a people, their implantation in a new land, and the harvesting of a new culture from the planting of the seeds of an older culture in new soil. Diaspora should be seen as a process of adaptation to Wetiko through the creation of a polycultural diasporan identity and practice rooted in African cultural retentions that takes the soil and the landscape of a new land and culture and transforms it for the needs of its people. Further, its rerootedness in the soil of the Americas is a reindigenization process: becoming a place-based people again.

We should see Black Americans and Mexican-origin people, the two ethnoracial communities in which I live and work, as active agents in our development. However, we should also be aware of the ongoing processes of colonialism that continually re-create the diaspora, reterritorialize urban space, and subjugate BIPOC. This critical reading of diaspora helps us see how identity is employed in building a food autonomy movement in the city. Moreover, through examining the interrelated food and environmental histories of Black and Indigenous Mexican-origin people and our current food autonomy work, we can see how diaspora operates, how it is used in food struggles, and the importance of place to ethnic renewal.

From Plantations to Urban Community Gardens:
AHK in the United States

Slavery created a paradoxical relationship between Black Americans and nature. On the one hand, nature was manipulated into the means of production for the development of the plantation economy and later, capitalist agribusiness, and thus it confronts slaves, sharecroppers, and, by extension, all Black Americans as a tool of oppression. On the other hand, slavery combined with AHK, especially as concerns ecology, continued an Indigenous African relationship to the land. This relationship led to a deep sense of kinship between enslaved Africans, sharecroppers, and small landowners and the landscapes of the eastern and southern parts of the United States. Later, rapid urbanization in the twentieth century displaced most Black Americans from the land and placed them in concrete environs in which the alienation from nature experienced during slavery and sharecropping took a new intensified turn. Yet many held on to their stewardship and food traditions.

In understanding Black Chicagoans' relationship to land through an analysis

of the food movement it is useful to keep in mind how political, economic, social, and cultural forces influence perceptions and feelings for nature, food, and
self. "Humans' relationship to the natural world is affected by the justice or injustice of their social arrangements."[3] Given the history of Black oppression and
Black displacement from the land, it is no wonder that Black Chicagoans are often dismissive of and derisive toward Black agrarian culture or what many label
derogatorily as "country." In addition to the horrid relations of agricultural production that Black Americans experienced under slavery and sharecropping, they
have had to endure cultural stigmatization related to Black American foodways.
Williams-Forson finds that Black women and traditional foodways continue to
survive and thrive in the face of food-related stereotypes such as the Black domes-
tic, fried chicken, and watermelon.[4]

Slavery and Plantation Agriculture

"Race slavery and post-Emancipation racial oppression put black Americans into
a conflicted relationship to the land—by coercing their labor, restricting their
ability to own land, and impairing their ability to interpret the landscape."[5] Enslaved Africans were not simply passive victims of the plantation system nor did
they often engage in mass acts of open rebellion (at least not until the middle of
the nineteenth century). "Instead, they creatively negotiated small portions of independence and autonomy from the master-slave relationship . . . Most of slaves'
waking hours were spent in labor on the land, but this labor gave them knowledge
of the land that was intimate and precise, and in turn had material, social, and
political usefulness."[6] Gardening, hunting, foraging, and religious practices that
took place in nature beyond the gaze of master provided enslaved Africans with
areas of freedom to practice their diasporan Indigenous culture and maintain an
interdependent relationship with nature. A diasporan African American culture
developed in these zones of freedom. Yet arguably most of contemporary urban
Black America associates nature with plantation slavery. Nature faces many Black
Chicagoans as an enemy, and thus they see work with the land as exploitative.
Amid the superexploitive economic and social system, it must be difficult for
many to appreciate the agrarian culture and AHK adopted, adapted, and renewed
in previous generations.

The cultures of many diasporan Africans encouraged seeing the interconnectedness of humans and all other species. "Broadly speaking, Africans believed in
the interconnectedness of the human, spiritual, and environmental realms and felt
that harm toward or care for one necessarily affected the others."[7] Indigenous people developed a relationship to more-than-human beings that includes reciprocity,
respect, equality, and diversity.[8] Kwasi Densu described five core features of Indig-

enous African agroecology, including viewing the earth as a living and spiritual reality, the use of the commons, and systems that were/are agroecological. Each of these is displayed by Black growers in my community suggesting the development of an Indigenous relationship to the land.[9]

Devastatingly, "slave agriculture and the systems of control it depended on put slaves in a conflicted relationship to the land, and they also created a strong association between the concept of freedom and certain ways of interacting with and controlling nature."[10] The plantation economy and its relations of production caused a change in the meaning of land for enslaved Africans. They made the quite accurate analysis that freedom in the South meant ownership and dominion over land and the use of monocultural industrial-agricultural techniques. They could be free if they could just own land and manipulate it to work for them; that is, if they could create monocultures of rice, cotton, or tobacco that could be sold on the market.

AHK in the Chi

In addition to the spiritual orientation toward interdependence and interconnectedness and the necessity of New World Africans to work the land to survive, they brought a wealth of agricultural techniques that spurred the land to produce the rice, tobacco, cotton, and other crops that enriched slave owners. For example, Dianne Glave writes that "in the rice culture of All Saints Parish in South Carolina, slaveholders purchased Africans who were experts in rice planting and cultivation."[11]

While slavery and sharecropping turned nature into an oppressive "factory" for Black Americans, we shouldn't simply see them as victims. As Kimberely Smith explains:

> The slave system forced slaves into an intimacy with the natural environment
> . . . The very skill and knowledge that slaves needed to be effective agricultural
> workers gave them the means to resist planters' control . . . knowledge was power
> on a plantation. Thus plantation agriculture could be a source of suffering and
> degradation for slaves, but it could also be a means to autonomy.[12]

The life of the enslaved African provided "an intimate knowledge of their local environment," especially through herbal medicines, gardening, animal husbandry, hunting and fishing. For example, "customary rights to a garden or to hunting privileges could become the basis for an attachment to place—an attachment based on one's positive relationship to the land rather than on the legal barriers to movement . . . Mastery of the natural landscape through knowledge of the local plant life was a source of spiritual power independent of the master."[13] Gardening provides us with an important example of the empowering and spirit-based relationship that many slaves and post-Emancipation Blacks had to the land. Today, Jacqueline A. Smith, Linda, Karlita, Quafin, Alexy, Melody, and others trade ideas and stories of African diasporic Indigenous ethics and economics and their empowering spiritual consequences. About gardening, Ms. Anglin said, "That's when the peace comes in." Tellingly, members of GLP named one of our gardens Sacred Greens, with a nod toward AHK (greens) and Indigenous spirituality (sacred).

Black Americans "created distinctively African American spaces that simultaneously mimicked nature and rejected white control . . . Although the gardens appeared chaotic, the disarray of plants also created a diversity that reduced opportunities for weeds and pests to take hold. Some gardeners sought ethical, moral, and spiritual enlightenment in these chaotic or wilderness spaces much as their African ancestors had."[14] This observation entails two points that are important for our understanding of contemporary Black American community gardening and the food autonomy movement in Chicago. First, control over space through the manipulation of our landscape is a powerful tool of independence. Today's "masters" of the global economic system can be undermined and marginalized with AHK. Second, urban space and ghetto environments can be seen and can mean something different than places of poverty, violence, and ugliness.[15]

Additionally, "many slaves engaged in gardening, hunting, and gathering roots and herbs. These production practices and the knowledge they reflected undoubtedly served as the basis of an attachment to place for plantation slaves, as well as a potential source of selfhood and social power."[16] The planting of medicinal herbs and the numerous discussions of their uses in food autonomy spaces reflects this diasporan tradition and AHK. Yarrow, mint, raspberry leaves, comfrey, lemon balm, sage, Echinacea, burdock, dandelion, and many others grow in the gardens of Black Chicago and are preserved and stored in the medicine cabinets and pantries of many in the food autonomy movement. Today's emphasis on self-determination and the idea of commUnity wealth fostered by BOC replicate these practices of social power in the Black food autonomy community.

Importantly, the maintenance of AHK did not rely simply on individual efforts but also collective work and intellectual leadership. Monica White's discussion of the maintenance of BAT during the twentieth century illustrates how AHK in the context of Wetiko becomes anticolonial and antiracist. AHK preserved in the gardens of enslaved Africans served as a rich source for Black thriving in the post-Emancipation period. Black elite and liberal white supporters established institutions of higher education and related programs where people like George Washington Carver, Booker T. Washington, and W. E. B. Du Bois helped preserve and expand AHK. These people and many others also helped distribute resources and organize Black farmers. Armed with AHK and support of people like Carver and Fannie Lou Hamer, southern Black farmers organized to protect their land, resources, and traditions. Their initiative and higher degree of self-reliance placed them in positions to assist others especially during the violence and terror of the civil rights movement period (1940s–1970). Black farmers created groups like Freedom Farm Collective and the Federation of Southern Cooperatives.[17] This legacy forms the foundation of much of the work that I have witnessed in the Black food movement in Chicago and elsewhere. Today, the Detroit Black Community Food Security Network, Black Urban Growers, National Black Food and Justice Alliance, and Urban Growers Collective practice and build on the work of our African ancestors.

Unfortunately, despite the efforts of Black food activists, much of this knowledge has been lost over the generations. Instead of seeing the transcendent and empowering AHK, many contemporary urban Blacks see such AHK as a past best forgotten. They, like earlier generations of Whites and many of today's Mexican diasporan community, stigmatize IK/AHK and those who practice it. This attitude began under Southern plantation slavery during which "that kind of knowledge (in contrast to scientific knowledge) also marked one's status as a slave. White elites often denigrated herb lore as 'Negro cures' and 'Negro superstition' (even while admitting it had some value) and cultivated scientific knowledge as a marker of their superior social status."[18] This antiagrarian, antinature attitude dominates contemporary urban Black relationships to nature. The steady migration of Blacks from the rural South to the urban North and Midwest facilitated the adoption of this perspective.

Urbanization and Alienation

Alienation from the land and nature characterizes northern urban Black experience today. Dianne Glave explains:

> African Americans' understanding of wilderness and the land began to transform with their increasing assimilation into American culture and the apparent possibility of their owning more land after Emancipation.
>
> This relocation to the increasingly urbanized North distanced them from the rural experiences of their parents and grandparents, who lived and worked in fields, gardens and woods. Scorn, distaste, and fear of nature became the emotional legacy of a people who had been kidnapped from their homelands.[19]

Urban Blacks adopted an "American" cultural attitude to nature that led them to have negative associations with "nature," "wilderness," agricultural labor, and the "country." Novice gardeners and visitors to gardens demonstrate a fear and hatred of insects that evidences this "antinature" attitude. Assimilation to Wetiko culture equates success, the "good life," or "the American Dream" with the accumulation of things as opposed to the close relationships that they had and have with others and the land. "Urban black culture, city culture, was just beginning to be the yardstick against which everything about blackness would come to be defined. All the aspects of our identity and culture that was deemed relevant came from the city."[20] Blackness starts to become defined by urban "cool," cosmopolitanism, consumerism, and economic success, all exemplary Wetiko values. Black agrarian culture and AHK become backward, inferior, and embarrassing.

Jacqueline A. Smith discussed this process in her own family:

> My paternal Great Grandmother, her name was Callie Glover, her children after her and her grandchildren after her did not take to growing food because of the Great Migration from the South to the North. They weren't really interested in growing food anymore or tending to anyone's land anymore. Industrial jobs were big. There was more money. They were more lucrative. It was a new way of life for my family. So they decided, I guess, that they weren't really interested in tending the land. I knew my Great Grandmother. I knew her but she passed away in 1990 or 1991. She was one hundred years old. I knew her, but I wasn't old enough to ask her questions about what she did, how she took care of almost twenty people in a shotgun house and tended to the land, grew hogs, slaughtered the hogs, had a smokehouse, had chickens running all over the place, and she would wring their necks and pluck their feathers and have it for dinner later on that night. She was very sustainable in what she did. Everything that the family ate came out of the ground. Only things she had to buy was flour and oats and maybe sugar . . . I think that's commendable. And I want to keep her legacy alive with GrowAsis [Urban Garden Consulting, Inc].

Ms. Smith's comments not only illustrate the problem of the Black American turn from nature but also the hope that many in the Black food autonomy movement have of an ethnic renewal through AHK practiced in food movement places.

In our dialogue quoted earlier, Mila Marshall discusses the difficulty of spreading BAT and AHK in urban spaces. She points out that what Ms. Smith and others in the movement are doing does not come easy. She observes that four or five generations in the city coupled with climate change and anti-Black racism limits urban Black acquisition of AHK and an Indigenous or African identity. In her work Dr. Marshall has seen not only the loss of AHK over the generations in the city but also the political economic conditions that combine with it, making food autonomy movement work in Black communities extremely difficult.

Black American alienation from nature extends to the fact that city life and "segregation [have] limited African Americans' access to parks and other public places."[21] This further alienation from nature has had devastating consequences. The early urban Black population was intellectually, emotionally, and physically separated from nature. This separation led to the withering of community solidarity that had once formed the foundation of Black agrarian life. Urban Blacks were becoming alienated from nature and one another.

> Estrangement from nature and engagement in mind/body splits made it all the more possible for black people to internalize white-supremacist assumptions about black identity. Learning contempt for blackness, southerners transplanted in the North suffered both culture shock and soul loss . . . Without the space to grow food, to commune with nature, or to mediate the starkness of poverty with the splendor of nature, black people experienced profound depression. Working in conditions where the body was regarded solely as a tool (as in slavery), a profound estrangement occurred between mind and body. The way the body was represented became more important than the body itself. It did not matter if the body was well, only that it appeared well.[22]

Psychic violence results from forced alienation from nature and AHK. An experience of depression can result from what we might call "nature-deficit disorder."[23] Urbanized Black Americans often believe that violence of poverty and its attendant ills could be lessened with an overemphasis on outward appearance. This consumer response to loss of AHK supports Wetiko and the ruling classes since Black people must purchase the commodities needed to approximate capitalist beauty, health, and other standards. This desire for things (rather than being) emphasized by advertisement and entertainment industries and "city culture" perpetuates the disdain for earlier Black agrarianism. The assimilation of Wetiko values intensifies an anticommunity, antinature value system.

Psychic violence extends to an injection of racist stereotypes of AHK and Black Agrarian life. Baba Fred explained,

> The distance started in my parent's generation. It started with them. They migrated to urban sections of the country. It was this great migration from the rural into the urban settings. That's where the disconnect occurred. That's one disadvantage of urban living. The urban living which is terrible nowadays. 70, 80 percent of the world's population now lives in cities. So it's a real big disconnect. They got so bad that they were shameful of that lifestyle. No one talked about it. It was a shame. Because when you got in an urban setting you were spoke down to. You was a "dirt farmer." [People would say,] "You live a low lifestyle."

However, many urban Blacks challenge the Wetiko values through community gardens and movement spaces. The Black food autonomy community around the

BOC and the GLP develops a politicized diasporan identity through reindigenization rooted in AHK.

Green Lots, Black Oaks, Sacred Greens

Writing about class-conscious Black "returning generation farmers" Leah Penniman and Blain Snipstal[24] assert that "our struggle is material, but it also deals with
our identities, assumptions and values. Bringing value and dignity back to the image of the Black farmer working with the land and nature is fundamental. Reval-
uing Black agrarian identity and Black agrarianism more broadly is a core task of
this 'returning generation.'" Food movement spaces address the urban problems
relating to loss of Black agrarianism, AHK and community as well as the incredibly
oppressive conditions of the late capitalist period in many Chicago communities.
These spaces are also places of recovery and resurgence of diasporic Indigenous
Africanness. In place of abandoned lots, drug spots, and gang territory, the gardens
offer flowers, fruits, friendships, and a deep connection to land through which we
can access a deeper understanding of ourselves. In a community suffering the consequences of a lack of access to healthy food, including high rates of diabetes and
heart disease, the gardens provide organic, healthy food options. Where people
are isolated from one another out of fear, they can come together on garden workdays. Gardens give kids a chance to explore freely and have fun safely instead of
dodging cars and gunshots in the streets where they are forced to play since there
are few indoor sources of recreation and safe parks in the neighborhood.

Gardens can be places of recovery. Identity and tradition can be remade
through work and communion in the garden. In 2008, Dominique R. Bowman,
GLP, and neighbors created an open garden, the Roseland Community Peace Garden (RCPG, now known as Roseland Community Forest Garden), where "those
who work, eat." We developed the space into an opportunity for community empowerment through collective work. We theorized that community resilience required overcoming the community's attitudes of indifference and derision toward
their environs and the recovery of Black agrarianism and AHK. Working with a
diverse, intergenerational group could provide solidarity, enhance knowledge, and
strengthen identity. RCPG members and gardeners have brought together neighborhood children, adults, and elders, as well as young adult and older adult students from nearby Chicago State University.

In the spaces of my food autonomy movement, accomplices such as CoGro
Farms, Reclaiming Our Roots, and Kuumba Tre Ahm Community Garden confront and continue to address loss of AHK and community in similar ways. BOC
uses the black oak as a metaphor for reindigenization. The Carters named their
land after the endangered dwarf black oak. In the essay, "Our Land, Our History,
Our Name" they explain,

The residents of Pembroke Township/Hopkins Park have been the succeeding stewards of what is now one of the most prized ecosystems in the state of Illinois referred to as the Kankakee Sands. This tradition of stewardship dates back to the care of the savanna by the indigenous people, the Potowatomi, who did controlled burns that maintained the savanna.

Later in the essay they discuss the African diasporan tradition in the area, its connection to autonomy and liberation movements, and the African diaspora's reciprocal relationship with the Indigenous of the region.

> Hopkins Park in Pembroke Township is one of the oldest black rural townships. It was founded by a runaway slave named Pap Tetter before the Emancipation Proclamation. Folk history tells us that he and his family of 18 children escaped from North Carolina around 1861. His originally acquired 42 acres of what is now called Hopkins Park created a safe place for other runaway slaves and the Potowatomi who did not go to reservations. Hopkins Park was a terminal for the underground railroad and became a secure space for ethnic diversity among the indigenous people and those who migrated there.[25]

BOC, like the many other places of food autonomy in Black Chicago, fosters ethnic renewal and resistance using AHK and the traditionally deeply important relationship that Indigenous people have with place. Several times per week in my work as scholar and participant in the food autonomy movement, I have had the good fortune to witness people engaged in the recovery of AHK and reindigenization including the examples below.

Food Travels: Loss, Memory, and Recovery in the Garden

"I've never seen that growing before" and "They grow that down south" are two oft-heard remarks in GLP gardens. They represent two competing experiences: the loss and the recovery of tradition and identity. The remarks of BT, an older student in my Food Justice class, reflect the conflicting relationships that working-class, urban Black people often have with the land. In the indoor classroom, when asked to reflect on the Black southern agrarian tradition, she described racist violence and backbreaking work. She told of how her mother had to escape the South under cover of darkness to avoid rape and other violence. Then, BT brought her grandchildren to the garden with her. While working in the garden she happily detailed her horticultural experience as a child in a southern sharecropping family and proudly demonstrated her expertise and skill. Indoors she expressed none of the enthusiasm that she displayed in the garden.

My interactions with BT suggest that pedagogy in the garden has the potential to help uncover pride in tradition, skills, and knowledge that has been lost in many cases in the urban Black United States. While Black students (and this extends to many Mexican students as well) are profoundly moved and find ethnic identity in African American and "Latino" Studies courses as well as others that center BIPOC experiences and cultures, practice of Black and Mexicanx traditions has a much deeper impact on them. The abstract theoretical and distant historical become real and hands-on in the garden. This active hands-in-the-soil garden pedagogy impacts both community and university students who work in and tour GLP's gardens.

Due to the concerns that many in the food autonomy movement in Chicago have regarding the loss of African diasporan traditions, we often emphasize intergenerational contact through land- and elder-based pedagogy. Indicative of this emphasis is the daily mentions of ancestors and elders. At GLP gardens, the HFH and the BOC members, visitors, and customers examine AHK and recognize the important work of ancestors and elders who have maintained and transmitted it. The logo of the HFH provides an example of our commitment to ancestral and elder knowledge and its transmission to future generations. In a December 19, 2013, post to HFH, the HFH's Facebook page, the author describes the logo and its connection to the HFH mission:

FIG. 11. First logo of the Healthy Food Hub. Photographer unknown.

Our updated HFH logo was reimagined to include our ancestral agricultural icons Wangari Maathai and George Washington Carver. These great figures represent our near and distant legacy of sustainability, environmental stewardship and utility. In the center of the logo is Africa which represents the abundant cultural, human and natural resources available for our responsible utilization. Rising above Africa is the Adinkra symbol, Aya, which is a fern representing endurance and resourcefulness. The fern is a plant which prospers in a wide variety of difficult ecosystems and circumstances. Representing our cultural foodways are the ears of corn and the okra, which find themselves a substantial part of our historical cuisine. This logo is now deeply aligned with our mission to transform urban and rural communities by restoring just practice and holistic awareness to our food system.

In many spaces of our movement, we continue the thousands-years old generational transmission of AHK and IK. BOC focuses on intergenerational teaching and write in their mission statement that a primary goal is to "educate and empower children."

Reindigenization and Adaptation in Diaspora

The teaching of las tres madres technology illustrates the nature of diaspora and the importance of interethnic cooperation of colonized and enslaved people. We show and tell how African diasporan communities adopted and adapted Amerindigenous foodstuffs as a means of survival and cultural renewal. Teosinte (corn) became a Black foodstuff in the Americas in the colonial period and could be found growing along with other Amerindigenous crops and African-origin crops in the gardens of enslaved and free persons.[26] Corn remains a staple of Black American cuisine. One is hard-pressed to think about a soul food meal without cornbread, for example. Within the local food movement, contemporary urban Black Americans continue this African diasporan tradition as they work to recover it and renew it for others.

There are numerous examples of the process of adoption and adaptation of Amerindigenous foodstuffs as an integral part of the survival and ethnic renewal of Africans in the Americas.[27] Africans brought an enormous amount of agricultural, culinary, and medicinal knowledge. AHK and the ethnobotanical knowledge of the Indigenous people of the Americas combined to create a new and vibrant culture that continues to thrive wherever people practice BAT. GLP gardens serve as a living museum of this process as Black Americans and Mexican Americans exchange information daily, and the perennial herbs and native fruit-bearing trees and bushes provide an outdoor pharmacy of sorts that members and neighbors continuously learn how to use. Through learning about the land, the specific land on which we grow in Chicago, and our place on it, Black Americans in the food movement continue the process of diaspora as well as become reindigenized and reconnected to land with a reverence for it and keen attention to human-nature relations. They are answering what John Mohawk calls the "spiritual call of the reindigenization of the world."[28] This reindigenization in diaspora mirrors what is happening in "Indian Country" in the United States and Canada, which Mohawk describes as "the re-biodiversity, recultural diversity, the rethinking of the Earth as a living being."[29] This diasporan process and reindigenization connects many to the AHK/IK principles of adaptation to change;[30] a dynamic understanding of what it means to be Indigenous. It is also a process of "recovering from Western culture. We're in recovery from that. It is that recovery that we must put our attention to—a recovery that involves the whole issue of medicine and plant life; the recovery of community."[31]

Practicing a Reindigenized Diasporan Identity

Addressing the oppression of Black people especially as it relates to the question of identity, community, and connection to an African past, Carl Anthony[32] writes that, "The knowledge of the earth, and of our place in its long evolution, can give us a sense of identity and belonging that can act as a corrective to the hubris and pride that have been weapons of our oppressors." Discussing contemporary Black urban culture with Wendell Berry, bell hooks remarks:

> Gone was a world where black folks understood the limitations of white power. My Daddy Jerry, my paternal grandfather, as he plowed with this mule would say; "you see that sun—the white man can't make it rise—no man can make it rise—man ain't everything." Daddy Jerry knew that there were limits to white power and to human power. We are living in a world right now where many black people and other people of color feel that white power is absolute. They see themselves as victims. They feel constant defeat and despair. In the culture of southern blackness, of Kentucky farm culture, you and I evoke, black folk were able to maintain integrity, dignity, creating beauty in the midst of exploitation and oppression.[33]

The loss of traditions and a sense of community have been lamented by BIPOC. hooks continues:

> If we think of urban life as a location where black folks learned to accept a mind/body split that made it possible to abuse the body, we can better understand the growth of nihilism and despair in the black psyche. And we can know that when we talk about healing that psyche we must also speak about restoring our connection to the natural world.[34]

Anthony and hooks suggest that AHK helps diasporan Africans in the United States to overcome some of the problems caused by Wetiko, including food injustice and lack of autonomy. Understanding the power of the earth and our relationship to it through AHK undermines capitalist ethics and the racist ideology that supports it. Black Americans, other people of color, and the Amerindigenous involved in community gardening and the food autonomy movement know that neither corporations nor powerful White men can make the sun rise nor rain fall. Wetiko is powerless in the face of nature and without our labor.

The food autonomy movement turns to urban community gardening and AHK/IK for solutions to many of our problems. We reason that through exposing ourselves to the wonders of nature and life we can begin to appreciate life more. Urban gardeners help turn Black neighborhoods into "communities of care."[35] Carolyn Thomas of God's Gang related to me how they care for children by instilling in them a positive Black American identity through teaching historical crops in their gardens:

> CT: God's Gang was asked to install a garden. We asked what she wanted to name it and she said, "Passion of Pullman." So we saw the opportunity to not only bring

some food but some passion in it . . . We usually grow cotton. We try to do things that when kids come is new, different, and historical. We always grow gourds, different gourds, every kind of gourd we can.

PM: You use those as a history lesson for the kids?

CT: Every time. Every time they come. We've got sorghum from a place called Macktown . . . That's where we originally got our sorghum seeds and we continue to use that sorghum and cotton . . . We do two kinds of cotton, sometimes three. We do white cotton, early green, and we do Nanking cotton because it has a wonderful story to the kids about one of the battles of the Civil War. It was lost or won, depending on what side you are on by a kid that was sent to enemy lines wearing a Nanking cotton shirt. And Nanking is the brown cotton that slaves were allowed to grow because master knew it wasn't his because it was brown. So we always do that and that provides that lesson.

We had a Hispanic garden which was kinda like a mandala. It had those kinda crops. We had an Indian garden with squash, corn, and beans. Then, we had a southern garden with collards, those kinda things. We had okra in our African garden and melons and peanuts and things that were appropriate . . . Not only our ethnicity but others'.

Importantly, Ms. Thomas models a radical polyculturalism as she connects the African heritage of the children and adults she works with to the foodways of people from other cultures and regions. Through the gardens we can teach awareness of self, our communities, and our connectedness to others. With the garden designs that she has developed, Ms. Thomas illustrates the ethic of diversity and polyculturality practiced in the Black food movement in Chicago.

Passing on AHK is a central activity in the Black food autonomy movement. Different aspects of AHK as practiced by members of Chicago's Black communities show up in food movement spaces. Paula Anglin teaches Black American religious practice, especially the brand of Black liberation theology common at Trinity, and AHK in the figure of Carver. Paula described how the mission of the church and the mission of the garden reinforce each other.

Well, I think it has been another way to reach the neighbors. I want the deacons to sit out here . . . Most of the people know me in the neighborhood. Sometimes people come by and say, "I see you out here working. It looks real nice." You know? I think it helps give more access, so to speak, to the church to the people.

One young man joined the church. I don't think it was because he came to the garden. Because he lives over here. But he was going somewhere else. I sat next to him one day and he told me he had been to the garden. So I don't know exactly the answer to that. I just know that everyone that comes here knows. I tell them. Sometimes they ask me if it is my garden. I tell them we belong to the church. I invite people in. I always give them food if we have some. Sometimes in the spring. It didn't happen this year. But the last two years in the spring people would be coming looking for the farmers' market before it opened. But I have been able to invite them in and give them a bag full of greens and, you know, herbs and stuff anyway.

Ms. Anglin is among many Black gardeners in Chicago who practice the Black and Indigenous tradition of giving thanks for our food and those things that sustain us to connect to ancestors, do our part to maintain respectful relationships with all our relations, and recognize a higher power.[36] On the topic of spirit in the garden she explained that if I "had come here ten minutes earlier you would've seen us standing in a circle out there praying. Part of that is Lauren's doing. So for me, gardening is meditative. It is meditative and relaxing." She claims that "that's where the peace comes in."

HFH promotes an Indigenous African identity through its symbolism. At the market members have discussions and practice a diasporan ethics. West African languages and symbols, especially Adinkra, create a cultural, educational, and political space for struggle and resurgence. Through clothing, art, music, and healing arts, people around the HFH and GLP develop and preserve AHK. As can be expected their diasporan culture and identity differs from those in previous generations given that native worldview and IK continue to be adopted and adapted and that economic conditions have changed.

Like members of the HFH, others in the movement look toward Africa to root their diasporan identities. Safia Rashid exemplifies this orientation stating,

> With me it primarily started from my work in the movement, Pan-African nationalist movement . . . I was thinking about "what can I contribute to this movement?" So it kinda came up because of the movement and saying, "What else can I do? What else can I contribute?"

Like Safia, who began her food work as an attempt to participate more fully in an ethnic renewal process, others re-Africanize through the local food movement. Food practices and Pan-African consciousness reinforce each other in the places of Chicago's Black food autonomy movement.

Importantly, many in the movement in Chicago emphasize "family" as a means to ethnic renewal and prosperity for themselves and their communities.

Children and elders can be seen at all the gardens, workshops, and markets that are the primary spaces of the movement. At the HFH children engage in numerous roles including as entrepreneurs, entertainers, and workers. Young children and teens often dance, play, and create music while the business of the market proceeds. They sell bean pies, popcorn, knitted items, pickles, hot sauce, teas, and other local, sustainably produced goods. Elders provide guidance, conversation, and love.

Mecca Brooks responded to well-worn stereotypes about Black people, nature, and sustainability. She wrote about the relationship between sustainability and her sense of self as a Black person. She recalls the stories of her grandmother that were lessons in energy and efficiency to point out that sustainability is not a new concept in the Black experience in the United States. After collecting stories, she concluded that "we can take ownership of our own work and at the same time provide access to the 'outside' about what it is we are doing to educate our young people." Like many in the Black food autonomy movement in Chicago, she reclaims her Blackness from Wetiko and remakes her identity through the Indigenous and diasporan BAT.[37]

Diaspora, Reindigenization, and Liberation

As a result of Wetiko's pressures, southern Blacks and Mexicanxs have had to move to different climes with different cultures. The cold, urban climates as well as commercial changes mean that strict adherence to IK is too distant from and unrealistic for our circumstances. In addition, as we assimilate aspects of the dominant culture and engage in exchange with one another, we change. Diaspora is an ever-changing process. Recognizing this helps movement members strategize about developing empowered identities that are a first step in establishing community solidarity, autonomy, and freedom.

Food autonomy spaces facilitate the development of a politicized diasporan identity rooted in reindigenization. Many reclaim an Indigenous African identity to achieve goals of autonomy and self-determination including the right to define their identity, culture, and religious beliefs. Food is obviously central to the survival of Indigenous people including those of the African diaspora and our cultures. Like the bison for the Lakota, manoomin (wild rice) for the Anishinaabe, and teosinte (corn) for Mesoamericans, food identifies people of the African diaspora. That these foods are grown and promoted in community gardens and the food autonomy movement means that African and Amerindigenous people and culture survive. Along with growing and distributing African heritage foods like greens, ngumbo (okra), and corn, members of the Black food autonomy movement further the process of diaspora and ethnic renewal and resistance by rein-venting and reproducing AHK. Diasporan identity work in the food autonomy movement promotes a radical subjectivity needed to combat racism and the various injustices of Wetiko and develop an African diasporan community based on Indigenous principles of reciprocity and respect for all our relations.

Kevin Triplett on Guerilla Gardening and the Gift Economy as Anticapitalist Solutions

Kevin has a consistent critique of the capitalist system and what ails us. He also sees the central role that food plays in our survival and in the coming revolution. As I discuss throughout this book, an analysis of capitalism is key to understanding the work that we need to do to solve the crises of food, climate, energy, and racism. However, our analysis of capitalism and colonialism is uneven and approached differently by movement participants. Kevin's analysis of capitalism and his application of communist ideas in the gardens is valuable to this project.

He started our taped dialogue on April 4, 2022, by discussing a recent war initiated

FIG. 12. Kevin Triplett. Photo by author.

when the Russian military invaded the Ukraine. The causes of this war are complex, important, and beyond the scope of this work. However, Kevin makes an important point that many of us in the food autonomy movement are beginning to understand. In this excerpt from our recorded dialogue, Kevin and I address the nature of revolutionary organization and how Marxist-Leninist-Stalinists see it differently than anarchists. These two groups have long quarreled over the proper organizational style for a revolution (centralization or decentralization) and for a new free and ecological society.

KT: That a place [Ukraine] can be talked about as the breadbasket of an entire continent shows you how the centralization of production is a danger. When I heard that I said, "Wow, Pancho would have a field day with this." The centralization of food production is an imperialist tool. No workers win from that. The planet does not win from the industrialization and centralization of food production. It is not a winning strategy for the human species.

PM: This had always been the beef between anarchists and Marxist-Leninists;

the question of centralization. Anarchists saying the Marxists want to centralize power in a party and that amounts to a state. And I know that the MLs (Marxist-Leninists) would argue with this, but the State is an instrument of coercion and can't be reformed. And that's why the ML version of organizing, of social organization, the centralization thing, is by its nature counterrevolutionary. I think that is the main issue that I see between anarchists and MLs.

KT: I can understand that stance, more now than I did before. There's always a balance that has to be struck between . . . , you know, people say, "If everyone is thinking the same, then no one is thinking." But, on the other hand, you can't have a million different ideas and think that they are all going to work. Because some of them are going to fail. You are not trying to compete with people. Part of cooperating is weeding out the things that we know don't work . . . There is going to be two steps forward and one step back. That is going to happen. There is no linear path toward utopia. We can have some centralized ideas about things: Racism is bad. Sexism is bad. Imperialism is bad. Harming the environment is bad. That's not group think. That's understanding.

PM: As an anarchist I am skeptical about attempts to centralize anything, but also as a permaculture designer, somebody who pays attention to how nature works, I recognize that nature is decentralized. That everything works. You have ecosystems that people fit into, plant people, insect people. People fit into different niches within the ecosystem. You know, not everyone is getting along in the ecosystem. But power is dispersed. I don't know that hierarchies really exist in nature. We project human hierarchies onto nature. You know, king of the jungle and all that kinda stuff. But there seems to be a much more cohesive, unified organization within nature. I see it that way and I know a lot of people, at least those that follow the permaculture that I do, see centralization of power as a problem.

KT: You have to keep thinking about what your relationship is to the factors of production. Because if you do not do that then you start to think that "I obviously know more than you." That doesn't matter. What is your relationship to the factors of production? I'm not saying that's all of it. But suppose you just keep asking that question. And in asking that it is not just what is your relationship to the land and or machinery. The other factor is what is your relationship to the other workers. How do you see them? That's the relationship that we need to talk about so that we are not alienated from one another.

PM: And you think that if we continue to ask that question that eventually we will get to the answer that we are all in this together because we are all working class folks?

KT: I think so but it's not that simple. That's a daily question.

PM: What about the question of race?

KT: Because we live in a racialized world, we can't ignore it. You can't ignore it in any place in the world. But I would still ask the question: What's your relationship to the factors of production? . . . So the question of race still comes back to the same thing. Am I dismissing people's cultural contributions? Nope. It's probably a good thing . . . But let's think about, not only the differences but the similarities. We live in a racialized world. In the United States anti-Black racism is terrible but anti-Indigenous racism is horrendous. We're talking about health outcomes, violence against women, all those measures are terrible. What do we get when we study a racialized world? We understand that imperialism has been devastating to everyone. Devastating! We don't ignore people's contributions, but we can't ignore that devastation of imperialism upon every single group you can name.

After discussing the current state of the world, especially as concerns BIPOC, we turned to discussing the project that he and I worked on together as part of the solution. When I asked him to talk about why he chose to initiate El Jardin Izquierdista, he emphasized land use, the reterritorialization of abandoned spaces of our city, and challenging capitalism through participating in a gift economy:

KT: Though we tried a little to go the legal route, what we did is expropriate this land and use it for, as you said, education for the people with whom you are dealing and then producing food and giving it away. There was never a farmers' market or any of that. There was food produced that was very, very locally distributed.

PM: Why is it important to give away as opposed to sell?

KT: I think it is important and not important. Because we live under capitalism, it is important to raise funds so we can do things. It is also important to give away to say, "Hey, the land is ours" and when I say "ours," I mean the collective, the community. "The land is ours therefore the fruits of what the land produces is also ours." And most of the stuff we distributed to senior citizens. Some of that is happenstance because that is what is in this neighborhood. And even that. Why are there only older people in this neighborhood? Well, that's the politics of racism. These black people got to be here in the late

1960s, early 1970s and their children and grandchildren did not have the same level of opportunities as when U.S. imperialism was on the rise. These people got to be teachers and postal workers and steel workers and stuff like that. So they were able to buy homes, and now they are in this neighborhood. This neighborhood is transitioning into being a Latinx neighborhood. Far more Latinx students at the school I teach, which is just a couple of miles away . . . That's that whole thing of two steps forward and one step back . . . I'm talking about the turnover, the gentrification, the elimination of the Black worker from homeownership.

We gave this stuff away to African American senior citizens. And the products that were made from them. We made pies from the squash and gave 'em away to African American senior citizens. Because that's who was right by us.

PM: When I describe to people what we were doing I say, "I have this friend Kevin. He lives next to this land. He took care of it for a while but then it became a hassle. He comes from a ML tradition. He saw the opportunity to teach people how to live differently. Kinda how we might be living in a communist society. The project was an example of how to do that." That's how I describe it and your motivation.

KT: I would say that is an accurate description of it. It's a laboratory of real practice. This is praxis right there. We took what they call private property and made it into something that was very public. Their paperwork, their understanding, that didn't matter to us. It was there, and we were going to use it for the good of the community. And it is interesting how . . . as it evolved and then taken back. It was taken back by the arm of the state. A person who knew the alderman, had funding, all of that. Think about how this . . . a microcosm of society. Who owned it? The state owned it. The state sold it to the Catholic Church. Then, the Catholic Church used state funds to pay young people to halfway put it together. The state stopped funding it, so then it goes into disrepair. Then, some private people try to take it over because they were going to be the real estate moguls, but that thing didn't work in this neighborhood, so then it reverted back to the arm of the state. The alderman's office takes it over. So it's the church. It's the state. It's all these things. It's happening right there. All the stuff that you read about in these history books and we're living right next to it.

PM: So, when I'm writing about it in the book so far, I say this is a great lesson in private property. That it can be taken you from you. No matter that we were doing a community good, an ecological service. It doesn't matter. We didn't have title. So I'm writing about it in that way, but it is good to hear about it from your perspective. I didn't know some of that. It is a microcosm. It is a model of all this theoretical stuff that we talk about relative to capitalism when we cite Marx. You can see it play out right there.

How do you feel about that project in general? I don't know that success and failure is the right terminology there. What do you think happened in those three years?

KT: I think what was important was the building of relationships that I saw there. And having an experience was so much a learning experience for me saying that this is what is possible. Even given what the limits are, we talked about private property. This is what is possible and how you can get people involved and how it can possibly be stronger if the people who were involved weren't so spread out from one another. I think that was it's one weakness. It didn't have as much local rooting as it probably should have. That's an organizing issue.

Say you took four square blocks, and you use that garden as a center to feed people. We are in a relative grocery desert over here. There is a Pete's Produce, but it is pretty small and it's expensive. Suppose you could figure how many people you can feed in this area. And to go beyond that with all these vacant houses and houses in disrepair. What if you trained people to fix houses in this area so that they can live in them. That's a way to fix urban blight that is not centralized. It's centralized to a small area, but it is not "Hey, Housing and Urban Development come help." I'm not saying those programs shouldn't exist. I'm saying they are not necessarily empowering for the people who live nearby. When shelter first had to be built, there was no centralized structure that was doing housing. It was whatever community people were in.

So I see it the same way with feeding people and housing in a neighborhood. That's how organizing needs to be done. That's how feeding people needs to be done. Of course, for the ecological reasons we discuss.

PM: How do you feel about what we did? There were really only a few people from the community that came out and worked and a few more got food. But in terms of organizing, it really wasn't. It was you going out and giving things away. They weren't involved in any way. What were your thoughts about that? Organizing people? What we did?

KT: I think we did what we could do. We tried handing out flyers. When people came by, we were very encouraging. We would say we are here at this time of day, and you are more than welcome to come. We put signs that said this is when we are here. There's no negative to that. It's just a matter of trying to do that and work a job or take care of a family. All those kinds of things. Those are things that happen when you are trying to be a revolutionary. There's no simple path to revolution.

PM: That's good. That's an important insight about why these things work or don't work or why they don't work as efficiently. It's an important insight to have about this system and how it makes this work very, very difficult. Once we figure out what the problem is then we can get to fixing it. Most of the time we don't even get to the point of understanding. We just get to blaming ourselves. We feel bad. We didn't put in the time. He didn't do what he was supposed to do or whatever. Instead of recognizing the limitations. That can be very valuable.

In this dialogue, Kevin and I discuss how we have identified capitalism as the system that causes the problems that are trying to address in the food movement. Ultimately, Kevin believes that nothing short of revolution will lead to justice, liberation, and the development of our full human potential. His perspective on this represents one of the major ways in which my camaradas in the movement approach our work.

Blackness, Ifá, and Liberation Struggles with Dr. Bonnie Harrison

Dr. Bonnie Claudia Harrison (Alalade Feyisara) is a confidant. I have known her for over twenty years, and our children are friends. We have worked together often. Her intellectual background as an activist-anthropologist working in the trenches at Chicago City Colleges positions her perfectly to be my sounding board and critic.

BH: I was not a food activist before I came to Kennedy-King. I was a social justice activist in general. I studied with Kwame Ture, Stokely Carmichael. I joined his All African People's Revolutionary Party, and I've worked with other people. I

FIG. 13. Dr. Bonnie Claudia Harrison. Photo by Blake Bonaparte.

worked with bell hooks just doing the kind of work that I do, which is hybrid identity, Blackness. One of the things I love to do the most is I like to look at and try to challenge people about what it means to be Black, what those values, behaviors, and beliefs are. One of my contentions is that most African Americans are really holding very tentatively to their Black heritage. They are not very clear what it means to be Black. Because it's hard to distinguish Blackness from "Americanness" in many ways cuz it's so folded in. Also, people are really taking American capitalist values as Black values. So there's a lot of loss of clarity about the struggle that is an African American struggle. And then, what is the larger social justice struggle that we are a part of? What will we stand for? What won't we stand for? Human rights? And then when we see other people's rights being violated, are we gonna stand up for them? Because that's really who we are. So we should not be standing for anybody's loss of human rights if we are standing for anything. Otherwise, we have lost our heritage. We have lost our struggle, and we're just trying to get ahead and consume goods and services and live the "good life" while other people suffer.

PM: I was writing about it from a colonial studies perspective. There are some people who say that everybody who is not Native is a settler. Other people say, "No, we have to be more subtle with these labels and understand that people are refugees, exiles, slaves." But then there becomes a point when those other groups take on settler values and settler ways. That was the language I was using yesterday.

BH: That's really illuminating because that's one of my goals: to more deeply understand the struggles of my allies . . . I find it so clarifying when I speak with an Indigenous person or an Indigenous activist, and they have a very different set of claims. That's really important especially for somebody like me who is a progressive and also very steeped in my tradition and my struggle and can take for granted that those are the same struggles.

The question is what would have happened if the colonial powers would have honored the treaties and honored their relationships instead of being bloodthirsty and lying thieves, murderers? Would there have been a natural human process of movement and migration? That is an important question to ask. People move around. Everybody comes out of Arica and moves around. On the other hand, I have to be very careful about how I treat my Indigenous heritage. I just wanna say I do want to talk about how I got into the food movement, but I wanna talk right now about my Indigenous heritage. As I was saying earlier, my grandpa . . . I was going to go to Africa and I was very excited about that and spent a lot of energy and time to get to Africa. I've been there three times to different places and felt very connected to what ends up being an ancestral homeland in Nigeria. But my grandfather always said, "I don't know anything about no Africa." He was notorious. He was a small man with a very big attitude, having shot at people. He was known as the Shotgun Man. He was very identified with his Indigenous identity. My grandfather along with his brother left Kentucky because they were aghast at the kinds of Jim Crow laws. He would say I have more of a right to go through the front door of this store than any of you people coming from the other side of the world. Because he identified with that, it's almost like, "You're a settler, and I'm Indigenous. I'm from here." He always said he was a colored man or Indigenous. Most of the photos of him are doing the sort of Western [crosses arms in stereotypical fashion] version on a painted horse with his arms across his chest . . . Where is he coming from with that? Most of my family their favorite shows are Westerns. This is their idea of indigeneity. Really, they are mulattos is what they are. They are a high mix of Indigenous, African, and European. They're really triguenos . . . tres raices. There's a lot of colorism.

I looked at one of my cousins and said, "You're so lucky. You're half black and half Puerto Rican." She looked at me and said, "Yo no soy negro." I'm not black. What are you talking about?" So that's what my master's thesis is about. How my cousin could reject blackness. So I thought my family just didn't want to be black . . . We are from a county in Kentucky, which is on the Trail of Tears.

Dr. Harrison and I have had numerous conversations over the years about her perspective on race, which comes from her complicated family history. Later, in the dialogue we pick up the thread of race through the issue of gender and politics.

BH: I was a punk rocker in school. In a sociological analysis of personality, I am a straight-up rebel . . . I wanted to change the world . . . I've been an activist since I was twelve . . .

Let me explain to you how hard it is to be a Black woman in leadership. That's not what people see me as. They don't see me as a leader. That is the last thing they think of. They think I'm the washer woman or, you know, I'm the cleaning lady or the caterer. They don't think "this lady is gonna lead us and we're gonna win." It's a very interesting road. I was very bitter about it for a long time. Now it's my secret weapon. They don't see me coming. They never know. I am a general. People don't recognize me as that, but that's what I do . . . I believe that is what I was trained to do. I believe that's what I'm doing. It's a campaign. It's a series of campaigns to win the war for survival.

PM: When you say this was a series of campaigns, are you seeing this as an extension of these earlier campaigns that you were a part of that are an extension of Black liberation struggles?

BH: Absolutely. Except for concretely I'm not just a Black person. I've been saying this for years. I'm blacker than most people and less Black than everybody. I don't fit the category.

PM: Knowing that about you, then, where do you say you fit what you have been doing? I'm saying that what we are a part of is the Black liberation struggle. Maybe it is more than that. What is it?

BH: I think it is self-evident, and I would be doing my ancestors a disservice if I didn't call it part of the Black liberation struggle. Let's be clear about that. Let's be real. Who do I come from?

From the cradle, I was raised in Black liberation struggles. So I must give them their due. You and I have this conversation about transcending categories that were handed to us by a colonial settler-capitalist system. I believe in that hybrid model of anti-antiessentialism. If it serves me to step away from that model, then I'm going to step away from that model. At some point, what struggle isn't limited by its own theology. I wanna win. I want Black people, etc. to be free. I wanna be free of this colonial system. I wanna be free of racism and sexism and White male supremacy. I'm tired of ableism and homophobia and transphobia.

PM: Is there a political label that you can put on that. As opposed to say Black liberation or Black nationalism?

BH: Socialist, democratic socialist. I'm not a sociologist or political scientist in that sense. What do you see?

PM: OK. This is important to me too. The last chapter of the book is trying to fuse these different traditions. Trying to see what are the things that we can learn from one another. What are the things that we have in common? What is fundamental to these struggles? So I'm thinking the Black agrarian struggle/Black freedom struggles, Indigenous . . .

BH: I'm a freedom fighter. That would be my label. Don't out me. Part of my strength is looking goofy and not being taken seriously. I believe in human freedom.

PM: I wonder if part of the limitations of political thought is that we are always putting labels on things. I am seeing so many similar things . . . I'm like you. I'm looking at hybridity quite a lot over my career and my life. I always talk about the limits we place on ourselves. You know, Chicanos are this, and it means you do certain kinds of things and if you don't, then you are not that. There are always these separations. So I'm trying to put together . . . what are the theories and practices of Black liberation struggles that people are using and that we can use to further our goals? And what are the Indigenous focus? What comes from an anarchist focus? Where can we see those in dialogue?

Part of the problem is the labels. I know most people who have these radical politics, who say they are freedom fighters and who would say "No, I'm not any of that. No, that doesn't define me." And have trouble putting a label on it. And maybe that's just what scholars do is try to put labels on stuff. I'm trying to say that these are the different political traditions that I do and see people doing around me in this part of the struggle in Chicago.

Dr. Harrison, like many of us, continues to develop a personal and spiritual relationship to the land. The seeds planted early in her life by her elders have been bearing fruit in her quest to be free and connected. Her ability to see past religious dogma and embrace the spiritual truths of various religions and the truly spiritual people who practice them began as a child seeing her uncle welcome people of different religions to his land. She recognizes that land-based spiritual traditions, no matter where in the world they come from, have some fundamental things in common. To me, she reflects the "eco-womanism" at the heart of our movement. She hopes to continue to build bridges between spiritual communities using her platforms including developing CoGro into a place for spiritual healing. We discussed the relationship between White Supremacy and colonialism and the deep historical and ongoing trauma found in BIPOC communities. Importantly, we don't stop at lamenting our misfortune at being colonized and racialized, but also focus on creating spaces for reindigenization.

BH: Being on the land allows me to practice my alternative vision of reality. I'm a utopianist and believe in a kind of social utopia. That it is possible. I know it is difficult and may take generations to achieve. I want to name this part of the world Earthseed as a new beginning.

Spirituality for me in many ways is a rebellion against the world that I was raised in; a very Christian world that I don't sit well with because it is the infrastructure of a world that doesn't see me as worthy or as worthwhile. The practice of this spirituality doesn't make a lot of sense to me; sitting in church trying to understand this theology that seems very hypocritical and strange and bent around and twisted around. Don't get me wrong, I respect Christianity. I learn from Christianity. Jesus is a cool dude [black power fist]. I literally had a conversation when I was eight years old . . . "This is our work but not in the church. You are supposed to be doing the work of your ancestors." Jesus told me to do my ancestor work. If I told this to my family, they would freak out. "You can't talk about Jesus like that." My experience of the world is one of magic from seed to spirit, seeing, feeling, doing, hearing, and seeking magic and transformation and elevation and healing. It's a really hard search cuz the world that we live in tries to take everything like it takes everything else. It tries to take from you, extract from you and use your spiritual energy for the production of other people's happiness, to make you into a slave.

My aunt is conflicted over Christianity and Indigenous spirituality, but my grandfather had no problem. He also practiced Yoruba and didn't have a problem. Why? Cuz both are land-based traditions. He would have Haitian voodoo people and Yoruba people come do their work on his land. Because primarily when you are doing this work with Yoruba and Haitian voodoo (I'm not an expert on voodoo, but I believe) you are addressing the earth. If you are doing a ritual, you are speaking to the earth. And if you don't speak to the earth, then you are not doing the work. A lot of people don't even know that. It is about who you are talking to or who has to witness your work. You may be talking to particular orishas and energies. The energy of Ogun, which is for me, and this is not orthodox, is gravity and Shango is lighting. The energy of that . . . Pulling back is Ogun and pushing forward is Shango. That is physics. What is physics but what we see and interact with the natural world.

My name, Alalade Feyisara, means the dreamer who pleases her mother and who is bonded to. The mother is the earth and my ancestral mothers. So that's my thing. I envision the next best thing. I see that things can be better. I see that Black people have a liberation theology, a liberation practice, but it takes the poets, art, creativity.

PM: One of the major themes that is coming up in this new way of thinking about activism and organizing is dealing with trauma and all of this self-care stuff. I find a lot of people use it in ways that are gross; just using it as an excuse to consume. "I'm going to take a break from all of this organizing and I'm going to go to the spa and get my nails done or spend a ton of money. I'm going to fly across the world, go to a beach somewhere." It seems very hypocritical and short-sighted. And more than short-sighted, it is voluntarily ignorant. People like to do a lot of high-performance, very dramatic organizing, a lot of events, fighting the police, doing those kinds of things. And I get that they are doing important stuff. They are falling apart like the rest of us are cuz they are working hard and not getting respect and stuff like that. So they go and they consume. And they don't connect what they are doing with the suffering of other people on the planet. And just looking like, this gets to the settler part. It looks like what settlers do. You go to other countries. You get someone else to do the work for you, and you live lavishly. And they call that self-care. That is an extreme kind of example of that behavior, but I just don't' see that as revolutionary. But because I have a bias. I grew up in a Marxist Chicano type of thing. We didn't talk about none of that shit, no self-care, none of that. What the fuck you talking about? We talked about our battle scars, and we fought them and all that. We don't self-care or none of that shit. So I get that that macho patriarchal shit is a problem. So I'm willing to entertain that the idea that I have of self-care is wrong cuz I can see where that masculinity and patriarchal stuff can creep in there. At the same time, I think I'm smart enough to understand healing and those kinds of things are necessary for our communities, so I can't figure out where the disconnect is with that word "self-care." Certainly, healing and all of that seems to be so central to what people are doing and I think in a good way it has to be talked about. bell hooks's love stuff and adrienne maree brown's new stuff or a lot of what I see the kids doing, this new generation of activists getting into their feelings and getting real with themselves and one another. There is some good stuff in there. I don't know how to get into that. I'm still trying to get into the herbs, you know, and getting right with the soil and the earth. I wanna talk about the trauma piece and the healing and what does that look like in your work.

BH: I'm glad you are willing to recognize your bias. What is it that our ancestors did for self-care? I think that's a really good model for us. For me as a person who practices an ancestral traditional religion. So when you were talking about getting on an airplane, people getting on an airplane and then spending money to have somebody else take care of them. I think the problem with that is that I see very clearly that self-care is community care . . . I was in a group . . . She had each of us sit back to back, and we did a meditation on holding one another up . . . I wonder if there aren't these kinds of somatic practices . . . This land that we are on one of our objectives, one of our missions is have people be able to come here and rest from their work. To enjoy nature, to go to Oshun, the river here, and have a restorative experience. It's a midterm goal. Have people be able to come and stay, declutter their lives, their minds. One of the primary goals of this property, CoGro, is to be a spiritual retreat. We have the extractive model of pleasure: taking away and consuming instead of giving and sharing. It speaks to our individualism. It speaks to maybe we need labels because we have a tribal mindset that puts us in a tribe. We are ailing and suffering from this individualism. There is something missing in that model of self-care . . .

Dr. Bonnie's thoughts on Africanity, spirituality, and social movements provides a useful segue into the discussion of spirituality as a key component of our movement. Her discussion of her struggles with race, Christianity, and colonialism provides valuable insight into these areas of conflict within our movement. Each of the dialogues that constitute the next chapter illustrate the various ways in which my camaradas in the movement navigate the treacherous waters of religion, spirituality, politics, and economics.

CHAPTER 7

A Sustainable Spirituality
OUR COMMUNITY SPEAKS ON FOOD AND SPIRIT

Sowing Sacred Greens

In January 2013, Jacqueline Smith and I, representing the Green Lots Project (GLP), met with Corey Buchanan and Dan Swets of Chicagoland Prison Outreach to discuss our partnership. They owned a large lot that included two very large growing beds. We spoke about how GLP would manage the lot and CPO would support in whatever ways they could. Interestingly, though, we spent most of the meeting discussing the goals and values of our two organizations and trying to find common cause so that we might work together. Upon reflection about our meeting, Ms. Smith and I realized that GLP and CPO felt a calling toward empowering community and building individual capacity.

At the first workday of the season, I explained to the teenage volunteers from Dayton Christian School that as urban growers and Indigenous people we know that land is sacred. That which provides life is worthy of reverence and care. Ultimately, as community gardeners with an Indigenous ecological view, we accept responsibility for the relationships that we have in the garden space and beyond. In the garden the relationships that I have with all my relations and those that they have with one another create interdependence. It has become my responsibility and privilege to be a good caretaker and to provide ecological services. In return I and other growers get to disconnect from Wetiko's soul-crushing and engage directly with soil and life-affirming processes. We know and constantly reiterate that all those life-affirming processes (sowing, planting, saving seed, having conversations, etc.) encourage a more-than-human community to develop. This community of interdependent relations bonds together through sacred rituals that take place throughout the season. Moreover, I explained, we live and work in Roseland, a Black American community. Greens play a significant role in the Black American diet and, importantly, though not always discussed, due to their high micronutrient and other nutrition content, can be credited with the survival of many in the Black diaspora. We wanted to acknowledge that this was an African garden and to exalt the often-maligned greens to their proper place in history. In addition, the garden is on the property of an organization with a Christian ministry that teaches formerly incarcerated men and women job skills while also engaging in Bible study and reflection.

For us, then, the name Sacred Greens Community Garden encapsulated a lot about how we thought of our work and our relationship to CPO. With the name Sacred Greens, we celebrated and committed to our place, our community and its food traditions, our spiritual worldviews, our guidance from the land and our culture. For me, as a Chicano anarchist, I felt that searching for and being guided by my connections to all my relations was a revolutionary methodology. If the colonizers always attack Native spirituality, then it must somehow be revolutionary. I became convinced, like Indigenous theologian George Tinker "that our American Indian image of the sacred can have potent and liberating political and social consequences, just as much as the colonizers' image of God has served historically to constantly reinforce and undergird the colonizers' control and domination in the world."[1]

My associations with the Black food movement strengthened my feeling that a place-based, earth-based spirituality is necessary in our quest for self-determination. This chapter presents the thoughts of some of my accomplices. The variety of land-based spiritualities among Black people in the food autonomy movement, while diverse, are means of connection since they share several principles whether Buddhist or Hindu,[2] Ifá or other Afrikan-based spiritual system, Muslim or Christian. These shared principles have been described as "an eco-spiritual worldview" that results from centuries of keen observation and understanding of the natural world.

> African peoples have through the centuries lived by farming, stock keeping, hunting and fishing, as well as by food gathering in some cases. Many rituals have been evolved to cover all these means of livelihood, incorporating what people believe, the values they attach to those activities and the right procedures or behavior required for making them run smoothly.[3]

Their commitment to peaceful coexistence rooted in African heritage knowledge (AHK) and intimate relationships with all our relations suggest an interdenominational Black environmental liberation theology/spirituality (BELT/S).

The development of BELT/S is rooted in the land-based spiritual systems of ancient and precolonial Africa. Penniman explains that, for example, "in Yoruba religion, nature is regarded as a divinity, and all plants, animals, and landforms have intrinsic value as Sacred Forces of Nature."[4] This orientation toward all our relations requires profoundly different behavior toward life than found in most of what we call Christianity. It requires that we care for the earth, not exploit it. As explained by Yeye Luisah Teish,

> All of the Orisas are associated with certain places in nature, and this gives worshippers a responsibility to that aspect of nature. I must go to the river respectfully,

make offerings, clean up the trash on the riverbank, and pay homage through ritual, because that is the body of my mother Osun.[5]

The "liberation" part of BELT/S comes directly from the Americas as New World Africans came to terms with enslavement, oppression, and estrangement from nature. Black preachers used the stories of Moses and the liberation of the Jews from their Roman oppressors and pointed to Jesus's work among the poor and marginalized as a means for understanding the violent circumstances thrust upon them by their enslavement and for uplift through developing an identity as God's chosen. Essentially, "slaves revolutionized the slave master's religion into a belief system that served, in Howard Thurman's words, 'the poor, the disinherited, the dispossessed.'"[6] James Cone in his influential set of books from the late 1960s and early 1970s first systematized an understanding of Christianity that put Black people at the center. He argued that Christianity is Black and is a liberation theology adhering to the Bible's continuous and consistent preference for the poor.

> Christian theology is a theology of liberation. It is *a rational study of the being of God in the world in light of the existential situation of an oppressed community, relating the forces of liberation to the essence of the gospel, which is Jesus Christ.* This means that its sole reason for existence is to put into ordered speech the meaning of God's activity in the world, so that the community of the oppressed will recognize that its inner thrust for liberation is not only *consistent with* the gospel but *is* the gospel of Jesus Christ. There can be no Christian theology that is not identified unreservedly with those who are humiliated and abused.[7]

Cone argues convincingly that Christianity is a religion of liberation, and that this interpretation of Christianity comes from canonical sources. He argues that "it is indeed the *biblical* witness that says that God is a God of liberation."[8] The Bible itself provides ample evidence for an argument of liberation and an interpretation of Jesus's resurrection as meaning that "the human being no longer has to be a slave to anybody but must rebel against all principalities and powers which make human existence subhuman."[9] Rebellion against illegitimate authority, that mantra of anarchists, decolonialists, and slave rebels, is according to Cone justified and encouraged in the Bible and the Christian tradition more generally. He even goes so far as to say that the state itself is the arbiter of violence and as such "is responsible for human enslavement and is thus the enemy of all who strive for human freedom."[10]

Cone and many after have seen an ecological liberation inherent in Christianity that gets buried under Wetiko. Cone's worked paved the way for a variety of "liberation" theologies, and later in his career he championed an ecological perspective:

People who fight against white racism but fail to connect it to the degradation of the earth are anti-ecological-whether they know it or not. People who struggle against environmental degradation but do not incorporate in it a disciplined and sustained fight against white supremacy are racists—whether they know it or not. The fight for justice cannot be segregated but must be integrated with the fight for life in all its forms.[11]

BELT/S is "a strand of black liberation theology" connected to Dr. King's final campaign fighting alongside the Memphis sanitation workers striking for better wages and improvement of environmentally hazardous working conditions. Black Americans concern for what we now call environmental racism is as old as slavery in the United States.[12] The aftermath of the civil rights movement and the grass-roots activism of Black working-class people throughout the southern Black Belt regarding toxic waste-dumping and other environmental concerns[13] led to the active engagement of the United Churches of Christ and Rev. Benjamin Chavis, whose 1987 study of environmental racism began to make it and environmental justice common concerns. Since then, many church leaders have turned their so-cial and theological efforts toward an environmental liberation theology. BELT/S, like Cone's and others' liberation theology, relies on a very different interpreta-tion of scripture than Wetiko's Christianity. Instead of focusing on the hierarchical and anthropocentric aspects of the Bible, BELT/S places emphasis on liberatory and biocentric stories, parables, and interpretations. Commonly, the Adam and Eve story is interpreted as granting humans domination over the rest of creation. However, a BELT/S interpretation shows Adam and Eve entering into a covenant with God for which in return for their ability to manipulate nature humans were responsible for stewarding all our relations. God commands humans to care for nature, not destroy it.

Importantly for this study of the food autonomy movement in Black Chicago, BELT/S sees the appropriate theology today as one of action. Thus, Glave proposes a "fifteen-point environmental justice agenda." Among the points that resonate with our work in Chicago are "self-sufficiency and autonomy in African Ameri-can communities," teaching the history of the Black church, the civil rights move-ment and environmental justice, creating coalitions "with other ethnic churches," modeling selfless Christian service, and "train[ing] many new leaders." While not always as radical as Glave asserts is necessary, many of my Christian-identified ac-complices engage in these practices and through their example have been incorpo-rated in the practices of GLP and many others.[14]

BELT/S resonates with eco-womanism. BELT/S comes directly from a Black environmental justice and Christian worldview, whereas eco-womanism comes from the wide variety of land-based spiritualities or "earth-honoring faiths" practiced by African women. Alice Walker's womanism is the basis for understanding the complexity and depth of Black women's experiences, understanding and interactions with all our relations. Michelle L. Harris summarizes womanism thusly: 1) "the first part [of the definition] identifies womanist with black feminism and feminisms of color"; 2) along with supporting "the love shared between women, sexual and nonsexual. This [second] part of the definition also celebrates the love shared between women and men, sexual and nonsexual"; 3) "a womanist 'loves the Spirit'" along with and inseparable from "nature and the cosmos," and, additionally, a womanist "*loves herself regardless*" of how others or "society" feels about her; 4) womanism is intersectional as it does not simply focus on "women's issues" but also on race, class, sexuality, and religious difference.[15]

From womanism, it is a small step to eco-womanism. Parts two and three of Walker's definition point directly to the more-than-human concerns of African women's spiritual traditions. Eco-womanism describes and theorizes a complex biological and spiritual world with profound and incalculable interconnections. Like all Indigenous religious systems, all our relations play determining roles in African eco-womanist thought and life. It also emphasizes the liberatory role that spirituality can play. Eco-womanism is a

> critical reflection, contemplation, and praxis-oriented study of environmental justice from the perspectives of women of color and particularly women of African descent. It links a social justice agenda with ecojustice, recognizing the parallel oppressions that women of color have often survived when confronting racism, classism, sexism, heterosexism, and similar oppressions that the earth is facing through environmental degradation.[16]

Eco-womanist praxis involves seven steps. Many can be found in the work and lives of the African diasporan women I work with and study under and my Indigenous Chicana mentors and family members. In addition, I hope that some of this method and praxis are used properly in this study to not use women's knowledge as a springboard for male advancement but as a means toward liberation work. Eco-womanists mine eco-memory and honor the counternarratives of Black women and other women of color and critically analyze them. In the food movement, women analyze the world not just as women but as Black, working- or middle- class, straight, queer, or two-spirited, Christian, or Indigenous African religious adherents. In other words, they experience the world intersectionally. Womanists also gain insight from African history, culture, and tradition. With memories, intersectional analysis, and grounding in African cultural understanding, womanists are then compelled to act on behalf of African liberation and the restoration of harmony, balance, and peace to all our relations.[17] Many of my accomplices exemplify this eco-womanist orientation. Ms. Thomas's insistence on growing African and Black American crops, Mama Safia Rashid's grounding in Pan-Africanism, and Dr. Mila Marshall's insistence on knowledge sharing and creation exhibit a womanist sankofa, reaching back to African traditions, history, and experience as a means to create an African future.

In our taped conversation, Jacqueline Abena Smith described the complexity and relationship between her emerging African-based spirituality and BELT/S. She briefly described her morning routine involving prayer, meditation, and plants. She told me, "First thing when I wake up in the morning, I am doing something [related to gardening] after I pray and meditate. Sometimes I don't even pray or meditate. I just do something with the plants." Ms. Smith experienced Christian spirituality as a biocentric, nature-loving connection to all our relations. She rejected interpretations of the Genesis story that emphasize God's words to Adam as meaning we should dominate and control "every wild beast of the field and every flying creature of the heavens" (Gen. 2:16). Instead, she understood the story to be a directive from God for us to be good stewards of the land. This BELT/S interpretation of Christian doctrine allowed Ms. Smith to see the connection between all our relations and the divine in all living things. Thus, time spent with plants and soil and insects is prayer and ceremony. Her ability to steward nature was a sacred gift that she connected to her ancestors and to the Spirit. Ms. Smith's journey from a Black American Christian perspective on the divine and spirituality based in the United Churches of Christ liberation theology at Trinity United where she was baptized by preeminent liberation theologian, Rev. Jeremiah Wright, and oriented toward the land-based African spirituality of Ifá, which serves as a metaphor for the interdenominational BELT/S that I witness in the Black food movement in Chicago and elsewhere. For Ms. Smith the "conversion" was smooth and natural. Her relatively easy transition to Ifá provided few, if any, mental, emotional, or spiritual problems since in her experience there were no hard and fast lines between her BELT/S Christianity and African-based religions. These different religions share a great deal regarding nature if we allow for BELT/S interpretation of the Bible.

Carolyn Thomas and God's Gang came directly out of a grassroots group of Black Catholic women, many who were postal workers. God's Gang is a social justice organization that uses food as a means of resistance beginning from a Christian principle of "brotherly/sisterly love." The origin story of God's Gang is a lesson in the importance of listening to youth and intergenerational relations as key to justice and resurgence. Ms. Thomas's son insisted on breaking down barriers between the "church kids" and the kids from the neighborhood projects who felt a distinct class difference. The neighborhood kids didn't want to have anything to do with the church kids, who were seen as just coming in on Sundays, having a good time, showing off and then leaving. Ms. Thomas's son wanted to break through a class barrier and expand and strengthen his friendships. They began with breakdancing, which was a "no-no" in the Church at the time according to Ms. Thomas. They then developed a breakfast program, an "adopt-a-grandparent" program, a library, and a dance team among other programs. They soon moved into aquaponics, vermicomposting, and horticulture. They led the youth charge in environmental justice in Chicago for several years based on a Christian-liberation orientation.

As explored more extensively in the final chapter, most Indigenous thought finds Christianity irredeemable. Christians took our land, clothes, language, and other lifeways. As I initially wrote these words in late 2021, more than 750 grave sites filled with more than 7,000 native children kidnapped from their homes and held as prisoners of colonial war in "residential schools" in Canada and the United States had been uncovered. Their Christianity is a colonizing, enslaving religion. Additionally, many "traditional" Indigenous people have problems with passages such as John 3:16 ("God so loved the world that he gave his only begotten son"). This "love for the world" "refers only to the world of human beings. God's salvific act in Christ Jesus is thought of as efficacious only for human beings." Humans begin to see ourselves in hierarchical relation to God, existing just below Him in the hierarchy of life. Our anthropocentrism seems to know no bounds as we even attribute humanlike qualities to God. For Christians, "human beings are significantly privileged over against the rest of creation."[18] How could it possibly be a religion of liberation? Christianity, even in its most liberatory versions, fails to examine the unnatural anthropocentrism of its views of life, spirituality, god, and the supernatural.

Native writers and thinkers show that instead of the individual, hierarchically ordered human detached from the rest of Creation our world rests on balance, harmony, interrelatedness, respect, and reciprocity. Generations of observation of the natural world led most Indigenous peoples to see the spirit force, god, or the Creator as manifest in a multitude of mundane everyday acts and experiences of all our relations. Everything is interconnected and this knowledge spurs acts of reciprocity and respect that lead to balanced, harmonious societies, ecosystems, and bioregions. Tinker sees the human arrogance, greed, and individualism that mark Wetiko society as stemming from the European, Judeo-Christian understanding of god, the spirit, and our relationships to one another. This religious perspective has led to the current abuses of Mother Earth and the continued violence against all our relations. The same perspective that abuses Mother Earth that has led to the climate, energy, and food crises leads to social injustice such as that suffered by native peoples the world over. Moreover, as Indigenous people, we continue to experience violence meted out against natives by White Christians and their White supremacist interpretation of the Bible that they use to justify it. So I and many of those with whom I work in the food movement have generally negative feelings about Christianity and seek out opportunities to enhance our Indigenous spiritual understanding.

For other of my accomplices, religion and spirituality are secondary or non-existent factors in their work. Safia Rashid rejects "religion" and "spirituality" as concepts because they are inadequate to explain her relationship to the land. Yet she and her family participate in spiritual rituals on their land and with their urban growing community to connect themselves to their African diasporan traditions, to the land they work, play, and pray on, and the community that sustains them.[19] The subject didn't come up during my conversations with most of my male accomplices. I asked Austin Wayne about it, and he said that it was too personal of a subject to discuss. My conversation with Dr. Mila Marshall kept to the academic and scholarly, but I know her to be a spiritual person and devotee and teacher of yoga. Interestingly, she discussed with me how she came to a spiritual understanding of the land through her scientific training and examination:

MM: My own spirituality has kept me. If I could ask god anything, Can I get on your shoulders and watch you make this world in present day? The reality is we're more than able . . . and we've been around and we have night and day and we have balance and all these things have DNA, just different letters that turn you from a person to a pig. Or you cut out a bone, and you cut a tree and it's that same pattern. We're connected in such an amazing reality to know that I'm 80 percent water. I can't live without it.

That came from science but the understanding of what I am, right. I have opposable thumbs. So does a gorilla. Similarities and dissimilarities that have been proved through science.

PM: But what makes that spiritual?

MM: It makes it spiritual because I can't explain it. I get into these conversations about evolution where we're taught not to challenge someone's religion, but also I'm a firm believer in god and science has been used against god in many different ways to control the options that we have in our lives. So I understand that people are extremely distrustful of science. Scientific chauvinists pick and choose when and what they believe . . . But then I think he is like "Watch me work. I made a single-cell organism and life comes from life and it gets more complex and then it gets more interesting and it gets more intelligent." And we can trace that. And things go in cycles. It is so perfect.

Many of our practices in our food movement show that spirituality and religion can be armed for our defense. Religion/spirituality does not have to be "like the opiate of the masses" as Marx and my ML (Marxist-Leninist) friends would deride them. Many scholars and activists show how our relationship to the spirit world and the fundamental questions of creation can be used to liberate. Those of us who are reindigenizing recognize the power of land-based spiritual systems. The eco-womanist praxis of most of my women accomplices in the movement show how our Indigenous religions/spiritualities remain fundamental sources for the resurgence of our people, which amounts to a revolution against Wetiko and for our self-defined humanity (to paraphrase the Zapatistas).

A Theology of Abandoned Lots

My place-based spiritual understanding, like much else, has solidified and deep-ened in the urban oases of South Side Chi by way of Mexican Catholicism, rituals in my grandpa's garden, Arizona sweat lodges, and anarchist religious skepticism. My experiences in Chicago's Black food autonomy movement have led me to what Gregory Cajete calls "a theology of place." While the abuses of Christianity drove me away from religion, the land brought me to spirituality and a recognition of the sacredness and connectedness of life—a "spiritual ecology." The South Side of Chicago, particularly the Roseland neighborhood, in all its beauty and decay taught me, like my traditionalist ancestors and elders, not only about the sanctity of all our relations but also about how I perceive myself and my relation to all else.[20] Driving or, better yet, biking through Roseland, the death and disease of Wetiko, illuminates our path with gaudy neon signs advertising alcohol, fried fast food, and sugary drinks. The broken streets and abandoned buildings provide the perfect backdrop for the spiritual death that accompanies displacement.

Under these circumstances it is hard not to adopt the spiritual death of Wetiko. Much easier it is to accept separation and alienation from ourselves and nature. Easier to pursue material comfort than personal and community health and spir-itual growth. Much easier it is to burn carbon than to regenerate our soils, lots, and communities. Yet if you spend enough time, pay enough attention, and ask the right questions, Roseland (and the rest of the South Side) will speak to you differently. Urban wildlife, native plants, and children and elders have deep-rooted knowledge that they will share. Learning the lessons of place requires patience and respect for all our relations.

The work of Bee Rodriguez and Reclaiming Our Roots based in Gage Park ex-emplifies how abandoned lots can be turned into sacred spaces of reindigeniza-tion and reconnection to all our relations. In the Reclaiming Our Roots garden, the young Chicanx land stewards created spaces for spiritual development. In the center of the garden, they built a temezcal/innipi/sweat lodge as a sacred space for doing our decolonial, reindigenization work. The temezcal

> is the representation of the womb of the Great Mother, our Mother Tonantzin Tlalli. It is also a reproduction of the cosmos . . . It offers the opportunity to see our conception and the possibility of rebirth and growth within the cosmos.[21]

In the temezcal, purifying and other medicinal herbs are used to assist us during the healing work that involves "unifying bodymindspirit."[22] In the temezcal, we seek an ecstasy that comes from "the sensation of being held, loved, advised, connected."[23] Through openness, honesty, and vulnerability, temezcalerxs open decolonial healing spaces that offer the possibility of connection to ourselves, one another, and all our relations. In the movement, we increasingly create opportunities for spiritual growth in our gardens and other spaces.

Below is further examination of the question of the Spirit in the words of some of my accomplices.

Jacqueline A. Smith

GROWING AS SPIRITUAL STEWARDSHIP

JS: My paternal great-grandmother, her name was Callie Glover . . . her children after her and her grandchildren after her did not take to growing food because of the Great Migration from the South to the North. They weren't really interested in growing food anymore or tending to anyone's land anymore. Industrial jobs were big. There was more money. They were more lucrative. It was a new way of life for my family. So they decided, I guess, that they weren't really interested in tending the land. I knew my Great Grandmother. I knew her but she passed away in 90 or 91. She was one hundred years old. I knew her but I wasn't old enough to ask her questions about what she did, how she took care of almost twenty people in a shotgun house and tended to the land, grew hogs, slaughtered the hogs, had a smokehouse, had chickens running all over the place and she would wring their necks and pluck their feathers and have it for dinner later on that night. She was very sustainable in what she did. Everything that the family ate came out of the ground. Only things she had to buy was flour and oats and maybe sugar . . . I think that's commendable. And I want to keep her legacy alive with GrowAsis [Ms. Smith's garden consulting business]. It's not even about GrowAsis at this point. It's about doing what's right because we don't have a lot of land left to grow on. I take land stewardship very seriously. I believe that's one of the most sacred and just things you can do as a human being living on earth . . .

   I believe that there is a force, a spirit, that is greater than us that created this earth and the heavens, the universe, the land and the sea and has given life and has given the opportunity to steward the land. Not dominate it and not exploit it but be co-stewards and take care of the animals and the insects and the seeds of original plant species. It's a spiritual thing to me to grow food on a mass scale or even a small scale. It's my purpose. It's my mission in life. I eat it. I breathe it. I sleep it. I dream it. I talk about it almost every day. First thing when I wake up in the morning I am doing something after I pray and meditate. Sometimes I don't even pray or meditate. I just do something with the plants. I'm growing cucumbers in my room right now.

FIG. 14. Sharon and Tommy Smith pose with painting of daughter, Jacqueline Smith. Stewart painted the photo of Smith. Photo by Tafari Melisizwe and Marilyn Stewart.

In her food work, Ms. Smith employed IK. She used heirloom seed, complimentary planting, raised beds/mounds, biological pest management related techniques. She explained her position:

> JS: Just because it is organic doesn't mean that it's sustainable. It could be a monocrop such as corn, a tomato, or what have you. It could be grown organically but where does the seed come from? Then, you have to talk about GMOs and the pesticides and the killing of the insects such as the monarch butterfly and the bumble bee and other pollinators that help make food what it is. Without them it can't happen. I can't do what I need to do if I don't have any insects. Although they are ugly and we don't like them and they are creepy crawly, they serve a purpose just like everything else that walks the earth.
>
> Permaculture, permaculture design, is involved in that. That's basically working with the natural resources of the earth. You work with what is already there in the earth. You don't make it work around you. You work around it. You're a steward. You're a co-steward in permaculture. It's sustainable. You don't add a lot of outside inputs. Not a lot of outside factors. In permaculture you work with what's there. It works with the community.

It works with the environment because it helps with the development of ecosystems . . . It's all connected . . . It's a means of Nature, Mother Nature, Mama Nature, as I call her, to teach us how we're supposed to treat the earth. In many cases, how we're supposed to treat one another because we are of the earth, but we don't treat the earth as such, we don't treat one another as such and we don't treat ourselves as such. We don't treat ourselves well. We don't treat one another well, and we don't treat the earth well. I think permaculture is a sustainable way of letting us know how we're supposed to function in the world.

"That's When the Peace Comes In"

PAULA ANGLIN AND TRINITY UNITED'S
GEORGE WASHINGTON CARVER GARDEN

Community is a common and controversial concept. It can refer to an insular and defensive means of defining us versus them. In social justice circles, including the food autonomy groups with whom I participate in Chicago, we use community to mean people who share our racial identity. In my food community, a variety of Black nationalism and Pan-Africanism influences our understanding of the term. In other instances, community refers to a geographic location whose boundaries are carefully policed. We often define, debate, and redefine community and who constitutes its members. Paula Anglin emphasizes her church community at Trinity United Church of Christ but also includes the surrounding geographic community, which she has gotten to know through her participation in the garden. She explains community in our taped conversation.

PA: A man came by here one day. He said, "In the summer I eat totally out of the garden." That's all he does. So this man came by, and he wanted to come in to have a tour. Everybody was astonished that you can grow grapes in Chicago and peaches or whatever. Watermelon. And this guy came in. I think he mighta done a little work. I think he did more talking than working, but he came in for a while. When it was time for him to go, he grabbed the lemon balm and he did like this [makes rubbing motion on armpits, chest, and neck]. And went on his way. We just kinda looked at each other. Cuz I never knew. I knew about mint. I thought, "OK." But, you know, they use lemon balm in perfumes. And, guess what, the extract of lemon balm is better than valium.

PM: Is that right? It mellows you right out. I can see that. It would be an aroma therapy-type of idea. Right? You were talking about these people coming by made me think of this question of community and about how you see the garden assisting the development of that.

PA: Well, I think it has been another way to reach the neighbors. I want the deacons to sit out here. Two of them. We go to the corner each year. "We pray for you." Come sit at the garden, and when people come by or back here, you know, that's what I think that might be effective. Most of the people know me in the neighborhood. Sometimes people come by and say, "I see you out here working. It looks real nice." You know? So I don't know. I think, um. I think it's . . . it helps give more access, so to speak, for the church to the people.

PM: An extension of the church. That's the whole idea of it right? The ministry?

PA: Yeah. And so I don't know. One young man joined the church. I don't think it was because he came to the garden. Because he lives over here. But he was going somewhere else. I sat next to him one day and he told me he had been to the garden. So I don't know exactly the answer to that. I just know that everyone that comes here knows. I tell them. Sometimes they ask me if it is my garden. I tell them we belong to the church. I invite people in. I always give them food if we have some. The last two years in the spring, people would be coming looking for the farmers' market before it opened. But I have been able to invite them in and give them a bag full of greens and, you know, herbs and stuff anyway.

PM: I did a thing, um, we did a season dedication in May at our other garden on Eggleston and when I told them that garden is called Sacred Greens and the reason it is called Sacred Greens is because it . . . Chicagoland Prison Outreach owns the land and they're a Christian ministry. So they asked us to come work with them, and then Jackie and I were talking last year and I came up with the idea. She's very attached to her church and her religion and spirituality and as a farmer. I'm getting to the point now, "As farmers," I said to them, "We know the land is sacred."

Indigenous peoples and farmers know because we see it happening. Now other people may not understand that, but we understand it. All the farmers I know are somehow spiritually engaged in what they are doing. For some of them it is very close to their church and their Christian ideas. For others it's more amorphous, but it is somehow spiritual. So the question is, How do you see that coming into play in your work?

PA: If you had come here ten minutes earlier, you would've seen us standing in a circle out there praying. Part of that is Lauren's doing. So, for me, gardening is meditative. It is meditative and relaxing. And, in fact, what is the name of that movie? Queen Latifah was a beekeeper in that movie. Anyway, one of her sisters had a learning disability. She would go to the garden. She would write down her problems. She would go into the garden and plant them. To me, *that* is composting! [laughter]. And so most of the time unless I'm overly stressed, that's how I relieve stress. That's how I relax. When I lost my brother, that's when I redesigned my backyard. It was just grass with a tree in the middle.

PM: Did you design it as a memorial?

PA: No. I was just planting. So a little girl said, "That looks like a coffin." I wasn't throwing the grass away. I was piling it up in a different area for the grass to grow. And that's what she saw. And I'm not sure why she thought she saw that except maybe she knew my brother had died. That's when I realized that it had something to do with that. And my grandparents had moved away, and that's where my garden was and so I was moving to gardening in my yard. It's how I relax.

PM: People go to church and they get their spiritual sustenance in church. Do you get some of that in the garden, too?

PA: Oh, sure. Yes. That's when the peace comes. Everyone says gardening is peaceful. That's where it's coming from. It's different than when you are in praise and worship. It's more like meditative. That's why I keep the gates locked. Dianne has been in here. And I've walked all the way up to her, and she never knew I was near because it is more meditative.

PM: Yeah, that's happened to me a lot, too, in the garden. It scared the heck out of me because I'm just so zoned out, so meditative. On little tasks that you are doing. I also ride my bike. It is a really good place to think. I also like the revelations. Like, "Oh! This is what I'm supposed to being doing!"

PA: Right. And I'm an intuitive gardener, so sometimes, you know, "Oh! This is how we are gonna do it." Sometimes it's in gardening, and sometimes it's in my life.

I think your mind has a chance to rest when you are actively meditating, which I'm not an expert on. In my mind, when you are meditating the idea is to have your mind blank, so to speak. And that's the challenge. But when you are gardening, most of the time all the busyness drifts away and you're able to just be peaceful, and that's when you know, as they say, that's when the Lord can speak to you.

People come cuz they want to be engaged in the earth. You know? People walk by. Homeless men. "Can I cut your grass?" People come in. He gave me his whole story. I guess he was living in the shelter. [I said] "Okay, come and pick some weeds." He said he didn't know anything about gardening. He picked weeds for about an hour. Then, he started telling me, "I'm from Mississippi and what you do over here is. And then . . . "You know? And I never saw him again. We always get one or two a year like that. People want to come in.

They want to get with the earth. They don't take any food. I guess, you know, if you've done it, you know, there is peace. Ten minutes in nature lowers your blood pressure.

PM: What else besides taking care of the garden do you do? Like, I was thinking about where does the food go?

PA: On Tuesdays I take it across the street to the church because the people that work at the church deserve healthy food too. We did spend some time trying to figure out what to do with the food. At the market the church has a table, but they don't want to sell what the other farmers are selling. They sell greens anyway, but they don't want me taking greens over there. So I take herbs over there and it's been an education for some. For a lot of people. They weren't sure that people would want them at first. But then turned a corner. It's been a learning curve. People are used to seeing their food released from a can.

PM: What kind of impact has it had on church members besides the ones that come? Do you see an impact on them at all?

PA: Yes. Dr. Mason started a twelve-week class that he called The Restart. Thursday nights they're starting a twelve-week program cuz he's a vegetarian. He always tells them to come to the garden.

PM: I was wondering how has the garden and the green ministry, in general, influenced church members besides the people who work in the garden?

PA: I'm not sure. I know that a lot of people appreciate getting the fresh herbs and things. That I'm not sure about.

PM: And that makes perfect sense because I think that in a lot of my work I'm never sure how it's impacting people. They might get exposed for the moment and you're not sure where that takes them. You know?

PA: A few people have told me that they've planted. I can say that. Some people already have gardens. A few people have told me they've started. Lauren has done some planting at her house. So I can say that and the people who work at the church do appreciate getting the fresh food because in the winter somebody said, "I can't wait till garden season comes." I said, "Oh, really?" Cuz I was hoping she was wanting to come work in the garden, but she was "Oh no. Those tomatoes. That squash. Those were really good." So that was nice. One lady, Miss Mary, she drinks sage tea. I try to make sure she has it. I tell them. "Bring you a ziplock bag to the garden and come on and get your herbs." So I don't know exactly, but I try to make sure she has her sage. When I've brought stuff over there, the people are excited. I can say that. But beyond that I don't really know exactly.

Carolyn Thomas, Mother of God's Gang

Ms. Thomas has more experience working in urban community gardens in Chicago than anyone I know. Her journey to the food movement began in the early 1980s through her church. In our taped dialogue, Ms. Thomas told the story of how her religious practices and beliefs led to the establishment of God's Gang.

CT: We would call them out[side], and everyone would be on the front breaking [i.e., breakdancing] That's not too cool for an AME church, but that's what we did. And then a woman by the name of Orinne Haynes and seven sisters of the Walt family of the church said, "Let's start a breakfast program." So we said, "Ok." We came early for church, and we served breakfast and we served elaborate breakfasts. People gave us, and we wouldn't serve commodities. We wouldn't serve regular breakfasts. We'd serve pancakes with cream and strawberries. And we would go to elaborate lengths to make these huge presentations of breakfasts.

PM: So your son had the idea, and you took it to the church?

CT: Exactly. It was Ms. Margorie Cheeks who was instrumental in funding us, in buying breakfasts. We would invite kids to come over and eat before church with no mention of staying for church. It was nothing that you would have to eat and listen to the minister. You could just come in and eat and go. It got kinda big where we were, and we didn't have a lot of money to do it. So we started a grandparents' program. So everybody in the church would say, "Well, I'm gonna have four kids, and I'll give four dollars for breakfast for them every week. If they wanna stay, they would sit with whoever their "grandparent" was. It got pretty big. We had like seventy-five kids, and then we had parents who'd come.

And then as kids started to stay, I don't know how it evolved but you certainly couldn't breakdance in the church. So we let the kids actually dance off gospel records. They would interpret it. We didn't have a dance teacher. We didn't have anything. My daughter went to Doris Jordan School [for] many years, and Michael, my oldest, and Marcus, my youngest. So they knew one dance in particular that was Aretha Franklin, "Mary, Don't You Weep," which was a finale that program did . . . The end of the year program from Doris Jordan that year was "Mary, Don't You Weep." So then we got invited to other churches and then we got invited to Kwanzaa celebrations and Black History and just went from there.

There was a community activist named Parris Thomas. He has now changed his name. He came to us and said, "You know, you guys have been everywhere." We just danced for everything that came up. We'd show up for free and we would dance. And another family in the church, the Westburys, would buy whatever we needed for clothing. We had a seamstress. One of the Westburys worked for the railroad. At the end of the year, they would discard the sheets and she would collect the sheets and they would make the kids skirts.

I think it was on Halloween. The church didn't want a Halloween party. So we didn't call it a Halloween Party. We called it a Harvest Fest though we grew nothing. And, um, one of the kids said, you know, "We're the baddest gang in town." And somebody said it was God's Gang.

Pariss came to Ms. Moore because she was a member of God's Gang; Barbara Moore she's deceased now. She really kept a handle on the kids and really encouraged kids to come. We asked what else we could do. We said to Ms. Moore, "Ok, we're going to meet with this guy is coming from Washington." He was from the Justice Department. He was saying, "You guys have a reputation. You could really do something. Think about what else you want to do and we'll give you a couple of thousands of dollars to help you do it." So the kids wrote the proposal. We asked them one thing that you can think of that you don't have to worry about what would it be? And they said, "Food." So we started a food pantry. It took almost a year to get the space and those buildings. We had no idea that the first or second year we had moved 42 or 43,000 pounds of food through some real challenging times. Through a bunch of gang wars. It was trying, but we did it.

PM: And you did this during the height of the gang wars, and you kept going every week?

CT: We served every week because the kids were on the Board we had to serve everybody. Most food pantries served by your zip code back then. The kids didn't understand that. If somebody comes and they say they need some food, if you had something saying who you were and your address or a lack of an address, they would be served. We had people coming from everywhere. One year the Salvation Army men's thing down on Ogden raised the amount the residents had to pay to eat in the commissary. We had people coming from the men's living quarters down there getting food, cooking in their little wherever they lived. It got crazy.

PM: So it started with the church, but you also had this woman who was running the building, Ms. Moore, did you have, was it a real church-community collaboration? Does it become that?

CT: Exactly. I mean, we were known everywhere as St. Mary's. It was definitely the church that supported it all. Then, the postal workers. I still worked eight hours. We had switched days of what we would do. My sister, who wasn't working . . . she was finally getting very ill . . . was there 24-7. It got pretty big. We still had the food pantry when the war was so bad. There was a big thing in the papers about the three buildings that were then at war. And literally shooting across from one building to one another. But we continued on, and then we ran out of money.

We ran out of money, and we had a woman named Allison Mears from the Heifer Project. She said, "You know, you guys could earn some money." We said, "We can't earn any money. I'm earning money to live. I have a job." She said, "No. You could raise livestock." She had offered this program all over Chicago and everybody had said, "No." She offered it to DuSable High School that then had a kind of a zoo in the middle of a pool. Anyway, she said, "Sure you could earn money. Heifer will give you money to buy livestock and then you sell the livestock. Sometimes you get donations from people, and we'd do some strategic planning to make the program work." What kind of livestock can you raise in CHA [Chicago Housing Authority]? Worms and fish. OK. So then a guy named Mark, I can't think of his last name. He's the largest worm farmer in Illinois. He was retiring and his worm farm consisted of a two-car garage. He raised red wigglers, and he gave us all his supplies. They pulled a guy in who wrote a book called *The Living System*, which was a system of raising tilapia in a three barrel system. He stayed with us a week, and my son learned how to build a system and we got space on the first floor for the worm and fish farm.

After a year, we were really trying to do too much as usual because after work we would go in and get the pantry. Food came in on Monday, and we'd distribute it all on Tuesday. It was hectic, but, in the meantime, we had a room where kids were doing their homework. Some of the volunteers who were working with the kids were really disgusted when they come back with homework that had smiley faces and it had eight wrong out of ten and you still got something saying it was great. So we decided, "Ok, now we need a library."

So then we got the first floor. Ed Moses was then the head of CHA. and one day Ms. Moore said, "Ed Moses says we're going to have a library downstairs."

In the space that was supposed to be originally the food pantry. So I said, "OK." They came in and less than a week, it was gone. The whole apartment on the first floor was gutted, new floor, new ceilings. It was a library. And at that time, there was a Chicago Post Office employees' library. Supposedly, it was started by Coretta Scott King. In the old post office, they told us when they built the new building that there was no space for it. So I lobbied the Recreation Committee and they agreed that they let me sit there a whole week and that anybody that worked in any post office could come in and take anything they wanted, any book they wanted, anything. And what was left went to Robert Taylor Homes. It went to the library we named Green-Cheeks after Maurice Cheeks's mother, Margorie Cheeks, who was our chief sponsor. And after Helen Green, who was secretary to Charlie Hayes and really provided a lot of educational stuff for the kids. So we named it Green-Cheeks Library. I was reading *Amistad* to two kids, and we had asked about us getting a worm and fish farm baseboard cuz we had thirty beds of worms against the wall in the back that used to be a coatroom. We had these three barrels of fish, fifty-five-gallon drums and the only window that was in the place. And we asked for space for the worm-fish farm, and we'd been told no, no, no. Ed Moses came on Valentine's Day to the Valentine's Day party. And I was sitting there reading in my uniform with two kids. He came in with Ms. Moore, and she was showing him and he was saying how beautiful it was with all the books that we'd gotten. And he walked to the back and he saw all these beds. He said, "What is that?" "That's the worm and fish farm." He said, "Ms. Moore, I don't know if anybody told you, but water and books don't mix." And the next day they came, and on the other end of the hallway they began constructing a worm and fish farm.

PM: This was made in CHA?

CT: CHA, CHA.

Habib

MECCA BROOKS'S SUSTAINABILITY JOURNEY

FIG. 15. Mecca Brooks. Photographer unknown.

MB: I designed this program called Art Up which is all about using art to develop relationships and connectivity. It was project based. The idea was that all of this would make them feel better about themselves and more confident when they go off to college. So right before funding got cut we had this project. We had to do one week. I decided that I was gonna do it. And my dad had just died so I was really sad . . . I was just really sad. So I didn't wanna go anywhere or do anything. I wanted to be close to home. I was walking down the street one day and I saw a friend of mine working on this garden and I was like "We're just gonna do the project here in the garden!" I had no idea what it was gonna be about. At that particular time, I was kinda used to just making things happen. It would just go my way. However, it was really hard to make it happen, and I had to convince them that we would do this around food. At the time, it wasn't so much that it was the furthest thing from my mind but I was like "How do you connect food and college readiness? This will be a tough one." So, somehow, I don't know. I'm pretty sure someone inspired me around this. I'm pretty sure it wasn't all my idea. So whoever reads this, so sorry. Somehow, we got this idea. This was when the Bronzeville Community Garden was just starting . . . Also, the other thing about what I was saying about college readiness that regardless of what you do after you leave your parents' home it is all of that stuff that made you who you are and that you take with you. You're gonna be fine wherever you go. That's the stuff that creates sustainability.

So I was like, "Ok, being in the neighborhood. Here they are with this socio-eco divide, taking this corner, building a garden. Who's the garden really for and how are the people who really hang out in the garden or hang out, at the time, in the lot really feel about what they are doing? Are they gonna feel included?" We decided that we would have the students do interviews of the people about food, about the space transforming and about how they would like to use the space. We made it into poems and then we made found poetry. At the same time, what was also happening losing my dad that was like a year of really rough family gun violence. So I had lost a few people that were young around gun violence. So I had this cousin who was Muslim, and the word "habib" just kept poppin out. So it was this project that we ended up doing was called "Habib," which means "to whom we hold dear." And it was the idea that it was all of the people that surround us in our lives that kind of grow from the ground. Cuz we did it all on photos that grow from the ground and actually offer this that is nurturing the food, fertilizing the food. This is what is giving life to everything. It's gonna come from the ground that we consider healthy eating. So if we, as a community, don't nourish one another, respect one another, hold one another up and actually rise together from the rubble, cuz that was what the lot was, then, what is our future? So it ended up being totems with images of people that we interviewed and the students and people in the garden and I put in a couple of pictures of my cousin who had just passed.

And that was it. That's how the whole food movement started for me which is really strange because the Bronzeville community garden is not a production space. It's really an education space. So life just takes you on this journey. At the same time that was happening someone was putting in an application for me for "Put Illinois to Work" under the HFH. At the exact same time. So the minute the layoff officially kicked in I rolled into working with the HFH. I think the Bronzeville community project, it was kinda like a portal into what's happening behind the scenes that I didn't know was happening. And that was because I knew Jifunza who runs BOC. She was our primary care physician, and she was handpicking people that she wanted to work with the HFH and I just happened to make the list. I didn't know about it. Someone did it behind my back. That was the next chapter in my life.

That was in 2010. The year my dad died.

PM: That's when we met. You had just started then. I had been in the food movement a couple of years at that point. I met Fred not long before. I didn't even know what Black Oaks was until just right before I met you. I met Fred working in a garden in South Chicago. That's when I was just being introduced to people. You know, I was sort of isolated with a few folks at that point and then once I went into the HFH was when I really got introduced to something larger, to the larger movement.

MB: We go back really. That was just here in Chicago and the notion of identity; what you do every day. But my real introduction came from my parents.
I grew up in a household where Dick Gregory was no longer a comedian. He
was the activist, the food activist. My cousin, Jimmy, I call him Uncle Jimmy,
my grandmother's first cousin, had a garden. He lived across the street from
us. He grew food in his yard. I mean, he's 80 plus. He tells this story about
when he was 30 he had an issue where he had to go to the hospital and his
lifestyle changed. It was like life or death and he promised if he made it out of
the hospital he would never, ever go down the path that he was going again.
He was totally doing a 180 and here we are fifty years later and that's what I
know of like what it means to really be a food revolutionary. I consider him
a food revolutionary because from a family standpoint he was the only one.
People ate pork, beef and here you are you have this man who was really
pretty cool. He played congas. He sung. He danced. He did the fur coat like
the whole pimp look but I mean . . . even that kinda died down a little bit,
the whole visual look. He just became the weird one in our family. He was
a baker, the best baker ever. He could make cakes without eating them. He
never tasted his food after he changed his lifestyle. That's what I knew.

I had pretty progressive parents. We grew up on rice cakes, sesame seed
candy and Jifunza mentored our family doctor in Philadelphia, Dr. Frederick
Burton. I mean the list is endless of the stuff that they were doing in the 80s.
But I didn't really think of those things cuz Uncle Jimmy was cool but, you
know . . . I didn't really, like, find it. I didn't really realize how much . . . it
influenced who I was until I became an adult.

PM: The creating of community and solidarity, intergenerational bonds. Those
relationships that create the resilience that you mentioned before. Those are
some really good words. OK, so thinking about that are there some other
words? You mentioned resilience. You mentioned transformative spaces.
We have all these words that we think about in the food justice movement.
People talk about organic, sustainable, and justice and security and access.
Are there certain kinds of concepts or theoretical frames or political frames
that are the foundation of what you do or how you think about what you do?
You use sustainability in a different way than I've heard it before. It's not even
an environmental kind of concept for you.

MB: Yeah. It's sustaining yourself. One of the big things that drives me and
my work is this notion of nonidentity. I don't know my . . . sustaining that.
When you sustain that part of who each of us are that's when you get into
this; when you are really able to be present in the work that you are doing.

The thing that comes along with identity. How do you put it? It comes with a lot, but it also comes with a rigidness and a wall and a barrier. And in a lot of instances, it's like hierarchical; this elitism. It can offer a lot of elitism. I like to take the approach, and it is a struggle every day, to try to be nonidentified. It doesn't mean that I don't have preferences and it doesn't mean that I don't have thoughts that come to my head. It's a mindfulness that everybody in this space is offering something and pretty much inform parts of what I am offering. The less I hang on to these notions of "This is Mecca," "She's from this place," "She studied at this place," "She's an expert in this," the more I'm able to really, really show up and develop a relationship that is going to transform things. When I say transformation and sustaining, I look at everything in vibrational frequencies and the more we are just there with no attachments, I think the higher the vibrations. Whatever is happening resonates longer and wider and larger and has deeper impact and meaning, than if you come with all that stuff.

Paula Roderick's Methodist Call to Action

PR: I go to a Methodist Church. John Wesley said, and I paraphrase, "Do all the good that you can with all the means you can for as long as you can." So if there is a spiritual sense for me, yeah, it is good work and you're supposed to do that as a part of the faith community. But my involvement at SEEDS isn't just because of that. It really does come from that activist sense of "Well, you know, you think the community needs some help and you're not there doing it. Who's going to do it?"

You put faith in it. Your faith has hands, I believe. You know? Hands and feet. So there's a part of it. But I know in our group there's a couple ⌊of⌋ people. One doesn't go to church, doesn't believe in church. She kinda goes, "Paula, I hear people talking about spirituality." It's not . . . we don't talk about faith in the garden but I know that people feel it's a spiritual thing that happens. I mean, I was thinking, you know, we started the season off with that wonderful concert with Reverend Billy [at Sacred Greens].

You know, and, uh, but everybody that was there was kinda looking around, going kinda, like, "That was a good thing to do." But if you looked at 'em they were people who probably would not have gathered together, yet they gathered together to sing and to garden. And when I look sometimes at the people who come into our garden. They're people who probably wouldn't gather together, but they do because it's kinda spiritual and nobody really knows how it's spiritual, how it is. Except I saw it in our first season when we worked with the Put Illinois to Work workers. They were young. Some of them were kinda, like, resentful; thought we were gonna wanna make them suffer by making them work out in the heat or whatever. And yet by the middle of the summer for some of them they were starting to see that amazing thing that happens when you put a seed in the ground and there's nothing there and six weeks later you're sitting there eating what you grew. It's a pretty miracle thing. So one of the workers who kinda had attitude when she started, she took over the corn. It became her patch, if you will. She got very interested in seeing how it was growing and how they were doing. Now that's a spiritual thing. It's not a religious thing. It's just somebody started out with attitude. They found out how engaging it could be to see something grow, and their attitude kinda shifted.

•   •   •

PR: I don't know that I see myself as a farmer even now. What keeps me invested is more the excitement that I see that happens when people, when they spend six, eight, ten weeks in the garden. And it's sort of like that transformative thing that happens, and that's farming. We provide a team leader. Somebody that knows a little bit more about gardening than the other people that are coming in. We draw on all our resources like you. When you came in, you and Dwight came in and said, "We're just gonna make this little space and we're gonna plant something here." So drawing on all our resources an amazing thing will happen to those people that have been working in that garden. That's not exactly farming. I believe in the community experience of growing, that growing things is very positive for the community. Now, I like to grow things. I've learned a lot. I'm still not the best. I joke a lot about the things that I don't know. But nothing else has this sort of capacity. You know? To be a metaphor. To be a metaphor for community activism, for growth in the community, for education. You know? I talk a lot about all the ways that you can look at a garden when I meet young people. It's a classroom. It can be a concert hall. It can be a kitchen. It has lots of things that it can be. I don't know that it means that I'm a farmer. I just love that that's what can be happening in the garden.

Land and Ancestral Connections

MAMA SAFIA RASHID ON SPIRIT

PM: Do religion and spirituality come into play in your work?

SR: For me, I'd probably say, no, because I'm an atheist. I don't usually think of it on that level. I usually think of it differently than some people. Kamau will probably totally respond a little bit differently. He doesn't even call himself an atheist. He calls himself something else. I forget what it is, but, me, I'm just like flat out I know that I don't believe in any kinda . . . in a single power. Not that I don't believe that there aren't energies and things . . .

PM: So I had this conversation with Mecca years ago, and she said, "I don't understand

FIG. 16. Safia Rashid.
Photo by Tafari Melisizwe.

atheists. I don't understand." I said, "Look, atheist means that you don't believe in a God, a deity. "Thei" being God and "a-" meaning "not." It's not that we don't believe in powers and energy or soul. You know, it could be any number of things. It's just that we don't believe in an all-encompassing God that just fixes everything. I'm an atheist, too, but I believe in the One Spirit and all that kind of stuff and that we are all connected. And we can have a better connection through the land. There is something about the land that helps us make those connections with other people, other . . . like we say, the Lakota say, "all our relations." Right? With other beings but also other humans in our community. So that's why it's important for me to be in the soil. That's the spirituality that I get from it. Not Jesus or, you know, whoever. That has nothing to do with it . . . That energy and that connection that you get from it, that seems to me to be that spiritual force.

SR: I mean I feel that connection. Like I said, I wouldn't necessarily call it spiritual or whatever. Only because I try to stay away from [the label] because people try to attach religion to it. I used to say spiritual, and then people would get all confused. And then I just backed away from it. Just because it gets people too confused. They are too wrapped up in the religion that they are connected too. So I just back away. I'll admit that. But, yeah, I mean for me I do feel like that there is something else going on. I kinda felt like that when I'm in the soil and working out there. There are sometimes that I do feel like there's this connection with my ancestors because on one side of my family, which is my father's side, we had sharecroppers. Then, on my mom's side we had family that owned land. They farmed land and they owned the land. So for me, sometimes when I'm out there and I'm just kinda like really in the zone where I'm not hearing too much that is happening . . . cuz people say, "How can you be out here by yourself with no music or whatever?" I'm like "I got plenty going on." I'm inside here [motioning to chest and body]. You know?

There is a lot going on in the land and in the things that I'm thinking about but there's also things internal that I'm just thinking about. Sometimes people walk up to me and scare me half to death because I'm like really in the zone. I didn't notice that until it happened to me a couple of times. I had people walk up on me, and I said, "Oh, I didn't even know you was there." I didn't even hear them walk up. So I mean you really do kinda feel that bigger connection to things and I think it definitely [happens] working with the land. You just really have a deep appreciation about how life is created and how it's all kinda connected. You start seeing all those connections to that. That's part of the reason why organic and being sustainable really pulled me in. Cuz I'm like, "You're killing that thing that helps keep us alive. That doesn't make any sense to me. How can you destroy what's keeping us alive? How can you destroy this ecosystem that we all need?" People don't even realize that it's all interconnected. And you really don't get that until you are out there and you realize I need this bug that I thought I should be spraying or stepping on or killing. We need those. There are certain ones that I really do need. Don't kill that wasp right away. You know? Things like that that I hadn't really thought about. People coulda mentioned it to me when I was younger, but it didn't really make that big connection until I got out there in the land and in the soil. Sometimes my kids will bring up stuff and I'm just like "I didn't even think about that." You know? They find little things. They found little connections.

PM: How many times do we get a chance to really see life and recognize it for what it really is from the beginning? I mean with pregnancy and stuff you get a sense of it. You put that soil in, and you get to see it grow and it really doesn't take that long. You wait a few months, and then you see it feed. There's something more than farming. Farming doesn't capture it. It's spiritual or its life force. Something that you can't really learn if you don't do this. Like you say, you don't know it until you are doing it. I try to explain to people about this, and they don't get it. They don't get it because they haven't done it.

Dwight Dotts

OUR NEED TO MEET GOD
ON A DIFFERENT LEVEL

DD: I see myself as a teacher. I'm an older guy in my sixties, so I don't have a whole lot of time on the planet and it's going to take a revolution, a change of mind, and a change of how we do things, where we're gonna have to change the system of capitalism, where everything is profit driven. And I believe talking to younger people saying the reason you might wanna think about doing it this way is because it is going to work out differently and we are not always gonna be in a situation where you can depend on giving your power to other people to feed you.

PM: Do you see Green Lots helping you accomplish that?

DD: Yeah. Because you are giving me a space to work. I see that there's going to be an urban thing and there's gonna be a country thing. And because I'm familiar with Pembroke and Hopkins Park I understand that you have got to have land that is undeveloped, that there is so much land that is being wasted in the city that can be used for something. You don't have to put a building on every vacant lot. So my thing is Chicago has already been messed up, the thirty square miles of the City of Chicago. You're not gonna turn Chicago back into pastoral land unless there is a nuclear explosion. Wipe it out. We're not talking about that because if it is nuclear we are all gone. But I do see that you've got to allow people a certain amount of land to play in the dirt. Now whether you're gonna be a farmer or you like to grow flowers or whatever. You've got to get to green space. I mean separate from parks, you know, go sitting in Grant Park. That's green space, but I'm talking about green space where if I want to grow flowers to eat or flowers to smell or things to eat. We need that. Because if you separate people from the land . . . A people without attachment to land has no roots to anything else. And you and I understand when you talk about Native American, Africans, people who come from the soil, you're gonna lose something with your kids over generations if they don't play in the dirt. With the City of Chicago you've got all this concrete, steel that's gonna be here for another thousand, two thousand years.

PM: What is it that we are going to lose?

DD: Attachment to earth. Spiritual. Everything. Emotionally, psychologically, spiritually, and physically. I can't exercise just for the sake of exercise. I can't do a treadmill. It bores the heck outta me. But if you put me out in the garden, I can pull weeds for two or three hours. Like Marlene, she can walk on a treadmill. I can't. It's boring, boring, boring. Now if you go outside and say, "Dwight you see these beautiful weeds. Can you weed 'em?" I can do that for two or three hours in the hot sun and feel that I had a good workout and . . . I can't go to Planet Fitness.

PM: I've been just recently doing a deep dive into spirituality and theology and stuff like this. Do you have any comments? You said something about spirituality. How do you see that in this work, in this movement for you? For us?

DD: Your family, your people, come from New Mexico. Correct? My parents moved to California in 1980. I've driven to California maybe fifty, sixty times over the course of thirty-eight years. When you get out beyond the city and you get out there in the mountains and the land, I believe you meet God on a different level. And I believe in church, but that's a structure, a physical building, and I think we are separated more because we think god is in church on Sunday instead of driving out to the Rocky Mountains; that awe of the land.

PM: Can we replicate that in the city? That awe for the land? I'm hoping that with Green Lots that there is some spiritual betterment.

DD: To see things grow. You and I are putting stuff in the ground. But when you are honest with it, you are putting some seed in dirt. The wonder of watching it grow. I have nothing to do with that. When you think about it how much do we devote to growing stuff. We don't do a lot of work. It's the one whether you want to call it god or Mother Earth, whatever you want to deal with, it's doing it all on its own. All I am is a curator, just snipping a little. That's all I am. I am not a creator of anything out there. I'm just preaching. That's how I feel about it. Do you realize that if we were the ones doing all of this we would have to be out here ten or twelve hours a day? It's been raining so I have no reason to go out and water because the water has been falling from the sky. Maybe in another two or three days I might say, "I better go check on the plants." But if I was the god that was making all of this happen, then I would have to be out there seven days a week.

PM: What is the main reason for doing this? My reason for doing this began as sort of to do my part in the revolution. Then, it started to change. Because once I started doing that, growing food and getting people involved, and all that it started to change where I'm doing it more for me and my family now.

Not only but to a great deal. Where it used to be the opposite. It used to be outward, for other people. Now it truly is internal. I like what you said about spiritual and health and all that. So what is your main reason for getting involved?

DD: You remember the Good Food Conference that comes to Chicago every year? I went to one of the early ones when it first started. Then, it became too commercial. I'm doing this because this doesn't have commercialism attached to it. I'm always concerned about Amazon and Whole Foods; whenever they see something happening they latch on to it and they change it. And here you have people not concerned with where their food comes from and that's OK. I'm concerned with where my food comes from. Has someone been exploited? You know? Like I drink coffee. Did the guy who grew the coffee beans, does he own the land? Would his great grandchildren be able to grow coffee beans on the land? Is he being paid for the labor? Not just you work fifteen hours a day, and you make a dollar. So I'm concerned that we're gonna have to change how we look at things about where our food comes from. I might not be able to have pineapples in December in Chicago in a climate where pineapples don't grow . . .

PM: Your concern is a concern for what exactly? We could get pineapples, and what's the problem?

DD: But it comes from two or three thousand miles away. I just worry that people need a full set of skills of things. Human beings have only been doing this urban experiment for the last . . . I'm going go back to the Romans. Two thousand years. And we've been living on the earth out of this experiment for two or three hundred thousand years. If you want to go back to eating woolly mammoths or eating buffalo or saber-toothed tigers. We were doing that a lot longer than we have been doing this. And I think that people are starting to see that this experiment, and we are an experiment, is going to be bad for the planet and is going to be bad for us. And I'm not against technology, but there's something to be said to leaving things separate from technology and that's why I think what we are doing comes into play.

Arming the Spirit with Kevin Triplett

KT: Here's what I think about the spirituality part, though. It doesn't make sense to me to try to deny spirit. I used to do that when I was first thinking about Marxism because I thought about the terrible role that organized religion has played. If your spirituality means that every day, whatever you call it, praying, meditating, whatever you do, and you think about the health, the healing, the safety, and well-being of every human being . . . if that is your spirituality, if that's your connection, what am I going to do? Am I going to debate that? Why would I do that?

PM: I'll tell you why. Because your abstract love for everybody is not going to overthrow the imperialist elite. I'm not saying that's true, but I can see somebody saying that. So what we see is people doing yoga and getting in touch with whatever, the plants, the cosmos, whatever. They're just sitting around "navel gazing" as they say. People say, "You're just sitting around navel gazing. You're wishing. You're just praying. Praying? That ain't gonna do shit. Pray all you want. They're still gonna come, and they're gonna bomb while you are praying." So a lot of people say you are gonna spend time praying and whatever, and bombs are dropping all around you. It's reactionary because you are not out fighting the fight or whatever. You are just staying home.

KT: I've adapted to my own use. If I am meditating on "May you be happy. May you be healthy. May you be safe. And may you live with ease." If I'm meditating on that, then the next part of that is if those things are not true, then what is keeping that from being possible? Well, it might be the imperialist.

Is it too much materialist determinist? If so, slap that label on me. I'm not just going to sit and contemplate my navel lint on global warming. Why is that happening?

PM: Do you think that meditating on love, everything is beautiful, does that automatically lead there or do you need some intervening thing to get you to that point?

KT: There has to be some kind of intervention, and that intervention is your relationship to other human beings. We don't live in a silo. You are going come up with everything by yourself cuz we don't live by ourselves. So I think

that it is absolutely worth the effort to meditate on these things and then figure out how to get there. Let's not blame one another. You know, "You didn't
do right because you don't have the right relationship with the creator." Let's
not do that.

PM: Can spirituality be a revolutionary tool?

KT: Yes and no. The negative end of spirituality is that it unites us with the ruling class. I can be sitting next to someone and say I believe in the same Jesus
as you do. So it goes back to my question about what is your relationship to
the means of production?

PM: A lot of people I work with are into Indigenous religions, African religions, and seeing them as tools of revolution. Because they seem them not
simply as a relationship to god or to the creator or whatever but they see them
also as things that hold real wisdom; that holds precapitalist, precolonialist,
non-European wisdom. So they really feel like it is a requirement to have a
connection to an Indigenous religious orientation of some sort.

KT: What you believe in doesn't affect anyone until you act on it in a way that
does not involve secular humanism. You have to see the importance of plants,
animals, the environment, all those things in your spiritual growth, then what
are you growing toward? Annihilation? You don't want people to sit and experience annihilation. Like you said, while you are sitting contemplating your
navel, there's bombs dropping around you. We don't want that. But you also
don't want people to express their spirituality to the exclusion of other people's humanity? Do we really want a battle between Hindus and Buddhists?
Do we want it between Catholics and Protestants?

PM: One of the ways I'm trying to make sense of it is: You have Indigenous
religions on the one hand. You have Abrahamic religions on the other. The
Abrahamic religions, being the spirit, is separate from the day to day. It is separate from politics, the economics. It's almost like you escape from the spirit.
Spirit is above us. It is in the sky. What I see with Indigenous religions is that
they are much more material. It's not just about being detached. It's being
attached to a god and the living, breathing, material plane. A lot of Christians
say, "What I'm waiting for is to get to Heaven." Indigenous religions are not
focused on that. They are focused on the relationship between yourself and
material things. You know, the plants, the animals and other material things as
well as supreme power or whatever you call it. In Indigenous religion, you are
honoring Sun Mountain because it gives you life. It really does give you life.
That is where the water comes from. That's where you forage. Whereas the
Abrahamic religions are so disconnected from the material. So I'm wondering

if that's what makes Indigenous religion a potentially revolutionary tool as opposed to these other religions.

KT: There are so many spiritualities around the world. You can practice that in whatever way you choose as long as you are not practicing that to the detriment of other human beings. I think these spiritual things help us just explain human relationships. I read little parts of the Bible every day. Just because it has snippets of wisdom. There are some miserable things in the Bible too. But there are things that help you understand how important human beings are. What god is? My mother was very religious. The two things I always remember my mother saying is "God is love" or she would say "Let brotherly love continue." Why would those two things stick in my mind? Probably because there is something about the importance of other human beings and what god is. God is love.

PM: So if we were to conclude, are we saying that religion and spirituality is a neutral in all this? It can be moved in different ways?

KT: Yeah.

PM: While I'm trying to suggest that we are in a dearth of spiritual depth, I also see that desperation for spirit has led to the manipulation of people and reactionaries are the ones that seem to be able to manipulate people's need for the spirit. So I'm wondering if leftist revolutionaries could arm the spirit in the same way that the right has done.

CHAPTER 8

Urban AlterNative Masculinity
MEN, LAND, AND REINDIGENIZATION

"Sorry for laughing, bro!" he blurted out between chuckles. "When I think of gardening, I think of old ladies!" My Chicano friend couldn't contain his surprise when I told him of my summer plans to spend most of my days in the community garden. In that same year when I described how I hosted "Preservation Parties" through our community organization, GLP, a friend and administrator on my campus, Chicago State University, could barely contain her fascination that a man would can and pickle. My colleagues' responses to my horticultural and preservation activities reflect central stereotypes about Chicano masculinity and masculinity in general, which serve to limit our possibilities for living full lives and for decolonizing and reindigenizing ourselves and our communities.

Importantly, my first memories of Chicano manhood involved waking up to my white T-shirt-clad, dark-skinned grandfather sitting at the kitchen table waiting for his grandkids to gobble up the French toast he prepared. My grandfather was the cook in our home when I had the good fortune to live with him. He was the most serene person I have ever met. He was strong, a former rural small-town cop who never pulled his gun in the line of duty and was respected by everyone including the cholos he had to bust on occasion. My best memories from my youth include my grandpa in the garden and on fishing trips. We regularly went for mile-long walks in the countryside, spending peaceful moments together. My grandpa didn't go to church. Nature seemed to be his temple. According to my mother, my maternal great-grandfather also passed on (Indigenous) tradition in the garden and the mountains of New Mexico. I only had eight years with my father before he died. This loving White American of Irish background also exhibited a masculinity that defied the hegemonic variety that dominates our understanding of gender and possibility in this country. While my memories of him are vague due to the trauma of his loss to me as a child, my mother always reminds us of who he was, which includes his love for the outdoors, his garden, and fishing. My mother claims that he exhibited the same serenity that my grandfather had; perhaps that is why she married him. Later, around my teen years, I learned something different about manhood. Through peers and pop culture I learned that men don't cry and that a "real man" was tough, violent, and emotionless. I learned to perform this gender role and began to define myself based on the "real man" stereotype. After failed relationships, study, fatherhood, and correction at the hands of Xicana and Black women, I began to develop an alterNative masculinity. My journey towards alter-Native manhood has brought me to the gardens and community care work where I can practice a manhood more in line with that of my father and grandfather.

Through my experiences in Chicanx communities and now in the Black food movement in Chicago, I have developed an autohistoriateoria that is both critical of Wetiko masculinity *and* strives toward an alterNative masculinity. My autohistoriateoria engages the possibilities for developing an antiauthoritarian, anticolonial alterNative (AAA) masculine praxis in urban settings. My critique of Wetiko masculinity and my understanding of an AAA masculinity developed because of my history in anticapitalist, antiracist activism epitomized by my deep involvement in the food autonomy movement in Black Chicago. My auto-historiateoria begins in the mountains of New Mexico and ends, for now, in abandoned lots turned urban oases on the South Side of Chicago. It moves from a childhood steeped in hypermasculine culture to a "macho" approach to revolutionary Chicanidad in my early adulthood to a deep study of gender in hip hop to lessons from elders and the land. I first outline a theory of AAA masculinity that I believe is necessary for any successful anti-/decolonial movement. Then, I briefly describe my journey from Wetiko hypermasculinity toward an AAA masculinity through practice and instruction in anarchist, Chicanx, and Black American movements. The bulk of the chapter examines how an alterNative masculinity does and does not develop in Chicago's food movement.

Antiauthoritarian, Anticolonial AlterNative Masculinity

Gender is performance.[1] Heteropatriarchal masculinity, though depicted as strong and resilient, is fragile. To be considered masculine under the Wetiko framework, one must continuously prove to be hypermasculine or risk the stigma of being called a "fag" or "pussy." Without evidence of masculinity, one is confined to the "inferior" realm of homosexual or woman. Thus, young and older men alike learn to act, move, talk, and emote in ways that make it clear that you are a "man." We perform despite desires to behave differently and despite what is good for us. Importantly, we pass on these ideas of masculinity to our children as they watch us act like "men." This is the essence of Wetiko masculinity, responsible for so much violence in my community and throughout the world.

Today, in the twentieth- and twenty-first-century United States, we equate masculinity with dominance and power over others. This power over manifests itself differently depending on one's social status but generally includes five ways to display one's conformity to the masculine norm: 1) violence; 2) power over women, including promiscuous sex; 3) daring and fearlessness (drug use, danger); 4) financial power; and 5) power over one's body (e.g., sports).[2] Economic status often determines how we perform our masculinity. Financial power is reserved for the wealthy men who can prove their masculinity through bank accounts and their positions. An employer can display masculinity through his money and his ability to control others including and especially women whose conditions of employment often include sexual harassment, sexual abuse, and constant reminders of their "inferior" gender status. Poor men, having no such financial power, must display their masculinity in other ways. For many, masculinity and consumerism come together as we go into debt through the conspicuous consumption of the accoutrements of masculinity such as cars, tennis shoes, and "bling." We may also make up for our lack of financial power by overemphasizing physical power. Some displays are considered legitimate, including sports prowess, while others are illegitimate, including violence aside from state-sanctioned police, prison, and military activity. If these schemes do not adequately prove one's masculinity, then we can take drugs or engage in other dangerous activities. All these aspects of masculine performance cause trauma to male performers as well as others in our society. Crime, violence, drug addiction, and many other social ills involve disproportionate numbers of men.[3]

More specifically, I argue that the masculinity I learned as a Chicano youth has detrimental effects for us, as individuals, community, and the planet.[4] The combination of hypermasculinity, heteronormativity, White supremacy/racism, colonialism, and capitalism direct Chicano masculinity in a toxic direction. It is a mix that contributes to higher-than-normal death rates from accidents, violence, and drug use, disproportionate incarceration rates, and intensified racist stereotypes of us as "macho." These facts have led me to the question, What should replace the hypermasculinity that dominates our ideals of manhood?

Over the past two decades my quest to answer this question has led me to what I call an antiauthoritarian, anticolonial alterNative masculinity.[5] I recognize that if we seek a better world, then it is not enough to "simply" change how we perceive our masculinity but rather to recognize and act on the understanding that our masculinity is intimately tied to Wetiko's authoritarian thought and culture. To decolonize Chicanx masculinity and destroy Wetiko's sex-gender system, we must address each of these pillars of domination. While we reject hypermasculinity and Wetiko's ideology, we look to our Indigenous traditions for a sex-gender system that is empowering for ourselves, our communities, and all our relations, sees gender in complex, multifaceted ways, and provides space for creative existence. An AAA gender politics recognizes the importance of two-spirit people to our cultures. Penniman explains, "in the past, queer, two-spirit, gender nonconforming, and transgender folks were often healers in many traditional societies across the planet. Existing between genders—neither male or female, or maybe being both—was thought to be a gift and considered sacred and balanced in some societies."[6]

I have distilled my study of Indigenous thought, anarchism, two-spirited insight and critique, and transnational feminism as they contribute to anticolonial masculinities to several components, including being:

Anticapitalist	Antistate	Anti-industrial	Antihierarchical
Antimisogynist	Place-based	Participatory	Decentralized
Gender fluid	Communal	Inclusive of all our relations	

AAA masculinity rejects capitalism, the state, and industry, which destroy life while elevating those men (and some women) who control the state and the economy. AAA masculinity also rejects all forms of domination, especially those resulting from patriarchy. In place of these Wetiko values and structures, AAA masculinity seeks an understanding and praxis of gender in which individuals and communities redefine or reject it. For the full development of our individualities and our communities, we must be able to express all aspects of our selves freely.[7] Instead of falling victim to hegemonic masculinity taught by Wetiko, AAA masculinity offers freedom and fluidity. AAA masculinity conforms to the needs of our communities and looks toward our more-than-human relations for lessons on how to be a "man." Our place and all our relations within it teach a liberatory, caring humanity.

Becoming Chicano

My childhood masculinity training involved my male peers, family, role models, coaches and others valuing the powerful, aggressive, dominating, sexist, and tough in me and shaming and stigmatizing the kind, caring, creative, and egalitarian tendencies I displayed as a male human of Mexican descent in Raton, New Mexico. Perhaps this is why I valued sports and hip hop. My socialization into Chicano manhood in the 1970s and 1980s came with a great deal of trauma since to perform my Chicano maleness, I often engaged in dangerous behaviors. Fights, running from various authorities, drugs, and other acts of bravado proved I was "crazy" or "loco" in our Chicano street talk.[8] Being described as "crazy" was a high honor. Our value system and behaviors as working-class Chicano men reflected our position in Wetiko society. As a working-class person, I had no financial power. I could not dominate someone by spending money or show my superiority through conspicuous consumption, though I often tried. I learned that my power as a working-class Chicano rested primarily on physical power and daring. I could fight, use drugs, and be sexually promiscuous. I drove fast down dangerous mountain roads, sometimes intoxicated. I learned that first-class maleness in the United States meant possessing things, so I learned consumerism. I aspired to trendy things that earned "respect" from my peers.

Before I learned the concepts, I understood well that full citizenship in the United States means hypermasculine upper-class Whiteness. Movies, music, sports, politics, school, religion, and family taught me to value a Euro-colonial capitalist heteronormativity and trained me to be a "macho" or stereotypical hypermasculine Mexican. I learned from boxing and my street mentors that the Mexican macho was the epitome of maleness. From many Chicano activist peers and mentors, I learned that to be a Mexican revolutionary was to be a "chingon," a big badass who would physically take on the gringo colonizer. Even our Indigenous ancestor heroes were depicted in words and symbols as chingones, and our history of resistance included mostly violent resistance. Never did I learn the possibility that resistance involved care work and the struggle to retain our ways. I learned of Zapata and Villa as the leaders of the Mexican Revolution and that women played secondary roles as illustrated by the Adelita stereotype. They were "macho" and men "led" while women played the patriarchal traditional role of helpmate.

Not only were women and their work less valued than men and theirs, but women were also reduced to sexual objects for male control and domination. Much of the media landscape during my youth from the movies I viewed to late night on HBO to *Lowrider Magazine* and MTV portrayed women as sexual objects for the ideal man's possessing. To come to terms with my own gender socialization through media, I researched and wrote the books *Chicano Rap: Gender and Violence in the Postindustrial Barrio* and *The Chican@ Hip Hop Nation: Politics of a New Millennial Mestizaje*. These books and the third in the triology, *Toward a Chican@ Hip Hop Anticolonialism*, aimed to help me and people like me, Chicanxs who love hip hop, understand the complexities of gender in our contemporary society and suggest ways to overcome Wetiko's heteropatriarchy.

Hip hop and other media showed me that men are sexually dominant. This belief is central to our gender identity development. Thus, we ruthlessly guard against the feminine. Our socialization tells us that we should stomp out anything that smacks of "women's roles" or "women's behavior" in our lives. The Chicano, the sexually dominant man, must be heterosexual according to heteropatriarchal logic since women are the submissive and subordinate in a sexual relationship. A "real" Chicano would never be sexually submissive like gay men are perceived to be. Becoming Chicano, I ridiculed any deviance from the heterosexual patriarchal norm, but most especially I and others learned to hate homosexuality. "Faggot" was a favorite epithet used to keep us sexually and otherwise in line. We could also hide our gender and sexuality insecurities behind it. We could use "faggot" to proclaim our macho heterosexuality.

Decolonial Beginnings

Three things began to alter my perception of Chicano manhood and my own Chicano identity: 1) corrections from Chicana/Mexican elders (primarily in my family) and activista/scholar camaradas; 2) Chicana feminist and queer theory[9]; and 3) fatherhood.

The rebellious and rough Chicanidad of my tías and their quiet knowledgeable indigeneity were my first teachers of xicanisma (Chicana feminism) and beginnings of my questioning of Wetiko masculinity masquerading as Chicanidad. They refused the role of the suffering mother or *madre dolorosa*. While the women of the Cortez family would kill for their children, they weren't simply tied to the role of mother. Nor were they housewives subordinated to their husbands who were the "true" head of the household. They were loud and brash, not pious. They fought racism and on behalf of workers. Their teachings of northern Nuevo Mexicana and southern Colorado foodways were subtle but all the more powerful for the lasting impact they had. Their lessons became clearer for me once I became enveloped in food autonomy work and in healing the land. Both their loud, warrior xicanisma and their stereotypically feminine roles as caretakers and food preparers became a coherent whole when viewed wholistically from the lenses of xicanisma, eco-womanism, and indigeneity.

The problems I was having with my masculinity and my understanding of the complexity of my tías and other elder women were the inability to disentangle "warrior" from "masculine" and the mixed messaging from family, church, and others. It felt contradictory and confusing. Eventually, I learned that my aunts, mother, and others were not living contradictions but examples of a complex Mexicanidad in between indigeneity and assimilation. In fact, their Xicana way of being provided early examples of decoloniality and how I might decolonize my own masculinity. By the time I read Xicana scholarship, ecofeminism, and queer theory, and participated in radical Chicanx spaces, I was ready for a more intense battle with Wetiko masculinity. The writings and actions of the Zapatistas, especially the women and their insistence on being seen and heard on their terms, provided a model to explore as I engaged the hegemonic masculinity of my youth and all that surrounded me. Their "Revolutionary Women's Law" and leadership helped me understand the complexity and fluidity of gender in an Indigenous context.[10] In the late 1990s, I spent time in Zapatista territory for my doctoral dissertation work. There I encountered a complex array of gender roles with women doing most of the care work (but certainly not all of it) as well as a good deal of physical, political, and intellectual labor. The men engaged in physical labor and politics but pursued this division of labor without notion of superiority and with love. Their quiet dignity and ethic of respect left no room for masculine violence. Of course, men in Zapatista territory do act out in hypermasculine ways. However, Indigenous governance structures mitigate the impact of patriarchal violence. It is relatively rare and is almost always related to colonialism either through the violence of poverty or substances like drugs or alcohol that are imported into communities and nearby towns. Indigenous forms of decision-making seek restorative and, occasionally, punitive justice.

On my return from Zapatista territory, fatherhood awaited. It also set me on a path of strong engagement with Wetiko masculinity and toward AAA masculinity. Having children is often life-altering for parents. It led me and others in my circles to question our lives and the direction of our lives. I now had to model the type of man that I agreed with Xicanistas and others would be ideal. Now, instead of theorizing it or critiquing it in others or in our world, I had to teach through example. I had to put theory into practice or risk replicating toxic masculinity in my sons. My sons grew up watching my complex masculinity change and develop. They saw Wetiko masculinity and its effects through my anger. They saw the reindigenizing and decolonizing masculinity in my care work with them from feeding, changing, and rocking them to sleep as babies to the breakfasts and dinners that I continue to make for them more than twenty years later and the heart-to-hearts we have. They saw—and continue to see—my commitment to caring and regenerating the land while helping people feed themselves and providing healthy food for my family.

My fierce commitment to reindigenizing my masculinity and caring for the land and the people in my community intensified when I moved to Chicago. There my decolonizing has matured and come together through lessons from elders and the land.

AAA Masculinity in Chicago's Food Movement

My autohistoriateoria relative to masculinity has matured in the fertile soil of the food movement in Black Chicago. Here in Chicago my community activism as executive director of GLP led me into liberatory anticolonial relationships with Black elders and the land. Through my deep, place-based education and praxis in sustainability and community organization, I was free to see my masculine Chicanidad (indigeneity) and anarchism for the truly anticolonial potential they had. The land and all our relations reject the fetishizing of a dominating hierarchical form of power over others found in Wetiko masculinity. My Indigenous Chicanidad, like that of many Indigenous scholars and others throughout Turtle Island,[11] is a source of knowledge in relationship with other humans and more-than-human beings. My anticolonial masculinity results from interaction with the land, with my hands in the soil and my body, spirit and mind working with and learning from all my relations in the gardens, fields, and prairies where I work and live.

The ecofeminism I began engaging with theoretically in the 1980s through my study with Devon G. Peña and encountered in real life through Indigenous Zapatista women and camaradas began to make sense. The language of Gaia or Pachamama concerning an alive, creative, and feminine world that I fully endorsed theoretically became a part of how I lived and interacted with all my relations. My daily practice involved working through the masculine violence of most of our actions under Wetiko. Through engaging the land and IK, I learned to act with all my relations in mind and toward practices that healed my landscape. I began to use my body to heal colonial wounds I suffered as well as those that have been inflicted and that I have inflicted on the land. And through this kinetic intellectual mode my understanding deepened and new decolonial behaviors emerged. This mode of being, learning and acting on and from the world, relied on making mistakes and careful observation of how my actions affected the world around me. As Simpson explains, this is a Native mode of knowing.

> Kinetics, the act of doing, isn't just praxis; it also generates and animates theory within Indigenous contexts, and it is the crucial intellectual mode for generating knowledge ... Practices are politics. Processes are governance. Doing produces more knowledge ... Mistakes produce knowledge. Failure produces knowledge because engagement in the process changes the actors embedded in process and aligns bodies with the implicate order.[12]

Certainly, my anticolonial journey in Chicago involves lots of failures, but the constant interaction and reciprocity, the doing of it, especially with elders in the movement is leading to an AAA masculinity that is self-reflexive, interactive, and flexible. It does not shy away from generative, creative, and loving acts. Through my land-based practices using IK, I see masculinity as demanding creativity and love. The more regenerative and loving the acts, the more I learn. Like a healthy ecosystem, the cycle regenerates itself producing knowledge and life and deepening my journey toward reindigenization.

Baba Fred always makes sure that we "check in" with our Indigenous ethics at every BOC course. Each session begins with a check-in and a discussion of Zone 0 or our "internal landscape." The check in serves to provide the people care of permaculture that is so often missing in Wetiko societies and to check how we are integrating respect, reciprocity, and relationships into our lives and our growing projects. Thus, caring and sharing are crucial parts of class. For me and my development of AAA masculinity within the confines of inner-city Chicago, the constant emphasis on caring and sharing at BOC and at my community gardens is necessary. The checking in with Indigenous ethics and ways of being as we understand them (remember we are reindigenizing and our journey is far from complete) epitomizes the constant vigilance required to combat the effects of Wetiko on our bodies, minds, and spirits. It also epitomizes the rewards of reindigenization. My gendered being could be free to engage in acts of creativity, regeneration, and love. Learning to care and share fully without expectation but with the certainty that I will be cared for has solidified AAA masculinity in me.

In addition to these valuable lessons from deep, sustained engagement with the land, I also learned from other men committed to a different life and world. In the community surrounding BOC and HFH, men express care and love. Baba Fred hugs men, women, and children alike. He is unafraid to tell male friends that he loves them. As a central figure in the community, he displays caring behavior that influences others. The words "peace," "love," and "blessings" are liberally infused in the conversations between men. Commonly men in this community touch their chest near their hearts and bow slightly in greeting and parting.

FIG. 17. Jason Jones. Photo by author.

Many men in this community model to varying degrees a liberatory masculinity. From the men in this community, I have learned a great deal about the freedoms and struggles associated with the decolonial and reindigenization processes. However, as always, in recent years my primary teachers of Indigenous ways especially as regards gender have been elder women. While Fred Carter and Gregory Bratton have been my primary mentors in horticulture, permaculture, and sustainability, I work daily alongside women like Dr. Wright, Dorothy J., Sandra P., Jacqueline Smith, Quafin and Alexy Irving. As in much of the radical resistance to Wetiko over the past five hundred years and more, women perform much of the regenerative work.[13]

From elder women I have learned most of what I know about the daily tasks and strategies of caring for and regenerating the land. To men and women alike, they teach their innate agrarian artistry and their womanist perspectives.[14] Importantly, women like Dr. Jifunza Wright, Safia Rashid, and Mama Dorothy have taught me key strategies, skills, and perspectives such as herbalism, foraging, and a better understanding of my place in relation to the plant nations who share the lands I occupy. Women lead our movement. While men are far from absent, women put in most of the work hours at the food autonomy events that I have participated in for eighteen years. Since 2011 I have kept daily records concerning participation in GLP gardens. More than 90 percent of the people who visit and work are women and their children. Additional evidence of women's leadership in our movement comes from our Lifeboats Permaculture course. Twenty-seven people completed the course. The class of community leaders consisted of nineteen women and eight men. Along with Dr. Jifunza Wright, one of the three co-teachers, women like Dr. Andrea Mason, Jacqueline Abena Smith, and Safia Rashid taught classes and used their expertise to assist novices. Others like Ana, Dr. Bonnie Alalade Harrison, Mama Jessie Avraham, and Rebecca did a great deal of organizing the class and making sure it ran on schedule.

A Persistent Malady

Heteropatriarchy is a key aspect of Wetiko. The resurgent revolutionary politics of decolonialism and reindigeneity that we practice in the food movement in Chicago must confront heteropatriachy with as much zeal as we confront private property, land grabs and land desecration, racism, wage labor and the state.

Wetiko's rigid sex-gender system has been an effective structure for dividing us from one another, creating hate for nonbinary/noncisgender people, and limiting the possibilities for expressions of gender and sexuality that are free and generative of knowledge and culture. Many Indigenous men including some Black Americans I am surrounded by in the food movement accept heteropatriarchy and are openly hostile toward LGBTQ2 people and culture. Cis-heteronormative (cis-het) men members of my food community have expressed in conversations with me their dislike for LGBTQ2 people, that there is a White gay agenda to feminize Black men, disrupt the Black family, and divert attention from "real" issues that Black people face, and they unapologetically state that they are homophobic. A recent Facebook thread from a member of our food community, "Joe," saddened me as it epitomized the anger and violence that many colonized and decolonizing men approach anything that does not resemble cis-het hypermasculinity. Joe posted a short video that discussed "Drag Queen Story Time." The video centered on a drag queen who went to elementary schools, read to children, and taught them to feel and act free and to express that through story and art. Joe commented with a series of violent epithets to drag queens and anyone who condones "these sick minded people."

What is significant about Joe's response is that he has been mentored in the community and his attitudes have not been significantly challenged. Joe has interned with and worked for many movement-related groups and with important elders in the community. He spends time on the land with Black elders. He is supported in our community. What does this mean about how our food community and the broader Black nationalist community sees gender and sexuality and how does this limit us in our efforts to decolonize and reindigenize? Significantly for this project of autoteoriahistoria, what does it say about my anticolonial masculinity that I did not denounce his heteromasculinist violence and have often failed to have this conversation with others holding similar views? Simpson answers this question without reservation in her clear-eyed analysis of the needs of Indigenous struggles for freedom:

> When we engage in gender violence or are silent in the face of homophobia, transphobia, heterosexism, discrimination, and ongoing gender violence, we are working in collusion with white men and on behalf of the settler colonial state to further destroy Indigenous nationhood.[15]

This includes women since men are not the only ones who assist Wetiko heteropatriarchy. Some women in my community including elder women have made it clear that they have accepted colonizer's gender-sexuality binaries and have a disdain for any that is not "straight." One leader had no qualms about labelling herself a homophobe in a group conversation. And to be absolutely clear, this heteropatriarchal plague is not unique to the Black decolonial food movement in Chicago. Chicanx students and collaborators have discussed with me how these phobias around gender and sexuality have cut deep wounds in our community. Sexual harassment, misgendering, homophobia, and hypermasculinity are topics regularly discussed by my Chicanx camaradas. Moreover, I have seen how a lack of recognition of genderqueer persons in their full personhood places limits on our relationships and has challenged our organizations and work. At GLP and with the Seedkeepers Collective, we have had difficult conversations about gender/sexuality identity and homophobia and transphobia that have caused some to distance themselves or leave the collective.

AAA masculinity and liberatory praxis have no room for hate and division of our people along Wetiko's gender and sexuality lines. We—and I—have room to grow and develop, but despite the trans- and homophobia that continues to limit our movement I am decolonizing and reindigenizing and see this hatred for what it is: a strategy on the part of the colonizer to undermine the power of women, two-spirit, lesbian, gay, queer, and trans people, to separate us from the knowledge that comes from two-spirit people, to drive a wedge between men and women, and to ultimately destroy Indigenous people.[16]

Homophobia, transphobia, and other heteropatriarchal orientations plague our movement as countless numbers of people have chosen their dignity over working with heterosexists and transphobes. Accomplices have discussed the fallout in numerous groups over the resistance to acknowledging gender queerness and defending masculinist perspectives and behaviors. We can never be sure how much of a wedge has been driven between members and organizations in the larger food movement due to this problem.

Fortunately, a new generation of urban BIPOC growers challenges Wetiko's sex-gender system that many of the rest of us in the movement have accepted. Groups like USAN, Urban Growers Collective, Reclaiming Our Roots, and Catatumbo Cooperative among others ensure that their gardens and other spaces of the food movement are open and inclusive. Moreover, they often center women and LGBTQ2 people in their work. Thus, more than being tolerant or mildly accepting these younger growers highlight marginalized people within our communities and the perspectives and culture of the more-than-cis-het communities. Trans- and homophobia are "called in," a term for establishing honest, open, and accountable relationships with movement members who express and act in damaging ways relative to inclusivity.[17]

The mere act of having people declare their desired pronouns at the beginning of meetings, for example, has a profound effect on those present. In conversation with Baba Fred Carter, I learned that at a national Black food movement organization of which he is a prominent elder member, they engage in this practice along with others that place issues of sex, gender, and sexuality front and center in their discussions. Baba Fred expressed to me that he had never had to do that before. Many elders, including him, have misstepped at meetings, including misgendering people. The result of this tension has been tearful, heartfelt conversations about gender and other areas of disagreement between younger (but not always) and older (not always) members. In his estimation, the conversations helped him and others to be aware of and sensitive to these issues.

Gage Park Latinx Council and Reclaiming Our Roots provide another example of the newer generation of food activists and their gender/sexuality inclusivity and vigilance regarding trans- and homophobia, and related issues. Bee Rodriguez along with the founders of GPLXC are explicit in their practices of gender/sexuality inclusivity as the "x" in Latinx suggests. But, rather than a mere symbolic gesture, the young leaders actively open space for gender and sexuality expression recognizing the power in the diversity of our community. When I have been around the young people mentored by GPLXC and Bee, they always engage me in questions addressing the colonial sex-gender system. Their reindigenization processes include challenges to Wetiko's sex-gender system as well as positive affirmations of Indigenous ways of being.

(In)Conclusion

My journey away from Wetiko masculinity has been fostered in the food autonomy movement. Healing from Wetiko has been difficult. I only began to make real
progress against this disease of greed and individualism once I put my hands in
the soil next to Mexicanx and Black elders. While my journey is far from complete
and I continue to encounter many roadblocks coming from inside and outside
our movement, I am certain that attention to IK is the correct path. As such, I have
distilled the best of what I know from Indigenous, anarchist and transnational
feminist scholars and activists into an antiauthoritarian, anticolonial, alterNative
framework whereby I can strategize and implement new (at least to some of us)
ways of being a man interdependently with all our relations. I learn from the land
and use my place and all my relations that reside upon it to engage my fellow humans in exercises of decolonizing our minds and bodies. Through intimate, sustained interactions with our place, we begin to dismantle master's hypermasculine
house with anticolonial tools. We reject the master's gender identities, roles, and
expectations and question all his categories including "Latinx," "Chican@," and
"Other." In further developing our urban alterNative masculinity, we can reach
back for our Indigenous stories that will move us beyond our current understanding. These anticolonial practices are the first steps toward the radical reorganiza-
tion of our world that we require.

Healing, Gender Identity, and Reindigenization with Bee Rodriguez

BEE RODRIGUEZ: I really want to say that I'm gender nonconforming, but that doesn't feel right. I'm still evolving. I'm still sitting with that. So I guess right now I'd say that I'm gender questioning as I continue to deconstruct the inherited masculinity and patriarchy that has been in my lineage.

Because in my gender identity it is not this monolithic green space [like industrial agriculture]. It's this deep gender identity that flows with the way the natural world works. Sometimes you don't see the beauty cuz a lot of times the beauty is under the soil. A lot of the beauty of the milpa is

FIG. 18. Bee Rodriguez. Photo by Simone Reynolds.

also under the soil. There's a lot of beauty that happens there too. And that's how I feel sometimes. There's a lot of internal beauty there that I haven't shared with the world or I haven't shared with my peers, but at the same time that internal beauty is helping the soil become more fertile for it to emerge in the next season. So that's kinda where I'm at with my gender identity, you know. Trying to prepare it and trying to feel comfortable in my own skin, in my own soil, so that I can fully be like my true authentic self.

PANCHO MCFARLAND: I feel that too. So much of what you said I want to talk about anyway. Your introduction jumps right in. That gender piece too. Not feeling comfortable saying gender nonconforming. I have the same thing too. I don't want to put words in your mouth, but this is how I feel. I don't want to be rigid. I don't want to follow the colonial sex-gender-sexuality system that has been forced upon us. But in my behaviors and in my history throughout my life, and I'm fifty-two, so imagine how long that has been, I've always been cis-het. I've always been a heterosexual man. I've only had sex with women and all that kinda stuff, so I would like to be gender nonconforming to say that but I don't know what people who are really gender nonconforming go through in this society. I don't want to steal an identity that is not mine. I do want to be able to think in a way that is more queered in that way. And then I can't figure out what is more natural to me. Is it natural to be cis-het in my sexuality the way that I've been? Or how much of that is actual colonial heteropatriachal mindset stuffed in me? So I feel you on that.

BR: I was thinking about that the other day. Growing up my experience has been cis-hetero. My lived experience hasn't been queer, hasn't been an open space for gender exploration. It really has been a rigid colonial patriarchy experience because that's what I inherited from my most recent abuelos and caretakers. That's what they were taught to assimilate to. I realize the harm I've done and hold myself accountable, but hold myself accountable in a soft way. Because I also realize the harm that patriarchy causes on the body, on land, on my queer peers, on myself most importantly. I get you. Growing up my experience has always been being masculine in the colonial ways. I've never been able to experience the multitude of my identity without backlash from my family. Without that trauma popping up. But that's the past me. Right now, as I come more aware of those realities, like I said, looking to transform and transmute the multitude and beauty of my identity. It is a scary journey of backlash from family, but that's why I think it's very important to relate to other folks, to have relationships with people who are affirming and understanding, who love you. In the queer world they call it chosen family. I think that's very important for my journey of self-discovery.

PM: What are your goals in this movement, in this life? What is it that you are trying to do here?

BR: There are people who manifest things like this [snaps fingers indicating "easily"] in their life. I'm not. I'm a slow manifester. It might take years. I'm more like a visionary. I'm able to see or have visions ahead of time through dreams or just through daydreaming, through writing. I'm a visionary, so I'm always dreaming. I'm always in a dream space or always imagining how I can design my life. How can I design my life according to the things I love and that I'm passionate about? I guess for me I really want to continue creating spaces for culturally appropriate ecological education. I have this seed that I'm dropping in my altar right now which is something I call La Escuelita Verde. La Escuelita Verde is exactly that. A space where young people from the community can come and have a culturally appropriate, affirming ecological education.

Every time I learn something new about practices, traditional soil practices, especially when it comes to our traditional food ways, maíz, frijol, squash, when I learn something about those things, about how they work, how they exist, it really awakens this inner-child feeling in me that gives me so much curiosity and ambition. Why not chase that feeling and that space for my entire life? Why not learn about these ways, remember these ways and create spaces to teach these ways? Not only to teach these ways but also to apply these to the land.

Maybe I'm making my healing work my life purpose. I don't know. Maybe but this feels right, right now. I do envision myself creating sustainable foodways within the urban city. Ways that folks can receive culturally appropriate food crops for free. Growing up we didn't get that. Government-assisted foods were not culturally appropriate. It was another way of making us sick but also creating a separation between people and the land, people, and food. Those are my visions. I want to continue creating spaces for me to connect to the land, teach about the land, and be able to design my life around the way the natural world works. I don't want to be working November to February. I want to be resting and celebrating and remembering rather than be working.

PM: I say this all the time during the hottest hottest days and the coldest snowiest days, we should not do anything. The whole city ought to shut down. "No, I'm not going to do anything." Cuz why? Why?

BR: Part of my design is making space to dream outside. Part of my design is also to do the things that my caretakers would never have imagined themselves doing because of colonialism and because of capitalism cuz they are always working their ass off. Part of it for me is to be able to go back and forth from here in the city to the place where my parents were born. To be able to have my safe place there too. And to be able to reconnect back and forth. It is very important to me, cuz even though I was born here in Chicago, I think the ties I have here in Chicago are more tied to the activism work rather than . . . I'm more tied to the work and to the journey. When I go back to my homeland I reconnect to the spirituality part. Cuz here in Chicago it is really difficult to connect . . .

PM: It is difficult to connect in Chicago. Why is that?

BR: What I mean by that is like if you do connect and you do center yourself there can be a lot of disruptions to that connection. For example, the way that I do things right now and the way I tend to the land right now is through guerilla gardening. There's always that fear of, like, trying to fight the system to grow food and that disruption . . . being at the garden is a place that I can connect besides my room. It is a place that I can connect and remember and practice our traditional medicine. If that gets disrupted, it is a way of displacing us. That's what disrupts that connection. We don't have access to green spaces like that. We don't have access to land like that. If we wanted to purchase the land, we don't have the resources right now to purchase it. I don't know if that's something we are looking to do. With all that and because of guerilla garden, that is a disruption and a fear that comes with guerilla gardening in the city . . . guerilla gardening, folks don't talk about the consequences that can happen when you are guerilla gardening. It is a radical thing to do. Pop up in an empty lot. Transform it into a garden without permission from the government or the city. Nobody talks about how the city can threaten you to take the garden. Nobody talks about the psychological effects that it has on your mind. So that's where the disruption comes from. Always trying to fight the system when you are just tryin to live. Just trying to grow corn.

PM: It made me think about the question of private property. The question of inequality. You said lack of resources. We can't be who we are and become more because we don't have security in land. It is fleeting security at best. It is impossible to connect fully. We are doing it. We are gonna do our best. As you mentioned, when you go to your garden you are able to connect. When I go to my garden, I'm able to connect but not as fully as we would like. That's related to the healing. That's one of the major themes that have been coming up in the dialogues with my accomplices and just in my experiences in the work we do. Everybody talks about it as doing healing work in the soil primarily being in the soil. I think the other aspects of it for us in the city because in the city we automatically have to become community organizers and activists. Whereas you had a piece of land out in the country, you'd just grow corn or whatever. But here politics is always involved. You have to be an activist too.

BR: Sometimes you have to be an "activist" without wanting to. It's not something you applied for or signed up for, but by nature and the things that you do and where you come from and your lived experience you have no other way but to fight for your struggles, to fight for a decent human life. That's what shocks me . . . The people around me do a lot of good work but it is necessary unnecessary work; unnecessary because we are not the ones who created this mess. We are not the ones who created the idea of industrialization and capitalism. We are just assimilating. Our ancestors, our relatives, are just assimilating to capitalism even just to have this conversation right now. The system wants us to clean up their mess . . . That's like something I'm trying to sit with and figure out. I don't want to be cleaning up their mess all of the time. You know?

PM: I want to go to this topic before I circle back to spirituality. The question I want to talk to about is around race and race relations. Especially Black/Indigenous, POC or cultural nationalism where it's just about us. It's just about Indigenous people or it's just about Black people or Mexicanos or whatever. The reason I'm asking you this is because in my work it is cross-cultural, cross-racial. It crosses boundaries. I think it almost has to cross boundaries. I can't imagine a liberatory practice that is only for one group of people. It doesn't seem right to me. So for me in my work I'm always thinking in that space of crossing bridges between people. And the major one is the race question. So I've spent fifteen years, in a primarily Black movement as a non-Black identified person. And the reason was because I think it is important to break these barriers down and to show people that it is possible. Through all the baloney that I have to go through over the years of people questioning my motives and still have to go through to show its importance. In particular for my generation of activists while solidarity is a question that is very important to us, meaning "I'm going to support your work," we still were focused on "our" issues. If it is "their" issues, then we are going to support "their" issues. And then we got "our" issues. And what I'm saying is "No, our issues are the same. If they are not, then what are we doing working together." They may manifest themselves differently. They may treat people who have darker skin and who are called Black in different ways, but at root the struggle is the same and the goals are the same. If they are not, I don't care what color you are, I don't want to work with you. I don't get the talk about "allies." That term "allies," I don't get that. And I don't get that talk about theirs versus ours. It is ours. I am equally in the fight with people who are not "like" me because we are fighting the same thing. We are fighting colonialism, capitalism, White supremacy, and the heteropatriarchy. If you are not down for that, then . . . ? I want my "we" to be expansive. I want my "we" to include. I want other people's to be too. I want them to call me "we," even if I don't share your sexuality or even if I don't share your race. You see what I'm getting at? That's what I've come to over the years with this stuff. So where are you on this?

BR: In Chicago, we live in silos. Every neighborhood lacks diversity. They say Chicago is diverse but segregated. The community that I am part of is majority of Mexican descent, predominantly Brown folks in a neighborhood that used to be predominantly Black relatives and before that used to be predominantly White . . . the history of the place is it started off White then Blacks came in and White flight. They got pushed toward Englewood, and then folks of Mexican descent came in. They started renting, they started moving in . . . I think we are still trying to figure that out. We are still trying to figure out how to relate to one another beyond silos, beyond borders, beyond race. Because the system doesn't want us to relate to one another. Doesn't want us to have conversations on how to be in right relationship with one another. Culturally, growing up there is a lot of anti-Blackness in the Mexican community . . . There is a lot of anti-Blackness that I'm holding myself accountable and things that I am unlearning so that when the time is right I can be in right relationship with folks that are different than me and who want to continue fighting against colonialism and building this new world. That's a space where a lot of conversation needs to be happening more; at least on the southwest side of Chicago. There's really no coalitions, no collectives, that cross cultures. There's nothing like that. I think the first time that I was able to be in a space where Black and Brown folks were together was the Chicago permaculture conference. I think that was one of the first spaces where myself as an urban campesino was able to begin to imagine a life together with Black and Brown folks.

So I do feel like we need to have more conversations and spaces to have those conversations. For me, ceremony and rituals are a good place to have those conversations, to build those relations. Traditional ceremonies and rituals to see one another eye to eye and heart to heart. That's a good way to see one another and build those relationships. I grew up in Little Village. My parents were so protective of who I went out with and where I went. They were very selective. A lot of that has caused harm between the way that I relate to folks who don't look like me. A lot of those things I'm still unlearning. It goes back to what we were talking about earlier about the rigidity in patriarchy and colonialism.

PM: I know that you work primarily with young people of Mexican descent. Almost exclusively. Is there in your practice some of the reaching across borders that you are talking about or are you still trying to figure out how to do that?

BR: Not by choice. It's not really by choice. When we recruit for programming that's what we get . . . We are in a pilot phase, the beginning phases. If I do wanna work with folks who are not of Mexican descent, it is important to bring on board in decision-making and curriculum-building, bringing, like, Black and other Indigenous folks into the curriculum-making and decision-making. When we are teaching and it is culturally appropriate, they can bring their piece of knowledge into the curriculum. I can teach certain things that I can read about the way Black folks tend to the land, but I'm limited to my experience. If I'm imagining building a cross-cultural curriculum, it makes sense to bring people, facilitators, educators from different cultures to the space. For me that will feel the safest. It will be the right move to do. In Gage Park majority is folks of Mexican descent, but the second biggest population is our Black relatives. I have seen how they are excluded in these resources, in these opportunities. That's a piece that I'm still trying to work out and imagine how to work through.

PM: We could talk a lot about this and our attempts at doing this and their failures and their successes. There are so many people who want to do that now. I think the young people are much more clued into our shared destiny and our shared futures and our shared current circumstances. People are much more sophisticated and know that it all stems from capitalism, colonialism, White supremacy, and heteropatriarchy. It all does . . . young people are much more keen to that. But the folks that I know are like you: geographically located in a particular area, expertise in a particular area, working with groups who have a certain type of mission that attracts certain folks. So as much as we want to cross and implement a much more [intense focus] on this, there are certain limitations on that. So the question is how do we do that. There are certain people like Alexy, who was at the conference, who work with young people. I was teaching for her yesterday. She wants to do the same thing. But because of who she is, working in a particular environment and the expectations of the people who give you jobs, funders. So funders sometimes say, "This is money that is going to this group." They may not have the vision of what we are talking about here that everything comes from the same source. They are very piecemeal, very locked in to the master's categories and the master's way of understanding things. I wonder to what degree that relations between subordinate ethnic groups, Mexicano, Black, Indigenous, what have you, are determined by White power structures. The degree to which we would love to do that, cross the aisle, cross the border, the power structures [that] implement certain types of things, sometimes not easily seen or understood, that limit our ability to cross borders. It's not always a simple lack, of not wanting to, or racism on the part of this group or that group. Sometimes there are real barriers to the ability to do so: institutional barriers and definitely cultural barriers in the larger white culture that is telling us how to think about Black people or Mexicans. Know what I mean?

BR: It's almost like a third person in the conversation. A lot of times it is . . . what White supremacy does to people of color at least in my experience trying to build these bridges. What White supremacy does is it creates this psychological manipulation. Saying that you shouldn't be doing that and you shouldn't be talking to Black folks and you shouldn't be building these bridges. It really is this psychological manipulation [that] takes time to heal from and unlearn that colonial voice that exists within the self. It's a real thing, man. It's a real fuckin thing.

PM: I'm even trying to figure out and there's a lot of push back on this. I've been saying this for years, in public conversations too. I wanna be able to say that it is not even about, as I'm saying this I'm critiquing myself. It's not even about crossing borders but realizing that there isn't a border. At the end of the day there are no borders. Those are only colonially erected barriers and borders that we are just choosing to accept. You are pissed off at the White man, but you go ahead and use his logic that says you are different than. I wanna say that we are all the same to the degree that we are all living souls. To the degree that we say we are relatives and not only across human groups but across species as well. I think that is the ultimate thing I want to get to. At the same time, recognize that diversity is part of the strength of any, of everything. Can we be the same, come from the same life force, and have individual and group diversity? That's what I'm hoping. I hope there is a politic for getting there too. But a lot of people reject that. They say, "This is who we are." And they talk more in solidarity and crossing borders as opposed to what I'm trying to suggest is that we eliminate the borders completely whether it is religion or gender or race or whatever it is. And maybe that is the way we might relate to one another better. You are talking about right relationship. I'm talking about "how do I need to be thinking so that I can begin to act in right ways with other people?" So that's what I'm thinking. I don't know if I'm right or wrong. I don't know if this is good or bad. But that's where I'm at.

BR: It's healing work, interpersonal healing work that needs to be done. I forget where I heard this. I don't want to be healing forever. I don't wanna be like healing forever, man. I wanna enjoy the perks of a healed person. You know what I'm saying? I've been doing healing work for a couple years now. The pandemic forced us to do healing work. At least for me. I'm learning that it's OK to take a break from healing and enjoy the perks, the things of earth throughout this journey. It goes back to some type of hyperpolicing yourself. The land is many things. It can be a space for healing when needed. The land can be a space for celebration. The land can be a space for manifestation. And sometimes the land can just be the land. It transforms into whatever relationship you need and have with the land in that moment. So do we. Sometimes we just need to celebrate and enjoy the perks of just existing. I don't wanna be healing forever. Eventually I want to celebrate myself. You know? I was gonna add to that, but period, that's it. Not in relation to any goddamn thing, but of course always we know we are in relation to everything. You deserve, and that's it. I wanna be healed, and that's it.

Dr. Jifunza Wright-Carter

COMMUNITY HEALER, MENTOR, AND ORGANIZER

Over the years, I have worked on numerous projects with Dr. J. She is a seemingly tireless leader of our movement. She explained to me that people always encourage her to slow down. She told me, "How can they really ask that of me? Do they know what they are asking? We have too many problems in our community. Slow down, rest? Not when we are experiencing what we are experiencing right now." Doc is a healer and believes that a key need in our struggle is to "raise the frequency, raise the vibration" of our interactions, words, ideas and actions. Mental, physical, emotional, and spiritual healing are key to developing our communities in ethical ways.

Doc describes herself as a Black woman but is quick also to remind people of her Amerindigenous heritage. During our Resilient Community Design course in June 2022, she explained her own experiences and why Black Americans are direct relatives to tribally recognized Indigenous people:

> When I was a little girl, I would listen to them speak the [Indigenous] language. There were all these little signs and things . . . My aunt told us that back in the day to be Indigenous was the lowest of the low. So many just claimed to be Black.

In that group of primarily Black-identified people, the discussion turned to each of their familial connections to recognized Indigenous Americans. Doc complicates further our understanding of the African American relationship to indigeneity:

> So, during slavery when the European brought Africans, they brought men. Who were they going to mate with? There were no African women. So all of us are likely to be Indigenous. But because of discrimination, records, we don't know this.

On May 5, 2022, Dr. Wright explained the values behind the BOC, Pembroke, Illinois, history, and BOC structures and strategies to a group of business development specialists. She explained that BOC had a philosophical/spiritual goal and a practical material goal.

> We want to be a catalyst for reclaiming Black folks' connection to this planet
> through agriculture, the earth and farming . . . We want to restore local food
> networks and pathways to generate economic opportunity for Black and
> Brown communities.

Explaining the Sustainable Agriculture tract at Black Oaks, she stated:

> With the Sustainable Ag tract, we want to return Pembroke to its place as an
> agricultural hub for Black people in the region. During the Great Migration,
> Black farmers in Pembroke fed Black people in Chicago. We found out that
> they fed people all the way in Michigan and Indiana. Black farmers were
> important to the whole region . . . We want what we call an endogenous eco-
> nomic development instead of the extractive type of economy of colonialism.
> We want the resources to be local and we want the resources generated to stay
> local.

Further on in the presentation, Doc stated,

> We want Black Oaks to become a catalyst for decolonization . . . With the Sus-
> tainable Building Tract, we are working toward some level of self-determina-
> tion. We have trainings. We have community-built buildings. We are building
> guilds that develop skills.

About the forty-acre eco-campus that is the headquarters, she said,

> We did not want to be an intentional community or an eco-village. Our aim
> was for people to visit and return to their communities and use the knowl-
> edge and the experience to improve their communities.

Doc explained that in their more than twenty years of experience with permaculture, intentional communities and related that eco-villages they have encountered
have been failures. She saw communities fall apart when new people move in, values change, and Wetiko ethics intrude. Her decades of experience have shown her
that the needed cooperation required to decolonize and move toward liberation
for Black Americans and others must come in different forms. A large part of what
Black Oaks does is work with others to figure out what types of cooperation work
best for Black and Indigenous people.

In 2020 extractive neocolonialism threatened to attack the Black communities
where BOC operates. Energy behemoth NICOR campaigned to run a natural gas
pipeline through the communities and the fragile Black Oaks ecosystem. NICOR
promises that the pipeline will bring much needed energy to the area. Black Oaks

and colleagues know that the pipeline, like all pipelines, will leak and its very construction will greatly damage the natural landscape including the water supply. Dr. Wright explained,

> With the Renewable Pembroke campaign, we have an environmental justice campaign going on. We are fighting the intrusion of a natural gas pipeline . . . With the solar array on the Black Oaks eco-campus, we want to be a model of sustainable energy. We want to be energy sovereign and support food sovereignty in the region.

Doc served as a lead organizer for the Renewable Pembroke campaign, which received support from Black environmental and food justice organizations throughout the country, including the Black Food and Justice Alliance. Numerous local activists worked on petition campaigns, political education, town hall meetings, and meetings with politicians.

As her name suggests, one of Doc's primary roles for our community is as a healer. Her knowledge of plant medicine, Indigenous healing modalities, nutrition, and the like have proved invaluable to hundreds, perhaps thousands, over the many decades of her community work. In our Resilient Community Design course in 2022, she often focused on the emotional needs that are going unmet in our communities. The emotional and spiritual lack is a primary driver of the difficulty we have working together to create community. So, while I focused on teaching our students "practical" skills related to water, soil, and trees, for example, Doc made sure we had some tools to think about and deal with the spiritual and emotional trauma that Black, Indigenous, and other people of color experience.

> I want to remind everyone of need. You know? The whole concept of need. Often times, the harm happens in the space of withholding of love, of needs. The prison-industrial complex has been allowed to flourish and create a subculture in our community as a result of our needs not being met. Inside of all of that is a lot of withholding of love. If we want to say, "I can design the most perfect places where people could actualize their potential. There would be peace and all those great things," then we kinda have to go back to the concept of needs being addressed and fulfilled . . . All too often people become angry and under the anger is hurt. So [we need to] literally address those things and not feed those things, neutralize things . . .

May 8, 2022, was Mother's Day on the U.S. calendar. Many of our students in the Resilient Community Design course expressed difficulty dealing with all that comes from this holiday. Difficult relationships with mothers and the desire to reject Mother's Day as a colonially imposed hypocritical holiday had many emotionally and spiritually stressed. Doc offered healing wisdom and invited us to think differently about this day. She said,

> When Pancho decided to have this class on the colonial "Mother's Day," I was like "Go with the decolonization process!" I was like "Whoa!" because unfortunately the colonialist "Mother's Day" is a very important holiday, at least in the Black American community. But I'm acknowledging that indigenously, you know, we all had our own individual "mother's day" and that was on the day of the birth of our children. That was our Indigenous mother's day . . . I want to invite everybody who is in transition with this just staying with the qualities of the earth. Mother is an endearing term for the earth. I was thinking about a spiritual. The words are: "My old Mother is a mighty good Mother. / My old Mother is a mighty good Mother. / You're gonna reap what you sow."

Doc encourages her students to look to our "mighty good Mother" for understanding ourselves in relation to our roles and responsibilities within community. On April 3, 2022, she taught the following:

> It's about ecological relationships. We are always within an ecosystem. The colonialist mentality is that ecosystems are outside us; humans reign. We should see ourselves differently. Every living thing has a function. We, each of us, has a function which is greater than serving ourselves . . . What we need to find out is who are you within the ecosystem? What niche do you fill? Be conscious that you are in relationships. But, also, what is the need that one has to be in ecological relationships? Often our needs are not met in this society. This is why we have all this lying, cheating, stealing. We need to be clear about we should fulfill people's needs.
>
> I want to invite you to walk through life like our ancestors: energetically. Everything has energy. There is no clear demarcation between living and nonliving things. We should be moving away from this Western insanity including the limits to language . . . We need to know who you are in creating a desirable outcome; be conscious of your connection to the collective consciousness and what are the needs of yourself and others that we can fulfill for one another to achieve the desirable outcome.

Doc's impact on our movement community is incalculable and not easily described in a few brief excerpts. The following chapter, "Mothers of the Movement," offers more insight into how Doc operates within our community and the innate agrarian artistry that she and others model.

CHAPTER 9

Mothers of the Movement

ECO-WOMANISM, INNATE AGRARIAN ARTISTRY, AND ANTICOLONIAL HEALING

Ipalnemohuani	You are the giver of life
No yolotl tatzin	We have your venerable heart
Tlazocamati	Thank you,
Tonanatzin	Venerated Mother

"HUEY TONANTZIN," MEXICA PRAYER

"The snakes were the worst part" my mom says during her retelling of living modestly and close to the earth as working-class girl of Mexican descent in New Mexico in the 1950s. The memory of her regular journeys to the outhouse at her grandparents' home in Jansen, Colorado, plays an important role in her *auto-historiateoria*. The story illustrates place, nature-human relations, poverty, racism, resilience, corrupt mining corporations, and many other aspects of life for her and other Indigenous and Mexican-origin people in the U.S. Southwest. She retold this story during a phone conversation in which I described many of the activities I was engaged in as part of my food autonomy practices. My stories of reindigenization prompted her to describe the close-to-nature lifestyle she experienced as a child. Our encounters with snakes at GLP gardens illustrating the natural abundance found there caused my mom to gleefully retell her stories of place. My story of being startled by snakes in our garden prompted my mother's memory and helped us both to "re-member" or put ourselves back together from the traumatic and dislocating effects of Wetiko.

My mothers and aunts filled my childhood with experiences of Indigenous/Mexicana agrarian artistry.[1] By the 1950s no one in our family was a farmer or relied on farm work to make a living. My tías and tíos were working-class people with jobs in coal, steel, policing, nursing, and education. Yet, due to their rural upbringing in Colorado and New Mexico, they held on to many land-based practices, a.k.a. Indigenous practices. Each had a good knowledge of how to grow annual vegetables in their climate, and most vegetables grew on small backyard plots. In addition, my tías had some knowledge of foraging, fishing, and other land-based practices. Indigenous-Mexicana culinary and celebratory traditions also grounded my youth in nature. On days of celebration, my cousins and I would smell and hear the tamale-making before we saw it. My aunts, mother, and grandmother talked loudly and sang along to Mexican rancheras. We also heard the slapping, scrapping, and boiling that accompanied the tamalada preparation. We came to-gether often for the millennia-old practice of the tamalada whereby Indigenous, corn-based communities celebrated and worshipped. The management of the tamalada, its food preparation and the mood, were set by the women of our family. The tamalada reaffirmed our indigeneity, which for us means, in part, our relation-ship to corn. Their cultural work consolidated our claim to our belongingness to the land—an anticolonial, antiauthoritarian alterNative existence.

By the late 1980s, I learned to call the agrarian artistry of my tias ecofeminism. While they weren't activists like so many who now wear the ecofeminist label, they were practitioners of IK. Indigeneity intersected with and came into conflict with Wetiko. Yet they held tradition and passed it on. They practiced a lifestyle that engaged nature and fought racism and capitalism. Their ecofeminism was antiau-thoritarian, anticolonial, and alterNative while also succumbing to the pressures of Wetiko. Women accomplices in the Black food movement in Chicago similarly demonstrate an innate agrarian artistry tying them to centuries of Black women's resistance on the land.[2] As keepers of the culture, Black women in our movement teach these Indigenous African landed traditions via multiple media including workshops, lectures, classes, field lessons, video, and writings.

In our community, many women describe their land-based practices as In-digenous. In a June 2019 visit to BOC, Mama Dr. Jifunza Wright explained that her plant-based medicinal practices, including the designing of herb gardens and planting, harvesting, drying, and prescribing of herbs, were Indigenous. She gave members of GLP and the Lifeboats Permaculture Guild lessons in plant identifi-cation (Indigenous, European scientific, and popular names of plants), mandala garden design, planting techniques, soil building, and a critique of Wetiko. Her workshops began with the lessons of the land and the time and pace of the Black Oaks woodlands and were eco-womanist, Indigenous, AAA, and filled with innate agrarian artistry.

The bulk of this chapter describes the Black eco-womanist praxis that I have experienced and learned from in the Black food autonomy movement on the South Side of Chicago. The Black women in our movement are the living legacy of the history of Black women's resistance to Wetiko and resilience through AHK. Like the "diasporadas" who used artistry to offer an internationalist "afrifemcen-tric" theory of resistance,[3] Black women accomplices in our movement use beauty and art to theorize and implement Indigenous ways of being. Through making connections between my accomplices in Chicago and the history of U.S. African diasporan women, we can add to the developing theoretical framework around the centrality of Black and Indigenous women to our community resilience and the revolutionary healing of the planet.

Black Women Build

The herstory of African women in the struggle for African liberation begins with Black women like the legendary Paanza, who would braid seeds into their hair and that of their children to enhance the possibility of survival in harsh and violent environments and to maintain cultural traditions.[4] Fannie Lou Hamer's work in the 1960s exemplifies the multiple and central roles that women have played in Black liberation movements, especially those keenly aware of the need for and power of food self-sufficiency and self-determination. She understood and developed two fundamental concepts to the Black radicalism of the time: 1) landownership; 2) collective and cooperative work.

Landownership allows people to have food autonomy, to be able to determine for ourselves what goes into our body, and how food is produced and distributed. As Hamer explained,

> Down where we are, food is used as a political weapon. But if you have a pig in your backyard, if you have some vegetables in your garden, you can feed yourself and your family, and nobody can push you around. If we have something like some pigs and some gardens and a few things like that, even if we have no jobs, we can eat and we can look after our families.[5]

The land and the knowledge of how to properly steward it are central to Black and Indigenous liberation. Hamer's theory and practice offer an example that many of my Black women accomplices adopt and adapt. In addition, my camaradas implement culinary justice. Michael Twitty argues that culinary justice includes learning and using AHK that contains valuable nutritional knowledge and stories of survivance: the active survival of African peoples amid colonization, slavery, and other manifestations of White supremacy.[6]

Women perform most of the invaluable socially reproductive and care labor. Women in our liberation movements extend this family care labor to the community level when they take their skills in organizing home economics to movement organizing spaces. Hamer serves as exemplar as she extended her practical knowledge of Black American foodways to her Mississippi community. She founded Freedom Farm Cooperative in 1967 "as a means to develop a sustainable black community on the foundation of agriculture [and] illuminated the relationship between economic self-sufficiency and political power and translated theory into action."[7] The Freedom Farm Cooperative served hundreds of local Black residents with many subsistence activities. All their services and projects sought to create a "cooperative intentional community" that "developed the kinds of economic autonomy that were a critical foundation for this self-determined, politically engaged, liberated community."[8] While the Freedom Farm Cooperative existed less than a decade, the strides they made toward Black autonomy through cooperative behavior offers many lessons for our current movement and illustrate how Black women keep and use the crucial knowledge of the BAT. That they were short-lived also suggests a weakness in Hamer's strategy that we can learn from; without political power, economic power can be easily undermined.

Harriet Tubman (Araminta Ross) serves as another example of Black women's key role in Black liberation. While Tubman is known by all who went to school in the United States as the key figure in the Underground Railroad, few of us know any details of her life and her work. Tubman was a "master herbalist."[9] Her knowledge of ethnobotany and plant medicine, along with that of astronomy and the natural world more broadly, allowed her to successfully help many Africans escape slavery. Tubman knew how to navigate by the stars and other natural phenomena and could identify plants and how to use them for the many maladies that escapees suffered along the way. Tubman's ethnobotanical knowledge exemplifies another survivance strategy for Black Americans: the knowledge of plant medicine that allows them to thrive amid medical neglect and malnutrition and to become independent of Wetiko's "health care" and food systems.

This crucial self-determination knowledge has been so threatening to dominant powers over the years that it has been outlawed, distorted, and co-opted. Much of the plant-based medicine of Indigenous and Black people has been attacked as "Voodoo" or some other form of sorcery. As such the women keepers of this knowledge have been targeted for violence and imprisonment. At best, the practitioners of these healing arts have been depicted as savage and backward while the male dominated, institutionalized allopathic medicine has been exalted. Apart from outlawing Indigenous American and African plant medicine and healers, corporate powers have consistently used this knowledge for profit in the creation of pharmaceutical drugs. Five thousand plants are used in Western pharmaceuticals. Scientists for pharmaceutical companies created a billion-dollar industry from the knowledge base of Indigenous and African people.[10]

Black women in our food movement are a wealth of ethnobotanical knowledge. Their use of plants in teas, tinctures, salves, and poultices provide our community with nature-based healing for our bodies, minds, and souls. Their use of plants as food and "root work" conjures up connections to an Indigenous past and to the land. Women accomplices in the movement adapt our ancestral healing wisdom to the oppressive conditions of the postindustrial city where colonially-induced trauma and susto (the effects of fright/fear on our bodies, spirits, and minds[11]) combine with our detachment from nature to infect us with victim identities, negative self-images, violent behavior, the denial of racism, and other symptoms of injected racism as well as pollution, high levels of toxins, malnutrition and diabetes.[12]

Black women and others do not have access to many of the plants of our ancestors, and thus substitute plants native to our region or are otherwise easily accessible. Moreover, their techniques, materials, and artistry differ from previous generations as we have had to adapt to new conditions. This adaptability is a cornerstone of the resilience necessary for survivance.

Eco-womanism and Innate Agrarian Artistry

Eco-womanism and innate agrarian artistry are invaluable to understanding our current situation and how to get out of it. I have already described eco-womanism as I understand it and so will discuss it only briefly here while I introduce innate agrarian artistry as theorized by Baxter and colleagues. For them, womanism

> articulates Black women's liberation as the seed to the collective liberation of humanity. When Black women, often thought to be the 'mule of the world' . . . are liberated, those depending on the physical, mental, and psychological toilage of supposedly mule-like Black women are also liberated.[13]

Innate agrarian artistry is "the creative, feminine use of land-based resistance to simultaneously preserve the people and the soil."[14] Innate agrarian artistry includes seed-saving, foraging, quilt-making, song-making, community organizing, gardening, food preservation, and food preparation developed, sustained, and adapted by Indigenous-African women over centuries.

Three consistent themes in the innate agrarian artistry are "healing creatively with the land; ancestral honoring/remembering; and community self-determination and liberation."[15] Women camaradas engage all these expressions of innate agrarian artistry. Innate agrarian artistry is Indigenous to the Americas too. Indigenous women possess this way of relating to the land. In Latin America they use embroidery, weaving, and hairstyles to express their relationship to our more-than-human relatives. Hernandez explains that "our huipiles carry our environments, and the elements embedded in them are collected from our local flora, fauna, and ecological histories."[16] Below I discuss further how Black women accomplices in our movement enact innate agrarian artistry to further our goals.

Women's Garden Artistry

From Dr. Carter's mandala garden, healthy and delicious soups and herbal drinks, and extensive knowledge of plant-based medicine to Jacqueline Smith's backyard oasis to Safia Rashid's lovingly designed urban mini-farm and community-focused business, Your Bountiful Harvest, examples of Black women's innate agrarian artistry abound in our food movement. This innate agrarian artistry is the perennial knowledge that, like native perennial plants, form the basis of a healthy ecosystem. The "mothers" of the movement combine sankofa with an adaptable and flexible knowledge that incorporates ideas from other traditions to form the fertile soil in which our movement can grow.

Mecca Brooks came to the Black food autonomy movement in Chicago through art. As she explained,

> So it was this project that we ended up doing was called "Habib" which means "to that to whom which we hold dear." And it was the idea that it was all of the people that surround us in our lives that kind of grow from the ground cuz we did it all on photos that grow from the ground and actually offer this that is nurturing the food, fertilizing the food. It's gonna come from the ground that we consider healthy eating. So if we, as a community, don't nourish one another, respect one another, hold one another up and actually rise together from the rubble, cuz that was what the lot was, then, what is our future.

In this brief passage Mecca provides an example of the eco-womanist theme of healing creatively with the land. Her beautiful photo exhibit at the Bronzeville Community Garden accomplished several things. The photos served as a center-piece for conversation. The attractive images drew people creating moments for exchange. The art also recognized community members of all sorts who are otherwise made invisible and easy to ignore. It also served as healing for Mecca and those who worked on the installation.

Storytelling is indispensable to eco-womanism and is a central medium for innate agrarian artistry. Women accomplices use eco-memory and honoring our ancestors to regularly spread AHK. This sankofa sensibility teaches through honoring. Jacqueline Smith regularly spoke about her great-grand-mother, Callie Glover, whose innate agrarian artistry helped her to raise "thirteen children in a shotgun house" as she described it. Through keeping Mrs. Glover on her mind and on her tongue, Ms. Smith's innate agrarian art-istry was enabled and she was able to pass on AHK. She told a story of Black women's resiliency in the face of the racism and sexism of the sharecropping system. Ms. Smith was a proud "granddaughter of a Mississippi sharecropper." Her pride came from knowing that it is the innate agrarian artistry of peo-ple like her great grandmother that not only kept tradition and their families alive but also built the country. Jackie not only told stories of innate agrarian artistry but also lived it. Her beautiful backyard garden included an annual keyhole bed, vertical growing techniques, an ancestral herb garden and a thirteen-chicken coop. All on a small twenty-five-by-twenty-five-feet space dominated by a two-car garage and a large concrete slab. Her garden artistry

FIG. 19. Seedkeepers Collective. Photo by Marcus Alleyne.

extended to her front yard with an herb spiral and circular garden of orange daylilies and purple coneflower. It extended to vegan, gluten-free baking, and crocheting. When the COVID-19 pandemic began in 2020, she used her artistry, like Black women before her, for community resilience. When she found out children at a local elementary were going without masks, she figured out how to crochet dozens of highly effective masks. Black women's innate agrarian artistry results from love of community and connection to the land.

When Dr. Wright welcomes people to BOC, she tells the history of Pembroke Township and how Black people's knowledge of the land and adaptation of Native knowledge allowed them to survive and thrive in the area. Sprinkled in with her history of the area is a heavy dose of eco-womanism expressed through her vast knowledge of plants and their medicines and the land-based ethics of African people. Sometimes the stories offer models of Black strength. At other times the stories pass on vital survival information. Often the stories strengthen and expand community. Dr. Wright and many others are participating in the "re-storyation" required for restoration of the land and healing of the people.

I believe that it was Linda who first pointed out all the red clover in our garden. She went on to explain that this was a "women's herb." She explained that we need only to harvest and dry the flowers to have medicine that works on several levels. Drinking a tea of red clover, she explained, assists symptoms related to menopause and other women's conditions. It is a great-tasting and beautiful tea with multiple health benefits. Since this discovery every season we at GLP harvest the flowers of this plant freely given by Mama Nature. We always care not to take too much to leave food for the bees and other relatives who depend on it for its nectar. Younger women in our crew such as Alexy Irving, DeVonya Shelley, Melody Gil, and Quafin continue to pass on this understanding to community members in our GLP gardens and at our annual event "Tinctures, Tonics and Teas."

One of the great joys of our work is passing on the IK that we have been given by others. I often get this joy when I overhear GLP members teaching newcomers and visitors. In 2018, while tending to an onion patch, I overheard a small gathering of GLP members discussing "women's herbs." Along with the perennial favorite, red clover, I heard Jill teaching about motherwort. She explained that the lovely pollinator-friendly plant has been traditionally used to treat an array of reproductive issues including menstruation. The lesson took a satisfying turn as they discussed how to use the plant and how important this knowledge is for the community. The very lessons that Mama J taught our permaculture class two years earlier as she provided us with motherwort seedlings and other native medicinals had been taught to GLP members who were now passing it on to others in our community. Their conversation provides a perfect example of how the land co-teaches with elders in Indigenous traditions. The motherwort plant in all its glory caused a group of young women to stop and admire it. This moment of awe led to a discussion of the plant and its importance. Undoubtedly, the GLP members will pass on the lessons of motherwort to future visitors to our gardens.

Mama Dorothy introduced me to the magic and beauty of comfrey. In 2009, she planted a piece of comfrey at the Roseland Community Peace Garden. She asked if I knew comfrey. I told her that I didn't, and she went on to expound on the wonders of what Jacqueline Smith taught me to call "Mama Comfrey." She explained that it is a great plant. It can be used as a fertilizer and mulch, internal and external medicine, and a pollinator. More than ten years later the small piece of comfrey that Mama Dorothy planted has spread to half a dozen gardens and has been a central element in my garden design and strategy. I and dozens of others know of and use Mama Comfrey in most of the ways that Mama Dorothy described on that hot day at the RCPG. Many GLP gardeners have used it as a poultice to heal wounds they receive in the garden. Having comfrey is like having an antibiotic ointment and band aids all in one and readily available. Importantly, women gardeners in my circle use it to heal themselves and all our relations while adding incredible beauty to gardens and growing projects. Lessons such as the complementarity of species are taught using comfrey. We see bees enjoying comfrey going about their work of pollination. They move in swirls and loops and figure eights about the garden spending time with Mama Comfrey before moving on to our annual crops helping our tomatoes, squash, and other favorites provide for us. In GLP and other gardens, we eat because of comfrey, the bees, and Mama Dorothy's innate agrarian artistry.

AlterNative Healing and Colonial Trauma

"Healing is an essential aspect of innate agrarian artistry."[17] Most of my women accomplices in Chicago focus their efforts on healing. Black women dispense plant-based healing information at nearly every community workday at GLP gardens. As the land and all our relations go through the cycles of the seasons, women describe which plants heal which ailments, how to grow, harvest and prepare plant medicines, and how to connect with our plant relatives and the land. The garden serves as a site of Black women's and others' physical, mental, emotional, and spiritual healing from the violence of Wetiko.

In October 2019, DeVonya proposed a healing workshop that the members of GLP could conduct that would use Sacred Greens Community Garden and its abundance to fulfill our mission to extend our IK that we are learning and developing to more in our communities. The workshop had the additional function of using the mint, lemon balm, sage, and goldenrod that grew abundantly in our gardens. We also raised funds for our organization. Six women and three men dedicated themselves to this healing mission. This group of primarily Black women tapped into the innate agrarian artistry of our mothers, grandmothers, and aunties to provide a healing experience. We organized a celebration of our land and taught our extended community about the ages-old practices of making tinctures, tonics, and teas from the plants that grow in our area and give of themselves for our healing. We taught the importance of interacting with our relations through reciprocity; we improve our ecosystem and return land to native and lightly cultivated earth and the earth reciprocates providing us medicine and beauty to heal our bodies, minds, and emotions. On October 5, 2019, more than fifty adults and a dozen children gathered at the garden to harvest, clean, prepare, and learn about plant-based medicines for our first annual medicine-making event.

It follows in the footsteps of the communal healing rituals of our African and Amerindigenous ancestors. The rituals and knowledge of plant medicine of the Lukumi and Vodou traditions influence our practices. In these spiritual traditions we understand that "soul force, or ase, can be found within the plants, imbuing herbal medicine with its power."[18] Our secular ritual of community medicine-making expresses much of the same understanding and spiritual connection to the land as ceremonies like pile fey in Haiti. Workshop attendees interact with healing herbs touching them to harvest, rubbing them to prepare for medicine, inhaling them, tasting them, and allowing them to teach us and experience a communal bonding over laughter and food sharing. Like our ancestors, we gather cultivated varieties of sage for drinking and burning and mint for its numerous health qualities including aiding in digestive and respiratory processes. We also gather wild, native herbs, which our ancestors believed contained "more ase," including red clover and goldenrod and both of which were key components in our ancestors' herbal apothecaries.[19]

One element of the the Wetiko monster emphasized by Mamas (term often used as an honorific in many sectors of our community, not to be confused with the pejorative homonyms "hot momma" or "sexy momma") and the Babas of the movement is geographical displacement, especially to cities for the Black population and detribalized Indigenous people including Chicanxs and migrants throughout Abya Yala and to cities and reserves for native people. The act of dislocation from land has measurable negative health outcomes.

> Environmental degradation resulting from pollution, poverty, and bio-social epidemiology such as diabetes, alcoholism, physical abuse, and high rates of suicide are all related symptoms of "ethno-stress" caused by the disruption of culture and loss of land base among Indigenous people.[20]

For Indigenous people, individual health is tied to community health, which is tied to ecosystem health in a cycle of unending reciprocity. Cajete sums up the Indigenous formula for health as "healthy environment, healthy culture, healthy people." Since the land is "the very center and generator of self-understanding," for Indigenous people its health and our relationship to it are key to healing all Wetiko-imposed maladies.[21]

Cajete writes of the emotional, mental, and spiritual trauma experienced by the Tewa of New Mexico (whose homelands are only miles from where I grew up in Raton) since Wetiko became entrenched in today's southwestern United States. The Tewa, whose ancestors have lived in the arid high mountains for thousands of years, now suffer under "ethno-stress."

> American Indian people today live a dual existence. At times, it resembles a kind of schizophrenia in which people constantly try to adapt themselves to a mainstream social, political, and cultural system that is not their own . . . .The results for many Indian communities are "existential" problems, such as high rates of alcoholism, suicide, abuse of self and others, depression, and other social and spiritual ills . . . Tewa people call this state of schizophrenic-like existence pingeh heh (split thought or thinking, or doing things with only half of one's mind).[22]

This is a universal experience of colonized people like the "double consciousness" of which Du Bois wrote or the experiences of native Algerians about which Frantz Fanon analyzed.[23]

Susto can come from living in a colonized world. Luz Calvo writes about how she suffered from susto after receiving a cancer diagnosis. This condition, "a fright that startles the spirit from the body,"[24] can have numerous symptoms. Susto can also be seen at the community level where Wetiko causes mass levels of consumerist behaviors and addictions, injected racism, and intracommunal violence. Calvo explains that decolonizing her diet and her mental and emotional states through adopting Indigenous land-based practices relieved her of susto. "Through the very act of getting my hands dirty and connecting directly with Mother Earth, my susto at last started to recede. I began to accept the cycle of life as I observed the seasons in my garden. I felt very connected to ancestors I never even knew. I developed a plant-based spirituality."[25]

The writings of Richard Louv and bell hooks extend our understanding of Wetiko-induced mental, spiritual, and emotional trauma by examining the effects of urban life on our health and, particularly, how the city has been a site of ongoing colonialism and White supremacy for BIPOC. Louv popularized the concept of nature-deficit disorder.[26] For BIPOC, Louv's insight is particularly valuable. Dispossession has exiled us to the steel and concrete environs of the cities. We are in Chicago. We are primarily on the South and West sides of the city with a polluted environment courtesy of Wetiko. We live with thousands of miles of pavement, millions of tons of steel, and un chingo of bricks! Living in the city causes all sorts of physical, mental, and spiritual maladies. From breathing in and otherwise ingesting toxins to constant noise pollution to fear and posttraumatic stress (*susto* in the city) to poor diets and lack of physical movement, the city provides the perfect conditions for poor health and trauma.

Nature-deficit disorder is

> the human costs of alienation from nature, among them: diminished use of the senses, attention difficulties, and higher rates of physical and emotional illnesses. The disorder can be detected in individuals, families, and communities. . . . Long-standing studies show a relationship between the absence, or inaccessibility, of parks and open space with high crime rates, depression, and other urban maladies.[27]

Numerous scientific studies link less meaningful interaction with nature to a whole host of illnesses, many of which are found disproportionately among BIPOC. Wetiko-induced stress and depression is a killer for us. Louv's review of the medical literature found links between the visual environment and mental and physical health and links between children's screen time and poor physical health and emotional issues. Numerous studies find that nature therapy and ecopsychology show great promise for healing. The evidence suggests that "nature experiences can relieve some of the everyday pressures that may lead to childhood depression" especially for "those experiencing the highest levels of stressful life events."[28]

Given the attack on our identities and sense of self heaped on us by Wetiko, it is important that any activity designed to conquer trauma for BIPOC take into serious consideration nature-deficit disorder. Our children must cope with the racist slander perpetrated by Wetiko's media and communications industry. Again, our visual environment seems to be an important factor in self-image, and nature, for multiple reasons, seems to positively impact children's sense of self. "Children with more nature near their homes also rated themselves higher than their corresponding peers on a global measure of self-worth."[29]

bell hooks adds that "many [Black] folks feel no sense of place. What they know, what they have is a sense of crisis, of impending doom . . . . This separation from nature and the concomitant fear it produced, fear of nature and fear of whiteness was the trauma shaping Black life."[30]

She provides a very useful understanding of the traumas of displacement to cities that many of us in Chicago experience. The land was placed in opposition to Black people because of slavery, sharecropping, and other Wetiko practices. The land, which for millennia has been for African people the source of life, spirituality, identity, and culture, became alien, "the scene of the crime"[31] or "original sin of America."[32] African cultures have been ridiculed and perverted so that "urban cool" and consumerist individualist behavior has become the hallmark of Black culture. The perversion of African cultures strikes at the heart of African survival found in the communal nature of most African societies. "Industrial capitalism was not simply changing the nature of black work life, it altered the communal practices that were so central to survival in the agrarian South. And it fundamentally altered black people's relationship to the body."[33]

Alienation from ourselves, our bodies, and the land as urban laborers "made it all the more possible for Black people to internalize white supremacist assumptions about black identity"[34]. The assault on Black and BIPOC sense of self may be the primary source of trauma in our communities. This realization led hooks, like many BIPOC in the food movement, to conclude that "when we talk about healing that psyche we must also speak about restoring our connection to the natural world."[35]

hooks takes this idea of a transformative connection to all our relations one step further in her series of books on love. hooks is not alone in seeing love as a key revolutionary principle. Che Guevara famously proclaimed, "At the risk of seeming ridiculous, let me say that the true revolutionary is guided by a great feeling of love. It is impossible to think of a genuine revolutionary lacking this quality." The source of much of our inability to heal and therefore get to the necessary revolutionary work of decolonization and reindigenization is our lack of understanding of love and means to engage the world from a place of healing love. hooks first helps us understand how Wetiko distorts and undermines love. Capitalism turns love, like everything else, into a commodity. Patriarchal institutions and culture turn love into a weapon for maintaining power. Colonial culture attacks the Indigenous sex-gender-sexuality system and love as intimacy and responsibility toward all our relations. She agrees with Erich Fromm, quoting him as writing that "the principle underlying capitalistic society and the principle of love are incompatible." When all the "dimensions of love—'care, commitment, trust, responsibility, respect, and knowledge'"—are considered, love defies private property, competition, commodities, and the other key aspects of capitalism. "Domination cannot exist in any social situation where a love ethic prevails."[36]

The spiritual traditions of Mexicanxs/Chicanxs, especially of those consciously reindigenizing, are also rooted in the land and in love. Medina and Gonzalez illustrate "Xicanx and Latinx spiritual expressions and healing practices" with their anthology of Xicana spiritual practices all based in care and connection to the land and love for all our relations. They explain that "reclaiming and reconstructing our spirituality based on non-Western epistemologies is central to our process of decolonization."[37] Women practicing Indigenous spirituality "acknowledge [themselves] in time and place" when they connect to the land and the elements.[38] Xicana spirituality includes taking care of others. Many Xicanas and Mexicanxs share a "strong sense of responsibility and attention to the needs and suffering of others."[39] For many Mexican-origin women, "to be human was to care for others, be it human or animal; we are supposed to care and support one another."[40] Karen Mary Davalos explains how she teaches her children respect for trees. She writes that "I wanted my children to know that the earth is alive and that we are her stewards. Again, this is ancient wisdom, which I learned from my Mexican grandmother and from my father, but they conveyed this knowledge in subtle ways."[41]

The lessons of AAA praxis through innate agrarian artistry have been abundant in my years of learning through doing in the food autonomy movement. Mama Dr. Jifunza Wright helps heal colonial wounds with her vast knowledge of plant-based medicine. At the HFH, Mama J directs the preparation of medicinal foods and whips up healing drinks from leaves, roots, bark, and other plant parts. She passes on her innate agrarian artistry and IK at markets, workshops, conferences and especially at the BOC's forty-acre eco-campus. Doc recognizes that the threat to the Black community manifests itself both in physical traumas (e.g., diabetes and high blood pressure) and intellectual, emotional, and spiritual traumas. In a July 2021 phone conversation and again at the First Chicago Permaculture Convergence and Urban Gardening Conference, Doc summed up the need for plant medicines since societal demands upon us have cost us a great deal of personal and community jeng (the Chinese medicine term for "the life force"). According to Doc, it is our job as healers to use our innate agrarian artistry to mitigate the draining of jeng. Dr. J's efforts around this area of healing are legendary. In 2019 (to cite one of dozens of examples), Dr. J. hosted a community event at which she directed those present in building a large mandala garden filled with medicinal herbs. Through working together and conversing, attendees learned about plant medicine, growing medicinal plants, and honoring the land, our ancestors, and all our relations. Doc explained that the shape or pattern of the mandala itself was healing. Its lines and repetition calmed and encouraged meditation. Planting it in curves with a diverse grouping of plants was healing for the land as well. Of course, touching the soil intimately and lovingly lifted our spirits and provided microbial protection to our bodies.

Before the building and transplanting, Doc gave an impassioned lesson about the state of Black people's health and our need to heal it through landed traditions. She contrasted the numerous health benefits of the cannabis plant with its adulteration under capitalism. Indigenous healing practices would use the entire plant for its numerous benefits. In our society the plant has been used as a smoking herb to "get high": a means of healing from trauma and attempt at more free thinking and creativity as expressed by so many BIPOC throughout hip hop culture; the same free thought and creativity squashed at every level by Wetiko. Doc explained how this sacred plant has become merely a drug for many of us; it may temporarily soothe our trauma but is insufficient to long-term healing. In addition to smoking cannabis, CBD, while an important plant extract helping thousands, has become an emphasis of industry to the detriment of an understanding of the entire plant. Moreover, agribusiness and chemical companies are growing cannabis in unsustainable and antilife ways using too much water, paying workers poverty wages, and experimenting with genetic modification. Corporations are beating the spirit out of this sacred plant. Doc finished her lesson inviting those present to join Black Oaks in cultivating cannabis in a healing way through their farmer training program.

Seven of us drove the fifty miles back to Chicago together. We discussed the healing that we experienced at Black Oaks with Doc and Baba Fred. The most common expression of healing involved merely being in nature away from the city and its noise and distractions. Participants enthusiastically expressed the inspiration they derived from seeing Black people, culture, land, and history in different, more liberating ways.

Eco-womanism sees memory and storytelling as central to healing for Black people; storytelling is emphasized in resurgence efforts of First Nations people in Canada and the United States as well.[42] Examples of using memory to heal abound in our movement especially in the gardens. It's as if the land provides the backdrop and inspiration for accessing our memories and the courage to tell our stories. Moreover, the stories are not merely retellings of history but opportunities for deep analysis of ourselves and our situation under Wetiko. They provide healing through empathy and laughter that brings us together. During a gathering on the Westside at Kuumba Tre Ahm Community Garden in 2018, Mama Gina (graduate of the Lifeboats Permaculture Design Certification course) honored tradition by telling her family's history with the piece of land that is now a beautiful and abundant garden. Her discussion of her family's use of the land to assist Black migrants from the South and at times as a place of unsanctioned economic activity offered a moment of profound community connection. Surrounded by natural beauty in the middle of a busy inner city the story of Mama Gina's ancestors healed. Her vision for honoring the legacy of that place with an even more effective practice of innate agrarian artistry connected us to our ancestors and revealed a possible future for our children.

In the spaces of our movement, especially the natural spaces of gardens and farms, we commonly pray or engage in other community rituals. Before a meal at Jacqueline Smith's house, Leah Penniman asked the attendees if we could sing a song of gratitude together. After a tour of Smith's impressive gardens on an average-sized lot on the South Side, Penniman, an Ifà priest, blessed the homestead through song and prayer while offering sacred corn. At Smith's home where she regularly hosted tours, workshops, and conversations with small groups of primarily Black women, she helped heal our community by turning plants into medicine, teaching others how to preserve healing foods, and helping them connect to our traditions.

We often address spirituality and repair of the Spirit in our movement. At Your Bountiful Harvest Family Farm, Mama Safia and Kamau Rashid heal through the nutritious food they grow and make available to our community and through engaging in community ritual. Collective workdays and tours at Your Bountiful Harvest, part of Urban Growers Collective based in South Chicago (land that needs a great deal of healing after the trauma meted out against it by the steel industry), begin with honoring ancestors. Kamau and Safia ensure that this space is an African space through ritual and constant discussion of African traditions and IK. Similarly, Dr. Alalade includes paying proper respect to our ancestors, elders, and all our relations at CoGro. At meetings, gatherings, and workdays she is keen to remind us of our spiritual connection to the work we do in building this movement and retaining IK. Her "alternative vision of the world," as she explained to me in our dialogue, is to "name this part of the world Earthseed as a new beginning." She and her partner are working to make CoGro a place where the power of Ologun, running as a river through CoGro property, welcomes people and groups for healing and spiritual regeneration. She hopes that CoGro can be a place of healing for an interdenominational group of spiritual warriors and others needing the healing that can only come from close connection to the land.

Importantly, for those of us reindigenizing, our elders teach communal healing. Mama J led our community in a Spring Healing. At the HFH she discussed a protocol for all of us to follow to cleanse and heal our bodies, spirits, and minds. Doing it together we can "check in" with one another and gain support and strength. Using Doc's example, a group of women members of the Lifeboats Permaculture Guild developed the Family Healing Center. Together, they provide plant-based medicine and advice about using it as well as nutritional information and other healing practices, including an innovative response to trauma, "Healing Through Play" started by Quafin in 2021. Her creative deep spiritual and healing "work" are inspiration to many in our community.

Activists and others in Chicago use healing circles as a method for dealing with Wetiko-imposed illness. Bee Rodriguez's Reclaiming Our Roots holds regular Indigenous rituals and celebrations, including the all-important temezcal (sweat lodge). Young people from Reclaiming Our Roots designed the garden for such spiritual and healing practices. They learn by doing in which the rituals and songs are adapted for the violent conditions of Wetiko's inner-city Chicago. Similarly, in 2018 GLP had the honor of hosting a Men's Healing Circle. For several weeks a small group of Black men met at Sacred Greens Community Garden in the Roseland community. Using the garden as metaphor, the facilitators encouraged the brothers to examine their lives as men from seed to harvest, both the traumas and triumphs. Then, the brothers got dirty. The garden transformed from metaphor to literal healer and teacher. One evening as we were wrapping up our session detailing the trauma and troubles of being Black men in Chicago, gunshots rang out and young men barely more than boys ran along the outside garden fence firing back as they ran from someone shooting at them. Not only did the garden provide healing and teaching but so, too, did the larger environment of the Roseland neighborhood. The shooting outside the garden served to remind us of the trauma of Wetiko and contrast it with the healing of nature. The troubled environs from which we sought escape provided evidence of the trauma caused by Wetiko, and the anticolonial garden gave us a space to express our fears and a place to release some of the trauma.

Healing Mother Energy

Our 2019 BOC Board of Directors Fall Retreat took place in the serenity of the forty-acre eco-campus. The board of directors and the founders of the BOC met for an all-day discussion of the direction of BOC. On the phone an overextended, exhausted, and energy-drained board member joined us in between meetings at her office. Dr. J began the meeting with recognition of the exhaustion that our member felt and that many in our community feel at this difficult time on the planet. She implored our very successful overworked colleague to visit Black Oaks ASAP so that she could be rejuvenated by the healing mother energy of the two-acres of mother hemp plants growing there. The peace of the land and the power of hemp and all our relations lovingly stewarded by Doc, Baba, and Akin detoxify and decolonize the body, mind, and spirit. The traumas of Wetiko are such that we are often unaware that we are sick or how to care for ourselves. Our colonized, racialized status often leads to an acceptance of our circumstances including Wetiko-induced illnesses. We may not know that the exhaustion, fatigue, and sadness we feel results from Wetiko and, therefore, don't know where to begin to heal.

The Healing Mother Energy of the women accomplices in our part of the Black food movement in Chicago can help us recognize our circumstances and our illnesses for what they are and to combat them. These women accomplices and many of the men in our movement see how Wetiko instills in us emotional and spiritual illness that exacerbates the violence of contaminated water, food, soil, and air. They know that diabetes, heart disease, interpersonal violence, and many other ills are political economic diseases caused by the greed of the new Wetiko—corporations.[43] I argue that their innate agrarian artistry and eco-womanism are key to liberation. Before any community-building, progressive, radical, or revolutionary work, we must interact with Healing Mother Energy provided by places like BOC, GLP, and similar zones of anticolonial autonomous activity.

PART IV

ARE WE TALKING ABOUT A REVOLUTION?

CHAPTER 10

Indigenous/Black Anarchism
LIBERATION THINKING IN THE FOOD MOVEMENT

The satisfaction of the wants of all must be the first consideration of the revolutionist . . . Our first object must be to care for providing this food and this shelter for those who are most in need of them, for those precisely who have been the outcasts of the old society.

PETER KROPOTKIN, "The First Work of the Revolution," in *Act for Yourselves: Articles from Freedom, 1886–1907* (London: Freedom, 1988), 59

Realistic day-to-day needs should be the basis of organizing people and making them conscious of revolution—that the world, the universe, must revolve—that it will stop, stagnate, and die for no man's privilege.

GEORGE JACKSON, *Blood in My Eye* (Baltimore: Black Classic, 1996), 56

Indian people who seek to realize the goal of harmonious coexistence within their communities find that this is impossible within the mainstream political system as it is currently structured.

TAIAIAKE ALFRED, *Peace, Power, Righteousness: An Indian Manifesto*, 2nd ed. (Toronto: Oxford University Press, 2009), 47

We do not seek that our ways of knowing, being, and acting ever be wrapped up into a fixed belief and presented as a pitiful rag. We do not wish that Indigenous anarchism ever be a flag that is planted anywhere on Mother Earth.

KLEE BENALLY, *No Spiritual Surrender: Indigenous Anarchy in Defense of the Sacred* (n.p.: Detritus, 2023), 324

Anarchists believe that it is the first duty of the revolutionary to feed the people, to provide us with what we need. We don't believe that "feeding the people" can be done by just any means. Rather, how we feed ourselves must match the desired ends of an antiauthoritarian, radically democratic, free world. Providing ourselves with what we need in a postcapitalist society requires a social organization flexible enough to be resilient in changing conditions and cultures.[1] Many revolutionaries emphasize food not only because hunger can cause people to engage in counterrevolutionary behavior but because it is a primary need of all species. It unites all of us. This fact means that those who seek wealth and power have used food as a weapon and a mechanism for social control.[2] Thus, revolution would require that workers, peasants, the Indigenous, and others seize or expropriate the means of food production and develop economic and political infrastructures that weaken capital and the state through taking away one of their primary weapons: dependence on Wetiko's food system.

Black revolutionaries including George Jackson, Fannie Lou Hamer, and the Black Panther Party understood the centrality of basic needs to revolutionary struggle. New Afrikan anarchist Kuwasi Balagoon argued and practiced the idea that "to fully take on the power structure in a given area, you got to not only provide alternatives but institutions that render the old ones useless."[3] For many the struggle for basic needs and "revolution" are one in the same. What is the goal of revolution, if not the complete emancipation of all from tyranny, hierarchy, and violence? Without control over our livelihoods, we are dominated no matter if you call it "communism" or "democracy." In addition, Black liberation struggles have often placed issues of the control of land at the forefront of their goals and strategies.

Many Amerindigenous people are reviving and fighting for our traditions. This is Indigenous resurgence.[4] These traditions offer important lessons in developing ecological, democratic, antiauthoritarian communities and societies. Reviving our cultures, our right livelihoods, is impossible under the current Euro-American state system. Indigenous ways of being are at odds with the idea of the state, industrialism, capitalism, and even, civilization.[5] The decades-long pan-Indigenous struggle for sovereignty and autonomy adds insight and exemplifies possibilities for a free, nonhierarchal postcapitalist society. Decolonial and anticolonial work guided by IK and using direct action provides models for revolutionary behavior in the food autonomy movement.

Principles, ideas, and organizational practices similar to those of anarchists, Black liberation efforts, and many Indigenous revolutionaries are found throughout the theory and practice of many in our movement. Movement work often mirrors anarchist social organization practices including small collectively managed, democratic units allied together in federations on a voluntary and temporary basis.[6] Many Amerindigenous nations and Black American communities use similar radically democratic frameworks for decision-making.[7] In varying degrees this type of organization is exhibited in Chicago's food movement. In this chapter I provide a discussion of Indigenous/Black anarchist thought for understanding the work that we do as well as to suggest an alternative future to strive for and challenge us to encounter one another despite the perceived differences.

My accomplices recognize that a collective, autonomous, self-managed food system is the type of organized revolutionary direct action required to undermine Wetiko.[8] These systems that we work to develop prefigure an ecological society that fosters the development of human potential. We believe that using locally focused, place-based systems will solve several Wetiko-induced crises. The crises of hunger, climate chaos, ecological ruin, and political disempowerment are addressed by local food systems informed by IK from peoples across the globe.

I begin this dialogue between revolutionary political traditions as pertains to our food autonomy work with a brief overview of Indigenous/Black (I/B) anarchism. I include Black anarchists in the United States in this discussion since we have established an argument for seeing Africans in Diaspora as strongly tethered to Indigenous African traditions. Then, I contribute to an I/B anarchist framework with a discussion of Indigenous knowledge that informs the work in Chicago's Black food autonomy movement. Next, I discuss the social organizational principles of anarchism and use them to examine our movement practices. At the same time, I refer to Indigenous social organizational principles that the food autonomy movement would do well to heed and that many of us implement in our communities and groups. Ultimately, I argue that the food autonomy movement in Black Chicago provides an imperfect model for a new free autonomous world and that our current practices are in creative tension with Indigenous ecological arts and sciences, I/B anarchist perspectives, and Black American liberation traditions. I argue for a deeper conscious dialogue between these differing groups of revolutionaries. For such a dialogue to occur, there must be respect for diversity. Revolutionary unity in diversity challenges much other revolutionary theory that would have working-class identity, consciousness, and culture be the only acceptable ways of being or excludes others based on race, gender, or nationality. Thus, I propose "revolutionary polyculturalism" as an additional guiding principle. I offer this as a summary of what I have learned through elders, the land, and others in my nearly two decades of participation in our struggle.

Indigenous/Black Anarchism

The antiauthoritarian, anticolonial, alterNative theory and praxis I put forth in previous chapters is a form of Indigenous anarchism that has come to guide my work and that can be found in various iterations throughout our movement. Since Taiaiake Alfred examined the term "anarcho-indigenism,"[9] several scholars and activists have attempted to better understand the links between an anticolonial indigeneity and anarchism.[10] We have sought to understand how these commonalities could be used as a basis for solidarity to undermine the state and reinvigorate ecological, place-based, nonhierarchical modes of living. Indigeneity is a place-based way of being and as such differs based on the limits established by geography. In the urban environs of the South Side of Chicago populated by members of the African diaspora, indigeneity is different than in rural areas inhabited by the Amerindigenous and members of the Mesoamerican diaspora. For my purposes in understanding the revolutionary potential of urban food autonomy work, AHK and place-based BAT are understood to be Indigenous traditions. Mays's recent work argues convincingly that members of the African diaspora are Indigenous and Black cultural retentions exhibit Indigenous thought and worldview. Obviously, this perspective is challenged by many but I believe it is an accurate position given historical geopolitical realities relative to settler colonialism and capitalism in North America. As discussed earlier, many of my accomplices in the movement (though clearly not all) share and promote this view of the BAT. However, it is important to be clear that Amerindigenous people's experience with Wetiko today differs from that of Black Americans.

Jacqueline Laskey offers this succinct definition of Indigenous anarchism:

> attempts to link critical ideas and visions of post-imperial futures in ways that are non-hierarchical, unsettling of state authorities, inclusive of multiple/plural ways of being in the world, and respectful of the autonomous agencies of collective personhood.[11]

Examination of pre-European invasion Indigenous societies in Abya Yala illustrates that they were based on principles that look a lot like what we call anarchism today. Amerindigenous social organization was typically nonhierarchical, did not have a notion of private property, emphasized personal autonomy within a collectivity, rejected coercive power, emphasized gender parity, and openness and diversity of sexuality, and practiced interdependence between human groups and between humans and our more-than-human relatives. Obviously, not all Indigenous groups organized their societies in this manner. The point is not that all Indigenous groups were ecological or democratic and free but that Indigenous peoples of the Americas have provided numerous models of ecological and free modes of societal organization resulting from their centuries-long residence in our place.

Observers including Benjamin Franklin and other "Founding Fathers" of the United States marveled at the egalitarianism of Indigenous societies and attempted to incorporate them into their political philosophies. IK found its way into the liberal philosophies of people such as Henry More and Jean-Jacques Rousseau. In the mid-nineteenth century, Amerindigenous principles of social organization had become part of the European working-class socialist movement. By the early part of the twentieth-century, European working-class revolutionaries had adapted the principles of Indigenous social organization and ethics into anarchism.[12]

It is no wonder then that Alfred sees a convergence of traditional Indigenous (Onkwehonwe) and anarchist social organization. To destroy imperialism and capitalism and "to recreate a life worth living and principles worth dying for," Onkwehonwe need to develop a warrior ethic. He proposes a framework made up of two elements:

> *indigenous*, evoking cultural and spiritual rootedness in this land and the Onkwe-honwe struggle for justice and freedom, and the political philosophy and move-ment that is fundamentally anti-institutional, radically democratic, and committed to taking action to force change: *anarchism*.[13]

Onkwehonwe ways of perceiving the problem and acting in the world have many commonalities with anarchist ways of being. He points out each group's "rejec-tion of alliances with legalized systems of oppression, non-participation in the institutions that structure the colonial relationship, and a belief in bringing about change through direct action, physical resistance, and confrontations with state power."[14] Alfred may have been thinking of Malatesta, the Italian anarchist who wrote in 1914 that all "socialists" must "keep outside every kind of compromise with the Governments and the governing classes."[15] In addition, both Indigenous and anarchist resistance to Wetiko has been met with fierce violence from the state including "communist" states.[16]

This isn't to suggest that anarchists, Africans, diasporic Africans, and the Amer-indigenous agree on everything or that they don't diverge in important ways. Over the history of anarchism, most anarchists trace our lineage to Europe and focus on the industrial working class. Anarchist heteronormative masculinity and an aggressive anti-religion/spirituality block communication and solidarity between anarchists and the Amerindigenous and Black Americans. Thus, many have called for a decolonization of anarchism.[17] Nonetheless, anarchists have proved to be a flexible and self-reflexive bunch. With guidance and dialogue, anarchists have the greatest potential of any White revolutionary group to overcome settler limita-tions as regards the creation of an ideal existence on stolen Indigenous land and to adopt an anticolonial perspective based in IK.

Additionally, Black anarchists have developed a political perspective and the-ory that challenges Black left thought and White anarchism.[18] Their ideas resonate with Black liberation practices throughout the centuries and show up in Chicago's Black food autonomy movement. Balagoon's writings provide us with key con-cepts and considerations for the development of an I/B anarchism. An excerpt from a letter dated May 2, 1984, establishes Balagoon's perspective on the relation-ship between New Afrikans and the Amerindigenous:

> Native Americans were indeed the first victims of imperialism in this hemisphere, and if we are to be anarchist in the here and now, and thus be anti-imperialist, as one cannot be an anarchist and not be against imperialism, we got to accept the Native struggle as our own. If the Greeds had not put the Natives in their position,

none of us would be in the position we are in. . . . It is clear to anyone that Native peoples are repressed more so than anyone else, that genocide has been practiced against them more so than any people who still exist as a people. Well that means we got to defend them—fight alongside of them, just like they fought alongside of the slaves.[19]

Balagoon offers a clear argument for the need for dialogue between Black American, Amerindigenous, anarchists, and other anti-imperialists. Our struggles are intertwined as they result from the same forces of Wetiko, and thus we must see one another's struggles as our own. This is perhaps the key insight from decolonial perspectives: the system and people responsible for our conditions are global and so should our struggle be. Second, he states plainly that anarchism must be anti-imperialist. His argument means that anarchists must examine, understand, and support nationalist movements that challenge imperialism.[20] This doesn't mean that we abandon our anarchist principles but that we understand the importance of the nationalist critique and should see them as "fellow travelers." Third, he recognizes and values the positive history of Indigenous-Black American solidarity in struggle against imperialism and racism.

Balagoon's writings and life are full of discussions of anarchist and Indigenous organizing principles and critiques of Wetiko. Like many Black (he preferred New Afrikan) revolutionaries of the time, he emphasized self-determination, self-defense, and expropriation of stolen wealth. He rejected all Wetiko's institutions and ideas including the European "race" and sex/gender systems (he was "bisexual").

William Anderson's Black anarchism rejects the state and concepts such as citizenship, writing that it is "an invention that is of no good use to us here. It has done much more harm than good. Anything that affords some people more rights than others based on borders, race, or class should be abolished. It has no redeeming quality for Black People and fighting to be recognized by or within it means seeking to be embraced by something that has our rejection, if not extermination, built into its very definition."[21] Klee Benally shows also how U.S. citizenship has been rejected by most Indigenous people since the European invasion began. Integrating with the U.S. empire through calls for full citizenship have weakened the fight for Indigenous sovereignty.[22] Since the state has only served as an instrument of domination, it is foolhardy to attempt to become part of it or to reform it. Furthermore, recognition by the empire has very little benefit for most Black and other BIPOC.[23]

Attempts at earning full citizenship in the U.S. empire have provided us with a few wealthy people and celebrities but have failed to provide freedom for the masses of Black people. In fact, these examples serve to undermine attempts at collective Black liberation. They get in the way of seeing the intricacies of the op-erations of Wetiko. The belief in and hope for citizenship, for being part of the empire, leads to a civil rights politics that argues for Black and other BIPOC having a piece of the imperial pie. Of course, the wealth of the empire is built on the suf-fering of BIPOC from within the United States and across the planet. No amount of reform or Black capitalism will change this. Thus, the need for internationalism or, perhaps, intercommunalism.[24] Zoe Samudzi and Anderson argue for a "land-based liberation" mindful of colonialism and say that "Black American land pol-itics cannot simply be built on top of centuries-old exterminatory settler logic of Indigenous removal and genocide. Rather, the actualization of truly liberated land can only come about through dialogue and co-conspiratorial work with native communities and a shared understanding of land use outside of capitalistic mod-els of ownership."[25] This "dialogue and co-conspiratorial work" is what many of us do within the Black food movement on the South Side of Chicago.

Indigenous Realism, IK, and AAA Foodways

Indigenous communities have a wealth of knowledge about and a method for in-forming the development of an ecological society. I argue that IK is the only epis-temic system that can lead to such a desired end. IK developed from long and deep analysis of place that allowed Indigenous communities to thrive in each locale for centuries while doing little ecological damage. Often these keystone communities provided ecological services to their place.[26] IK is

> the culturally and spiritually based way in which indigenous peoples relate to their ecosystems. This knowledge is founded on spiritual-cultural instructions from "time immemorial" and on generations of careful observation within an ecosys-tem of continuous residence.[27]

IK is scientific, "based on empirical knowledge that has been collected over long periods of time."[28] Dr. Bonnie Alalade Harrison argued vehemently that IK, in-cluding Ifá, is science and that to only apply this label to accepted European sci-ence is racist. Because the analysis has been so systematic for so long IK is typically based on the premise that change is inevitable and any ethical, political, economic, epistemological, or social system must be adaptable. IK incorporates a (home) land ethic. Indigenous peoples' attention to our place leads to "a relationship with nature that corresponds to the biogeographical regions that sustain local com-munities." It recognizes "the importance of biological and cultural diversity."[29] Its spiritual aspects including ritual and ceremonies come from the desire to use ob-servation and adaptability to learn to live in correct relationship with one's place as well as confront enemies and hardship.[30]

Deep Experiential Knowledge: The Foundation of IK

Tyson Yunkaporta addresses the key questions for our examination of IK and its centrality to our revolutions in the garden. He asks, Who are the real Indigenous people? Who among them carries the real Indigenous knowledge, and what aspects of that knowledge are relevant in grappling with the design of sustainable systems today? Yunkaporta's initial answer is informative: "an Indigenous person is a member of a community retaining memories of life lived sustainably on a land base, as part of that land base. Indigenous knowledge is any application of those memories as living knowledge to improve present and future circumstances."[31]

He emphasizes the "application of [IK] as living knowledge," not as conversation pieces or internet memes but information used to live correctly. IK requires praxis; we must do something. Permaculture founder (sometimes derided as a colonizer) Bill Mollison borrowed this understanding in establishing an important permaculture principle. He writes that "information is *the* critical potential resource. It *becomes* a resource only when obtained and acted upon."[32] I have seen this versed as "each one, teach one" in many Black homes. We must obtain IK and then put it to use in our gardens and our revolutions. Otherwise, it becomes a museum piece or another privilege for the overprivileged who can use it to "become one with nature" while leaving out the all-important and necessary decolonization. Information about how to live sustainably becomes IK only when it is used "to improve present and future circumstances." The appropriation of IK for the self-improvement of the individual lives of settlers or by corporations to improve their bottom line is common throughout the history of colonialism and even in justice-seeking movements such as permaculture. Yunkaporta's definition warns against this misuse of IK. Finally, this definition points out that IK is not information from a bygone era but an ever-adapting living knowledge. The colonial project, while unfathomably violent and destructive, is unable to completely destroy our IK. It lives within us and our memories or every time we eat una tortilla de teosinte.[33]

Being Indigenous is not simply about blood quantum but about behaving as instructed by the Original Instructions. Measuring the genetic material of Indigenous people is not an Indigenous way of understanding. The settler-colonial U.S. government introduced the idea of measuring blood to determine a person's Native status as part of the land grab known as the Dawes Act of 1887. As a tactic of the enclosure of Native land, the United States designed a pseudo-biological category and measurement of blood quantum. Blood quantum determined whether a person was Native and eligible for an individual allotment on a reservation. Once the government made a count to determine how much native land would go to those they determined Native, the remaining land was sold cheaply to settlers.

Currently blood quantum measurement has evolved into DNA testing. Some Native scholars and activists point out that membership in a Native nation has traditionally been determined as a political and cultural designation. The political definition of Native community membership emphasizes citizenship whereas a cultural designation would emphasize the practice of Indigenous culture.[34] Alfred answers his question, "What does it mean to be Onkwehonwe?" by emphasizing behavior:

> In fighting for our future, we have been misled into thinking that "Indigenous,"
> . . . is something that is attached to us inherently and not a description of what we
> actually do with our lives . . . much more than applying a label to ourselves and
> saying that we are indigenous to the land. It means looking at the personal and
> political choices we make every day and applying an indigenous logic to those
> daily acts of creation. It means knowing and respecting Kanien'kehaka, Innu, and
> Wet'suwet'en teachings and thinking and behaving in a way that is consistent with
> values passed down to us by our ancestors.[35]

This way of understanding indigeneity is not confined to the Americas. Yunka-porta of the Australian Apalech clan emphasizes memory and place-based sustain-ability. As he brilliantly illustrates throughout his yarns (Indigenous Australian storytelling), remembering an ancient past is central to being Indigenous.[36] Im-portantly, ritual, ceremony, dance, carving, temezcal, drumming, and other music bring cohesion to Indigenous communities as they tell of our history, traditions, and beliefs. Throughout the history of our interaction with colonial powers, we have used memory and storytelling to resist and retain our culture.

IK comes out of a long history of land-based living and observation; a "deep ex-periential knowledge." Daniel Wildcat explains that deep experiential knowledge is a

> living system of knowledge . . . that is capable of change and innovation, the ability
> to figure out what works in a particular place for the people of that place. One
> advantage of knowledges arrived at in the processes of experiments in living, as
> Fleener described them, is that such knowledges result in worldviews that are
> intrinsically open-ended or unbounded.[37]

It is part of "indigenous realism," an Indigenous epistemology. To understand re-ality, one must have

> respect for the relationships and relatives that constitute the complex web of life
> . . . that we, members of humankind, accept our inalienable responsibilities as
> members of the planet's complex life systems.[38]

In this high-context culture, everything provides opportunities for understanding how to exist ecologically; in relations of interdependence. Indigenous political traditions exhibit

> a commitment to a profoundly respectful way of governing based on a world view that values autonomy but also recognizes a universal interdependency and promotes peaceful coexistence among all elements of creation.[39]

IK is rooted in a flexible longitudinal study of a particular place over generations and centuries. Intergenerational residency along with place-based spiritual knowledge is the foundation of Indigenous environmental ethics.[40] The primary observational method begins with a holistic epistemology incorporating a wide range of experiences and interactions with more-than-human relatives. Differing from a European reductionist science that dismisses the agency of more-than-human life and privileges the general over the specific, the goal of IK is not simply to know but also to live responsibly with all our relations. It is to know our geographic place and our social place within our ecosystem.

IK emphasizes observations of and meditations on our interactions in our environment.

> We can know ourselves only through our relationships with relatives in the natural world—the nature-culture nexus . . . Indigenous realism suggests a dynamic and active construction of knowledge.[41]

The development of knowledge is interactive. The "scientist" is humbled as their understanding is informed by affirming his relationships. Scientific knowledge in the European tradition is hindered by faux objectivity, whereas the science of IK is created precisely because of the recognition of the "real" subjectivity of all parties involved.

In IK systems, the observer/human/scientist interacts with and understands the world using respectful attentiveness.[42] This outlook sees interdependence between all beings as primary in terms of our responsibilities as humans and as a natural fact. About the term "metakuyeayasi" (all my relations) in Lakota spirituality, Frank Black Elk writes,

> Everything in the universe is related within the tradition of Lakota spirituality; everything is relational and can only be understood in that way . . . Lakota spirituality is . . . the pursuit of a true understanding of the dialectical nature of the universe. That, and to conform our lives to living relationally, as a relation among relations; not at the expense of our relations.[43]

Wildcat adds the idea of the "nature-culture nexus, a symbiotic relationship that recognizes the fundamental connectedness and relatedness of human communities and societies to the natural environment and the other-than-human relatives they interact with daily."[44] Metakuyeayasi is similar to other indigenous ethics such as the Lacandon Mayan idea of in lak' ech (you are my other me), the Diné concepts hozho (harmony, balance, the good life) and ké,[45] and the Bantu notion of ubuntu (I am because we all are). In biocentric cultures, nature informs culture. At the same time, nature is changed by culture. In the nature-culture nexus, one cannot exist in the same form without the other. Importantly for our discussion here, anarchists, especially those informed by Murray Bookchin's social ecology, see the world similarly "with ecosystems in which living things are interdependent and play complementary roles in perpetuating the stability of the natural order."[46]

Minobimaatisiiwin (continuous rebirth) is concept fundamental to Anishinaabeg and Cree worldview with basic principles common to the worldviews of many Indigenous peoples. Two central tenets define Minobimaatisiiwin: cyclical thinking and reciprocal relations. Cyclical thinking recognizes that everything in the world flows in cycles. Reciprocity "defines responsibilities and ways of relating between humans and the ecosystem."[47] Similarly, the New Mexican ethic of verguenza derives from biocentric values that govern the affairs and relations among equals within nature.[48] Indigenous Mexican ethics in New Mexico are taught through cuentos such as the story of the Forest Spirit that banishes greedy people who cut too many trees and otherwise abuse the life-giving mountains. Minobimaatisiiwin and verguenza imply an ethic of "you take only what you need, and you leave the rest."[49] Since all our relations are animate and interdependent, it makes no sense to take from our ecosystems and not give back. The White anarchist-leaning founders of permaculture, Bill Mollison and David Holmgren, use this wisdom in their efforts to create an ecological design system that non-Indigenous people could use to live right. For example, the original third ethic is "setting limits to population and consumption: by governing our own needs we can set aside resources to further the above principles [of care of the earth and care of people]."[50]

Indigenous ethics lead to a system of production and distribution that is "decentralized, self-reliant, and very closely based on the carrying capacity of that ecosystem."[51] Each ecosystem is unique, therefore decisions about what to do with a land base or a resource, for example, must be made at the local or bioregional level.[52] Decision-making power must be decentralized in a similar manner to anarchist principles discussed below. Indigenous place-based, biocentric values result from long observation of place, which allow us to engage in mutually beneficial and sustainable relations with our ecosystems.[53] Our longevity on the continent should make this point obvious.

IK in Indigenous American Horticulture

Devon G. Peña provides important and consistent analysis of Mexican IK includ-ing horticultural and organizational philosophies, ethics, and practices.[54] His re-search shows that the deep spatial knowledge of Mexico's Indigenous led to the development of important agroecological innovations. The "Mayan managed mo-saic" was based on the understanding that species within an ecosystem are inter-dependent. He uses *in lak' ech* to describe this biocentric ethic.[55]

From this basic ethic, a tradition of land stewardship developed that includes practices such as biomimicry, complementarity, and agroforestry. Biomimicry re-sults from ancient Indigenous observations regarding how life grew without hu-man intervention. They saw that nature works well by itself to sustain life. Thus, in their relationships with nature, Indigenous Mexicans would not stray far from the lessons that land and nature taught them. They observed that a healthy ecosystem has a wide variety and diversity of species growing together. We often call the In-digenous observation of this fact of nature polyculturalism.[56]

Mesoamerican science discovered the centrality of soil to the web of life. Thus, soil maintenance and categorization were key to their stewardship. The Indige-nous practice of composting is now common in organic gardening circles. Today, we take for granted the necessity of a compost pile, crop rotation, cover crops, and other soil maintenance techniques. The centuries-old technique of the chinampa similarly illustrates the emphasis that early Indigenous Mexicans placed on soil. The ingenious technology of the chinampa takes advantage of the naturally oc-curring fertility of lakes to create floating beds of high productivity. Like all the Indigenous technologies previously mentioned, permaculture designers incorpo-rate this into our system.

The soil, la tierra, is central to the sustainability of any local food movement project. Food autonomy movements can benefit from treating land with respect and reverence as Indigenous peoples have done. Many in the food autonomy movement in Chicago already engage in this practice, but it is remarkable how many see land as inanimate and here for human use. Many urban gardeners and farmers approach their understanding of food justice from Wetiko's perspective that treats land as a commodity and the Christian perspective that sees humans as superior to other beings. Those attached to the BOC, the HFH, and GLP revive AHK/IK and its emphasis on land care while extending BAT in an urban setting.

AHK in Chicago

bell hooks calls BAT "a culture of place." It shares many of the characteristics of Am-erindigenous IK discussed above. This tradition begins from respectful relation-ships among humans and between humans and all our relations. She explains that living close to nature, black folks were able to cultivate a spirit of wonder and reverence for life. Growing food to sustain life and flowers to please the soul, they were able to make a connection with the earth that was ongoing and life-affirming.[57]

Emigration from the rural South had a devastating impact. In the cities away from nature many urban Black Americans have few opportunities to access the "personal power and well-being" that rural southern Black people felt from being co-creators with nature. The argument goes that without nature urban Blacks seek out sources of personal power and well-being offered by Wetiko. The primary outlet for this is conspicuous consumption. In the virulently racist society of the United States, Black people and other BIPOC are disproportionately kept from societal wealth and a sense of dignity. In addition, the good life is defined by the quantity and trendiness of the things one possesses. Things began to take an inordinate place in our value system. Rather than seek out life-affirming opportunities, many urban Black Americans, like most Americans, focus on achieving material wealth at the expense of spiritual and emotional well-being.[58] Wetiko consumerism has captured us all. IK is the way back to health.

The BAT I learn from elders in Chicago is a form of AHK and shares many elements with other forms of IK. AHK is "a cultural fund of the individual and collective knowledge of African peoples, which has endured through time and draws on a critical linkage of culture, race and politics in coming to know."[59] Black agrarian AHK developed over centuries in Africa, transported to the United States, and mixed with Amerindigenous IK, and, later, migrated to the North, Midwest, and West where many continue the tradition.[60] The copious use of greens by Black Americans is exemplary. Greens served several gastronomical, horticultural, nutritional, and economic functions in West Africa and later in the U.S. South where Africans survived the horrors of slavery using AHK. Currently, Black elders in Chicago are encyclopedias of greens. Every collective harvest of greens that I have attended over the years has included discussions about which greens to grow, how to grow, how to harvest, and how to cook and eat them.[61]

Many in Chicago have retained African land stewardship technology. In 2011 one elder described the importance of the hoe to several gardeners in the Outdoor Community Classroom of the Roseland Community Peace Garden. While weeding and tilling a garden bed with a hoe, he explained that "you can do anything with a hoe. Chop weeds. Dig. Make trenches. This is a good tool. The hoe." Through demonstration of its usefulness and a brief narrative, this teacher passed on an important part of a centuries-old Western African agricultural system that used multiple different hoes. It is such a useful system of agriculture that many plantation owners in the Americas had enslaved Africans use hoes instead of the animal-powered plow.[62] The multiple uses of hoes by Black American elders in Chicago is testament to the resilience of AHK.

Gardens throughout Chicago's South Side are a wealth of AHK concerning land maintenance and food production and consumption. For many, the food movement is a means of survival using AHK. Mecca Brooks explains that sustainability practices are nothing new in Black America. She explains that this sustainability and its pedagogical practices developed out of necessity rather than awareness. Black Americans adapted AHK to new surroundings of the slave economy. AHK allowed enslaved Africans to survive the horrors of slavery, apartheid conditions, urban migration, and racism. According to Brooks, the food and justice movements in Chicago require such AHK transmitted under the ethic of sankofa:

> It is also necessary to place value in informal access to knowledge. For the health of culture, it is essential to have community members sharing across generations what they do (and have done) to maintain the ecosystem using knowledge that has been passed down from previous generations. This is a part of the legacy which some define as sankofa.[63]

In the spaces of the Black food autonomy movement in Chicago, you find a continuous educational process in which AHK is transmitted. Importantly, Brooks and many others emphasize intergenerational communication. Blacks in Green and GLP emphasize this concept in their work. Blacks in Green, directed by Naomi Davis, has developed the idea of "grannynomics" which emphasizes the importance of elders' wisdom regarding sustainability and the need to transmit it across generational divides. GLP's mission statement includes an emphasis on intergenerational interaction and communication. Importantly, the HFH's and BOC's other spaces are designed for intergenerational exchange.

Colonialism and Autonomy

Indigenous resistance movements use the language and perspective of anti- and decolonialism. This perspective is often referenced among my accomplices in the food movement in Black Chicago. Anticolonial analysis provides significant insight into food injustice and corporate control of the global food system. The realization that the European bourgeoisie (and later the global bourgeoisie) relies on colonialism, especially the theft of material and human resources and the psychological oppression of native populations,[64] helps us connect material deprivation with psychological and spiritual oppression in food-deprived communities. Decolonial theories allow us to see how racism develops under capitalism as the colonizer uses settlers or "settler-rangers" as the front line in the attack on the Native population.[65] The manufactured opposition of the White settler/working class to BIPOC and Whites' acceptance of their "privilege" (relative to BIPOC) maintains racial divisions. White settlers feel privilege and often engage in violent acts against the native population. The Native population understands their oppression in racial terms. Decolonial theory provides a means to understand racism in psychological terms as well as material terms. It informs us about revolutionary organizing with a multiethnic population.

Decolonial theory helps us understand the ruling class liberal strategy of integration, assimilation, and inclusion. Wetiko often seeks to integrate natives and people of color into its system. Capitalism needs the oppressed classes and colonized peoples to work and buy. It needs labor like it needs the other natural resources stolen from the lands previously occupied by the formerly enslaved, the Indigenous, and migrants. Subaltern populations can even speak their minds on occasion; witness the hundreds of peaceful marches of people "speaking truth to power" every year in the United States alone. The ruling class often accommodates the expression of free speech and freedom of assembly. However, the ruling class fears autonomy.

> What settler society fears more than the disruptive potential of Indigenous speech is the inevitability that Indigenous peoples, once released from an imposed duty to justify themselves to the colonizer, will turn that massive investment of energy back into being truth to power. Being truth to power is reflected in those embodied practices of love for community and for the land.[66]

Decolonial analysis allows us to confront the key issue: land. Who owns it? Who manages it? Who determines? Any revolutionary theoretical perspective and praxis must address these questions if it seeks to understand, explain, and solve inequality, racism, hunger, and other symptoms of Wetiko while bringing about a new society. Ward Churchill adds,

> Unless and until this population [Indigenous Americans] is addressed on its own terms and in accordance with its own definition of its human needs, any conceivable revolutionary theory can only amount to a continuation of "the invasion of America.[67]

Alfred, tying the psychological components of colonialism with the material, explains that assimilation is at "the root of the problem." He writes, "Colonization is a process of disconnecting us from our responsibilities to one another and our respect for one another, our responsibilities and our respect for the land, and our responsibilities and respect for the culture."[68] Simpson comes to the same conclusion in her study of Indigenous life. Indigenous people cannot be Indigenous people without land and all our relations.[69] Since many in the Black food autonomy movement in Chicago attempt to reindigenize culture, self, and land, these are key issues. They are difficult, and there is no consensus on how best to solve the problem. Continued attention to Indigenous perspectives and claims to land can assist any revolutionary organization or movement with their goals of bringing about better societies. Ultimately, to end ecological and racial violence land stewardship must be turned over to Indigenous people. This is the basis of the recent push for #landback as a rallying cry for decolonial movements. Further addressing the twin colonial evils of psychological warfare and land dispossession, many Native scholars argue against liberal settler-government strategies of integration and reconciliation. They argue for Indigenous resurgence and rejection of settler society[70] and, even, civilization, itself.[71]

The decolonial process is necessary for developing "a world in which all worlds fit." According to this Indigenous insight, working people, colonized people, and others must come together and assert right livelihood. This struggle for autonomy and right livelihood is at the heart of much of the work in the food autonomy movement in Chicago. Moreover, Indigenous ethnic renewal or reindigenization provides the most viable long-term strategy for human survival and environmental justice.[72] A society based on the ethic of respect for and reciprocity with our more-than-human relatives leads to a more peaceful, liberated interdependence. Seeing more-than-humans as part of our community, we value them and take our interactions with them seriously. We recognize that humans "exist within mutual relationships."[73] Using ecosystemic logic, IK, or native ecosophy,[74] we can create a society based on equity through cooperation.

Decolonial Food in Chicago

Food autonomy movement work in Chicago reflects the analysis of decolonial scholars and activists. The BOC bases the HFH on African land ethics. BOC explains:

> The mission of the HFH is to create a just, holistic local food system to transform urban to rural communities through education, entrepreneurship and access to healthy, affordable food." In 26 words, the HFH sought to scale a massive vision of interwoven community processes down into a statement more easily digestible while still communicating our core commitment to the work of food justice as a launchpad for community governance. It was a subtle attempt to reclaim the connotation of the "marketplace" from being viewed solely as a space where one puts up money in exchange for goods. The marketplace in the traditional sense was a center of economic, commercial, social and political activity. It remained a common ground where everyone met in order to trade in both goods and ideas.

The marketplace was an open community curated space where everyone could find a voice and fill a need.

The HFH was formed to provide one such open community curated space where we have offered classes, workshops, food demonstrations and an open mic for community announcements. The market is more than a marketplace. The HFH is a form of community propaganda.[75]

HFH calls into question the capitalist understanding of the market simply as a place of economic exchange. Instead of a strict divide between the business and the consumer, the market becomes an open community space where social, political, and cultural development occurs. They practice "a more sustainable notion of the marketplace."

In resisting Wetiko ethics of domination and individualism, BOC follows in the BAT of collective work and organization. African people brought their traditions of mutuality to the Americas. Here they adapted these traditions and adopted others. The Underground Railroad, maroonage, and guerrilla warfare are early examples of Black American cooperative behavior. Black communities have managed to survive and improve their lives by building solidarity, taking collective action, pooling monies and other resources, creating mutual-aid societies and intentional communities, and working land collectively. Throughout the Black food movement, growers are reviving these traditions and adapting them to current conditions.[76]

Efforts to practice Indigenous foodways requires a decolonization of the mind using Indigenous epistemologies. BOC and the HFH use the "Akan philosophical system of Adinkra" as a counter to Wetiko worldview. Adinkra is reinterpreted in the urban U.S. context to determine health needs and to organize efforts to develop a local, community-controlled food system.[77]

Decolonizing the mind occurs through a reframing of the contemporary Black American relationship to the land, because as bell hooks points out "unmindful of our history of living harmoniously on the land, many contemporary black folks see no value in supporting ecological movements or see ecology and the struggle to end racism as competing concerns."[78] Schools, churches, and the media almost never examine the wisdom of AHK and its centrality to the survival of the African diaspora.[79] Instead, the only discussions of Black people and the land involve slavery and violence.

BOC and the HFH attempt to reclaim BAT worldview through communication, storytelling, and humor. Their members explain, "Our legacy lives in the land and the relationships our ancestors cultivated throughout the history of human agriculture."[80] HFH becomes a hallowed center for passing on AHK.

In this sacred space of communication we found that stories shared by others act as a catalyst in restoring aspects of our own memories which may have faded. In the collective memory, there is an incredible strength to reclaim, recapture and archive our history.

The marketplace becomes a meeting place where these stories can be reframed in their entirety as each of us contributes a single square of fabric to the quilted tapestry.[81]

At its eco-campus in Pembroke, Illinois, Black Oaks reclaims AHK through several programs and workshops transmitting AHK to hundreds who have made important impacts on our movement.

The "commons" adds to our understanding of the Black food autonomy movement in Chicago. Describing a new revolution consisting of people across the planet taking back and developing the idea of commons, Peña writes,

The "social common," involves the entire web of social knowledge and relationships produced across the multitude of humanity, especially when people pursue—out of sheer metaphysical necessity—what Marx terms "species life." This includes all the unique life-ways and right livelihoods of ethnic cultures, place-based communities, as well as the always shifting rhizome-like networks of subaltern affiliations of persons based on qualities related to shared trades and crafts or associations springing from the value persons agree to place on affective and artistic skills.[82]

The food autonomy movement in Black Chicago exemplifies this social common practice. Teaching and learning happen daily in gardens, markets, and other movement sites. In addition, movement members and groups have numerous affiliations and work with one another on many short-term projects while trying to develop a lasting local, community-controlled food system.

Anarchist Horticulture

Peter Kropotkin claims that "the chief aim of Anarchism is to awaken those constructive powers of the laboring masses of the people."[83] It is especially crucial to develop a plan for production during and after the revolution. Malatesta added that the food supply is fragile, we are constantly on the verge of famine, and that any major upheaval will cause many to starve needlessly.[84] George Jackson famously stated "realistic, day-to-day needs should be the basis of organizing people and making them conscious of revolution."[85] Service to the Black community and solving day to day problems was central to the Black liberation movement out of which anarchists Balagoon and Lorenzo Komboa Ervin developed. Balagoon argues that we must develop "an actual infrastructure" "that render the old ones useless."[86]

Such logic suggests that we must not simply discuss the destructive nature of revolution but also its constructive nature. We must build the world we wish to inhabit along with our more-than-human relatives. In the struggle for a liberated world, the tools of mutual aid, solidarity, and direct action are crucial. In the numerous spaces of the food autonomy movement, people are doing just this. Individual and community self-empowerment are evident in ideas such as Black Oaks' "commUnity wealth" and the educational work taking place in gardens and markets. Many of the urban community garden projects and local food movement initiatives in the Chicago region exhibit practices and ideals that model I/B anarchism. Direct action, worker self-management, direct democracy, shared responsibility, distribution by need, autonomy and federation are found in varying degrees throughout the Black food movement. While these anarchist elements exist, most in the Black food autonomy movement would not readily accept the label "anarchist" nor would they accept all basic anarchist tenets. They have their own revolutionary ideas, traditions, and identities. The point is not that they are anarchist but that with the leadership of Black and Indigenous people anarchists can learn from and participate in the sites of the BIPOC food autonomy movement and that anarchists and Black, Indigenous, and other food autonomy movement groups learn about justice and revolution from one another. Finally, I/B anarchists have much to offer the Black food movement and White anarchists.

Gardening as Direct Action for Indigenous/Afrikan Identities and Lives

Black people/New Afrikans have engaged in direct action since European slavers brought masses of Africans to Abya Yala. It is no surprise, then, that Black/New Afrikan anarchists would see direct action and alternative institution building as key tactics in their revolutionary strategy. As Balagoon explains,

> Set up communes in abandoned buildings. Sell scrap cars and aluminum cans. *Turn vacant lots into gardens.* When our children grow out of clothes, we should have places where we can take them, clearly marked anarchist clothing exchanges, and have no bones about looking for clothing there first. And, of course, we should relearn how to *preserve food.* We must learn construction and ways to take back our lives, help each other move, and stay in shape (emphasis added).[87]

Direct action can be defined simply as "acting for yourself against injustice and oppression"[88] or "the habit of direct action is the habit of wresting back the power to make decisions affecting us from them."[89] With indirect action such as voting and peaceful protest marches, you seek an end to your suffering and disempowerment by asking others to do it for you; the "begging" that in our dialogue my accomplice Austin Wayne argues limits our energies for developing self-determination. Glen Coulthard defines direct action simply as acts counter to the colonial system "performed by the colonial subject themselves which seek to produce a more or less immediate effect."[90] Direct action such as road blockades and reoccupying Indigenous lands is seen as illegitimate by the settler-coloniaL state because it is less mediated and more destructive of colonial privilege and structures. He opposes this to "legitimate action" (or indirect action) such as negotiations and symbolic, peaceful protests that are controlled by the state, abide by the law, and are not disruptive to Wetiko.

Through acting for themselves, people develop a sense of power and dignity required to end hierarchy and domination and create a liberated society. One group of anarchists explain,

> Direct action is the means of creating a new consciousness, a means of self-liberation from the chains placed around our minds, emotions and spirits by hierarchy and oppression ... Direct action is the means by which people can liberate themselves and educate themselves in the ways of and skills required for self-management and liberty.[91]

Direct action, working together such as we do in community gardens, strengthens solidarity, the "building of links of support, of common interests, of organization."[92] This practice opposes a great deal of "revolutionary communist behavior" which takes place in coffee shops owned by corporate America. Often, the "revolutionary Left" criticizes capitalism but does little to begin to implement communism in everyday life. Direct action opposes "coffee shop communism." It is a prefigurative activity in which participants build an antiauthoritarian anarchist community in the now while engaged in undermining the current social system. Politicized, liberated community gardening is direct action against domination and for a new society.

> Even the hobby gardener has added a portion of freedom to life simply through direct experience of growing, smelling, tasting. But the politically conscious gardener does more. By realizing the garden not only as a kind of autonomous zone but also as an act of resistance, the avant gardener raises the stakes, adds meaning to action, sets a standard, and joins deliberately with others in a common cause.[93]

At their best, urban community gardens enact conscious revolutionary direct action. Some enact freedom from Wetiko's antilife ethics and practice forms of communism. Wetiko is weakened through refusal to play the roles reserved for us. Liberated tendencies, structures, and systems are strengthened as workers and others labor collectively without wages and the exploitation that attends them. Direct action is a force for redefining ourselves and all our relations to one another. Direct actions such as land reoccupation, guerilla gardening, and reterritorialization help us reconnect to land and our indigeneity.

For many Indigenous radicals, indigeneity is about being and doing indigeneity, being a part of a community that knows how to live sustainably. From this perspective decolonization requires direct action that emphasizes a reindigenization process based on reconnection to the land. Klee Benally offers a framework they call Indigenous-Rooted Direct Action:

> The organizing framework we utilize is based on Diné iiná (our life/lifeways). So it goes beyond activist interventions and tactics and applies to how we live our lives. ... When we assert these contextual frameworks, we build on the understanding that action is our prayer when we live our lives in accordance with our beliefs, or our reverence with the sacred. ... We affirm that our power is rooted within our mutuality with existence, with the sacred. Indigenous-Rooted Direct Action means being a force of nature.[94]

Many Black and Indigenous urban farmers and food autonomy advocates recognize this important process and consciously focus our efforts on developing a relationship to the land. We engage in direct-action gardening to confront Wetiko, to decolonize and reindigenize.

Unfortunately, we often fall short in our efforts due to an analysis of racism/White supremacy and capitalism without attention to decolonization. Decolonization would return the stolen resources of the Indigenous people who cared for these lands before the European invasion. The "civil rights" discourse that has predominated in Black, Chicanx, and other people of color movements from the 1960s until today seeks an equal amount of the things that our society has to offer. This discourse recognizes the centuries-long inequality to which Black, Latinx, and other POC suffer as the consequences of racism that can be righted if we more fairly distribute the wealth of our society. It rarely questions the violent imperialist origins of that material wealth. This perspective on Black and Indigenous politics lacks the internationalist understanding and solidarity that has long been part of our liberation struggles.[95] Unfortunately, this sharing of "the American Dream" discourse has won over most activists and social movements.

Fortunately, the discourse of decolonization has begun to spread in the movements of a new generation of activists. Building on the hard work of their elders, these young people speak about, debate, and attempt to implement ideas like "sovereignty," "Indigenous leadership," and "decolonization." BIPOC activists/

revolutionaries are decolonizing their minds and organizing spaces. They now implement as one of their pillars "land back," meaning the return of stewardship of these lands to Indigenous peoples. We recognize that the only solution to the climate and numerous ecological crises requires "rematriation" of these lands.

Anarchist Land Use

The collectively run, self-managed urban garden exemplifies the potential effectiveness of I/B anarchism in creating a revolutionary new world. If an egalitarian society, free of exploitation, is to be created, it must be based on the principle that no one individual is more valuable or has more power than any other individual. Thus, decision-making must be based on direct democracy. In addition, an ecological community would insist that actions are taken with attention to the needs of all our relations. In the words of accomplice Jacqueline Abena Smith, we "co-steward with the earth" to help provide for all our relations. Or to paraphrase the eco-warrior character, The Lorax, from Dr. Seuss fame, "We speak for the trees." To engage in ecologically sound, democratic practice, White anarchists are challenged to learn from and with Indigenous people, work alongside and live with colonized peoples. Balagoon's central critique of anarchists, Black nationalists, and other Black radicals of the time is that they don't work with "people outside of the movement" and instead "simply refuse to organize in the Black community."[96] His critique is more relevant than ever as new generations of activists struggle with how to effectively organize especially those of us who have succumbed to the seduction of working within the nonprofit-industrial complex. Often, we spend more time in meetings talking with one another and potential funders than with people engaged in survival or revolutionary work. Without immersion alongside and communion with human people, plant people, the winged, and other relatives, democratic practices are impossible.

Land is key to Wetiko control and the continued subjugation of Indigenous people. We don't own or control land upon which to pursue self-determination and express our indigeneity. Anarchist and similar community garden projects also understand the importance of landownership and management. Anarchists oppose the private ownership of the means of production. Ideally, land is socialized; that is, community residents collectively "own" it. Collectively managed land helps fulfill the anarchist goal of attaining the most individual freedom and creativity. It should be noted that the concept of land "ownership" runs counter to most Indigenous understanding of land as a relation to which we have a responsibility to serve.

While those who use a resource have the right to do so and "those who work, eat," anarchists typically do not believe in inviolable property nor hunger. A well-run community garden would yield an extraordinary abundance of food that would be based on individual and family needs. This distribution by need principle is common throughout the history of the broader socialist movement including those branches of the movement that believe in the ideal of "from those according to ability, to those according to need."

We aspire and adhere to these principles in varying ways throughout the local food movement in Chicago. GLP attempts to implement these organizational principles in the most effective manner possible. Like all manner of worker-run revolutionary practice under Wetiko, the project is a work in progress. We practice worker self-management through collective work and decision-making. Each piece of land managed by GLP has been owned by different entities causing the members of the GLP to have different relationships with each. The RCFG sits on land owned by two different entities. The founder of GLP, Dominique Bowman Vining, owns one parcel, and the other is owned by the City of Chicago and controlled by the alderman's office. Chicagoland Prison Outreach owned the land that we called Sacred Greens Community Garden. They allowed us to use the garden and their water and provided valuable assistance. El Jardín Izquierdista was on land owned by the Archidiocese of Chicago and controlled by St. Sabina Church. They ignored our attempts to purchase the land or otherwise use it, so we guerilla gardened on it for three seasons until they sold it to a different church.

The degree to which we have the freedom to interact with the land affects how we feel about and interact with it. We know that the lands that we do not own can be easily taken from us. The loss of El Jardín Izquierdista and Sacred Greens provide cautionary tales. Our lack of legal ownership to most of the land means that our work suffers at the hands of landlords and we must question the wisdom of working so hard to rehabilitate and improve the land. Yet we care for it as if we are its morally and legally designated caretakers because that is what we do and for now that is all we have.

We continuously re-examine policies and practices in GLP gardens. This re-examination takes place through the Managing Collective that we develop each year. In recent years, the Seedkeepers Collective has fulfilled this role. We meet before planting to discuss the upcoming work. As the season progresses those of us active in the maintenance of the garden continue to meet and assess our work and relationships. In this way we try to be democratic and collective in our decision-making. On the distribution side, we aim for a distribution by need system that favors those engaged in the work of stewarding our land. The open portion of the Roseland Community Forest Garden, for example, allows residents of the neighborhood to access highly nutritious food, whether they have worked the land. However, the threats of Wetiko's values including private property, ownership, authority, and hierarchal leadership are ever-present. The local food movement and community gardening harbors a wide variety of people and perspectives including liberal philanthropists and right-wing survivalists. Moreover, in the communities in which we organize, Wetiko's values reign and conditions of desperation lead many to behave in violent, greedy, and selfish ways. We expect this response as the Indigenous principles of reciprocity and interdependence and anarchist solidarity are kept from masses of the working classes and BIPOC, and Wetiko's ethics of individualism and consumerism are ubiquitous in our culture. Moreover, the structures of Wetiko society make it difficult for us to survive otherwise.

Many radicals and revolutionaries engage in land takeovers, rematriations, and occupations. I/B anarchists have a history of expropriation. Indigenous revolutionaries routinely use and blockades in our anticolonial struggles. Unauthorized land reclamations have long histories on Turtle Island. Building squats, urban reterritorialization,[97] and land takeovers by groups like Movemento Sem Terra are the precursor to today's guerrilla gardening. Importantly, these types of gardens display our lack of respect for Wetiko law and our belief that the land should be stewarded for the good of all our relations. They also have the potential to feed a lot of people. Each of the guerrilla gardens that I have had the opportunity to work with has provided food for Black and Brown communities. Given our lack of police or military to enforce our land claims, guerrilla gardening can only be a temporary autonomous zone, a place where human potential and self-determination are practiced and experimented with.

While many anarchist and Indigenous principles find resonance, each of these groups views our relationship to land differently. Given the centrality of land both to Indigenous identity and any economy, anarchist theory and practice would do well to incorporate an Indigenous anticolonial perspective—a decolonizing of anarchism.[98]

Community-Controlled Food Systems

After the overthrow of Wetiko, we will need to create a system of human organization based on principles of freedom, love, and community. Like Balagoon, we work toward a new system "built around collectives, rather than capitalism or state capitalism. All railroads, ship lines, airlines, phone companies, oil, gas, and electric companies will be socialized, all trucking will be put into the collective ownership of drivers, all overseas possessions left to sink, all textile mills collectivized, all military industries and arms manufacturers taken over by militias." These collectives and coops provide a good deal of relief from Wetiko, but "the trick is to form a federation that takes care of the needs of its members and invites more."[99]

Isolated individuals and communities cannot be successful at achieving a liberated world. For the food autonomy movement to yield a freer life today and a free society in the future, gardens, farms, communities, co-ops, and other groupings cannot become small isolated and insulated groups. A liberated future will have systems of interconnected or federated, autonomous collectivities. An ecologically oriented anarchism would consider ecological boundaries and limitations. Community and regional boundaries follow bioregional, watershed, ecosystem, or other natural boundaries. For permaculturalists, decentralized organizational structures are necessary for designing sustainable human settlements and preserving and extending nature.[100]

Ecological principles would insist on local food systems. The needs of the local population and the carrying capacity of the land would be the principal concerns; exchange with other communities or in some sort of market and sourcing necessities from distant lands would be secondary considerations. Today's global food system relies on burning fossil fuels and war. Moreover, we will be forced to develop local food systems when we run out of petroleum. A return to Indigenous and small farmer practices is inevitable. The adoption of the sensibilities of place-based people would have us seek and conservatively use renewable sources of human, animal, and other organic energy. An I/B anarchist community would adopt sustainability as a framework for decision-making. Governance based on the probable impact that current decisions will have on future generations (i.e., the Haudenosaunee seventh-generation principle) would extend democracy into the future and across species.[101] The science and art of permaculture can contribute to a decentralized, ecological model. As such, many anarchists, anti-colonialists, and urban guerrilla gardeners have used its principles, strategies, and techniques. Some have extended such organizational and moral principles by creating eco-villages, communes, or other intentional communities. Black people have practiced versions of intentional communities throughout history including maroon communities and MOVE in Philadelphia.[102]

For direct democracy to work in the creation of an I/B anarchist society people must be able to engage in face-to-face politics. Community decision-making bodies and communities themselves must be structured so that each has an opportunity to voice their opinion on any given subject. Like many in the international Indigenous movement including the Zapatistas, we propose autonomous communities federated with many others on a regional, temporary, and voluntary basis. Communities and their resources will be collectively managed. Everyone will have a say in the general issues facing them. This type of collective work and management has a long history in the BAT.[103] The history of Black cooperative economics illustrates the advantages and challenges of self-managed, collectively owned enterprises. Black urban growers adapt these lessons each season. Alliances like Urban Growers Collective, Urban Steward Action Network, Grow Greater Englewood, and the Lifeboats Permaculture Guild engage in collective management and federation.

Ideally, each community would answer questions about how much food is needed, how it is tended, and how it is distributed. In such a societal organization, the central decision-making body is the general assembly in which all community members participate. From the activities and decisions of the general assembly, we delegate particular responsibilities and authority to individuals or small groups. Many of the day-to-day tasks required to meet the needs established by the community would be determined by work groups or individuals based on community need and individual expertise. Collectives could be established for community needs. For example, our Lifeboats Permaculture Guild established the Chicken Co-op in 2021 for the expressed purpose of fulfilling some of our protein needs. The guild itself is an example of a collective established to help fulfill one another's needs.

A federated, autonomous, self-managed collective social organization is put into practice in a limited manner in our food movement and serves as goal that many try to achieve. While a local food system based on these principles has not developed, elements of it surface often. Many participate in autonomous, self-managed community gardens federated with others. Members determine the season's goals and delegate individuals to perform certain tasks. Generally, those who have more experience, skills, or knowledge exercise rational authority exemplified by the centrality of their opinions and perspectives in final decisions. However, the ideal is for all members to develop a wide range of skills. Those with well-developed skills or knowledge feel obliged to assist other members in learning all they can about important subject matter.[104] This sentiment sparked the Local Food System Development with Permaculture Design Certification course initiated by BOC. In line with anarchist, Indigenous, and permaculture perspectives, the three teachers desired to disseminate as widely as possible the skills and knowledge they acquired and to create a guild whereby graduates could practice permaculture and local food system development outside of class. Entities like the Lifeboats Permaculture Guild and other affinity groups serve as a foundation for establishing a federated, autonomous, rhizomatic network similar to those desired by anarchists. For this reason, our PDC and Resilient Community Design course and many other elements of work focus on food system development and creating conditions for successful communities built on ecological relationships.

REVOLUTIONARY POLYCULTURALISM

Leave to each its sentiments, its affections, its beliefs, its languages and its customs . . . The first effect of centralization is to bring about the disappearance, in the diverse localities of the country, of all types of indigenous character.[105]

[Colonial] myths and attachments are rooted in a simplistic liberal ideology that has as one of its core premises that unity requires homogeneity: we can all get along only if we are all made to be the same.[106]

Decolonial perspectives and revolutions can retreat to xenophobic nationalism when they lack an ethic of solidarity, mutual aid, mitakuyeayasi, and critique of capitalism. The strategic essentialism that often results from "closing ranks" against Wetiko uses "master's tools" (the concept of race) to "dismantle master's house" (racism, capitalism, colonialism). Thus, the inverted racialist logics of Wetiko become a dogma that limits our understanding of land-based ethics while narrowing our knowledge of self in relation to others. Bourgeois cultural nationalism is an important limiting factor to an accurate analysis and praxis regarding the problems of our world and effective solutions. Redefining taken-for-granted notions of ourselves using the flexible, relational perspectives of our Indigenous ancestors and constant appraisal of movement work can help solve the problems of rigidity, dogmatism, and xenophobia. Many, especially younger activists, are addressing this in movement spaces in ways that the older, dominant sectors of Black, Indigenous, and other people of color Left do not. Race exclusivity as the conceptual foundation for bourgeois cultural nationalism must be interrogated and challenged since it is a concept developed to create divides between the working classes and between Indigenous and non-Natives. The racialist lens, while separating the masses from one another, also narrowly defines "us" by skin color. This often leads to violent members of a given race being allowed to do damage to that population simply because they share "race." The colonizer has always used the comprador class or petit bourgeois members of an oppressed group as a tool of exploitation and social control. The political histories of the United States and Chicago illustrate how the Black comprador class has been used to stifle Black revolution. Much can be said about how tribal councils play a similar role in Indigenous communities in settler nations.

To combat the errors of nationalist exclusivity, some revolutionary antiracist, anticapitalists emphasize the commonality of the working class across the globe. According to this line of reasoning, since we are all workers, we should not focus on differences that divide us but see ourselves as one. My accomplice Kevin Triplett often convincingly argues this point with me. In addition, they insist that all nationalist and tribalist perspectives undermine the revolution against capitalism. This perspective limits much needed conversations about how the recognition of ethnic diversity has liberatory potential. Further, it undermines the goal of solidarity since many people wish to remain seeing themselves in and behaving in the culturally prescribed ways of their people. They wish to continue to be who they are ethnically and not be pushed into the homogenous entity of the working class. The desire to require the adoption of a working-class identity recalls the colonial desire to "Americanize" Indigenous people or to "bring Christianity to the savages." Visions of homogeneity are authoritarian and counterrevolutionary. Thus, I argue that revolutions against domination of all sorts require unity in diversity. For example, Cedric Robinson's corrections to Marxist theory and practice shows clearly how the Black radical tradition is replete with unique methods of struggle based in African cultures.[107]

Respectful coexistence and interdependence are Indigenous principles that guard against xenophobia and homogenization.[108] Moreover, hostility to diversity goes against natural laws required to sustain life on the planet.[109]

> Unity in diversity . . . is not only the determinant of an ecosystem's stability; it is the source of an ecosystem's fecundity, of its innovativeness, of its evolutionary potential to create newer, still more complex life-forms and biotic interrelationships.[110]

Life according to this understanding is a set of complex interrelationships that have developed over a long historical period. Complex food webs and the wide diversity in human cultures and relationships to other species demonstrate a scientific grounding for the encouragement of unity through diversity. Of course, Indigenous people who study nature recognize that "diversity is the heart of evolution"[111] and some of us have made diversity the heart of our revolution.

The Zapatistas took up arms against the Mexican federal government and the global capitalist system in 1994. Among their numerous demands for a new world was a call for un mundo donde caben todos los mundos (a world in which all worlds fit). They resist the homogenizing call of the powerful who deny us our dignity by making us all the same. They seek a world in which we are allowed to be ourselves, to achieve our full human potential as we see fit in our cultural groups. So the Zapatistas say, "I am as I am and you are as you are. Let's build a world where I can be, and not have to cease being me, where you can be, and not have to cease being you, and where neither I nor you will force another to be like either me or you."[112] They recognize the necessity of diversity for creating a world that is just for everyone. Diversity is no less necessary for an egalitarian human social world than it is for healthy ecosystems. Importantly, isolated individual distinct units by themselves are not enough for a sustainable system. The key to a sustainable, just, free system is the relationships between the various components including plants, animals, energies, and human groups.[113] This Indigenous perspective on diversity stems from a religious or spiritual recognition of human relations with the more-than-human world. Vine DeLoria, Jr. explains that "to exist in a creation means that living is more than tolerance for other life forms—it is recognition that in differences there is the strength of creation and that this strength is a deliberate desire of the creator."[114] The mindset and culture of sameness is a sickness. The colonial mentality that brought about industrial monocultures also brought about a mono-culture of the mind that threatens Indigenous existence and the IK that might save us all from climate chaos. This same monocultural mind has thrown us headlong into a rapidly increasing era of species extinction. I argue for "pledging allegiance to all sorts of biodiversity" as opposed to pledging allegiance and identifying with any human colonial nation.[115]

Urban community gardening and the development of a community-controlled food system in Black Chicago demonstrates how we daily pledge allegiance to revolutionary diversity. While remaining steeped in AHK, this work often models interethnic mutual recognition and cooperation and the respect for difference required as a precondition for a truly revolutionary society. At the same time, many members of the food movement retreat to a xenophobic, racist bourgeois national-ism or practice willful ignorance of others through choosing to interact only with those who are somehow "like them." Unfortunately, often the spaces of food "justice" in Chicago are racially segregated spaces. My experience as a non-Black identified human of Mexican descent in the Black food movement in Chicago is marked by questions about my motives, suspicion, and occasional hostility as well as being grounded in interethnic decolonial love. The racial history of Chicago, including continuous attacks against Black residents, has created a powerful nar-rative among Black activists and community organizers of racial separation and retrenchment. Black media outlets such as WVON encourage a "Black first agenda" and a hostile orientation to those who are not Black, especially "foreigners" and "immigrants" who are seen as "jumping the line" required for realization of the the American Dream. Currently, this is most popularly expressed in the concept of "African Descendants of Slaves" or ADOS. An example from our food commu-nity occurred on the day that I initially wrote these lines. A friend and long-time conspirator in the food movement posted a status on Facebook that culminated in the hashtag, #separateorelse. As a non-Black identified human, my immediate response was "Where does that leave me?" Would my children be included but not me? Further, how does "separation" of the races fit with the universal prin-ciple of diversity and interdependence that Indigenous people have honored for centuries? How different is #separateorelse from the logics of racism, colonialism, genocide, slavery, and dispossession that is the foundation of Wetiko in Abya Yala and throughout the planet?

In the best examples of community gardening and the food movement, polyculturalism reigns. A wide variety of individuals from different ethnic, racial, generational, gender, and national groups work together in a garden full of diverse species and relationships. For example, the food arts and sciences of Black Americans mingle with those of Mexican Americans and Africans in GLP gardens to expand the knowledge base of each and to bring members closer. Younger food warriors have been at the forefront of rejecting divisive political philosophies and practices, including "separate or else," heteropatriarchal behaviors, and transphobia, ableism and ageism. Groups like Urban Steward Action Network (USAN), Reclaiming Our Roots, and the Gage Park Latinx Council insist that the members of our community are included in the decision-making and benefits of the work as well as working with anyone regardless of race, skin color, gender identity, and so on who is sincere and recognizes the primacy of IK in our work. The IK shared in the gardens undermines both ruling class efforts to divide and conquer through race *and* the erroneous belief that revolutionary unity can only be found through homogeneity as one global working class as most Marxist-Leninists would have it. Sharing knowledge in the gardens not only shows us the strength of diversity but conversations about horticulture, food preparation, and life illustrate commonalities and collective struggles. Our unity in the gardens comes not from an abstract homogenous working-class identity nor from a racially exclusive self-understanding but from respect for diversity and experience working side by side in a commons.

A Model for an Ecological Autonomous Society

The food autonomy movement I participate in and describe in these pages is a prefigurative practice. Like anarchist economics and politics, it is a practice "that seeks to lay the foundations of a future society in the present"[116] or as the Wobblies of the Industrial Workers of the World described as "forming the structure of the new society within the shell of the old."[117] They are attempts at "the reinvention of everyday life."[118] The nearly two-centuries long critique of capitalism and other hierarchical economic and political systems and their examination of humanity has led anarchists to propose and practice several economic forms that differ drastically from capitalism and that are present in Chicago's food movement as well as provide a guide for future developments within it.

At minimum, gardening and the development of a community-controlled food system takes money, power, resources, and control away from landowners, bosses, and corporations. Growing our own food has numerous benefits as a tactic in dismantling Wetiko as we withdraw from its economy and food system. IK is disruptive of capitalist globalization because those of us who practice it reduce our consumption of food created through the destructive "capitalist commodity chains."[119] For example, the home-kitchen garden practices of Mexicanxs in San Jose, California, disrupt capitalist commodity chains and logics by overcoming transportation inequality, creating social networks of cooperation, safety and trust, developing an informal sharing economy, impacting health care inequality, and producing a socially meaningful life.[120]

Such practices improve the lives of working-class people and as such are necessary to the development of revolution. Beyond food many participate in various exchange relationships and networks such as The Kola Nut Collaborative; a time bank developed through the persistence of Baba Mike Tekhen Strode; an integral and early member of BOC and HFH. Many members of the Lifeboats Permaculture Guild and students from the Local Food System Development course participate in The Kola Nut Collaborative. Through this web-based skills/labor sharing platform we strengthen our community and efforts toward self-determination through "do for selves" outside the logic of capitalism.

Importantly, developing a gift economy also withdraws our energy and resources from Wetiko. Gift economies develop when

> individuals freely give goods or services to one another without immediately receiving anything in return. Yet by maintaining through their actions the practice of gift giving, they too can expect to receive gifts themselves as part of a generalized culture of reciprocity. In attempting to launch an entirely different culture of exchange, anarchist practices of gift economy are the most distant from capitalism and the least to partake in its structures.[121]

The gift economy relies on ethics of reciprocity and community well-being. Reciprocity plays a central role in Indigenous thought and social organization because it "allows people to build a reputation of generosity based on sharing to ensure ongoing connectedness and support"[122]. Moreover, such practices replace our faith in the economic system with faith and trust in one another. The permaculture design system that we at GLP and BOC use includes the ethical principle of fair share or the practice of limiting consumption and sharing of surplus.[123]

Serving others or contributing to society is a natural process undermined by Wetiko. Studies of child psychology demonstrate the tendency for children to help. Labor has become a burden and a commodity under capitalism. Those things that we would normally take pride and pleasure in, such as producing goods that benefit our communities, become toil only undertaken to benefit personally through monetary compensation. The capitalist ethic of individualism and competition makes communal labor absurd in the minds of many. Ideas of sharing labor and resources so common throughout much of human history have become abnormal, even deviant in our society. Moreover, the capitalist consumer ethic causes many to reject labor of service or community labor that does not lead to the ability to purchase commodities.

Fortunately, our movement attempts a return to communal practices, shared labor, and reciprocity. One of the primary pleasures of community gardening and developing food communities is giving away wealth in the form of sharing resources. Members of the food movement give and receive mulch, soil, seedlings, seeds, tools, labor, and harvests. In much of this book, I've described the numerous members of my community who have offered gifts of immense wealth. Dr. J. has been integral to spreading medicinal plants such as Cup, Joe Pye, gynura procumbens, and motherwort to me and our GLP gardens as well as dozens of gardeners throughout the South and West sides. The Community Nursery Program at Sacred Greens Community Garden and the In Lak' Ech CommUnity Wealth Program are slightly more formalized efforts to establish a gift economy within our community. At Sacred Greens, gardeners and farmers were able to dig out native perennial plants to transplant including raspberry, sunchoke, and currant. The In Lak' Ech program started as a memorial to Jacqueline Abena Smith also aspires to extend this cycle of reciprocity.

Our primary gift is food. Food autonomy-oriented land stewards give to neighbors, friends, and extended families after harvesting together. Efforts like Seedkeepers Collective member Luis Rafael's "love cabinet" (a locker at RCFG containing food, plants, seeds, books, and other resources) in 2023 are common throughout our movement. With an ethos of "to each according to their needs," often community gardens are completely open and members work knowing that much of the harvest will go to many in the community who do not work in the garden. In addition, gardeners, especially ecological gardeners, give the products of their labors to thousands of other species and in so doing provide ecological services. Those of us who take seriously our responsibility to be good stewards to our relatives extend our understanding of yield to include the habitat and food that we provide our more-than-human relatives. The ethos of the gift economy is revolutionary under Wetiko's individualism, competition, and consumption. Mutual aid, working on behalf of others in our communities, strikes at Wetiko's heart. Developing a consciousness around the gift economy, mutual aid, reciprocity, and shared labor has enormous potential benefits for the struggle to create a revolutionary new society based on IK.

For revolutionary antiauthoritarians, the fact that we keep resources out of the Wetiko's economy provides a great deal of satisfaction. Wetiko cannot survive without our acquiescence. Corporations, bosses, and landowners rely on us as workers and consumers. Freely giving the products of our freely given labor means that our labor power and our bodies are not expended to enrich the ruling classes and that we work, instead, for one another. Intelligent garden work puts into practice working class solidarity.

Anarchist and Black agrarian organizational strategies such as cooperatives (co-ops) provide further outlet for revolutionary direct action.[124] Jessica Gordan Nembhard's history of Black cooperative economics shows how rural Blacks developed co-ops and related strategies early in the twentieth century that followed practices of their African ancestors. Ideally, they can become the basis for ecological living since "cooperation, not competition, is the very basis for existing life systems and for future survival."[125] Many in the food autonomy movement develop food cooperatives to provide for one another and practice more ecological, equitable means of food production. BOC and others are combining food co-ops with energy and housing initiatives based on the Black economic cooperative tradition. This vision is like anarchists' emphasis on the commune as the basic unit of an anarcho-communist society.

> The bases of this new organization will be the free federation of producer groups and the free federation of communes and of groups of independent communes.[126]

The consumer and producer coops created in the food autonomy movement in Black Chicago cannot be accurately described as anarchism and not always anticapitalist. Too often they seem to be liberal band-aids reliant on foundation support. So while many in the movement would not recognize the language of anarchism nor identify with it, much of what goes on resembles anarchist theorizing in action. Importantly, the BAT of co-ops, collectives, and networks informs the work being done in Chicago's Black food autonomy movement and is an area of commonality between Black growers, anarchists, and Indigenous people. My accomplices in the Black food autonomy movement urgently revive these traditions out of necessity and survival.

Efforts at reindigenization have helped many to decolonize our minds, diets, and relationships. The best of our work exemplified by BOC, GLP, and most of those who have contributed their wisdom to this project seeks to reindigenize and desires self-determination. We exhibit anticolonial behavior and seek reindigenization processes while engaging in political and organizational practices reminiscent of anarchism. The limits of our thought and action are at the level of ownership or stewardship of the land that we occupy and reactionary understandings of "race" and gender. None of our efforts have decolonized land in terms of rematriating it to its original human caretakers, the Native nations of the Great

Lakes region. Thus, our impact on dismantling the settler-colonial system is limited. The central issue is the rematriation of land to Native stewards, and this defining element of decolonization is at odds with the projects of White supremacy *and* rights movements of BIPOC based on sharing the spoils of settler-colonialist and imperialist genocide since "the promise of integration and civil rights is predicated on securing a share of a settler-appropriated wealth (as well as expropriated 'third-word' wealth)."[127] In this conceptualization of settler colonialism, BIPOC can be "brown settlers" for whom "becoming a subordinate settler is an option even when becoming white is not."[128] This settler consciousness, desire, and behavior are at odds with the decolonial project.

While much of our behavior as regards advocacy for BIPOC amount to supporting the imperial status quo, seeing Black people, immigrants, and refugees as "subordinate settlers" elides much of our history and current political economic arrangements. A more nuanced analysis accounts for how imperialism causes the violence of war leading to immigration, exile, and refugee status. This analysis recognizes the history of U.S. imperialism and the role of Black people and Blackness. We would do well to include in our analysis the differing economic niches in which BIPOC are forced and how the position of BIPOC in the capitalist system along with consumerist ideology and "savagism" (the colonial narrative about Indigenous people) influences the behavior of Black people, immigrants, and other POCs. Building relationships between Indigenous people and non-Native BIPOC requires nuanced understanding of the political economic system and our positions within it. Kyle T. Mays provides some of this as he argues for seeing Black people as Indigenous and for a deeper historical understanding of the relationships between Indigenous and Black Americans.[129]

The central premise of much anarchist and Marxist-Leninist revolutionary thought places the working classes or securing workers' rights or a workers' state as the primary interest or goal. Once again, while this perspective has the potential to disrupt capitalism, it does nothing to decolonize and as history has shown will lead to the genocide of Native people.[130] Without the rematriation of land and its management to Indigenous people, attempts at a revolutionary ecological society will likely fail. IK is the only thing that can continue our existence on the planet. But this knowledge must be practiced by Indigenous people on Indigenous land while everyone else follows along and learns.

Additionally, in the movement we often fall short of values associated with an antiauthoritarian, anticolonial, alterNative ideal as I have articulated them. A reindigenization process that many believe is required for revolutionary anticolonial behavior includes a challenge to the system of race and gender/sexuality established by the colonizers. The Black supremacy, separatism, and hostility toward other groups that rears its ugly head on occasion in our movement are at odds with an antiauthoritarian, free world. Homophobia and transphobia also make appearances in movement spaces. In fact, some of the leaders of the movement adhere to a very conservative social agenda that includes heteronormativity, patriarchy, and fear of a "gay agenda." A recent example of this is the enthusiastic support that many figures in our community have shown for comedian Dave Chapelle, that he should be able to verbally attack the transgender community.[131] A new generation of activists provides hope that these reactionary aspects of our movement will be eradicated soon. The gardens of the younger members of our movement seem to be spaces that value LGBTQ2 presence.

We are often less than revolutionary as bourgeois values, consumerism, and individualism led us down reactionary paths. Entrepreneurship as a value in Black and Mexican-origin radical spaces often leads us further into capitalism and relationships with capitalists as many in the movement focus on a limited definition of self-determination as individual business ownership. With profit becoming the motive force behind their efforts, large corporations and those with money increasingly become their business partners while community members get left behind. "Black buying power" and "Black capitalism" are creations of White capitalists with an assist from the mainstream Black media outlets that further drain Black resources and undercut Black revolutionary behavior. Capitalism, no matter the adjective put in front of it, is detrimental to Black freedom.[132] Thus, our movement would do well to reject "Black capitalism" and other cynical iterations of Wetiko.

Finally, we have spent thousands of hours trying to develop a local food economy based in liberatory practices. Yet we have yet to develop a single functioning cooperative or worker-owned farm/garden. All the reasons listed above contribute to our inability to form a sustainable solidarity economy of any significance.

In sum, I contend that a revolutionary vision of food autonomy requires an understanding of the convergences between the practices of Indigenous and African peoples, anarchists, and food activists in Chicago and a dialogue between all parties. These exchanges can teach us a great deal about how to develop autonomous food systems and an antiauthoritarian world. Many in the food autonomy movement emphasize the process of learning and relearning ecological and communal behaviors. An email from the BOC (September 3, 2013) explains their understanding of the issues:

> I am of the strong opinion that people learn best by working in close proximity
> with one another where accountability matters most deeply. Here is the place
> where conversations occur and patterns are revealed. It begins with the simple

act of purchasing goods together and becoming familiar with one another. In familiarity, we are more willing to learn from the best habits of those around us. Our thoughts and perspectives are most closely aligned with those whom we frequently associate.

This email emphasizes one of the most coveted principles common to anarchism, Marxism, and socialism: solidarity. Solidarity, according to this email, results from doing. Deeds, more than words, illustrate political perspectives and serve as political education. Moreover, one cannot learn to feed oneself or others from a book. The act of learning to grow food can only take place with one's hands in the soil. An Indigenous pedagogy requires that we learn from the land in reciprocal relationships. Intergenerational sharing of knowledge and resources is essential to our revolution.

Occasionally, our work in the local food autonomy movement illustrates I/B anarchism. We try not to be coffee shop communists, philanthropists, or business-people. We strive to create the world we wish to see in the here and now. There is no waiting for the overtheorized big-"r" Revolution. These are the little revolutions in action. Members of the food autonomy movement in Chicago actively re-create Indigenous human relations and modes of living. Within this movement the human need to cooperate is beginning to overcome the other human tendency toward selfishness and conflict.[133] Wetiko's systems have caused the latter to surge to the fore of human behavior in recent centuries. The memories and lived experiences of Indigenous peoples, the displaced, the racially or ethnically oppressed, and those in the food autonomy movement challenge Wetiko's private property regimes and individualism. In place of the antihuman, antilife social organization of Wetiko, we insist on ecological existence and practice our revolution in gardens and farms throughout Chicago and the world.

Red, Black, and Green Futures

Against the backdrop of a Black Lives Matter mural, a masked man wearing an "EDUCATED BLACK MAN" T-shirt and a white Black Lives Matter baseball cap holds and examines his gun while an elder woman narrates, "We have to get a grip on the gun violence that is devastating our communities or more innocent lives will be cut short." The camera pans so that we now see walking between two rows of funeral attendees a Mother Goddess carrying a funerary box with the letters "G.R.I.P." inscribed in it. The scene takes place within the lush backdrop of a garden. The camera comes closer to the Mother Goddess played by Chicago-based singer and actress, Laura Walls, who says "Guns, rest in peace." The man places his gun in the box adorned with an ankh and places it in a hole next to a potato patch. The video ends with the masked man throwing a shovelful of soil over the box and the Mother Goddess saying, "Let's bury the guns, not innocent lives."[1]

This two-and-a-half-minute video shot at GLP's Sacred Greens Community Garden in 2021 encompasses many of the themes addressed by our food movement. The earth, well-tended by Indigenous women, offers peace, liberty, and the opportunity to live right by all our relations. While the video does not explicitly locate the source of Chicago's gun violence in Wetiko, it does argue for self-determination and autonomy as solutions to the problem. Gun violence in U.S. ghettoes and barrios is unlikely to be stopped by its source, the state and corporations, since "the state itself is white supremacist."[2] We will solve the problem. Importantly, Maurice Walls, writer and director and graduate of CSU, located the burial for violence and our resurrection in a community garden.

I asked Maurice for some thoughts on the video. He described Roseland where Sacred Greens is located as a "food desert." His job as a "Hitchcockian filmmaker" is to present ideas in "unexpected ways like horror movies or thrillers." He wants to prompt conversations about how to solve important problems. He chose to shoot the funeral for gun violence at the garden because it "represents vitality of life and something missing from our diets. Food contains minerals and vitamins that not only affect our biological framework but our neurobiology . . . Bad foods can trigger negative behavior patterns. Good food leads to positive behavior and cohesiveness." Like many in our food movement, he recognizes the connection

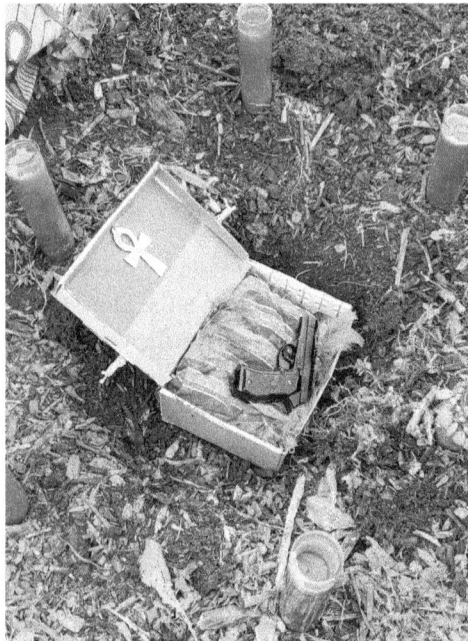

FIG. 20. Still from "G.R.I.P." short video.
Photo by Maurice Walls.

between what we put in our bodies and how we behave. In addition, he likes that through gardening "we get something [food and beauty] off of something [abandoned lots] that we don't need."

As a lifelong resident of the South Side of Chicago, Maurice bears witness to social injustice and sees gardens as a solution. He expressed the importance of a resurgence in African identity and modes of being. Maurice and his collaborators filled "G.R.I.P." with symbols of AHK. The only speaking character dressed in green West African print and orange headwrap carries the red, green, and black funerary box with an anhk dangling from the inside top. They bury Wetiko's gun inside their symbol of African culture.

The fertile, deep-green spring garden represents the earth. Central to the earth-based narrative is the Mother Goddess character who Maurice describes as

> symboliz[ing] Mother Earth, Giving Earth, giving life and the green [of her dress] represents Mother Earth, life-bringing, life-giving Earth, bringing forth life . . . the gun has nothing to do with life. Life is everything in that garden. People held candles, light, knowledge. The vegetables, the potato patch that we kept stepping on. Sorry about that!

Life and the life-giving light that comes from AHK are central to the story. Maurice described their use of African symbology in this way:

> African symbology endorses the embracing of cultural identity. Unfortunately, Brother Pancho, through chattel slavery we've been culturally circumcised. Mentally we have carbon-copied the behavior of our oppressors, taking on a new identity. That identity has more violence. The Eurocentric ideology has been rooted in manipulation, deceit, and conquering. That wasn't the African way.

Unlike the violent image of many Black, Indigenous, and Mexicano men who mimic Wetiko hypermasculinity, Maurice agrees with many in our food movement that African humanity is more complex and life-affirming. Wetiko put the guns and the consumerist, hypermasculine identity into the hands and hearts of some Black men in our poorest communities. In place of Indigenous African culture, many "carbon-copy" the oppressor. His perspective mirrors how some in the movement see the current situation. Dr. Harrison addressed this loss of African culture similarly in our dialogue when she described how the psychology of some colonized Black Americans makes them similar in values and behaviors as White Americans, a state that Fanon describes in his works on the psychology of colonized Algerians.[3] This problem drives many to teach and learn Indigenous African ways.

Music sets the tone for the video and adds depth to the message of burying Wetiko violence and the resurgence of African culture. "Countdown to Infinite," composed by Harvey Davis, consists of intense and distorted electronic violin and sparse bass drum music. It evokes the sad and depressed state of the situation that many colonized people experience. The music is foreboding and melancholic. With the burying of Wetiko's handgun, Wetiko violence, represented by the music, ends. As the credits roll against a black backdrop, we get a sense of the resurgence that we seek. The song, "Mojuba," by Art Turk Burton and the Congo Square Ensemble, evokes African cultural resurgence relying on multilayered rhythms played by congas, bells, a bass, timbales, and drumkit. It connects us to African Indigenous tradition because as Leah Penniman explains, "The iba or mojuba is a prayer of homage that is recited to open morning devotion in traditional Yoruba households, a practice that has spread across the African diaspora. We pour water or alcohol on the ground as an offering, and turn our hearts toward our ancestors, to our respected elders and teachers, and to the benevolent forces of nature."[4] The song is celebratory and fast-paced, urging you to dance and evoking the joy of African being and signaling a new morning. The conga and timbal solos and multiple rhythms move participants to ecstatic moments of liberatory possibility and offer a space for "freedom dreaming"[5] about an Afro-Indigenous future of endless possibility.

Members of our food movement have internalized sankofa and seek out IK at every opportunity and attempt to implement it in our lives. In these pages I have attempted to show how daily we adopt and adapt Afro-Indigenous lifeways as means of survival and prosperity. In the face of an enormously powerful Wetiko monster, we engage in life-affirming Indigenous behavior. But Wetiko is persistent, and we don't always get it right. Our biggest "internal" contradictions come from Wetiko's tentacles: greed, heteropatriarchy, and bourgeois nationalism.

How We Might Get Here: Dreamspace and Innate Agrarian Artistry

In the summer of 2021, at an imagination session in the Gage Park Latinx Council offices, Diego, a youth leader at GPLXC asked what I saw in this new generation of Black and Brown activists. I responded to them that I saw three important things that activists of my generation struggled with: 1) a recognition of the value of LGBTQ2 people and making space for them/us and our/their perspectives, 2) an understanding of the need for Black-Indigenous and/or Black-Brown solidarity and Afro-Indigenous understanding, 3) their attention to creativity and care as revolutionary practices. The youth activism that I have had the honor to witness keeps these issues at the forefront of their activity. They might agree that

> Black and Indigenous survival after centuries of violence has been about creating a future. Survival has never been passive. It has been a sustained creation of possibility for living in a white supremacist world. Caring for one another is the only way we can actually imagine and then envision the society that we actually want to live in. This will not be easy . . . Liberation takes work; it takes compassion, love, and patience.[6]

And it takes one another. The era of chauvinistic nationalisms is over because "if settler colonialism is global, and it is linked with racism—even while considering the specificity of its operation—understanding connections with other peoples is crucial for liberation going forward."[7]

Anarchists and gardeners are often accused of being utopian. To that accusation, I say, "Thank you!" Without creative, mindful, and purposeful dreaming about the future, we have no chance of changing the present. An Afro-Indigenous future requires the creative minds of my accomplices who garden, tend to chickens and all our relations, make art, music, and food, as well as design spaces and our lives upon an Indigenous foundation. Bee Rodriguez describes themself as a dreamer. Their garden, art, and writing projects with neighborhood youth ask them to imagine an Indigenous future. At the First Chicago Permaculture Convergence and Urban Gardening Conference in 2021, an intergenerational mix of Black and Indigenous/Chicanx added to a collective art piece started by GPLXC youth. Bee invited us to add our dreams to those of the young interns. The expressions of the future were distinct, yet all were embedded in Indigenous values.

The art, music, and gardening pedagogies advanced in Bee's spaces and that of others in the movement ask us to imagine utopia, an Afro-Indigenous future. For most the dreaming begins from an Indigenous foundation of interdependence with all our relations, responsibility toward one another, reciprocity, and balance. Along with our Indigenous foundation, I and others use insight from anarchists and disciplines like permaculture. The mezcla of traditions has driven my work over the years and resonates with what I have experienced and learned in our movement.

Permaculture is a Westernized ordering and synthesizing of IK from across the planet. It takes the values and strategies of Indigenous communities and codifies them for the European mind. Its set of ethics, principles, and design methodologies provides a conceptual vocabulary for designing sustainable lives. Permaculture also takes the best of European design science, ecology, and other things and conjoins them with Indigenous thought. For those of us overeducated in Wetiko ways, permaculture provides an intermediate step to get to a more deeply Indigenous way of being. Alone it promises great improvement in humans' relationship to all our relations. But it is not Indigenous, and we require more.

There is plenty to quarrel about concerning "the permaculture movement," as it has often taken the insight of IK and exploited it for profit and individual improvement for a small number of White people. IK has once again been extracted, commodified, and adulterated with few positives trickling down to us. The public face of permaculture is a colonial, capitalist, White male face and thus a major turn-off for many. For these reasons many BIPOC growers and land stewards run from permaculture. Fewer disagree with the content of the permaculture system.[8] It contains amazing insights into how to live right by all our relations. Bee, who earned a permaculture design certificate from Jacqueline Smith and I in 2021, conceives of it as a toolbox that can help them create an excellent garden and a more sustainable lifestyle.

I and BIPOC camaradas claim the knowledge of permaculture as ours—Black and Indigenous ethics and logics. Some in the Black food movement in Chicago believe that we can reorient permaculture on an Indigenous path. The attempts to do so by the the Permaculture Institute of Chicago and BOC have furthered many of the goals of our movement. We have taught hundreds how to grow and steward the land, to be conservative in our use of earth's beings and gifts, and to see more-than-humans as our relatives.

Unlike many White permaculturalists, we include the spirit, ceremony, and prayer in our design. Bill Mollison and many since have been explicit about the importance of keeping religion and spirituality out of permaculture. It is a design science based on data and the scientific method that Eurocentric scientists juxtapose to spirituality. Moreover, permaculturalists see religion as a potential source of conflict and division and is thus better left out of the sustainability conversation. The Indigenous and Black growers and stewards who I work with see spirituality as central to our endeavors. Ceremony and ritual transmit knowledge and understanding, focus a community on a common goal, reinforce community identity and provide opportunities for reflection about and connection to life. Place-based

FIG. 21. Permaculture
Conference. Photo by
author.

Indigenous spirituality comes out of material experience. It doesn't purport to be universal, as do permaculture and the Abrahamic religions that are colonizing in their logics and behaviors.[9]

For these reasons, permaculture can help us get to the desired Afro-Indigenous future, but it cannot get us there alone. According to my accomplices, IK, African/Indigenous identity and an understanding of the sacredness of all life are required to defeat Wetiko. Land, we know, is the basis of our culture, our spirituality, our knowledge, and our revolution. Through our innate agrarian artistry, we learn about ourselves and how to live right as well as demonstrate to others our radical imaginary. In anarchist language, it is in the gardens where we prefigure a free, sustainable world. In the gardens we experiment with AAA ways of being, thinking, and relating.

A Red, Black, and Green Future

Engaging with hundreds of accomplices in nearly two decades of work in the Black food movement in Chicago leads me to an optimism that other aspects of work and life do not. From my dreamspace in the gardens and other movement spaces, the future looks red, black, and green. It's redness and blackness is anarchist, African, and Indigenous. The future is green: a reciprocal, interdependent and respectful relationship between humans and our more-than-human relatives. I dream of this future while surrounded by life in the garden. The smell of the soil, plants, and rotting wood evokes memories of an Afro-Indigenous future.

As people with intimate relationships with "nature," we recognize patterns. We find the spiral everywhere. We know too that "what goes around, comes around."

Time moves like a spiral. We see time in a manner that differs from Europe's progressive linear time. For Mayans, December 2012 marked the end of the Fifth Sun and beginning of the Sixth. Five hundred and twenty years earlier, the Fifth Sun began when Columbus invaded the land now known as Hispaniola. The first few years of the European invasion foreshadowed Wetiko's dominance of Abya Yala as hundreds of thousands of Europeans conquered (for the time being) and killed tens of millions of Indigenous Americans and kidnapped Africans to toil for the empire.

However, the Sixth Sun, as we dream it and bring it into being through our food autonomy work, is a new era that promises a revolution. If the Fifth Sun initiated colonialism, then the Sixth Sun will see a resurgence of Indigenous, place-based ways of being. So prepped with a foundation of indigeneity from my ancestors and family and blessed with two dozen years of Black community wisdom and anarchist organizing and study alongside my accomplices in this movement, I dream the memories of a red, black, and green future.

.

PARTICIPANTS

NAME	AFFILIATIONS	DATE OF DIALOGUE
Jacqueline A. Smith	GrowAsis Urban Gardening Consulting, Inc. Green Lots Project Urban Stewards Action Network Lifeboats Permaculture Guild	November 4, 2014
Paula Roderick	Southeast Economic and Environmental Development, Inc.	August 30, 2015
Paula Anglin	George Washington Carver Community Garden Trinity United Church of Christ	August 25, 2015
Austin I. Wayne	Indigenous Style Foods Healthy Food Hub	December 14, 2017
Fred Carter	Black Oaks Center for Sustainable Renewable Living National Black Food and Justice Alliance	March 2, 2016
Gregory Bratton	I Grow Chicago	August 11, 2016
Mecca Brooks	Healthy Food Hub	2015
Safia Rashid	Your Bountiful Harvest Family Farm Lifeboats Permaculture Guild	March 2015
Carolyn Thomas	God's Gang	November 2015
Kellen Marshall		December 1, 2015
Dwight Dotts	Green Lots Project	Summer 2018
Maurice Walls		October 2021
Dr. Bonnie Harrison	CoGro Biodynamic Growers Lifeboats Permaculture Guild	October 2021

NAME	AFFILIATIONS	DATE OF DIALOGUE
Bee Rodriguez	Reclaiming Our Roots Gage Park Latinx Council Green Lots Project	November 18, 2021
Dr. Jifunza Wright-Carter	Black Oaks Center for Sustainable Renewable Living	Various
Kevin Triplett	Chicago Public Schools	April 2019

NOTES

CHAPTER 1. Okichike Ka Centeotzintli: Bienvendios a Mesoamerica en Shikaakwa

Roberto Cintli Rodriguez, *Our Sacred Maíz Is Our Mother: Indigeneity and Belonging in the Americas* (Tucson: University of Arizona Press, 2014), 3. The author writes: "The concept okichike ka centeotzintli . . . means 'made from sacred maíz.'"

1. Jeffrey Pilcher, *Que Vivan Los Tamales! Food and the Making of Mexican Identity* (Albuquerque: University of New Mexico Press, 1998).

2. Luz Calvo and Catriona Rueda Esquibel, *Decolonize Your Diet: Plant-Based Mexican-American Recipes for Health and Healing* (Vancouver: Arsenal Pulp, 2015).

3. Jack Forbes, *Columbus and Other Cannibals: The Wetiko Disease of Exploitation, Imperialism and Terrorism* (New York: Seven Stories, 2008).

4. Rodriguez, *Our Sacred Maíz*; Judith Carney and Richard Nicholas Rosomoff, *In the Shadow of Slavery: Africa's Botanical Legacy in the Atlantic World* (Berkeley: University of California Press, 2011)

5. Pancho McFarland, *Toward a Chican@ Hip Hop Anticolonialism* (New York: Routledge, 2017); Pancho McFarland, *The Chican@ Hip Hop Nation: Politics of a New Millennial Mestizaje* (East Lansing: Michigan State University Press, 2013).

6. Ashante Reese, *Black Food Geographies: Race, Self-Reliance, and Food Access in Washington, D.C.* (Chapel Hill: University of North Carolina Press, 2019), 135.

7. Qtd. in AnaLouise Keating, "Risking the Personal: An Introduction," in Gloria E. Anzaldua, *Interviews/Entrevistas*, ed. A. Keating (New York: Routledge, 2000), 12.

8. Ibid.; Hannah Garth and Ashante M. Reese, eds., *Black Food Matters: Racial Justice in the Wake of Food Justice* (Minneapolis: University of Minnesota Press, 2020), 14–17; Dara Cooper, "Foreward," in Reese, *Black Food Geographies*, xi–xiii; Psyche Williams-Forson, "Afterword: Problematizing the Problem," in Garth and Reese, *Black Food Matters*, 280.

9. Cooper, "Foreward."

10. Reese, *Black Food Geographies*, 9.

11. Anzaldua, *Interviews*, 242–43.

12. David Graeber, "Anarchism, Academia, and the Avant-garde," in *Contemporary Anarchist Studies: An Introductory Anthology of Anarchy in the Academy*, ed. R. Amster, A. DeLeon, L. A. Fernandez, A. J. Nocella, II, and D. Shannon (London: Routledge, 2009), 103–12.

13. Ibid., 112.

14. I use the terms "ally" and "accomplice" similarly to Klee Benally who understands "ally" to refer to those who engage in temporary and often meaningless or harmful symbolic demonstrations of support. "Accomplices" take risks and listen to, rather than impose on, Indigenous and other marginalized people. Benally writes, "Ally has become an identity disembodied from any real mutual understanding of support . . . When we fight back or forward, together, becoming complicit in a struggle towards liberation, we are accomplices." Klee Benally,

"Accomplices Not Allies: Abolishing the Ally Industrial Complex," Indigenous Action Media, May 4, 2014, www.indigenousaction.org/accomplices-not-allies-abolishing-the-ally-industrial -complex/.

15. Monica M. White, *Freedom Farmers: Agricultural Resistance and the Black Freedom Movement* (Chapel Hill: University of North Carolina Press, 2019), 19.

16. Rodriguez, *Our Sacred Maíz*, 22.

17. Melissa K. Nelson, ed., *Original Instructions: Indigenous Teachings for a Sustainable Planet* (Rochester, Vt.: Bear, 2008).

18. Leanne Betsamosake Simpson, "Land as Pedagogy: Nishnaabeg Intelligence and Rebellious Transformation," *Decolonization: Indigeneity, Education and Society* 3, no. 3 (2014): 1–25.

19. "Observing and interacting" is one of David Holmgren's twelve permaculture principles. Dave Holmgren, *Permaculture: Principles and Pathways beyond Sustainability* (Hepburn Springs, Australia: Melliodora, 2002).

20. Simpson, "Land as Pedagogy," 12–14

21. For useful discussions of "Indigenous permaculture" and the history and development of permaculture as IK, see Woodbine Ecology Center, accessed May 23, 2024, woodbinecenter .org/indigenous-values (site currently under maintenance); and International Institute of Indigenous Science, "Indigenous Permaculture," accessed May 23, 2024, www .indigenouspermaculture.org. See also Devon G. Peña, "On Intimacy with Soils: Indigenous Agroecology and Biodynamics," in *Indigenous Food Sovereignty: Restoring Cultural Knowledge, Protecting Environments, and Regaining Health*, ed. Devon A. Mihesuah and Elizabeth Hoover (Norman: University of Oklahoma Press, 2019), 276–99.

22. "Black History Month: Black Heroines, Part 5: Paanza: Mother of Two Great Saramaka Nations," Beautiful, Also, Are the Souls of My Black Sisters, Feb. 11, 2009, https:// kathmanduk2.wordpress.com/2009/02/11/black-history-month-black-heroines-part-4 -paanza-mother-of-two-great-saramaka-nations/

23. Tata Cuaxtle Felix Evodio, in Rodriguez, *Our Sacred Maíz*, 57–58.

24. Ibid., 119.

25. Carney and Rossamoff, *In the Shadow of Slavery*, 93

26. Psyche Williams-Forson, *Building Houses Out of Chicken Legs: Black Women, Food and Power* (Chapel Hill: University of North Carolina Press, 2006), 2.

27. White, *Freedom Farmers*.

28. Leah Penniman, *Farming While Black: Soulfire Farm's Practical Guide to Liberation on the Land* (White River Junction, Vt.: Chelsea Green, 2019).

29. Brit Reed, "Food Sovereignty Is Tribal Sovereignty." Last Real Indians. March 24, 2015. https://lastrealindians.com/news/2015/3/24/mar-24-2015-food-sovereignty-is-tribal -sovereignty-by-brit-reed

30. Kitrina Baxter, Dara Cooper, Aleya Fraser, and Shakara Tyler, "Womanism as Agrarianism: Black Women Healing through Innate Agrarian Artistry," in *Land Justice: Re-imagining Land, Food, and the Commons in the United States*, ed. Justine Williams and Eric Holt-Gimenez (Oakland, Ca.: Food First, 2017), 94–110.

31. X. Banales, "Joteria: A Decolonizing Political Project," *Aztlan: A Journal of Chicano Studies*, 39, no. 1 (2014): 155–65; Q. Driskill, C. Finley, B. J. Gilley, and S. L. Morgensen, eds., *Queer*

Indigenous Studies: Critical Interventions in Theory, Politics, and Literature (Tucson: University of Arizona Press, 2011).

32. Simpson, "Land as Pedagogy."

33. Baxter et al., "Womanism"; Williams-Forson, *Building Houses.*

34. Baxter et al., "Womanism."

35. Baxter et al., "Womanism," 96, 107.

36. Carney and Rossamoff, *In the Shadow of Slavery.*

37. Bill Mollison, *Permaculture: A Designers' Manual* (Sisters Creek, Australia: Tagari, 1988).

38. Eric Holt-Jimenez, *A Foodies' Guide to Capitalism* (New York: Monthly Review, 2017).

39. Richard Day, qtd. in Jesse Cohn, *Underground Passages: Anarchist Resistance Culture, 1848–2011* (Oakland, Ca.: AK Press, 2014), 380.

40. Glen Coulthard, *Red Skin, White Masks: Rejecting the Colonial Politics of Recognition* (Minneapolis: University of Minnesota Press, 2014).

41. W. J. Wright, T. McCreary, B. Williams, and A. Bledsoe, "Race, Land, and the Law: Black Farmers and the Limits of a Politics of Recognition," in Garth and Reese, *Black Food Matters,* 228–50.

42. Kyle Powys Whyte, "Indigenous Food Systems, Environmental Justice, and Settler-Industrial States," in *Global Food, Global Justice,* ed. Mary C. Rawlinson and Caleb Ward (Newcastle upon Tyne, U.K.: Cambridge Scholars, 2015), 24.

43. Raul Zibechi, *Territories in Resistance: A Cartography of Latin American Social Movements* (Oakland, Ca.: AK Press, 2012), 38.

44. Cohn, *Underground Passages.*

45. Andrej Grubacic, "Exit and Territory: A World-Systems Analysis of Non-State Spaces," in *Grabbing Back: Essays against the Global Land Grab,* ed. Alexander Reid Ross (Oakland, Ca.: AK Press, 2014), 169.

46. Ibid., 173.

CHAPTER 2. People, Places, and Spaces: Our CommUnity

1. Arnold Hirsch, *Making the Second Ghetto: Race and Housing in Chicago, 1940–1960* (Chicago: University of Chicago, 1998).

2. "Roseland neighborhood in Chicago, Illinois (IL), 60619, 60620, 60628 detailed profile," City-Date.com, accessed Dec. 17, 2022, www.city-data.com/neighborhood/Roseland -Chicago-IL.html

3. Ashante Reese, *Black Food Geographies: Race, Self-Reliance, and Food Access in Washington, D.C.* (Chapel Hill: University of North Carolina Press, 2019); Hannah Garth and Ashante M. Reese, eds., *Black Food Matters: Racial Justice in the Wake of Food Justice* (Minneapolis: University of Minnesota Press, 2020).

4. Bill Mollison, *Permaculture: A Designers' Manual* (Sisters Creek, Australia: Tagari, 1988), 34.

5. Ibid.

6. Dania C. Davy, Savonala Horne, Tracy Lloyd McCurty, and Edward "Jerry" Pennick, "Resistance," in *Land Justice: Re-imagining Land, Food, and the Commons in the United States,* ed. Justine Williams and Eric Holt-Gimenez (Oakland, Ca.: Food First, 2017), 55.

7. Leah Penniman and Blain Snipstal, "Regeneration," in *Land Justice: Re-imagining Land, Food, and the Commons in the United States,* ed. Justine Williams and Eric Holt-Gimenez (Oakland, Ca.: Food First, 2017), 63.

8. "Home," Black Oaks Center, accessed, June 1, 2016, www.blackoakscenter.org

9. "Our Mission Is To . . . ," Black Oaks Center, accessed June 1, 2016, www.blackoakscenter .org/mission-approach

10. Austin is adamant in his opposition to terms such as "Black" and refuses to be identified as such. He calls "race" and "racism" color games.

CHAPTER 3. Key Concepts for Our Food Fights

An earlier version of this chapter was coauthored with Kourtney Craigmiles McFarland and published on the *Environmental and Food Justice* blog: Pancho McFarland and Kourtney Craigmiles McFarland, "Overcoming the Violence of Injustice," 2010, https://ejfood.blogspot .com/2010/02/food-justice-in-city.html?q=pancho+mcfarland.

1. Kierin Gould, "Deep Food Autonomy," Indigenous Research Center of the Americas, University of California, Davis, unpublished report, 2004), 2.

2. Brit Reed, "Food Sovereignty Is Tribal Sovereignty." Last Real Indians. March 24, 2015. https://lastrealindians.com/news/2015/3/24/mar-24-2015-food-sovereignty-is-tribal -sovereignty-by-brit-reed.

3. Devon Mihesuah, "Searching for Haknip Achukma (Good Health) Challenges to Food Sovereignty Initiatives in Oklahoma," in *Indigenous Food Sovereignty in the United States: Restoring Cultural Knowledge, Protecting Environments and Regaining Health,* ed. Devon Mihesuah and Elizabeth Hoover (Norman: University of Oklahoma Press, 2019), 95.

4. Rosalinda Guillen and C2C, "Growing Justice in the Fields: Farmworker Autonomy and Food Sovereignty," in *Mexican-Origin Foods, Foodways and Social Movements: Decolonial Perspectives,* ed. Devon Peña, Luz Calvo, Pancho McFarland and Gabriel Valle (University of Arkansas Press, 2017), 236.

5. Peña et al., "Autonomia," in *Mexican Origin Foods.*

6. Klee Benally, *No Spiritual Surrender: Indigenous Anarchy in Defense of the Sacred* (n.p.: Detritus, 2023), 31.

7. Gould, "Deep Food Autonomy," 2.

8. Peña et al., "Autonomia," 26.

9. Eric Holt-Jimenez, *A Foodies' Guide to Capitalism* (New York: Monthly Review Press, 2017); Raj Patel, *Stuffed and Starved: The Hidden Battle for the World's Food System* (New York: Melville House, 2008).

10. Vandanna Shiva, *Soil Not Oil: Environmental Justice in an Age of Climate Crisis* (Boston: South End, 2008).

11. Anonymous, "How Fertilizers Harm Earth More Than Help Your Lawn," *Scientific American,* July 20, 2009, www.scientificamerican.com/article/how-fertilizers-harm-earth/.

12. Holt-Gimenez, *Foodie's Guide.*

13. Mae-Wan Ho and Lim Li Ching, "The Case for a GM-Free Sustainable World," Institute for Science in Society, 2003 (accessed August 2014), https://www.isaaa.org/kc/inforesources /publications/mythsandfacts/ISP_Draft3.pdf; Mae-Wan Ho and Eva Sirinathsinghji, "Ban GMOs Now: Health and Environmental Hazards Especially in The Light of New Genetics,"

Institute for Science in Society, 2013 (accessed August 2014), https://www.isis.org.uk/Ban
_GMOs_Now.php.

14. Ibid.

15. Gould, "Deep Food Autonomy," 11.

16. Luz Calvo and Catriona Rueda Esquibel, *Decolonize Your Diet: Plant-Based Mexican-American Recipes for Health and Healing* (Vancouver: Arsenal Pulp, 2015), 30.

17. Simone Adler, "Dangers of the Gates Foundation: Displacing Seeds and Farmers," Grassroots International, 2015, https://grassrootsonline.org/learning_hub/dangers-of-the-gates-foundation-displacing-seeds-and-farmers/.

18. Karl Marx and Friedrich Engels, *The German Ideology* (1845; Amherst, N.Y.: Prometheus, 1998).

19. Louis Althusser, *Lenin and Philosophy and Other Essays* (1971; New York: Monthly Review Press, 2001).

20. Ashley Lutz, "These 6 Corporations Control 90% of the Media in America," *Business Insider,* 2012, http://www.businessinsider.com/these-6-orporations-control-90-of-the-media-in-america-2012-6.

21. Roberto Cintli Rodriguez, *Our Sacred Maíz Is Our Mother: Indigeneity and Belonging in the Americas* (Tucson: University of Arizona Press, 2014); Robin Wall Kimmerer, *Braiding Sweetgrass: Indigenous Wisdom, Scientific Knowledge, and the Teachings of Plants* (Minneapolis: Milkweed, 2013).

22. Brit Reed, "Food Sovereignty Is Tribal Sovereignty." Last Real Indians. March 24, 2015. https://lastrealindians.com/news/2015/3/24/mar-24-2015-food-sovereignty-is-tribal-sovereignty-by-brit-reed.

23. D. R. Block, N. Chavez, E. Allen, and D. Ramirez, "Food Sovereignty, Urban Food Access, and Food Activism: Contemplating the Connections through Examples from Chicago," *Agriculture and Human Values* 29, no. 2 (2011): 203–15.

24. Leah Penniman, *Farming While Black: Soulfire Farm's Practical Guide to Liberation on the Land* (White River Junction, Vt.: Chelsea Green, 2019), 4.

25. Jasmine A Delk, Brittany A Singleton, Sara Al-Dahir, William Kirchain, and Janel Bailey-Wheeler, "The Effect of Food Access on Type 2 Diabetes Control in Patients of a New Orleans, Louisiana, Clinic," *Journal of the American Pharmaceutical Association* (2022): 1675–79, https://pubmed.ncbi.nlm.nih.gov/35738993/; Enza Gucciardi, Mandana Vahabi, Nicole Norris, John Paul Del Monte and Cecile Farnum, "The Intersection between Food Insecurity and Diabetes: A Review," *Current Nutrition Reports* 3 (October 2013): 324–32, https://link.springer.com/article/10.1007/s13668-014-0104-4.

26. Pattrice Jones, "Afterword: Liberation as Connection and the Decolonization of Desire," in *Sistah Vegan: Black Female Vegans Speak on Food, Identity, Health, and Society,* ed. A. B. Harper (New York: Lantern, 2010), 196.

27. Douglas C. Lummis, *Radical Democracy* (Ithaca, N.Y.: Cornell University Press, 1996); Subcommandante Marcos, *Our Word Is Our Weapon: Selected Writings of Subcommandante Insurgente Marcos,* ed. Juana Ponce de Leon (New York: Seven Stories, 2001).

28. Harry Cleaver, "Food, Famine and the International Crisis" (1977), accessed June 14, 2023, available at zerowork.org/CleaverFoodFamine.html.

29. Gustavo Esteva and Madhu Suri Prakash, *Grassroots Postmodernism: Remaking the Soil of Cultures* (London: Zed, 1998).

30. Vandanna Shiva, *Stolen Harvest: The Hijacking of the Global Food Supply* (Boston: South End, 2000), 97, 103.

31. Vasile Stanescu, "'Green' Eggs and Ham? The Myth of Sustainable Meat and the Danger of the Local," *Journal of Critical Animal Studies* 8, nos. 1–2 (2010): 8–32, citing p. 29.

32. Michael Carolan, *The Sociology of Food and Agriculture* (New York: Routledge, 2012), 323.

33. Steven Best, "Rethinking Revolution: Total Liberation, Alliance Politics, and a Prolegomena to Resistance Movements in the Twenty-First Century," in *Contemporary Anarchist Studies: An Introductory Anthology of Anarchy in the Academy*, ed. R. Amster, A. DeLeon, L. A. Fernandez, A. J. Nocella II, and D. Shannon (London: Routledge, 2009), 190.

34. A. Breeze Harper, "Introduction: The Birth of the Sister Vegan Project," in *Sistah Vegan*, xii–xix; Layli Phillips, "Veganism and Ecowomanism," in *Sistah Vegan*, 8.

35. A. Breeze Harper, "Social Justice Beliefs and Addiction to Uncompassionate Consumption: Food for Thought," in *Sistah Vegan*, 20–41.

36. Ibid.

37. Ibid., 21.

38. Gail Wadsworth. 2014. "What does Food Justice Mean for Farmworkers?," Food First, January 15, 2014, https://archive.foodfirst.org/what-does-food-justice-mean-for-farmworkers/.

39. Anne Shattuck, Eric Holt-Gimenez, and Zoe Brent, "Food Workers Food Justice: Linking Food, Labor and Immigrant Rights," *Food First Backgrounder* 16, no. 2 (Summer 2010), available at www.foodfirst.org/publication/food-workers-food-justice-linking-food-labor-and-immigrant-rights.

40. J. Imig, dir., *Immokalee: Story of Slavery and Freedom* (Tucson, Ariz: Pan Left Films, 2010).

41. Tomás Madrigal, "We Are Human!" Farmworker Organizing across the Food Chain in Washington," in Peña et al., *Mexican-Origin Foods*, 259.

42. Rosalinda Guillen and C2C, "Growing Justice in the Fields," in Peña et al., *Mexican-Origin Foods*; Devon Peña, Luz Calvo, Pancho McFarland and Gabriel Valle, "Introduction," in Peña et al., *Mexican-Origin Foods*.

43. Enrique Salmón, *Eating the Landscape: American Indian Stories of Food, Identity and Resilience* (Tucson: University of Arizona Press, 2012), 46.

44. See Vijay Prashad, *Everybody Was Kung Fu Fighting* (Boston: Beacon, 2002), for an excellent study of the complexities of cultural exchange and the history of Asian-African interaction.

45. Gilles Delueze and F. Guattari, *A Thousand Plateaus: Capitalism and Schizophrenia*. Alexander Reid Ross, ed., *Grabbing Back: Essays*, 2nd ed. (Minneapolis: University of Minnesota Press, 1987).

46. AFAQ Editorial Collective, *Anarchist Frequently Asked Questions* (Oakland, Ca.: AK Press, 2000); Bill Mollison, *Permaculture: A Designers' Manual* (Sisters Creek, Australia: Tagari, 1988).

CHAPTER 4. Learning from the Land: CommUnity Pedagogy in Place

1. Leanne Betsamosake Simpson, "Land as Pedagogy: Nishnaabeg Intelligence and Rebellious Transformation," *Decolonization: Indigeneity, Education and Society* 3, no. 3 (2014): 1–25; Leanne Betasamosake Simpson, *As We Have Always Done: Indigenous Freedom through Radical Resistance* (Minneapolis: University of Minnesota Press, 2017).

2. Gustavo Esteva and Madhu Suri Prakash, *Grassroots Postmodernism: Remaking the Soil of Cultures* (London: Zed, 1998), 9.

3. Qtd. in ibid., 74.

4. Simpson, "Land as Pedagogy, 11.

5. Rosalinda Guillen and C2C, "Growing Justice in the Fields: Farmworker Autonomy and Food Sovereignty," in *Mexican-Origin Foods, Foodways and Social Movements: Decolonial Perspectives*, ed. Devon Peña, Luz Calvo, Pancho McFarland, and Gabriel Valle (Fayetteville: University of Arkansas Press, 2017); Devon Peña, Luz Calvo, Pancho McFarland and Gabriel Valle, "Introduction," in Peña et al., *Mexican-Origin Foods*, 20.

6. Devon Peña et al., "Autonomia," in *Mexican-Origin Foods*.

7. Simpson, *As We Have Always Done*, 146–49.

8. Ibid.

9. Borrows, qtd. in Simpson, "Land as Pedagogy," 156.

10. Ibid., 4.

11. Antonio Gramsci, *Selections from the Prison Notebooks of Antonio Gramsci* (New York: International Publishers, 1971), 3.

12. Gramsci, *Prison Notebooks*, 5.

13. Pancho McFarland, *The Chican@ Hip Hop Nation: Politics of a New Millennial Mestizaje* (East Lansing: Michigan State University Press, 2013); Pancho McFarland, "Organic Intellectuals and Direct Action 50 Years Past Chicago's 'War on Poverty,'" in Peña et al., *Mexican-Origin Foods*, 291–310.

14. Gramsci, *Prison Notebooks*, 9–10.

15. Paolo Freire, *Pedagogy of the Oppressed* (New York: Continuum, 2000) 48, 18.

16. bell hooks, *Teaching to Transgress: Education as the Practice of Freedom* (New York: Routledge, 1994), 8.

17. Judith Carney and Richard Nicholas Rosomoff, *In the Shadow of Slavery: Africa's Botanical Legacy in the Atlantic World* (Berkeley: University of California Press, 2011); Daniel R. Wildcat, *Red Alert! Saving the Planet with Indigenous Knowledge* (Boulder: Fulcrum, 2009).

18. Ashante Reese, *Black Food Geographies: Race, Self-Reliance, and Food Access in Washington, D.C.* (Chapel Hill: University of North Carolina Press, 2019); Hannah Garth and Ashante M. Reese, eds., *Black Food Matters: Racial Justice in the Wake of Food Justice* (Minneapolis: University of Minnesota Press, 2020); Psyche Williams-Forson, *Building Houses Out of Chicken Legs: Black Women, Food and Power* (Chapel Hill: University of North Carolina Press, 2006).

19. Carney and Rosomoff, *In the Shadow of Slavery*, 112, 94, 16.

20. Carney and Rosomoff, *In the Shadow of Slavery*, 178.

21. These gardens are used by many practitioners of permaculture and Indigenous food systems. They have many practical uses including water preservation and efficient use of space and connect gardeners to the spiritual uses of mandalas in Indigenous cultures.

22. Jeffrey Pilcher, *Que Vivan Los Tamales! Food and the Making of Mexican Identity* (Albuquerque: University of New Mexico Press, 1998); Roberto Cintli Rodriguez, *Our Sacred Maíz Is Our Mother: Indigeneity and Belonging in the Americas* (Tucson: University of Arizona Press, 2014).

23. Robin Wall Kimmerer, *Braiding Sweetgrass: Indigenous Wisdom, Scientific Knowledge, and the Teachings of Plants* (Minneapolis: Milkweed, 2013), 139–40.

24. Devon G. Peña, *Mexican Americans and the Environment: Tierra y Vida* (Tucson: University of Arizona Press, 2005), 51.

25. This story was first published in Pancho McFarland, "Organic Intellectuals and Direct Action" in Peña et al., *Mexican-Origin Foods*.

26. William Morris, "Useful Work versus Useless Toil," in *Why Work? Arguments for the Leisure Society* (London: Freedom Press, 1983), 35–52.

27. Carney and Rosamoff, *In the Shadow of Slavery*; Dianne D. Glave, *Rooted in the Earth: Reclaiming the African American Environmental Heritage* (Chicago: Lawrence Hill, 2010).

28. J. Imig, dir., *Immokalee: Story of Slavery and Freedom* (Tucson, Ariz: Pan Left Films, 2010).

29. bell hook *belonging: a culture of place* (New York: Routledge, 2009); Kimberly K. Smith, *African American Environmental Thought: Foundations* (Lawrence: University Press of Kansas, 2007); Carney and Rosamoff, *In the Shadow of Slavery*.

30. Paul Gomberg, *How to Make Opportunity Equal: Race and Contributive Justice* (Malden, Mass.: Wiley-Blackwell, 2006); Morris, "Useful Work."

31. Morris, "Useful Work."

32. Guillen and C2C, "Growing Justice in the Fields," 240

33. Luz Calvo and Catriona Rueda Esquibel, *Decolonize Your Diet: Plant-Based Mexican-American Recipes for Health and Healing* (Vancouver: Arsenal Pulp, 2015); A. B. Harper, ed., *Sistah Vegan: Black Female Vegans Speak on Food, Identity, Health, and Society* (New York: Lantern, 1996).

34. See Sadhu Muri Prakash and Gustavo Esteva, *Escaping Education: Living as Learning in Grassroots Cultures* (New York: Peter Lang, 2008).

35. John Byrne, "Chicago Mayor Lori Lightfoot Spent 281.5 Million in Federal COVID-19 Relief Money on Police Payroll," *Chicago Tribune*, Feb. 18, 2021, www.chicagotribune.com/politics/ct-chicago-lightfoot-covid-19-police-spending-20210217-uohx77y36nblrf2526whoedkgi-story.html.

36. Quelites refers to a category of wild edible greens of which there are hundreds. I grew up calling lamb's quarters "quelites" since this is what my grandmother called them.

37. Steven Foster and James A. Duke, *A Field Guide to Medicinal Plants and Herbs of Eastern and Central North America* (New York: Houghton Mifflin, 2000).

38. "Ethnoecology Blogs—Autumn 2012— Dandelions II," Environmental and Food Justice, http://ejfood.blogspot.com/2012/12/ethnoecology-blogs-autumn-2012_30.html.

39. Peña, *Mexican Americans*; Pilcher, *Que Vivan*.

40. Rodriguez, *Our Sacred Maíz*, xxv.

41. See Murray Bookchin, *The Ecology of Freedom: The Emergence and Dissolution of Hierarchy* (Oakland, Calif.:AK Press, 2005); Murray Bookchin, *The Murray Bookchin Reader* (Montreal: Black Rose Books, 1999).

42. Peña, *Mexican Americans*, 51.

43. Murray Bookchin and Peter Kropotkin are among the central figures of anarchist theory who propose that these principles be part of an anarchist society.

44. Glenn Coulthard, *Red Skin, White Masks: Rejecting the Colonial Politics of Recognition* (Minneapolis: University of Minnesota, 2014); Frantz Fanon, *Black Skin, White Masks* (New York: Grove Press, 1952).

45. It is a good source of vitamins A, C, K, and B6 and minerals thiamin, riboflavin, calcium, potassium, copper, and manganese. It is also a good source of protein.

46. Calvo and Esquibel, *Decolonize Your Diet*; Peña et al., *Mexican-Origin Foods*; Pilcher, *Que Vivan*.

47. Dave Holmgren, *Permaculture: Principles and Pathways beyond Sustainability* (Hepburn Springs, Australia: Melliodora, 2002). It should be noted that these were not the original ethics as expressed by Bill Mollison in his seminal book, *Permaculture: A Designers' Manual* (Sisters Creek, Australia: Tagari, 1988). Instead, "fair share" is of newer origin and is meant to replace the Mollisonian ethic of "setting limits to population and consumption."

48. Mollison, *Permaculture*, chapter 3.

49. bell hooks, *all about love: New Visions* (New York: William Morrow, 2011), 105.

50. Ibid., 115.

51. Mollison, *Permaculture*, 2.

52. Simpson, *As We Have Always Done*; Simpson, "Land as Pedagogy."

53. Freire, *Pedagogy*; Prakash and Esteva, *Escaping Education*.

54. Leah Penniman, *Farming While Black: Soulfire Farm's Practical Guide to Liberation on the Land* (White River Junction, Vt.: Chelsea Green, 2019), 263.

55. Eric Holt-Gimenez, *A Foodies' Guide to Capitalism* (New York: Monthly Review Press, 2017).

56. Calvo and Esquibel, *Decolonize Your Diet*.

57. Prakash and Esteva, *Escaping Education*.

58. Will Allen, *The Good Food Revolution: Growing Healthy Food, People, and Communities* (New York: Gotham, 2012), 51.

CHAPTER 5. Race Other

1. Angela Davis and Elizabeth Martinez, "Coalition Building among the Poor," Center for Cultural Studies, University of California Santa Cruz, accessed June 20, 2023 (*Inscriptions*, vol. 7, 1993), https://culturalstudies.ucsc.edu/inscriptions/volume-7/angela-y-davis -elizabeth-martinez/.

2. William C. Anderson, *The Nation on No Map: Black Anarchism and Abolition* (Oakland, Ca.: AK Press, 2021), 48.

3. Ibid., 50.

4. Ibid., 65.

5. Luis Alvarez, *The Power of the Zoot: Youth Culture and Resistance in World War II* (Berkeley: University of California Press, 2009); Gerald Horne, *Black and Brown: African Americans in the Mexican Revolution, 1910–1920* (New York: New York University Press, 2005); Marco Polo Hernandez Cuevas, *African Mexicans and the Discourse on Modern Nation* (Dallas: University Press of America, 2004); Pancho McFarland, *The Chican@ Hip Hop Nation: Politics of a New Millennial Mestizaje* (East Lansing: Michigan State University Press, 2013)*!*

6. Horne, *Black and Brown*.

7. Kyle T. Mays, An *Afro-Indigenous History of the United States, (Boston, Mass.: Beacon, 2022)*, xix–xx.

8. Ibid., ix.

9. Joanne Barker, *Red Scare: The State's Indigenous Terrorist* (Berkeley: University of California Press, 2021), 119.

10. Mays, *Afro-Indigenous History*, xxi.

11. Ibid., chapter 5.

12. Paul Ortiz, *An African American and Latinx History of the United States* (Boston: Beacon, 2018), 6.

13. Anderson, *Nation on No Map*, 20–21.

14. Ivan Van Sertima, *They Came before Columbus: The African Presence in the Ancient Americas* (New York: Random House, 1976), among others, argues that first contact between Amerindigenous and Africans is ancient. While Van Sertima's most controversial claims have been debunked by many archaeologists and others, his Afrocentric re-examination of this relationship suggests a much more complicated history of interaction between the two groups. On the flip side, many Afro-supremacists have taken his ideas and used them as means to claim ownership over Indigenous land, technology, and culture and to undermine Indigenous struggle.

15. Hernandez Cuevas, *African Mexicans*; Sagrario Cruz-Carretero, "The African Presence in Mexico: La Presencia Africana en Mexico," in *The African Presence in Mexico: From Yanga to the Present*, ed. Sagrario Cruz-Carretero, 14–59 (Chicago: Mexican Fine Arts Center Museum, 2006).

16. Hernandez Cuevas, *African Mexicans*.

17. For an examination of zoot-suiting, see Alvarez, *Power of the Zoot*; for lowriding, see J. Yamoaka, dir. *The History of Hydraulics* (Los Angeles: Lowrider Magazine, 1998); for hip hop, see McFarland, *Chican@ Hip Hop Nation*; for the third world resistance movement, see Laura Pulido, *Black, Brown, Yellow and Left: Radical Activism in Los Angeles* (Berkeley: University of California Press, 2006); for street style, see James Diego Vigil, *A Rainbow of Gangs: Street Culture in the Mega-City* (Austin: University of Texas Press, 2002).

18. Hernandez Cuevas, *African Mexicans*.

19. Anani Dzidzienyo and Suzanne Oboler, eds., *Neither Enemies Nor Friends: Latinos, Blacks, Afro-Latinos* (New York: Palgrave, 2005).

20. Mays, *Afro-Indigenous History*, xxi.

21. Qtd. in Anderson, *Nation on No Map*, 147.

22. For details, see "Black Excellence Hour, WVON 1690AM—The Talk of Chicago," 53:35 video, www.facebook.com/watch/live/?ref=watch_permalink&v=572500411287108.

23. Ibid.

24. Ortiz, *African American and Latinx History*, 1.

25. Ibid., 29, 45.

26. Ibid., 4–5.

27. Ibid., 52.

28. Simpson, *As We Have Always Done*, 80.

29. Estevan Arellano, 2010, "Convide," *Environmental and Food Justice*, https://ejfood.blogspot.com/2010/03/guest-blog-estevan-arrellano.html?q=convide.

30. "Urban Stewards Action Network," accessed June 8, 2021, www.facebook.com/usanchi.

CHAPTER 6. Diasporic Foods: Race, Place, and Identity

1. See Leah Penniman, "These Roots Run Deep," in *Black Earth Wisdom: Soulful Conversations with Black Environmentalists* (New York: Harper Collins, 2023), for outline of Black environmentalism.

2. Robert E. Fox, "Diasporacentrism and Black Aural Texts," in *The African Diaspora,* ed. Isidore Okpewho, Claire B. Davies, and Ali A. Mazrui (Bloomington: Indiana University Press, 1999), 369.

3. Kimberly K. Smith, *African American Environmental Thought: Foundations* (Lawrence: University Press of Kansas, 2007), 11.

4. Psyche Williams-Forson, *Building Houses Out of Chicken Legs: Black Women, Food and Power* (Chapel Hill: University of North Carolina Press, 2006), 3–4.

5. Smith, *African American Environmental,* 8.

6. M. Stewart, "Slavery and the Origins of African American Environmentalism," in *"To Love the Wind and the Rain": African Americans and Environmental History,"* ed. D. D. Glave and M. Stoll (Pittsburgh: University of Pittsburgh Press, 2006), 11.

7. Dianne D. Glave, *Rooted in the Earth: Reclaiming the African American Environmental Heritage* (Chicago: Lawrence Hill Books, 2010), 44.

8. Taiaiake Alfred, *Peace, Power, Righteousness: An Indian Manifesto,* 2nd ed. (Toronto: Oxford University Press, 2009); Gregory Cajete, *Native Science: Natural Laws of Interdependence* (Sante Fe, N.Mex.: Clear Light, 2000); Melissa K. Nelson, ed., *Original Instructions: Indigenous Teachings for a Sustainable Planet* (Rochester, Vt.: Bear, 2008); Raymond Pieroti, *Indigenous Knowledge, Ecology and Evolutionary Biology* (New York: Routledge, 2011); Daniel R. Wildcat, *Red Alert! Saving the Planet with Indigenous Knowledge* (Boulder: Fulcrum, 2009).

9. Kwasi Densu, "Theoretical and Historical Perspectives on Agroecology and African American Farmers: Toward a Culturally Relevant Sustainable Agriculture," in *Land and Power: Sustainable Agriculture and African Americans,* ed. J. Jordan, E. Pennick, W. Hill, and R. Zabawa (Waldorf, Md.: Sustainable Agriculture Research and Education, 2009), 99–102.

10. Smith, *African American Environmental Thought,* 37.

11. Dianne D. Glave, *Rooted in the Earth: Reclaiming the African American Environmental Heritage* (Chicago: Lawrence Hill Books, 2010), 85; see also Judith Carney, *Black Rice: The African Origins of Rice Cultivation in the Americas* (Cambridge: Harvard University Press, 2002).

12. Smith, *African American Environmental,* 10, 19.

13. Smith, *African American Environmental,* 27–29.

14. Glave, *Rooted,* 117.

15. Murray Forman, *The 'Hood Comes First: Race, Space and Place in Rap and Hip Hop* (Middletown, Conn.: Wesleyan University Press, 2002).

16. Smith, *African American Environmental,* 38.

17. Monica M. White, *Freedom Farmers: Agricultural Resistance and the Black Freedom Movement* (Chapel Hill: University of North Carolina Press, 2019); Jessica Gordon Nembhard, *Collective Courage: A History of African American Collective Thought and Practice* (University Park: Pennsylvania State University Press, 2014).

18. Smith, *African American Environmental,* 31.

19. Glave, *Rooted,* 9, 5.

20. bell hooks, *belonging: a culture of place* (New York: Routledge, 2009), 195.

21. Dianne D. Glave and M. Stoll, "African American Environmental History: An Introduction," in *"To Love the Wind,"* 1.

22. hooks, *belonging,* 38.

23. Richard Louv, *Last Child in the Woods: Saving Our Children from Nature-Deficit Disorder* (Chapel Hill, N.C.: Algonquin, 2005).

24. Leah Penniman and Blain Snipstal, "Regeneration," in *Land Justice: Re-imagining Land, Food, and the Commons in the United States,* ed. Justine Williams and Eric Holt-Gimenez (Oakland, Ca.: Food First, 2017), 62.

25. "Our Land, Our History, Our Name," accessed May 29, 2024, https://www.blackoakscenter.org/our-story.

26. Carney and Rosamoff, *In the Shadow of Slavery*; Dianne D. Glave, *Rooted in the Earth: Reclaiming the African American Environmental Heritage* (Chicago: Lawrence Hil, 2010), 88, 97.

27. Ibid.

28. Qtd. in Gregory Cajete, John Mohawk, and Julio Valladolid Rivera. "Re-Indigenization Defined," in *Original Instructions: Indigenous Teachings for a Sustainable Future, ed.* M. K. Nelson (Rochester, Vt.: Bear, 2008), 260.

29. Ibid., 255.

30. Raymond Pierotti, *Indigenous Knowledge, Ecology and Evolutionary Biology* (New York: Routledge, 2011).

31. Cajete et al., "Re-Indigenization," 263.

32. Carl Anthony, "Reflections on the Purposes and Meanings of African American Environmental History," in *"To Love the Wind and the Rain": African Americans and Environmental History,"* ed. D. D. Glave and M. Stoll (Pittsburgh: University of Pittsburgh Press, 2006), 203.

33. hooks, *belonging,* 195.

34. Ibid., 39.

35. Ibid., 226–29.

36. Pierotti, *Indigenous Knowledge.*

37. Mecca Brooks, "Black Bioneers," *Sacred Keepers Sustainability Lab Newsletter,* February 21, 2014.

CHAPTER 7. A Sustainable Spirituality: Our Community Speaks on Food and Spirit

1. George Tinker, *American Indian Liberation: A Theology of Sovereignty* (Maryknoll, N.Y.: Orbis, 2008), 29.

2. A. B. Harper, ed., *Sistah Vegan: Black Female Vegans Speak on Food, Identity, Health, and Society* (New York: Lantern, 1996).

3. John Mbiti, qtd. in Owusu Bandele and Gail Myers, "Roots!," in *Land Justice: Re-imagining Land, Food, and the Commons in the United States,* ed. Justine M. Williams and Eric Holt-Gimenez (Oakland, Ca.: Food First, 2017), 21.

4. Leah Penniman, *Black Earth Wisdom: Soulful Conversations with Black Environmentalists* (New York: Harper Collins, 2023), 5.

5. Qtd. in ibid., 9.

6. Paul Ortiz, *An African American and Latinx History of the United States* (Boston: Beacon, 2018), 72.

7. James L. Cone, *A Black Theology of Liberation* (1970; Maryknoll, N.Y.: Orbis, 1990), 1.

8. Ibid., 33.

9. Ibid.

10. Ibid., 35.

11. Cone, qtd. in Melanie L. Harris, *Ecowomanism: African American Women and Earth-Honoring Faiths* (Maryknoll, N.Y.: Orbis, 2017), 71.

12. D. D. Glave, "Black Environmental Liberation Theology," in *To Love the Wind and the Rain": African Americans and Environmental History*," ed. D. D. Glave and M. Stoll (Pittsburgh: University of Pittsburgh Press, 2006), 189.

13. Robert L. Bullard, *Dumping in Dixie: Race, Class and Environmental Quality* (New York: Routledge, 2000).

14. Glave, "Black Environmental Liberation Theology," 198

15. Harris, *Ecowomanism*, 86–95.

16. Harris, *Ecowomanism*, 141–42.

17. Harris, *Ecowomanism*, 23–58.

18. George Tinker, American Indian Liberation: A Theology of Sovereignty (New York: Orbis Books, 2008), 156, 158.

19. Eugene Mason, "3-H Apprenticeship Video Series: Your Bountiful Harvest Family Farm," 5:40 video, www.facebook.com/coachgreengene/videos/684608871962196/

20. Gregory Cajete, ed., *A People's Ecology: Explorations in Sustainable Living* (Sante Fe: Clear Light, 1999), 3.

21. Estela Roman, "El Temezkal, a Place for Rest and Purification," in *Voices from the Ancestors: Xicanx and Latinx Spiritual Expressions and Healing Practices*, ed. L. Medina, and M. R Gonzalez (Tucson: University of Arizona Press, 2019), 188.

22. Ibid., 189.

23. Ibid., 189.

CHAPTER 8. Urban AlterNative Masculinity: Men, Land, and Reindigenization

1. Judith Butler, *Gender Trouble: Feminism and the Subversion of Identity* (New York: Routledge, 1984). My notion of an antiauthoritarian, anticolonial alterNative politics was first developed in my book *Toward a Chican@ Hip Hop Anticolonialism* (New York: Routledge, 2017).

2. L. Baker-Kimmons and P. McFarland "The Rap on Chicano and Black Masculinty: A Content Analysis of Gender Images in Rap Lyrics," *Race, Gender and Class* 19, nos. 3–4 (2012): 331–44, citing p. 20; Pancho McFarland, *The Chican@ Hip Hop Nation: Politics of a New Millennial Mestizaje* (East Lansing: Michigan State University Press, 2013).

3. Sut Jhally, dir., *Tough Guise: Violence, Media and the Crisis in Masculinity* (Media Education Foundation, 1999); M. Kimmel, "Masculinity as Homophobia: Fear, Shame and Silence in the Construction of Gender Identity," in *Theorizing Masculinities*, ed. H. Brod and M. Kaufmann (Thousand Oaks, Ca.: Sage, 1994), 119–41.

4. McFarland, *Chicano Rap: Gender and Violence in the Postindustrial Barrio. (Austin: University of Texas, 2008)*; McFarland, *Chican@ Hip Hop*; McFarland, *Hip Hop Anticolonialism*.

5. McFarland, *Hip Hop Anticolonialism*.

6. Leah Penniman, *Black Earth Wisdom: Soulful Conversations with Black Environmentalists* (New York: Harper Collins, 2023), 43.

7. Individual freedom is perhaps the highest good under anarchist systems. As well, individuality, including as regards sexuality, is encouraged in most Indigenous communities as we recognize that what is best for our community is that individual members of our communities are encouraged to pursue their talents and desires.

8. For an analysis of the "loco episteme," see McFarland, *Chican@ Hip Hop Nation*.

9. See X. Banales "Joteria: A Decolonizing Political Project," *Aztlan: A Journal of Chicano*

Studies 39, no. 1 (2014): 155–65; Q. Driskill, C. Finley, B. J. Gilley, and S. L. Morgensen, eds., *Queer Indigenous Studies: Critical Interventions in Theory, Politics, and Literature* (Tucson: University of Arizona Press, 2011); L. Hall, "Indigenist Intersectionality: Decolonizing and Reweaving an Indigenous Eco-queer Feminism and Anarchism," Perspectives in Anarchist Theory, 29 (2016): 81–94>; E. Perez, *The Decolonial Imaginary: Writing Chicanas into History* (Bloomington: Indiana University Press, 1999).

10. Anonymous, *Zapatistas! Documents of the New Mexican Revolution* (New York: Autonomedia, 1994).

11. See Taiaiake Alfred, *Wasase: Indigenous Pathways of Action and Freedom* (Toronto: University of Toronto, 2005); Taiaiake Alfred, *Peace, Power, Righteousness: An Indian Manifesto*, 2nd ed. (Toronto: Oxford University Press, 2009); Glenn Coulthard, *Red Skin, White Masks: Rejecting the Colonial Politics of Recognition* (Minneapolis: University of Minnesota, 2014); Leanne Betasamosake Simpson, *As We Have Always Done: Indigenous Freedom through Radical Resistance* (Minneapolis: University of Minnesota Press, 2017); Daniel R. Wildcat, *Red Alert! Saving the Planet with Indigenous Knowledge* (Boulder: Fulcrum, 2009).

12. Simpson, *As We Have Always Done*, 20.

13. Kitrina Baxter, Dara Cooper, Aleya Fraser, and Shakara Tyler, "Womanism as Agrarianism: Black Women Healing through Innate Agrarian Artistry," in *Land Justice: Re-imagining Land, Food, and the Commons in the United States,* ed. Justine Williams and Eric Holt-Gimenez (Oakland, Calif.: Food First Books, 2017), 94–110; Monica White, *Freedom Farmers: Agricultural Resistance and the Black Freedom Movement* (Chapel Hill: University of North Carolina Press, 2019).

14. Baxter et al., "Womanism"; White, *Freedom Farmers*; Melanie L. Harris, *Ecowomanism: African American Women and Earth-Honoring Faiths* (Maryknoll, N.Y.: Orbis, 2017).

15. Simpson, *As We Have Always Done*, 52.

16. See ibid.; and Driskill et al., *Queer Indigenous Studies*.

17. adrienee maree brown, *Emergent Strategy: Shaping Change, Changing Worlds* (Chico, Calif.: AK Press, 2017).

CHAPTER 9. Mothers of the Movement: Eco-womanism, Innate Agrarian Artistry, and Anticolonial Healing

1. Kitrina Baxter, Dara Cooper, Aleya Fraser, and Shakara Tyler, "Womanism as Agrarianism: Black Women Healing through Innate Agrarian Artistry," in *Land Justice: Re-imagining Land, Food, and the Commons in the United States* ed. Justine Williams and Eric Holt-Gimenez (Oakland, Ca.: Food First, 2017), 94–110; L. Medina and M. R Gonzalez, eds., *Voices from the Ancestors: Xicanx and Latinx Spiritual Expressions and Healing Practices* (Tucson: University of Arizona Press, 2019).

2. Baxter et al., "Womanism."

3. Bonnie Claudia Harrison, "Diasporadas: Black Women and the Fine Art of Activism," *Meridians* 2, no. 2 (2002): 163–84.

4. Carney and Rosamoff, *In the Shadow of Slavery*; Dianne D. Glave, *Rooted in the Earth: Reclaiming the African American Environmental Heritage* (Chicago: Lawrence Hill Books, 2010); and Leah Penniman, *Farming While Black: Soulfire Farm's Practical Guide to Liberation on the Land* (White River Junction, Vt.: Chelsea Green, 2019).

5. Qtd. in Monica M. White, *Freedom Farmers: Agricultural Resistance and the Black Freedom Movement* (Chapel Hill: University of North Carolina Press, 2019), 65.

6. Ibid. For a critique of Vizenor's concept of "survivance," see Klee Benally, *No Spiritual Surrender: Indigenous Anarchy in Defense of the Sacred* (n.p.: Detritus, 2023).

7. White, *Freedom Farmers*, 71.

8. Ibid., 86–87.

9. Penniman, *Farming While Black*, 191.

10. Ibid., 190.

11. Luz Calvo and Catriona Rueda Esquibel, *Decolonize Your Diet: Plant-Based Mexican-American Recipes for Health and Healing* (Vancouver: Arsenal Pulp, 2015).

12. Penniman, *Farming While Black*, 273–75; Richard Louv, *Last Child in the Woods: Saving Our Children from Nature-Deficit Disorder* (Chapel Hill, N.C.: Algonquin, 2005).

13. Baxter et al., "Womanism," 95.

14. Ibid., 96.

15. Ibid., 100.

16. Jessica Hernandez, *Fresh Banana Leaves: Healing Indigenous Landscapes through Indigenous Science* (Berkeley, Ca.: North Atlantic, 2022), 163.

17. Baxter et al, "Womanism," 101.

18. Penniman, *Farming While Black*, 200.

19. Ibid., 201.

20. Cajete, *People's Ecology*, vii.

21. Ibid., viii, 6.

22. Ibid., 16.

23. Frantz Fanon, *Black Skin, White Masks* (New York: Grove Press, 1952).

24. Calvo and Esquibel, *Decolonize Your Diet*, 136.

25. Ibid., 137.

26. Louv, *Last Child*.

27. Ibid., 34.

28. Ibid., 46–49.

29. Ibid., 49.

30. bell hooks, *belonging: a culture of place* (New York: Routledge, 2009), 1.

31. Penniman, *Farming While Black*.

32. Jared A. Ball, *I Mix What I Like: A Mixtape Manifesto* (Oakland, Ca.: AK Press, 2011).

33. hooks *belonging*, 37.

34. Ibid., 38.

35. Ibid., 39.

36. Ibid., 98.

37. Medina and Gonzalez, "Introduction," in *Voices from the Ancestors: Xicanx and Latinx Spiritual Expressions and Healing Practices*, ed. L. Medina, and M. R. Gonzalez (Tucson: University of Arizona Press, 2019), 4.

38. Medina and Gonzalez, *Voices from the Ancestors*, 32.

39. N. E. Cantu, "Teachings from Mami," in Medina and Gonzalez, *Voices from the Ancestors*, 139.

40. Medina and Gonzalez, Medina and Gonzalez, 39.

41. K. M. Davalos, "Be Stewards of the Earth," in Medina and Gonzalez, *Voices from the Ancestors*, 260.

42. Robin Wall Kimmerer, *Braiding Sweetgrass: Indigenous Wisdom, Scientific Knowledge, and the Teachings of Plants* (Minneapolis: Milkweed, 2013).

43. Ibid.

CHAPTER 10. Indigenous/Black Anarchism: Liberation Thinking in the Food Movement

1. Errico Malatesta, *The Method of Freedom: An Errico Malatesta Reader* (Oakland, Ca.: AK Press, 2014), 478; Wayne Price, *The Value of Radical Theory: An Anarchist Introduction to Marx's Critique of Political Economy* (Oakland, Ca.: AK Press, 2013), 170.

2. Harry Cleaver, "Food, Famine and the International Crisis" (1977), accessed June 14, 2023, available at zerowork.org/CleaverFoodFamine.html; Pancho McFarland, "From Weapon to Sovereignty," *Environmental and Food Justice* (blog), January 15, 2012, https://ejfood .blogspot.com/2012/01/food-fights-hunger-politics-and.html?q=From+Weapon+to +Sovereignty.

3. Kuwasi Balagoon, *Soldier's Story: Revolutionary Writings by a New Afrikan Anarchist* (Montreal: Kersplebedeb, 2019), 188–89.

4. Glenn Coulthard, *Red Skin, White Masks: Rejecting the Colonial Politics of Recognition* (Minneapolis: University of Minnesota, 2014), 201.

5. Taiaiake Alfred, *Peace, Power, Righteousness: An Indian Manifesto,* 2nd ed. (Toronto: Oxford University Press, 2009); and Benally, *No Spiritual Surrender*.

6. See numerous works in anarchist theory and descriptions of anarchist practice. A few important titles include the following: AFAQ Editorial Collective, *Anarchist Frequently Asked Questions* (Oakland, Calif.: AK Press, 2000); Balagoon, *Soldier's Story*; Murray Bookchin, *The Murray Bookchin Reader* (Montreal: Black Rose Books, 1999); Peter Kropotkin, "The First Work of the Revolution," in *Act for Yourselves: Articles from Freedom, 1886–1907* (London: Freedom, 1988); Iain McKay, ed., *Direct Struggle against Capital: A Peter Kropotkin Anthology* (Oakland, Calif.: AK Press, 2014); Chris Wilbert and Damian F. White, eds., *Autonomy, Solidarity, Possibility: The Colin Ward Reader* (Oakland, Calif.: AK Press, 2011); Colin Ward, *Anarchy in Action* (London: Freedom, 1973); and Errico Malatesta, *The Method of Freedom: An Errico Malatesta Reader* (Oakland, Ca.: AK Press, 2014).

7. Alfred, *Peace, Power*; Jessica Gordon Nembhard, *Collective Courage: A History of African American Collective Thought and Practice* (University Park: Pennsylvania State University Press, 2014).

8. Balagoon, *Soldier's Story*, 154

9. Taiaiake Alfred, *Wasase: Indigenous Pathways of Action and Freedom* (Toronto: University of Toronto, 2005).

10. Benally, *No Spiritual Surrender*; R. J. Day, "Anarcha-Indigenism: Encounters, Resonances, and Tensions," International Studies Association 2008 Conference, San Francisco, unpublished conference paper, 1–30; L. Hall, "Indigenist Intersectionality: Decolonizing and Reweaving an Indigenous Eco-queer Feminism and Anarchism," *Perspectives in Anarchist Theory* 29 (2016): 81–94; Jacqueline Laskey, "Indigenism, Anarchism, Feminism: An Emerging Framework for

Exploring Post-Imperial Futures," *Affinities Journal,* special edition on Anarch@Indigenism (August 2011), https://ojs.library.queensu.ca/index.php/affinities/issue/view/572; and E. M. Lagalisse, "Marginalizing Magdalena: Intersections of Gender and the Secular in Anarchoindigenist Solidarity Activism," *Signs* 36, no. 3 (Spring 2011): 653–78.

11. Laskey, "Indigenism, Anarchism, Feminism" 3.

12. Ibid.

13. Alfred, *Wasase,* 45.

14. Ibid., 46.

15. Malatesta, *Method of Freedom,* 383.

16. Ward Churchill, *Marxism and Native Americans* (Boston, Mass: South End, 1983).

17. Maia Ramnath, *Decolonizing Anarchism: An Anti-Authoritarian History of India's Liberation Struggle* (Oakland, Calif.: AK Press, 2011).

18. See the works of William Anderson, Zoe Samudzi, Ashanti Alston, Lorenzo Komboa Ervin, and Kuwasi Balagoon.

19. Balagoon, *Soldier's Story,* 185.

20. See also Ramnath, *Decolonizing Anarchism.*

21. Anderson, *The Nation on No Map,* 21.

22. Benally, "Voting Is Not Harm Reduction," in *No Spiritual Surrender.*

23. Coulthard, *Red Skins.*

24. Huey P. Newton, *To Die for the People* (San Francisco: City Lights, 2009).

25. Zoe Samudzi and William C. Anderson, *As Black as Resistance: Finding the Conditions for Liberation* (Oakland, Ca.: AK Press, 2018), 31.

26. Devon G. Peña, *Mexican Americans and the Environment: Tierra y Vida* (Tucson: University of Arizona Press, 2005); see Bookchin, *Murray Bookchin Reader,* 68–66 for a view contrary to Peña's and others' argument concerning the ecological nature of Indigenous peoples.

27. Winona LaDuke, *The Winona LaDuke Reader: A Collection of Essential Writings* (Stillwater, Minn.: Voyageur, 2002), 78.

28. Pieroti, *Indigenous Knowledge,* 14.

29. Devon G. Peña, "Los Animalitos: Culture, Ecology and the Politics of Place in the Upper Rio Grande," in *Chicano Culture, Ecology, Politics: Subversive Kin,* ed. D. G. Peña (Tucson: University of Arizona Press, 1998), 39.

30. On living in correct relationship with one's place, see ibid.; on confronting enemies and the Nndáá' (Enemy Way Ceremony), see Benally, *No Spiritual Surrender,* 381.

31. Tyson Yunkaporta, *Sand Talk: How Indigenous Thinking Can Save the World* (New York: Harper One, 2020), 36.

32. Bill Mollison, *Permaculture: A Designers' Manual* (Sisters Creek, Australia: Tagari, 1988), 35, italics in original.

33. Rodriguez, *Our Sacred Maíz.*

34. Kim Tallbear, *Native American DNA: Tribal Belonging and the False Promise of Genetic Science* (Minneapolis: University of Minnesota Press, 2013).

35. Alfred, *Wasase,* 32–3.

36. Yunkaporta, *Sand Talk,* 36.

37. Wildcat, *Red Alert!,* 70.

38. Ibid., 9.

39. Alfred, *Peace, Power*, 14.

40. LaDuke, *Reader*, 177.

41. Wildcat, *Red Alert!*, 69.

42. Ibid, 21.

43. Frank Black Elk, in Churchill, *Marxism and Native Americans*, 148–49.

44. Wildcat, *Red Alert!*, 20.

45. Benally, *No Spiritual Surrender*, 212.

46. Bookchin, *Ecology of Freedom*, 69.

47. LaDuke, *Reader*, 79–82.

48. Devon G. Peña, "Los Animalitos: Culture, Ecology and the Politics of Place in the Upper Rio Grande," in *Chicano Culture, Ecology, Politics: Subversive Kin*, 40.

49. Robin Wall Kimmerer, *Braiding Sweetgrass: Indigenous Wisdom, Scientific Knowledge, and the Teachings of Plants* (Minneapolis: Milkweed Editions, 2013).

50. Mollison, *Permaculture*, 2.

51. LaDuke, *Reader*, 80.

52. Peña, *Mexican Americans*.

53. LaDuke, *Reader*.

54. Peña, *Mexican Americans*; *Environmental and Food Justice* (blog).

55. Peña, *Mexican Americans*.

56. Vandanna Shiva, *Soil Not Oil: Environmental Justice in an Age of Climate Crisis* (Boston: South End, 2008); Peña, *Mexican Americans*. Permaculturalists base their entire system around these indigenous observations and innovations. Unfortunately, permaculture remains on the margins of organic, noncorporate, noncapitalist food production. Equally problematic is that many within permaculture credit Bill Mollison with creating permaculture and its practices instead of recognizing its origins in Indigenous horticulture, social organization, and ethics.

57. bell hooks, *Belonging: A Culture of Place* (New York: Routledge, 2009), 36.

58. Ibid.

59. George Sefa Dei, "Indigenous Anti-colonial Knowledge as 'Heritage Knowledge' for Promoting Black/African Education in Diasporic Contexts," *Decolonization* 1, no. 1 (2012): 105.

60. Leah Penniman, "These Roots Run Deep" in *Black Earth Wisdom: Soulful Conversations with Black Environmentalists* (New York: Harper Collins, 2023).

61. Judith Carney and Richard Nicholas Rosomoff, *In the Shadow of Slavery: Africa's Botanical Legacy in the Atlantic World* (Berkeley: University of California Press, 2011); Dianne D. Glave, *Rooted in the Earth: Reclaiming the African American Environmental Heritage* (Chicago: Lawrence Hill Books, 2010); hooks, *Belonging*; Penniman, *Farming While Black: Soulfire Farm's Practical Guide to Liberation on the Land* (White River Junction, Vt.: Chelsea Green, 2019).

62. Carney and Rossamoff, *In the Shadow of Slavery*, 117–18.

63. Brooks, "Black Bioneers," *Sacred Keepers Sustainability Lab Newsletter*, February 21, 2014.

64. Frantz Fanon, *Black Skin, White Masks* (New York: Grove, 1952).

65. Roxanne Dunbar-Ortiz, *An Indigenous People's History of the United States* (Boston: Beacon, 2015).

66. Tobald Rollo, "Sage against the Machine: Being Truth to Power," in *Unsettling America:*

Decolonization in Theory and Practice, vol. 2, issue 2, December 10, 2013, https://unsettlingamerica .wordpress.com/2013/12/10/sage-against-the-machine-being-truth-to-power/.

67. Ward Churchill, "Introduction: Journeying toward a Debate," in Churchill, *Marxism and Native Americans*, 5.

68. Alfred, *Peace, Power*, 5.

69. Simpson, *As We Have Always Done*.

70. Coulthard, *Red Skins*.

71. Benally, *No Spiritual Surrender*.

72. Wildcat, *Red Alert!*

73. Pierotti, *Indigenous Knowledge*, 217.

74. C. Anthony, "Reflections on the Purposes and Meanings of African American Environmental History," in *"To Love the Wind and the Rain": African Americans and Environmental History*," ed. D. D. Glave and M. Stoll (Pittsburgh: University of Pittsburgh Press, 2006).

75. Email to members, May 29, 2013.

76. Nembhard, *Collective Courage*; White, *Freedom Farmers*.

77. Email to HFH members, February 15, 2014.

78. hooks, *Belonging*, 39.

79. Glave, *Rooted*; Glave and Stoll, *"To Love the Wind"*; Will Allen, *The Good Food Revolution: Growing Healthy Food, People, and Communities* (New York: Gotham, 2012).

80. Email to members, Mar. 29, 2014.

81. Email, Oct. 29, 2013.

82. Devon Peña, "Revolutions Happen: Notes on the Crisis of Neoliberalism and the Subversiveness of the Commons," *Environmental and Food Justice* (blog), accessed April 18, 2014, www.ejfood.blogspot.com.

83. Iain McKay, ed., *Direct Struggle against Capital: A Peter Kropotkin Anthology* (Oakland, Calif.: AK Press, 2014), 189.

84. Malatesta, *Method of Freedom*, 425–29.

85. Jackson, *Blood in My Eye*, 55–56.

86. Balagoon, *Soldier's Story*, 188–89.

87. Balagoon, *Soldier's Story*, 154.

88. AFAQ Editorial Collective, *Anarchist Frequently Asked Questions* (Oakland, Ca.: AK Press, 2000), 1018.

89. Colin Ward, "The State," in *Autonomy, Solidarity, Possibility: The Colin Ward Reader*, ed. Chris Wilbert and Damian F. White (Oakland, Ca.: AK Press, 2011), 18.

90. Coulthard, *Red Skins*.

91. AFAQ Editorial Collective, *Anarchist Frequently Asked Questions*, 1018–19.

92. Ibid., 1059.

93. Peter Lamborn Wilson, "Avant Gardening" in *Avant Gardening: Ecological Struggle in the City and the World*, ed., Peter Lamborn Wilson and Bill Weinberg (New York: Autonomedia, 1999), 26–27.

94. Benally, *No Spiritual Surrender*, 168–69.

95. Bonnie Claudia Harrison, "Diasporadas: Black Women and the Fine Art of Activism," *Meridians* 2, no. 2 (2002): 163–84; and Paul Ortiz, *An African American and Latinx History of the United States* (Boston: Beacon, 2018).

96. Balagoon, *Soldier's Story*, 180.

97. Raul Zibechi, *Territories in Resistance: A Cartography of Latin American Social Movements* (Oakland, Calif.: AK Press, 2012), 38.

98. Ramnath, *Decolonizing Anarchism*.

99. Balagoon, *Soldier's Story*, 184, 189.

100. Mollison, *Permaculture*, chapter 14; and the idea of decentralized structures appears on p. 1 and is focused on in chapter 14.

101. LaDuke, *LaDuke Reader*, 276. She writes that the seventh-generation principle is "the Iroquois Confederacy philosophy—that we must consider the impact of a decision made today on the impact on the seventh generation from now."

102. Nembhard, *Collective Courage*.

103. Ibid.

104. This commUnity pedagogy occurs daily in GLP gardens and is examined more in part II.

105. Iain McKay, ed., *Direct Struggle against Capital: A Peter Kropotkin Anthology* (Oakland, Calif.: AK Press, 2014), 28–29.

106. Alfred, *Wasase*, 112.

107. Cedric Robinson, *Black Marxism: The Making of the Black Radical Tradition* (Chapel Hill: University of North Carolina Press, 2021).

108. Alfred, *Wasase*.

109. Shiva, *Soil Not Oil*.

110. Bookchin, *Murray Bookchin Reader*, 41.

111. Kenny Ausubel, "'It is Time to Plant' the Real Green Revolution," in *A People's Ecology: Explorations in Sustainable Living*, ed. Gregory Cajete (Sante Fe, N.Mex.: Clear Light, 1999), 63.

112. Subcommandante Marcos, *Our Word is Our Weapon: Selected Writings of Subcommandante Insurgente Marcos*, ed. Juana Ponce de Leon (New York: Seven Stories Press, 2001),162.

113. Mollison, *Permaculture*, 39.

114. Vine Deloria Jr., *God is Red: A Native View of Religion*, 2nd ed. (Golden, Colo.: Fulcrum Publishing, 1994), 89.

115. Gary Paul Nabhan, *Cultures of Habitat: On Nature, Culture, and Story* (Washington, D.C.: Counterpoint, 1997), 244.

116. Deric Shannon, Anthony J. Nocella, II, and John Asimakopolous, eds., *The Accumulation of Freedom: Writings on Anarchist Economics* (Oakland, Calif.: AK Press, 2012), 12.

117. Qtd. in Uri Gordon, "Anarchist Economics in Practice," in Shannon et al., *Accumulation of Freedom*, 213.

118. Situationist slogan, qtd. in Carol Ehrlich, "Socialism, Anarchism and Feminism," In *Quiet Rumours: An Anarcha-Feminist Reader*, ed. Dark Star (Oakland, Calif.: AK Press, 2012), 57.

119. Devon G. Peña, "Revolutions Happen: Notes on the Crisis of Neoliberalism and the Subversiveness of the Commons," *Environmental and Food Justice* (blog), accessed April 18, 2014, www.ejfood.blogspot.com

120. Gabriel Valle, "Food Values: Urban Kitchen Gardens and Working-Class Subjectivity," in Peña et al., *Mexican-Origin Foods*, 49.

121. Gordon, "Anarchist Economics," 211.

122. Yunkaporta, *Sand Talk*, 28.

123. Mollison, *Permaculture*.

124. Gordon, "Anarchist Economics"; Nembhard, *Collective Courage*.

125. Mollison *Permaculture*, 2.

126. Kropotkin, in McKay, *Direct Struggle*, 501.

127. Eve Tuck, and K. Wayne Yang, "Decolonization Is Not a Metaphor," *Decolonization: Indigeneity, Education and Society* 1, no. 1 (2012): 7.

128. Ibid., 18; and Bonita Lawrence and Enakshi Dua, "Decolonizing Antiracism," *Social Justice* 32, no. 4 (2005): 120–43.

129. Kyle T. Mays, An *Afro-Indigenous History of the United States* (Boston: Beacon, 2022).

130. Churchill, *Marxism and Native Americans*.

131. In October and November 2021, a controversy arose around Dave Chapelle's comedy special on Netflix *The Closer*. The vast majority of the special focused on his ongoing disagreements with many in the transgender community and their allies. Anecdotal evidence from my colleagues associated with the movement I am analyzing shows a good deal of transphobia and homophobia while supporting Chapelle's "right" to earn a living as a Black man in America.

132. Jared A. Ball, *The Myth and Propaganda of Black Buying Power* (Cham, Switzerland: Palgrave Pivot, 2020).

133. Peter Kropotkin, *Mutual Aid: A Factor of Evolution* (Mineola, N.Y.: Dover, 2006).

EPILOGUE. Red, Black, and Green Futures

1. Maurice Walls, dir., "G.R.I.P" (2021).

2. William C. Anderson, *The Nation on No Map: Black Anarchism and Abolition* (Oakland, Ca.: AK Press, 2021), 122.

3. Frantz Fanon, *Black Skin, White Masks* (New York: Grove, 1952).

4. Leah Penniman, *Black Earth Wisdom, Black Earth Wisdom: Soulful Conversations with Black Environmentalists* (New York: Harper Collins, 2023), xxv.

5. Robin D. G. Kelley, *Freedom Dreams: The Black Radical Imagination* (Boston: Beacon, 2002).

6. Kyle T. Mays, An *Afro-Indigenous History of the United States* (Boston: Beacon, 2022), 168.

7. Ibid., 172.

8. Bill Mollison, *Permaculture: A Designers' Manual* (Sisters Creek, Australia: Tagari, 1988).

9. Vine Deloria Jr., *God is Red: A Native View of Religion*, 2nd ed. (Golden, Colo.: Fulcrum, 1994).

INDEX